INTERNATIONAL LIBRARY OF
AFRO-AMERICAN LIFE AND HISTORY

 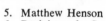

1. Blanche K. Bruce
2. A group of black soldiers in Cuba
3. Migrant workers in Alabama
4. Walter White
5. Matthew Henson
6. Recipient of a Small Business Administration loan
7. Upward Bound students at Johns Hopkins University

INTERNATIONAL LIBRARY OF

AFRO-AMERICAN LIFE

AND HISTORY

THE QUEST FOR EQUALITY

From Civil War to Civil Rights

BY

CHARLES H. WESLEY

THE PUBLISHERS AGENCY, INC.

CORNWELLS HEIGHTS, PENNSYLVANIA

under the auspices of

THE ASSOCIATION FOR THE STUDY OF AFRO-AMERICAN LIFE AND HISTORY

LIBRARY OF CONGRESS CATALOG CARD NO. 68-56835

INTERNATIONAL STANDARD BOOK NUMBER 0-87781-210-1

PRINTED IN THE UNITED STATES OF AMERICA

REVISED EDITION

EXCLUSIVE WORLD-WIDE DISTRIBUTION BY

THE LIBRARY COMPANY, INC., WASHINGTON, D.C.

To

CHARLOTTE WESLEY HOLLOMAN

Preface

THE Association for the Study of Afro-American Life and History joins with Pubco Corporation in presenting this new series of volumes which treat in detail the cultural and historical backgrounds of black Americans. This Association, a pioneer in the area of Afro-American History, was founded on September 9, 1915, by Dr. Carter G. Woodson, who remained its director of research and publications until his death in 1950.

In 1916 Dr. Woodson began publishing the quarterly *Journal of Negro History*. In 1926 Negro History Week was launched, and since that time it has been held annually in February, encompassing the birth dates of Abraham Lincoln and Frederick Douglass. The *Negro History Bulletin* was first published in 1937 to serve both schools and families by making available to them little-known facts about black life and history.

During its sixty-one years of existence, the Association for the Study of Afro-American Life and History has supported many publications dealing with the contributions of Afro-Americans to the growth and development of this country. Its activities have contributed to the increasing interest in the dissemination of factual studies which are placing the Afro-American in true perspective in the mainstream of American history.

We gratefully acknowledge the contributions of previous scholars, which have aided us in the preparation of this *International Library of Afro-American Life and History*.

Our grateful acknowledgment is also expressed to Charles W. Lockyer, president of Pubco Corporation, whose challenging approach has made possible this library.

Though each of the volumes in this set can stand as an autonomous unit, and although each author has brought his own interpretation to the area with which he is dealing, together these books form a comprehensive picture of the Afro-American experience in America. The three history volumes give a factual record of a people who were brought from Africa in chains and who today are struggling to cast off the last vestiges of these bonds. The anthologies covering music, art, the theatre and literature provide a detailed account of the black American's contributions to these fields—including those contributions which are largely forgotten today. Achievement in the sports world is covered in another volume. The volume on the Afro-American in medicine is a history of the black American's struggle for equality as a medical practitioner and as a patient. The selected black leaders in the biography book represent the contributions and achievements of many times their number. The documentary history sums up the above-mentioned material in the words of men and women who were themselves a part of black history.

CHARLES H. WESLEY

Washington, D.C.

Editor's Note

I WISH to thank the following people for the contributions they have made on behalf of this volume: Patricia W. Romero, who supervised the research and editing with the able assistance of Gretchen Fox and a staff of dedicated young people, among them Anita Baly and Christine Kent; and Allan Kullen for collecting photographs and handling the layout of the volume. Particular gratitude is owed to the following for their invaluable aid in providing material and photographs to illustrate the book: the Moorland Room of Howard University; and the staffs of the Library of Congress, the New York Public Library, the Historical Society of Pennsylvania, the National Archives, the Department of Labor, the Pentagon and the New York Public Library-Schomburg Collection.

CHARLES H. WESLEY

Washington, D. C.

Table of Contents

Introduction

WHEN THE Civil War ended, the nation faced a number of new problems. A major one was the plight of the four million freedmen who had to be provided with jobs, housing and education. The Freedmen's Bureau, which had been established in 1863, assumed most of the responsibility for the ex-slaves in the South. The period of transition from war to peace did not provide for any systematized settlement of these black people, and many of them wandered over the countryside seeking a livelihood where they could find it. Others settled on the land they had worked as slaves, contracting as laborers for their former masters. A few found employment and living accommodations in the towns and cities of the South.

The few blacks who had been educated or trained outside the South found new opportunities with the restoration of peace and the military occupation of the former Confederate states. These men returned and became part of the political Reconstruction which began in 1865 and lasted more or less until the later 1870's. Hiram R. Revels was elected by the state legislature of Mississippi to serve out the unexpired term of Jefferson Davis in the United States Senate. He was followed by Blanche K. Bruce, also from Mississippi. Twenty blacks were sent to the House of Representatives between 1869 and 1901. P. B. S. Pinchback of Louisiana was briefly governor of that state and was later elected to the U.S. Senate, but was refused his seat. History books covering this period have sadly neglected the story of the black man's participation in government at this time, and one of the purposes of this volume is to supply the missing chapters.

The quest for education was an important one to the newly freed people. One of the functions of the Freedmen's Bureau was to establish schools wherever its agents could find schoolrooms and teachers—both in short supply. Negro colleges also made their appearance during this initial period of freedom.

The increasing participation by black people in government and other areas declined rapidly as the old leadership was restored to the South. This, together with the withdrawal of federal troops in 1877 and the fact that former abolitionists in the North no longer concerned themselves with his plight, removed the black man from public life and, in the South, reduced him to a state not much better than slavery.

Those who could left the South. Some moved to the West and others traveled to the northern cities in search of jobs and fulfillment. In the last three decades of the century, a literary and cultural movement arose within the newly closed society. George Washington Williams wrote his two-volume *History of the Negro Race in America*. William Wells Brown, who had earlier written the first novel to be published by a black man in this country, recorded the achievements of many successful Afro-Americans in his book *The Rising Son*. Paul Laurence Dunbar, poet of the people, published a succession of works —fiction as well as poetry. These men and many others set the stage for the black cultural "renaissance" of the twentieth century.

With the rise of Booker T. Washington at Tuskegee, black leadership was accorded national recognition. Washington was followed by W. E. B. Du Bois, who advocated a more militant attitude for the Afro-American. Later other black leaders—both men and women—took up the fight for equal rights. In 1909 the National Association for the Advancement of Colored People was founded. This was followed, some ten years later, by the National Urban League. Both worked with the National Association of Colored Women's Clubs and with churches and local organizations, and all contributed to the rise of the civil-rights movement.

World War I brought a new flood of immigration from the South to the northern cities. Defense industries were in urgent need of labor, regardless of color. Many Afro-Americans felt a new hope as they left their old surroundings for better jobs and decent living quarters. The war ended, and in many cases so, too, did the jobs. There was a wave of prejudice, accompanied by riots and lynching.

However, the 1920's saw the rise of a vital literary, theatrical and musical movement among blacks. This included such personalities as Langston Hughes, Claude McKay, James Weldon Johnson, Countee Cullen, Georgia Douglas Johnson, Arna Bontemps and Waring Cuney in poetry; Jean Toomer, Eric Walrond, Walter White and Zora Neale Hurston in prose; Paul Robeson, Charles Gilpin, Jules Bledsoe, Rose McClendon and Abbie Mitchell in the theater; Bill Robinson, Florence Mills and Ethel Waters in show business; Duke Ellington, Louis Armstrong, Shelton Brooks, W. C. Handy and Bessie Smith in music.

Then came the Depression, and with it came more poverty, unemployment and discrimination. The black middle class which had developed in the early part of the twentieth century often suffered along with its poorer brothers.

World War II brought the promise, once again, of better conditions for black Americans. And again, the trend was to move to areas where defense jobs were available—or to enlist in the nation's armed forces. The first war hero was Dorie Miller, a black seaman trained to serve as a mess steward. At Pearl Harbor, he manned a ship's gun and shot down four Japanese planes. World War II marked a turning point in race relations in the United States and was followed by the rapid rise of the civil-rights movement.

The civil-rights movement took on a national significance when a black woman, Mrs. Rosa Parks, refused to move to the back of a bus in Montgomery, Alabama. A then unknown minister, Martin Luther King, Jr., organized the black citizens of Montgomery into a successful boycott of the public transport system and thus demonstrated to Afro-Americans that by joining together in nonviolent resistance they could bring about changes in the status quo.

People of all complexions joined the established civil-rights groups, and students flocked to the new organizations that were formed at this time. New legislation was passed by Congress to guarantee the rights of black people; an informed citizenry seemed to be ready for the democracy their country stood for; and black people all over the country felt that true equality would be achieved in the not too distant future.

Today black Americans find themselves historically where they have been before. There are again representatives in Congress; equality of education is more of a reality than ever before; a larger middle class enjoys better jobs and housing; more professional positions are available, and the economic situation is improving steadily. Yet the unsolved problems of prejudice and segregation remain for the masses.

The above is a brief outline of this volume, which fills in the story of the Afro-American from the end of the Civil War to the present day and details the contributions and achievements of black Americans during this time.

CHARLES H. WESLEY

Washington, D.C.

CHAPTER ONE

Black Reconstruction— The Southern Negro as Statesman

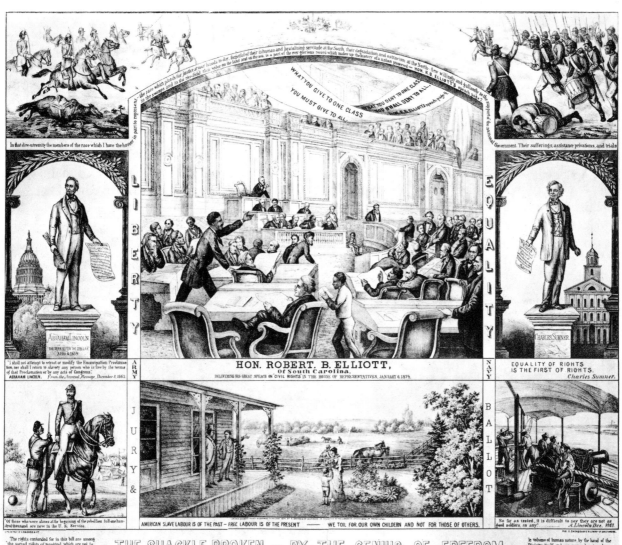

THE Civil War was over—slavery ended. But the relief and rejoicing following these victories were short-lived, for reunification was but a military fact. Binding together North and South would not resolve fundamental differences in economic, social and political values and institutions. Just as these roots of hostility remained between North and South, the reality of defeat for the white southerner and of a tempered freedom for the black southerner bred its own hostility.

Because the freedmen had not been part of the informed citizenry, they had no way of knowing the meaning of freedom; they knew only that they were no longer property, no longer slaves. For many, therefore, freedom merely meant not obeying orders and not working. Following the war, many Negroes rushed to Union army camps. Others remained on the plantations waiting—usually in vain—for the army to come. Most of those who left the plantations had no jobs, no friends, nowhere to go; many wandered about the countryside, fearful of the present, and anxious about the future. Thousands of freedmen died of privation.

The aristocratic planter class, the old Confederate leaders, had suffered huge financial setbacks in the war. When they lost their slaves as well, many gave up all hope of regaining their losses. This was why, in isolated areas, Negroes were

not told of their freedom by their owners. Some of the planters used every means to keep the former slaves dependent—but in fact it was the planters who were dependent on the cheap or slave labor. The poor whites, too, were anxious to preserve what little status they had. They based their "superiority" on their color, and often cruelly persecuted the Negroes.

The Union army was governing the South; the military rulers were as unpopular as forces of occupation ever are with a conquered people. The Freedmen's Bureau, an army agency, increased its efforts to secure and protect the rights of the ex-slaves, but while the bureau was successful in some areas, it was hampered by the animosity of the whites and by the enormous task before it.

The defeated South, then, could not even unify itself, and later historians would charge that the northern victors took unfair advantage of their victims' internal conflicts. The formidable task of rebuilding the Union, which would have tested the finest statesmen of any era, fell principally to northern Republicans, who dominated Congress. One of the first Reconstruction Acts passed by Congress provided for a free election in each former Confederate state. The vote was to determine whether or not the state should call a convention to rewrite its constitution so that it might be admitted once more to the Union.

Having won the right to vote, Negroes participated actively in electioneering in the South.

This election marked the first time Negroes voted in the South. Aided by the Freedmen's Bureau and Republicans anxious to have the support of these new voters, thousands of Negroes registered to vote, and many of the potential convention delegates whose names were on the ballot were Negroes. In many places the Negro vote outnumbered that of the whites. Not only had many old Confederate leaders been barred from voting (disfranchised) by Congress, but many more refused to participate in politics which threatened to destroy their values. For the next few years the old aristocracy would be politically powerless as the new Republican leadership took over.

NEGRO PARTICIPATION IN STATE CONSTITUTIONAL CONVENTIONS

The 1867 election results ensured that each former Confederate state would hold a constitutional convention. The delegates to these conventions were both black and white, but the great majority were allied in politics: the liberal or "radical" Republicans were now in firm control.

A leadership less informed than any which had previously governed in the South now came to the forefront. Though many delegates of both racial groups were uneducated, these assemblies wrote and adopted constitutions that set forth worthy guidelines for state government. Black Reconstruction, moreover, was not as bleak as some historians have maintained. Some conventions found in their midst an educated Negro leadership which had gained its freedom before emancipation. Other black members had as much native talent as the white delegates. Many were unlearned men, but they earnestly sought solutions to their states' problems. In fact, South Carolina's *Charleston Daily News* observed that "the best men in the convention are the colored members."

The constitutions framed by these delegates were to remain in effect for many years. A major issue was free public schools for all—a new concept in the South, where taxation for any kind of public welfare was virtually unknown and where education had generally been reserved for the upper classes. Constitutional provisions

JOHN R. LYNCH

for such necessities as relief measures and free education for all seemed outlandish to the Old South, and those who framed the constitutions were subject to criticism and branded as radicals. Each state's constitution had to meet the approval of both the voters in that state and the U.S. Congress. The conventions worked long and hard, often against great odds, to write laws which would serve the citizens and yet not be so offensive that they would be rejected at the polls.

In Mississippi, for example, the delegates found it nearly impossible to frame a suitable constitution. Among the delegates (eighteen Negroes and eighty whites) there was much hard feeling and racial prejudice, which greatly hampered their efforts to work together. When the convention opened, a white delegate proposed that the word "colored" be entered after each Negro delegate's name in the rolls. John R. Lynch, a black delegate, sprang to his feet and dryly proposed that the color of each delegate's hair also be entered, showing just how pointless such discrimination would be among men whose purpose was lawmaking. For many days this convention debated whether Negroes could use the ballot intelligently. They finally inserted a universal enfranchisement clause—at which point fourteen white delegates resigned. Measures for integrated schools were defeated, as were measures for segregated schools. This issue was finally left out of Mississippi's constitution altogether. Similar difficulties existed at the conventions meeting in the other southern states.

In Louisiana, half the delegates were Negroes, a stipulation agreed upon before the election. Most had been free men before the Civil War, and were landowners. They served on convention committees and several acted as chairmen. The Negro members objected to the disfranchisement of the Confederate leaders and proposed that they should only be restricted from holding office. But that in itself rebuffed the old aristocracy. Compromise was nearly impossible, yet Louisiana's new constitution provided for equal rights, public schools, suffrage for men of both races and annulment of the old discriminatory laws regarding labor.

In South Carolina's convention particularly, the subject of Negro land ownership touched off much debate. Since the South's economy rested on agriculture, owning land was almost essential to earning a decent living. Many of the plantation owners who had suffered severe setbacks were forced to sell their land at low prices to any buyers available. A Negro tailor and Republican leader from Charleston, Robert C. DeLarge, noted that more than one thousand Negroes had bought land from the whites. But DeLarge, who had worked as an agent for the Freedmen's Bureau, also told the convention that many other Negroes could not afford to purchase their own farms, and as a result they were forced to roam the land, unemployed and most of them unskilled. These freedmen had been led to believe that the government would give them land with their freedom. But that wish was never to materialize. Even though the federal government allowed homesteading in certain southern areas, this solved no problems. Now these poor ex-slaves desperately needed education to prepare themselves for new lives.

Delegates to the South Carolina convention finally agreed on setting up public schools—the need was obvious. But whether the new schools should be integrated caused more debate. A Scottish-educated Negro delegate, Francis L. Cardozo, spoke about the inevitability of segregation even though it might not be legalized by the state's constitution.

"There can be separate schools for white and colored," he stated, "[and] if any colored child wishes to go to a white school, he shall have the privilege of doing so. I have no doubt, in most localities colored people will prefer separate schools, particularly until some of the present prejudice against their race is removed."

Incorporation of the public schools bill in the constitution was probably due to such assurances from the black delegates that segregation would be acceptable as long as free schooling was available to all.

Despite the pains taken by these delegates to frame acceptable constitutions, almost all of the new documents met with objection at the polls. Anxious to have the Confederate states back in the Union, Congress enacted the Fourth Reconstruction Act in 1868, providing that only a majority, instead of two-thirds, of the voters should decide whether a state constitution would be ratified. This law resulted in the adoption of new constitutions in the states of Alabama, Georgia, Louisiana, North Carolina and South Carolina.

By presidential order Mississippi held a special election and finally ratified her constitution. Not until 1870 would that troubled state, along with Florida and Texas, be readmitted to the Union.

With the new laws in effect and equal rights "guaranteed" for all, the army felt the work of the Freedmen's Bureau had been accomplished. The military governors now curtailed their role as protectors of Negro rights. Many agents packed their bags and returned to the North. The South grudgingly proceeded to grant its freedmen the right to vote, at least on paper, but the opposite was happening in the North. In 1865 three northern states—Connecticut, Wisconsin and Minnesota—declined to adopt Negro suffrage. In 1866 Congress extended to Negroes in the territories the right to vote, but in the same year the states of Arkansas and Kentucky rejected it. Kansas and Ohio refused in 1867 to adopt Negro suffrage. In 1868 Michigan and New York followed suit.

ROBERT C. DeLARGE   FRANCIS L. CARDOZO   JOHN P. GREEN

NEGRO PARTICIPATION IN THE STATE LEGISLATURES

Massachusetts, the hotbed of abolitionism, became the first state to elect Negroes to its legislature. In 1866 it sent Edwin G. Walker, the son of the abolitionist David Walker, and Charles Mitchell to the State House in Boston. Other colored members followed them to the gold-domed capitol on Beacon Hill: George L. Ruffin, John B. Smith, Joshua B. Smith and William J. Walker.

John P. Green was elected to Ohio's legislature in 1881. Born in New Bern, North Carolina, he was a graduate of the Ohio Union Law School in Cleveland. Green was elected justice of the peace in 1875. The Republicans nominated him for the legislature in 1877. He lost that election, but ran again, successfully, four years later. The *Ohio Historical Quarterly* notes that he served creditably during his years in Columbus.

Negroes sat as Republican members of all the southern state legislatures. In three states—South Carolina, Mississippi and Louisiana—blacks had considerable influence and power. Many were former slaves, crude in manners but capable public servants. Many spoke ably and worked hard as lawmakers. As a rule, they performed on a par with the white "carpetbaggers" and "scalawags" among their colleagues. Both these terms were coined by southern foes of Reconstruction; the first term described the northern agents who arrived, with carpetbags in hand, to oversee the postwar reforms; the second singled out southern whites who collaborated with them.

Although they never dominated the South Carolina legislature as a whole, as some critics have suggested, Negroes exercised great influence there—as great as in any state's postwar legislature. Two speakers of the house were Negroes, and three times a Negro was chosen to act as the president of the white-controlled senate. An Englishman who observed the Negro officials in action in 1872 concluded that they would have "creditably presided over any Commonwealth's legislative assembly."

In contrast to those passed by the pre-Civil War aristocratic government, the laws passed by this body aided the common man. Homes for orphans, the poor, the blind, and a hospital for the mentally ill were founded. Paramount to these legislators, however, was free education for all. One of their priorities was instituting the public school system provided for in the new state constitution. Segregation was not put into the law at that time: no dual "separate but equal" system was established.

There were many problems in the administration of the schools, and this left the lawmakers open to much criticism. But critics found the absence of a segregation provision in the common school acts just as serious an offense as any real administrative flaw.

South Carolina's antebellum government, with its low public expenditures, had spent $12 million in 1860. Despite a rise in taxes, the state debt rose to $22 million by 1871. A convention, with Negro members present, met to protest the mounting state debt. It leveled charges of bribery, fraud and corruption at the legislature. This kind of protest is often used as proof of the evils of black Reconstruction. But white officials, elected by both white and Negro voters, held most of the state administrative offices in which wrongdoing occurred.

The Mississippi house of representatives of 1871 numbered thirty-eight Negro and seventy-seven white members. Only seven Negroes ever sat in that state's senate; Negroes never controlled the Mississippi legislature or any branch of the state government. Hence no basis exists for the charges of "Negro misrule" in that state's Reconstruction legislature.

A former slave, John R. Lynch, served as speaker of the Mississippi house of representatives in 1872. He was born in 1847 in Concordia Parish, Louisiana, and freed during the Civil War. Lynch attended night classes in Natchez, Mississippi, acquired further education by self-study, and entered the photography business. Soon he showed a flair for politics, and in 1869 Governor Ames appointed him a justice of the peace for Natchez County.

Lynch won a seat in the lower house in the same year and was elected speaker. His colleagues later gave him a testimonial for his services. He was presented with a resolution commending his house leadership and "the impartial manner in which he had presided over its deliberations." Later he was elected to the U.S. Congress, and he also held other important posts.

The Mississippi legislature set up a new public school system, rebuilt penal and charitable institutions and enacted civil-rights laws. Charges of corruption were few, yet the state debt rose as a result of both the necessary reforms and the liberal spending.

No one knows the exact number of Negroes in Louisiana's Reconstruction legislatures. The varying shades of color made it difficult to determine the race of its members. The senate in 1868 was thought to include seven Negroes out of a membership of thirty-six. In the lower house, Negroes held nearly half of the seats. A Negro, R. H. Isbell, served as speaker of the house in 1868.

Factions developed among the Louisiana Republicans, which weakened the party's powers. Secret groups, such as the Ku Klux Klan, worked within the legislature, and the resulting intimidation of both whites and Negroes almost provoked open civil war.

In Alabama, Georgia and Florida the Negro's voting influence seldom equaled his ratio in the population. The Alabama legislature of 1868 had twenty-six Negroes as delegates in the house and only one Negro senator. Conflicts between Negroes and whites often arose at election time —particularly in Alabama where the Ku Klux Klan was active.

The outstanding Alabama Negro, James T. Rapier, had been educated in Canada. Rapier held local offices and in 1870 ran for the office of secretary of state. In 1872 he ran successfully for the U.S. House of Representatives, but in 1874 he was defeated by a white candidate. Caught in the Republican Party split, he failed to win another election.

The voters elected twenty-nine black house members and three senators to the Georgia legislature of 1868-69. But the white legislators voted in September 1868 not to seat the Negro members-elect. They appointed the whites with the next highest vote to serve in the Negro legislators' places. Finally, in 1869, the state supreme court ruled in favor of the Negroes, and they took their seats.

Two Georgians, Aaron A. Bradley and Henry MacNeal Turner, stood out from the rest of Georgia's Negro legislators. Bradley, an eloquent speaker who fearlessly attacked discrimination, was soon defeated at the polls. But the voters later rallied to his support and returned him to his seat in Atlanta.

Turner, born in South Carolina in 1833, had worked as an office boy in a white law firm and had studied law, history and theology. He became a licensed preacher in 1853. A man of marked ability, Turner served as the Union army's first Negro chaplain upon his appointment by President Lincoln in 1863. Following his discharge, he served as a minister in the African Methodist Episcopal Church. He was later recommissioned and detailed as an agent of the Freedmen's Bureau.

Turner was a member of the Georgia state convention, then won election to the legislature in 1868. During his tenure, he served on the committee on education and helped to develop

JAMES T. RAPIER

ALBION W. TOURGEE

HENRY M. TURNER

the public school system. As a Republican Party leader, Turner was assailed with many charges—all of which he disproved. In 1869 President Grant named him postmaster for Macon, Georgia, and he later served as a customs inspector and a government detective. The University of Pennsylvania awarded Turner an honorary degree in 1872. He was elected a bishop in the African Methodist Episcopal Church, as well.

The Florida legislature's Negro members sought alliances with farmers, carpetbaggers and poor whites, but the farmers and poor whites united to remove Negroes from the lawmaking branch.

When the North Carolina legislature met in 1868, it included 149 whites and twenty-one Negroes. The fifteen-man senate had three Negro members. Though few legislators of either race could claim much formal education, two of the Negroes served as speakers of the house. The situation in North Carolina resembled that in many other states. The northern carpetbaggers, southern scalawags and old Confederate leaders struggled among themselves for power. When the occasion demanded it, the poor whites and blacks took sides with one faction or the other. Eventually, just as in Florida, the southern whites united against the blacks to expel them from the

legislature. The same pattern was apparent in Texas, Maryland, Kentucky, Tennessee and Missouri.

The postwar legislation adhered to the federal Reconstruction Acts and ratified the new amendments to the U.S. Constitution, under which Negroes were given equal rights and the right to vote and hold office. Without the liberal Republicans, both black and white, in the southern states' legislatures, Reconstruction would not have taken place as quickly as it did, and the United States would have remained divided for many more years.

The Negroes' legislative record hardly deserves the criticism that some historians have heaped upon it. Corruption, extravagance and other government failings did exist. This was a corrupt period from the national level down to state and local governments. Political graft flourished in the North, where scandals broke around the Tweed Ring, the Salary Grab Act, Black Friday, the Credit Mobilier, the Whiskey Ring and other shady dealings in railroad high-financing, stock watering and bribery. Maladministration was confined to no one race, class or party.

A North Carolina judge during Reconstruction, Albion W. Tourgee, recorded his own opinions of the black statesmen. Summing up the

Negro's imprint on southern politics during his brief ascendancy under Reconstruction, Tourgee attested to the new governments in action: "In all that time," he stated, "no man's rights were invaded under the forms of law. Every Democrat's life, home, fireside and business were safe. No man obstructed any white man's way to the ballot box, interfered with his freedom of speech or boycotted him, on account of his political faith." Tourgee recalled the clash of opinions during the Civil War. Two peoples had grown up within the United States. They were called "the North" and "the South." One believed that all men were "created equal and endowed with certain inalienable rights, among which are life, liberty and the pursuit of happiness." The other held that such rights belonged only to white men, whose privilege it was to grant favors to Negroes as they saw fit. Tourgee also observed that "when the ostracism, proscription, outrage, abuse and murder in the South first began, there was no provocation; the victims had not done a single act which ought to have provoked wrath." Tourgee's novel *Fool's Errand* sold nearly 200,000 copies when it was published in 1879. It depicted the brutality of the Ku Klux Klan, gave an account of the South during Reconstruction and noted its failure to grant justice to its Negro citizens.

The Negroes voted the Republican Party ticket, but they showed a desire to cooperate with southern Democrat planters, many of whom actively encouraged their cooperation. Some of these whites joined the Republican Party and became leaders whom the Negroes followed. Other old aristocrats were torn between trying to re-establish the antebellum way of life and beginning a new, more democratic system. In any case, their relationships with Negroes, both personal and political, were invariably better than the poor whites'. The latter were jealous of the Negroes' new power and only rarely cooperated with blacks to achieve common goals. They continually pushed the Negro down, and this gave the oppressors the illusion of rising to the top, socially, economically and politically. So, owing to intimidation and fraud and their own lack of political organization, Negroes were eventually removed from the state political scene.

OTHER NEGRO OFFICEHOLDERS

Many Negroes served in other public offices during Reconstruction. Some owed their election to an alliance with Republican Party leaders. Others held appointive offices. South Carolina alone had two Negro lieutenant governors, a Negro associate justice of the supreme court, a Negro secretary of state, a Negro adjutant and inspector general and two Negro speakers of the house. Most of these were educated men who showed above average ability. Negroes also served as legislative clerks, postmasters and sheriffs. Some traveled to Chicago in 1868 as delegates to the Republican Party convention and some to the 1872 convention in Philadelphia.

Several of these Negroes were especially outstanding. Lieutenant Governor Alonzo J. Ransier of South Carolina had been auditor of Charleston County and a member of the constitutional convention before he assumed the state's second highest post in 1870. His successor, Lieutenant Governor Richard H. Gleaves, had served as a probate judge and president pro tem of the state senate. He remained the state's lieutenant governor until 1876. Associate Justice Jonathan Jasper Wright was the only Negro to sit on a state supreme court during Reconstruction. Born in Pennsylvania in 1840, he had studied in that state and in New York before leaving the North to organize schools for the freedmen in South Carolina. Justice Wright served as legal adviser to General Oliver Otis Howard after being admitted to the bar in 1866. Two years later, he sat as a member of the state constitutional convention. As a state senator, Wright was "clearheaded, quick as a flash, and could out-talk any man on the floor." He won election to the supreme court in 1870 and remained on the bench until his resignation in 1877.

Fewer Negroes gained public office in Mississippi, but those who did served well. Isaiah Montgomery, a former slave of Jefferson Davis, was named a justice of the peace in 1867—the first Negro to hold such office in the state. In 1873, Mississippians elected A. K. Davis lieutenant governor and James Hill secretary of state. Blanche K. Bruce, a future United States senator, first held minor offices in Bolivar County.

He was an assessor and tax collector before winning higher office. Of the state's seventy-two counties, twelve elected Negro sheriffs.

Louisiana, unlike the other southern states, before the war, had had among its citizens a large number of free Negroes who were both educated and prosperous. Some of them had owned thriving plantations and many slaves. In 1864 Louisiana, by popular vote, was the first state to free its slaves. But a strong white minority violently opposed this, and, as elsewhere in the South, the Negroes' potential political power was greatly feared. Louisiana Negroes organized themselves politically and voiced their opinions in the country's first Negro daily newspaper, the *New Orleans Tribune*, which began publication in 1864.

From this background, Negro leaders in Louisiana quickly rose to places of prominence. Oscar J. Dunn, a former slave who had purchased his own freedom, became one of three Negro lieutenant governors. He was well educated and showed both courage and ability during his tenure.

Dunn's successor, P. B. S. Pinchback, was born free in Georgia and educated in Cincinnati. His father, Major William Pinchback, was a white planter, his mother, a woman of mixed Indian and black parentage. After working as a cabin boy and then as a deckhand on boats traveling on the Missouri and Mississippi Rivers, Pinchback made his way to New Orleans about 1862, when Union Generals Benjamin Butler and N. P. Banks appointed him a recruiter of infantry and cavalry units for the Louisiana Native Guards. He resigned from his army appointment in 1863. After the War, Pinchback served as a state senator, delegate to Republican conventions and member of the city and state boards of education. He was elected a United States senator in 1873, but was never permitted to take his seat. He also edited a weekly newspaper, and was an internal revenue agent, surveyor of customs and practicing attorney.

When Louisiana's Governor Warmoth was removed from office in 1873, Lieutenant Governor Pinchback governed the state for thirty-five days —the first Negro to act as governor of a state for an extended period. Dunn had earlier acted as governor during Warmoth's absence from the state. Many white Louisianans were said to prefer a Negro governor to a carpetbagger.

Other high-ranking Negro officials in Louisiana included Lieutenant Governor C. C. Antoine, Secretary of State P. G. Deslonde, State Treasurer Antoine Dubuclet and Superintendent of Public Education W. G. Brown. Negro leadership was so powerful and federal control so complete in Louisiana that some state offices remained in Negro hands for many years.

The outstanding Negro leader in Florida was Jonathan Gibbs, a Dartmouth graduate. He was an able orator and great champion of equal rights. He served as secretary of state (1868-72) and was later superintendent of public instruction when Florida was establishing its public school system. H. S. Harmon and the Rev. J. W. Hood were also leaders in this field.

An outstanding Texas Negro, Norris Wright Cuney, worked as customs inspector, as sergeant-at-arms of the legislature and as school director for Galveston County. He was a candidate in Galveston's mayoralty election of 1875.

JONATHAN GIBBS

ALONZO J. RANSIER

P. B. S. PINCHBACK

ISAIAH MONTGOMERY

OSCAR J. DUNN

In other states Negroes also took an active part in Reconstruction politics, but black officials grew fewer in number as the race's voting power was obliterated by terrorism and fraud.

NEGROES IN THE UNITED STATES SENATE

Two Negroes represented their states in the United States Senate during Reconstruction. Both men, Hiram R. Revels and Blanche K. Bruce, were Mississippians by adoption. Revels was born of free parents in Fayetteville, North Carolina, in 1822. Bruce was born in 1841 of slave parents in Farmville, Prince Edward County, Virginia.

Revels moved to Indiana, then to Ohio, and then on to Illinois, where he attended Knox College in 1847. The same year he entered the ministry of the African Methodist Episcopal Church and traveled in several states as a preacher. At the outbreak of the Civil War, Revels was pastor of a church in Baltimore and aided in forming the first Negro Regiments there. He founded a school for freedmen in St. Louis, then joined the army as a chaplain in Mississippi. He later settled in Natchez, where he was once again a pastor and where he became active in politics.

HIRAM R. REVELS

While serving as a Natchez alderman in 1869, Revels was chosen to represent his county in the state senate. Then in January 1870, Revels succeeded to the United States Senate seat vacated by the Confederacy's ex-president, Jefferson Davis. He took his seat in February and served the final year of Davis' unexpired six-year term. This was the peak of irony—a black man succeeding the president of the Confederacy in the United States Senate.

A debate over Revels' admission lasted three days. His opponents insisted that their chief objections were that Governor Adelbert Ames, who signed his credentials, was not legally the state's governor, and that Revels had not been a resident of the state for the length of time required to qualify as a senator. In addition, they argued that because Revels was a Negro he was not a United States citizen—the Fourteenth Amendment notwithstanding. These charges were leveled prior to the date when the Fifteenth Amendment was ratified, legalizing the Negroes' right to vote and, by implication, to hold office.

Before a packed gallery of Negroes and whites, Senator Henry Wilson of Massachusetts ridiculed these arguments as "the slave power dying in the last ditch." He called the occasion "an historic event, marking the triumph of a great cause." The Declaration of Independence, he added, was now made a reality. On the vital roll call, forty-eight senators voted to admit Revels and eight opposed seating him. Revels was escorted to the bar of the Senate where he took his oath—the first United States senator of known African ancestry.

During his year in office, Senator Revels served on the committee on education and labor. He spoke out forcefully on an issue related to the District of Columbia public schools. He supported a bill to bar discrimination because of race, color or previous condition of servitude in the admission of pupils to any of the District schools. The bill also banned any racial discrimination in the education and treatment of pupils. He spoke out against prejudice, and against its practice in the South.

Although he represented Mississippi, and did so conscientiously, Negroes from all parts of the country looked to Revels as a leader. Among many petitions presented to him was one from

BLANCHE K. BRUCE

the Negro citizens of Philadelphia, asking for legislation to ensure equal protection of the law for all citizens.

The senator favored giving the vote back to disfranchised ex-Confederates. He told his colleagues what he had vowed to his constituents in Mississippi—that he "would abandon the Republican Party if it went into any measures of legislation really damaging to any portion of the white race." In fact, Senator Revels did leave his party after his term expired, claiming that it had been corrupt and had forfeited its right to political control. After he left the Senate in 1871, he was appointed president of Alcorn College by Reconstruction Governor Ames, who succeeded him in the Senate. Later, Revels was *ad interim* secretary of state for Mississippi. He returned to Natchez after this term, and died in 1901.

The second Negro in the Senate, Blanche K. Bruce, was born a slave in Virginia. He began his education with his master's son. He continued to study while he served as a printer's assistant, reading books and newspapers in his spare time. During the Civil War, Bruce went to Hannibal, Missouri, where, like Revels, he opened a school for Negroes. Then in 1866 he went to Oberlin College, one of the very few colleges which welcomed Negro students. From Oberlin he moved to St. Louis to seek a steamboat job. He traveled to Arkansas and Tennessee and finally settled in Mississippi in 1869. Bruce was then twenty-eight. Shortly thereafter he was appointed to positions of trust and honor.

Governor Ames chose Bruce as Tallahatchie County's conductor of elections. He served as sergeant-at-arms in the legislature of 1869-70. Then in 1871 Governor Alcorn appointed him assessor of Bolivar County. The same year he was elected sheriff, and later became superintendent of schools.

Bruce took his United States Senate seat in 1875 and completed a full six-year term. Senator Roscoe Conkling of New York, for whom Bruce named his son, became Bruce's close friend. He escorted the young Negro to the bar of the Senate to take his oath.

Senator Bruce served on a half-dozen committees, among them education and labor, pensions, and manufactures. As chairman of the committee which supervised the Freedmen's Bank, he ordered a thorough investigation of its failure. He sponsored a bill to reimburse those who had lost their savings in the bank's failure.

He was a fine orator, and spoke out on many occasions. On the death of Senator Morton he delivered a eulogy in which he declared: "No public man of his day, with the possible exception of Abraham Lincoln and Charles Sumner, was better known to the colored people of the South than Oliver P. Morton, and none more respected and revered."

His maiden speech had supported a resolution by Senator Morton concerning setting up a committee to investigate election frauds in the South, as well as the withdrawal of the remaining federal troops. He later spoke against a bill restricting Chinese immigration, pointing to "the strength and assimilative power of our institutions." He denounced in the same vein the United States policy toward American Indians. He proposed that they be granted citizenship and insisted that they be treated fairly. One of his bills would have set up a national academy of education "giving preference to the genius and talent of the land and to the orphans of the republic."

One of Senator Bruce's greatest concerns was the worsening political developments in his own state. He was alarmed by the intimidation of colored voters and by other acts intended to terrorize Negroes.

When the Senate denied admission to P. B. S. Pinchback, who had been elected senator from Louisiana, Senator Bruce championed his seating. He stated in an 1876 speech that the state's Negro majority of nearly 46,000 was sufficient reason to accept the legislature's selection of Pinchback as the state's spokesman.

When Bruce presided over the Senate on February 14, 1878, the *New York Tribune* remarked editorially: "Senator Bruce is universally respected by his fellow senators and is qualified both in manners and character to preside over the deliberations of the most august body of men in the land."

Bruce sat with the Mississippi delegation to four Republican conventions. In 1880 the senator was proposed as a nominee for vice-president, but he withdrew in favor of Chester Arthur. Bruce also presided over this convention for a period. He turned down an appointment as minister to Brazil and another as third assistant postmaster. At the end of his term in 1881, he was named register of the United States Treasury by President Garfield. President McKinley reappointed him in 1897. He served as a trustee of Howard University for many years and in 1898, shortly before he died, the school conferred an honorary Doctor of Laws degree upon him.

NEGROES IN THE UNITED STATES HOUSE OF REPRESENTATIVES

Twenty Negroes sat in the House of Representatives after the passage of the Reconstruction laws—between 1869 and 1901.

The first Negro to claim a seat in Congress was J. Willis Menard, elected from a New Orleans district. Born on a farm in Kaskaskia, Illinois, in 1838, he remained there until sent to school at the age of eighteen. He attended Iberia College, then won an appointment to a clerical position in the Department of the Interior in 1862, stirring up a storm of protest. One of his responsibilities was to make a study of a tract

of land in Belize, Central America. The site was under consideration as a possible Negro colony—a plan which never materialized. He moved to New Orleans in 1865 when he was made inspector of customs. During this period he edited a newspaper, the *Radical Standard*.

Menard ran in 1868 for a seat vacated in Congress. He was opposed by a white man, General Seldon. Both men ran on the same ticket, gained the same number of votes and were given certificates of election. Governor Warmoth signed Menard's credentials, but Warmoth's right to office was questioned by the House of Representatives. Though Menard was officially listed as a congressman, General Seldon claimed the seat and was sworn in. In defense of his election, Menard told the House: "I do not expect, nor do I ask, that there shall be any favor shown me on account of my race, or the former condition of that race. I wish the case to be decided on its own merits and nothing else." It was the first time that a Negro had spoken on the floor of Congress.

Although Menard failed to secure approval in the House, he was allotted full congressman's pay. It remained for Jefferson F. Long, a tailor from Georgia, to qualify as the first legally recognized Negro congressman. He served a term in the Forty-first Congress but declined to seek reelection.

The first of South Carolina's eight Negro House members, Congressman Joseph H. Rainey, took his oath late in 1870. He was born in 1832 in Georgetown, South Carolina—the son of parents who had purchased their freedom from slavery. Many of his black fellow members of the House were also representing South Carolina. This group of men included Richard H. Cain, Robert C. DeLarge, Alonzo J. Ransier, Robert Smalls, and Robert B. Elliott. Nearly all of these men had gained experience in the state legislature or in other public offices.

Congressman Rainey had been barred by law from attending school. But by his own efforts he obtained some education, and trained to be a barber. Later the Confederate army forced him to serve as a laborer. He escaped and took refuge in the West Indies. After the war he returned to South Carolina to sit in the constitutional con-

FFERSON F. LONG   J. WILLIS MENARD   JOSEPH H. RAINEY   ROBERT B. ELLIOTT   RICHARD H. CAIN

vention of 1868 and in the state senate. In Congress, the South Carolinian argued forcefully for civil rights. He and Robert Smalls both held office for five terms.

A dramatic incident occurred in the House when Congressman Alexander Stephens of Georgia, former vice-president of the Confederacy, spoke against the civil-rights bill. A South Carolina Negro member, Robert Brown Elliott, delivered a celebrated reply. He called on Stephens to accept the great doctrine of American citizenship.

"Let him lend his influence . . . ," Congressman Elliott said, "and he will have done that which will most nearly redeem his reputation in the eyes of the world, and best vindicate the wisdom of that policy which has permitted him to regain his seat upon the floor."

Born in Boston in 1842, Elliott attended schools in Jamaica and in England, where he studied law. When he returned to the United States he settled in South Carolina, where he edited a newspaper. He gained a seat in the state legislature in 1868 and was later adjutant general of South Carolina. In 1870 he was elected to Congress. He resigned the same year, then regained his seat in 1872.

Congressman Richard H. Cain, a native of Virginia, moved to Ohio as a child. He studied at Wilberforce University, but at the outbreak of the Civil War he moved to New York. There he became active in the African Methodist Episcopal Church, and was sent to South Carolina as a missionary to the freedmen. He ran for the state senate, served two years there, then won a seat in Congress.

These Negro congressmen fought not only for civil rights and equality, but for better public schools, Indians' rights and enactment of the two special-interest measures that concerned the South—lower cotton taxes and higher protective tariffs.

Congressman John R. Lynch of Mississippi spoke eloquently of the need for a civil-rights bill in this speech of 1875:

> I love the land that gave me birth; I love the stars and stripes. This country is where I intend to live, where I expect to die. To preserve the honor of the National Union of the States, hundreds, and I may say thousands, of noble, brave and true-hearted colored men have fought, bled and died. And now, Mr. Speaker, I ask, can it be possible that the flag under which they fought is to be a shield and protection to all races and classes of persons except the colored race? God forbid! . . . I appeal to all the members . . . to join with us in the passage of this bill, which has as its object the protection of human rights. When every man, woman and child can feel and know that his, her and their rights are fully protected by the strong arm of a generous and grateful Republic, then we can all truthfully say that this beautiful land of ours, over which the Star Spangled Banner so triumphantly waves, is in truth and in fact, the land of the free and the home of the brave.

After his retirement from Congress in 1883, Lynch was named fourth auditor of the United States Treasury for the Navy Department. He presided as chairman of the Mississippi Republican conventions from 1881 to 1892.

Secretary of State James G. Blaine commented on these Negro members of Congress in his memoirs:

> If it is to be viewed simply as an experiment, it was triumphantly successful. The colored men who took seats in both Senate and House did not appear ignorant or helpless. They were as a rule studious, earnest, ambitious men, whose public conduct . . . would be honorable to any race. Coals of fire were heaped on the heads of all their enemies when the colored men in Congress heartily joined in removing the oppressors, and who, with deep regret be it said, have continued to treat them with injustice and ignominy.

THE TWILIGHT OF THE NEGRO IN CONGRESS

In the post-Reconstruction period, new ways were found to subjugate the Negro. Whites had returned to their dominance in southern government, and every effort was made to end Negro voting by electing a "lily white" bloc to represent the South in Congress. Nonetheless, the Forty-ninth Congress (1885-86) included two Negro congressmen—Robert Smalls of South Carolina and J. E. O'Hara of North Carolina. The Fifty-first Congress (1889-90) also withstood the inevitable. It counted three Negroes—Henry P. Cheatham of North Carolina, Thomas E. Miller of South Carolina and John M. Langston of Virginia—among its members. After this Congress, only one Negro member sat in the House during each succeeding Congress prior to 1901. Cheatham served during the Fifty-second Congress. Then George W. Murray of South Carolina captured a seat in 1893. He held it until 1897. Finally, George H. White of North Carolina, elected in 1896, remained in Congress two terms before his defeat in 1900 at last broke the chain of victories.

The backgrounds and training of these black congressmen provide a study in contrasts. John Langston had given up the presidency of Virginia Normal and Collegiate Institute to enter Virginia politics. With his flair for oratory and mass appeal, Langston ran for Congress as an independent Republican. He attracted enough votes—mostly from Negroes—to win the election. But only after one of the most sensational challenges in House history did he gain his seat. The contest wore on until September of 1890, when the congressman-elect was finally sworn in. It was the last week of the Fifty-first Congress.

Langston later became inspector general for the Freedmen's Bureau and professor, dean, vice-president and acting president of Howard University. Before coming to Congress, he acted as minister-resident and consul-general in Haiti from 1877 to 1885. While in the House, he sat on the committee on education. He made efforts to establish a national industrial university for Negroes and to provide for the direct election of all congressmen and the President. Langston, a brilliant and eloquent debater, was the most scholarly Negro member of Congress during the Reconstruction era. He often disagreed with Frederick Douglass on political questions involving the Negro. He remarked sardonically, after his defeat in 1891, that "when it comes to the race question, the Republicans are all Democrats." He retired to the District of Columbia and died there in 1897.

Langston's colleague in the Fifty-first Congress, Henry P. Cheatham, had been born a slave in 1857. Nevertheless, he attended school in North Carolina, then went on to Shaw University. He graduated in 1883. Cheatham performed creditably during his two terms in Congress, but hardly in the spectacular manner of Langston in his freshman term.

The third Negro member of the Fifty-first Congress, Thomas E. Miller, was born of free parents in 1849. A native of Ferebeeville, South Carolina, he attended schools in Charleston and in Hudson, New York. He graduated from Lincoln University in 1872 and was admitted to the South Carolina bar in 1875. He served in both houses of the South Carolina legislature before taking his seat in Congress. After his term ended, Miller returned to the state legislature. He rounded out his career as president of the State College for Negroes at Orangeburg.

The last two Negro congressmen of the nineteenth century—Congressmen Murray and White—each served two terms. George Washington Murray, born a slave in 1853, received his early education through a tutor. He entered college in South Carolina in 1874 and remained there two years before entering politics. After filling several jobs at the state level, he entered the House in 1893. When the free-silver issue raged before Congress, Murray used the occasion to stress the patriotism of black Americans. "The Negro is always found voting and shouting for America and Americans," he said, "and on this currency question, he is in favor of an American instead of an English, German, French or Belgian policy." Murray favored expanding industrial training and proposed federal aid for the Cotton Exposition in Atlanta. During his second term, the South Carolinian laid petitions from Negroes before Congress protesting election injustices and pleading for federal intervention. When the Re-

JOHN M. LANGSTON

JAMES E. O'HARA

ROBERT SMALLS

HENRY P. CHEATHAM

THOMAS E. MILLER

GEORGE W. MURRAY

GEORGE H. WHITE

publican Party divided into separate "lily white" and "black and tan" conventions, Murray committed a political blunder which led to his defeat. He first joined the "lily white" group, then switched his affiliation to "black and tan." It was too late. After leaving Congress, Murray tried his hand in real estate—with disastrous results. He moved to Chicago, and lived there until his death in 1926.

George White, the last Negro survivor of Reconstruction in Congress, was destined to become a brilliant spokesman for his race. He attended public schools in Rosindale, North Carolina—his birthplace—and later entered Howard University. He studied law at Howard and was admitted to the North Carolina bar. White sat in the state legislature during the

1880's, then served as solicitor of the second judicial district of North Carolina. In 1897 he replaced Congressman Murray as the lone Negro in Congress.

White often managed to steer discussions toward civil rights. He argued for the passage of a tariff law so that Negro laborers and other workers would benefit from the bill's protection. "Bread and butter are what we want," White said, "not finespun Democratic campaign theory."

White urged that the South's representation in Congress should be reduced in accordance with the Fourteenth Amendment, since the Negro role in southern politics was restricted. (The clause, providing for reduced representation in the event of the South's practice of discrimination, was never implemented.) During his second term White introduced an anti-lynching bill. It met with strong opposition and was never passed. He turned to another issue: the status of returning Negro veterans of the Spanish American War. White fought to pass a bill to build a home for the aged and infirm out of unclaimed funds due to Negro soldiers. After his defeat at the polls, he correctly assumed no Negro would be elected to the next Congress. His farewell message drew loud applause from his House colleagues:

> This, Mr. Chairman, is perhaps the Negroes' temporary farewell to the American Congress, but let me say, Phoenix-like, he [sic] will rise up some day and come again. These parting words are in behalf of an outraged, heartbroken, bruised and bleeding, but Godfearing people, faithful, industrious, loving people—rising people—full of potential force. . . . The only apology that I have to make for the earnestness with which I have spoken is that I am pleading for the life, the liberty, the future happiness and manhood suffrage for one-eighth of the entire population of the United States.

CHAPTER TWO

The Birth of a Myth—
Separate but Equal

THE Fifteenth Amendment to the Constitution, passed by Congress in 1870, was the last and greatest of the Republican reforms during Reconstruction. After this, they seemed to feel that they had done their best and could rest their consciences. While the Republican Party had led the Negro out of bondage and into politics, it was also the party interested above all in economic recovery for northern business interests. Sometimes this goal conflicted with the Republicans' role as the Negro's protector. Gradually the northern politicians began to give more and more responsibility for the South back to the southerners. This meant one thing for the Negro: return to his old status—not slavery now, but something not much above it.

THE SEPARATION OF THE RACES

A new policy of racial separation began to replace the former relationship between whites and Negroes. Once there had been bonds of intimacy and family connections which had drawn whites and blacks together. There had been a freedom of association with pleasant personal contacts on the basis of merit. "The humblest black rides with the proudest white on terms of perfect equality," one English traveler had written after the war.

With Reconstruction reforms and the new black advances in political equality, however, whites came to consider these relationships as privileges temporarily bestowed on Negroes. Few southern whites recognized the Republican governments and black elected officials controlling their states. The old-line Democrats stood ready to reinstate their own leaders and to see that the Negroes, once ousted, would "stay in their place."

Soon new policies prevailed: segregated schools; separate churches and public accommodations; finally, voting booths for "white only." The gulf between the races widened, with the Negroes occupying the lowest status level in the rigid system. Southern whites saw this as a process of redemption with themselves as the redeemers. This meant nothing more nor less than canceling out the gains made during Reconstruction and reverting to the antebellum way of life, insofar as that was possible. That was an illusion, however. Redemption philosophies were no real substitute for the Old South, which lay buried in the rubble of the war. Nor were "Jim Crow," or anti-Negro, laws any real replacement for slavery.

In 1875 Tennessee passed a law granting railroads the privilege of refusing service to Negroes as first-class passengers. The other southern states passed laws between 1887 and 1892 segregating the races on railroads. The Georgia legislature approved a measure, soon copied by other southern states, to enforce streetcar segregation. Negroes boycotted in protest, but with little effect.

Tennessee moved to outlaw interracial marriages in 1870. Virginia and North Carolina passed similar laws in 1873, and again the other states fell into step. Then came a series of statutes aimed at reducing the Negro to an inferior role. "White only" signs went up in the schools, libraries, theaters, parks, hotels, hospitals, jails and even in cemeteries. A strong wall had been erected between the races, built of prejudice and buttressed by terror.

THE LAST FEDERAL CIVIL-RIGHTS LEGISLATION

The most eloquent and influential Senate Republican during the stormy postwar years, Charles Sumner of Massachusetts, was a firm and insistent champion of equality. He fought against segregated schools in his home state. Arguing before the Massachusetts supreme court in 1849, he maintained that the equality asserted by the founding fathers was an equality of law: "Its object was to efface all political and civil distinctions and to abolish all institutions founded on birth—Here nobility cannot exist because it is a privilege from birth. But, the same anathema which smites and banishes nobility must also smite and banish every form of discrimination founded on birth— Separation of children on account of color or race is in the nature of caste and, on this account, is a violation of equality."

Sumner believed that his party had not fulfilled its mission to bring about full emancipation. He opposed southern states-righters and Re-

CHARLES SUMNER

publicans as well as Democrats who upheld "white only" in public accommodations—whether they were hotels, hospitals or horse-drawn buggies. "I singly insist," he told his colleagues, "that in the employment of these institutions there shall be no exclusion on account of color." Sumner had sponsored legislation in 1861-62 to permit Negro witnesses to appear in the District of Columbia courts. He led the attack on the Washington and Alexandria Railroad's charter, which discriminated against Negro passengers. He fought to equalize pay for Negro soldiers. Sumner also spoke out for individual Negro petitioners seeking equal rights. Congressman Richard H. Cain sent Sumner one petition approved by seven thousand ministers of the African Methodist Episcopal Church and their membership of 375,000. The resolution declared that the churchmen "would never rest until, as American citizens, our race shall enjoy all rights and privileges on all the highways on this continent as any other class of people." Protests such as this emphasized the renewed effort to separate the races—a trend in process as Reconstruction ended and "home rule" returned to the South.

To the Deep South, Charles Sumner's zeal for equality might have seemed insincere. To New England, however, Sumner was real and true. He spent his life defending equal rights and attacking the premise of slavery. When the Senator died in 1874, a strong civil-rights bill was under consideration. Sumner himself had first introduced this bill in 1870; it provided for equal access to all public conveyances and public accommodations, including schools, theaters and cemeteries, and also to federal and state juries. It was the most far-reaching civil-rights legislation ever introduced—before or since—and it was, simply, too broad, too liberal, for many members of Congress. It died in a congressional committee.

Sumner introduced the identical bill again, and again it was killed in committee. He tried a third time, and the bill was ignored by the committee. So Sumner tried to attach the civil-rights bill as an amendment to another bill. Animosity was so high that the bill and its civil-rights amendment were both voted down. When Sumner tried this a second time, it was defeated again. Finally,

much against Sumner's wishes, the provisions for equal rights in schools and on juries were taken out of his bill, and it passed in the Senate but failed in the House.

In 1873, Sumner, still fighting for his original bill, re-introduced it, and it went to the Senate's judiciary committee. One month passed, two months, three months, four months. It was April, 1874. Senator Sumner was fighting to keep the bill alive, when he died. But his death spelled life for his civil-rights bill. Sumner's friends urged his Senate colleagues to adopt his civil-rights bill as a tribute to him and his cause. The Senate complied; the bill was reported out of committee and passed.

The Civil Rights Act of 1875 took effect on March 1 of that year. Unfortunately the school clause was dropped, but the bill did guarantee to Negroes the privileges accorded other citizens in inns, public conveyances, theaters and places of public amusement without discrimination due to race or former condition of servitude. This was the last of the Reconstruction Acts to protect the rights of Negro citizens.

The funeral of Charles Sumner in Washington, D.C.

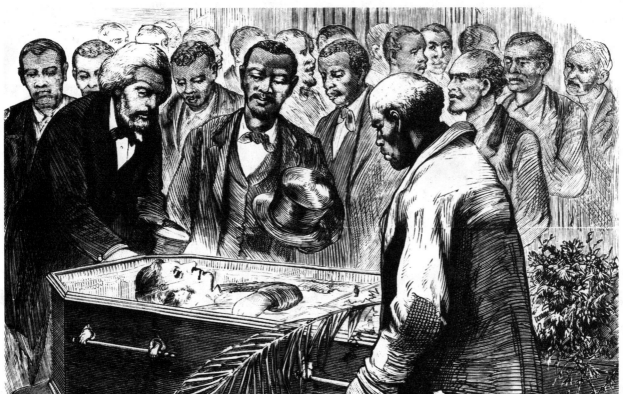

RECONSTRUCTION LEGISLATION AND THE SUPREME COURT

The next important concern was the effect the new legislation would have in reforming the southern temper. Some quarters had already seen an end to bigotry in sight. "It has been said that feeling cannot be changed by legislation," *Harper's Weekly* observed in 1874. "The moment the law enables the guest to call the offending host to account and the host is taught he cannot enforce whimsical distinctions among proper guests, the prejudice will soon wane." The same optimistic tone rang out in speeches by General Ben Butler and the Speaker of the House, James A. Garfield. In the Senate, Morton of Indiana and Edmund of Vermont shared this optimism.

In a short time liberal hopes received a blow. A case which had come to the Supreme Court in 1877 had already challenged the 1875 law before it was passed. *Hall* v. *DeCuir* actually tested a similar Louisiana statute, but the court's decision had a national impact. The Louisiana law required equal rights and privileges for both races on public carriers. A Mississippi River steamboat captain contested the law by refusing to admit a Negro woman to a white cabin as the boat traveled within the state of Mississippi. He held that the law interfered with interstate commerce, since cabins could not be integrated in every state through which the boat passed. The court sustained the captain's view and declared the law unconstitutional, ruling, in effect, that a state could not *prohibit* segregation on a public interstate carrier. Only Congress, in the court's opinion, could regulate interstate commerce.

Then the court considered a series of appeals known as the Civil Rights Cases. These five cases challenged the Civil Rights Act of 1875. They came to the high court from federal circuit courts and were finally decided in 1883. Two of the appeals, one from Kansas and the other from Missouri, resulted from Negroes being denied restaurant and inn services. Two other cases, from New York and San Francisco, stemmed from Negroes being barred from theaters. The final case was the only one originating in a former

Confederate state. In this instance, a railroad was indicted for refusing to allow a black woman to ride in a "ladies'" railroad car in Tennessee.

The court voted eight to one against the blacks in each case. The majority opinions were based on a strict interpretation of the Fourteenth Amendment, which prohibits any "state" from discriminating in its laws. The 1875 Civil Rights Act, however, had prohibited "individual" discrimination as well, and the court held that Congress lacked the power to extend such additional protection to Negroes. Nearly a century later the Supreme Court, under Chief Justice Earl Warren, would review that decision in upholding the 1964 Civil Rights Act. Under the Constitution's commerce clause, the Warren court ruled, congressional powers extend further than the 1883 court ruled in deciding the Civil Rights Cases. If that court had given more consideration to the commerce clause, perhaps the outcome of the 1883 decision would have been favorable.

The Civil Rights Cases were also judged in the light of the Thirteenth Amendment, which bars both slavery and involuntary servitude, but the court held that racial discrimination was not a form of slavery. "It would be running the slavery argument into the ground," Justice Joseph Bradley said, "to make it apply to every act of discrimination which a person may see fit to make as to the guests he will entertain, or as to the people he will take into his coach or cab or car, or admit to his concert or theater, or deal with in other matters of intercourse or business."

The Supreme Court justice suggested that Negroes had ceased to seek merely equal citizenship but sought to be "the special favorite of the laws." Recalling the prewar conditions of free Negroes, Justice Bradley mused that "no one, at that time, thought it was any invasion of his personal status as a freedman that he was not admitted to all the privileges enjoyed by white citizens, or because he was subjected to discrimination in the enjoyment of accommodations in inns, public conveyances or places of amusement."

Thus the court struck down the Civil Rights Act of 1875. Congress could adopt laws to bar the states from denying citizens their rights, it said, but could not prevent private individuals or corporations from discriminating.

JOHN MARSHALL HARLAN

RESPONSE TO THE DECISION

Negro citizens lost no time in expressing their dismay over the court's ruling. A mass meeting of civil-rights supporters convened on October 22, 1883, in Washington, D.C. Professor James M. Gregory of Howard University presided over the gathering at Lincoln Hall. Frederick Douglass delivered the main address. Resolutions urged Negroes not to vent their indignation in disrespect toward the court. Not only would this be useless, but it would lose vital friends, the resolutions maintained. The meeting voted instead to hold the political parties to their platforms in regard to the equality of all men before the law.

The civil-rights meeting adopted a statement declaring that "the progress of the colored American citizen in morality, education, frugality and general usefulness as man and as citizen makes it the part of sound policy and wisdom to maintain and protect him in the enjoyment of the fullest and most complete rights of citizenship." In this way, various Negro groups thought that their cause would be advanced rather than neglected

Justice John Marshall Harlan, the court's "great dissenter," took issue with the majority. He stated that its opinion was "entirely too narrow and artificial." The ban against Negroes could one day be extended to other groups, he warned. The Constitution, according to Justice Harlan, forbade placing "any class of human beings in practical subjection to another class, with power in the latter to dole out to the former just such privileges as they may choose to grant." Envisioning the growth of a color-caste system, the justice foresaw that "we shall enter upon an era of constitutional law when the rights of freedom and American citizenship cannot receive from the nation that efficient protection which heretofore was unhesitatingly accorded to slavery and the rights of the master."

Justice Harlan reasoned that "since . . . [slavery] rested wholly upon the inferiority, as a race, of those held in bondage, their freedom necessarily involved immunity from, and protection against, all discrimination against them because of their race, in respect of such civil rights as belong to freemen of other races." Many decades were to pass, however, before this thinking would stand as the law of the land.

JAMES M. GREGORY

as a result of Justice Bradley's ruling. In an 1889 meeting in the District of Columbia, however, Congressman John M. Langston of Virginia lashed out at the decision as "a stab in the back." Across the nation, other Negroes denounced the court's "betrayal" and charged it with "selling out" to the ex-Confederates.

Generally speaking, whites were apathetic to the decision, but a minority—especially in the South—received the decision with a feeling of victory. The *Arkansas Gazette* editorialized in 1883 that the law would not have been enforced anyway. "Society is a law unto itself," the *Gazette* remarked approvingly, "which in matters social in their nature overrides the statutes against its decrees; the written law is powerless." Between acts of an opera performance at the Georgia Opera House, the ruling was announced. The audience, reported the Atlanta *Constitution*, broke into a thunder of applause such "as was never before heard within the walls of the opera house."

The decision was taken more calmly in the North. The *Nation* mused on "how completely the extravagant expectations as well as the fierce passions of the Civil War died out." It concluded that "the decision settles the point forever that the Fourteenth Amendment merely adds new limitations upon state action." The *Independent* added: "In this way—in no other way—can our duplicate system of government be harmoniously and successfully worked. Several leading colored men have expressed great indignation and disappointment, [but] the court is clearly right." *Harper's Weekly* paid no editorial attention to the ruling. This in itself showed how quickly the North had lost the crusading spirit of the war. The one-time outspoken abolitionist Horace Greeley snapped that it was "time to have done with Reconstruction."

Negroes did find some support in the North, but it was temporary. The editorial pundits of the *Nation* declared that America had "no political machinery to protect ignorance and inexperience completely against skill, vigor and unscrupulousness, and the southern whites boast the possession of all three." Thirteen northern states' legislatures adopted their own laws to protect citizens' civil rights, in response to public

indignation. Still, this liberal sentiment gradually vanished. Slowly the northern states moved closer to the South in dealing with racial issues. Merchants, especially, saw practical business grounds for adopting southern attitudes.

By 1897 many states had taken advantage of the court's rulings to pass their own laws permitting discrimination—especially in public accommodation. Four states—Connecticut, Iowa, New Jersey and Ohio—adopted such statutes in 1884. Seven more—Colorado, Illinois, Indiana, Michigan, Minnesota, Nebraska and Rhode Island—followed their example in 1885. Pennsylvania took the same step in 1887, then Washington in 1890, Wisconsin in 1895 and California in 1897. It was clear that the Negro would be accorded separate treatment in the schools, the courts, libraries, theaters, hotels, hospitals, asylums and even in the graveyards.

RELATED RULINGS BY THE SUPREME COURT

Another series of Supreme Court decisions severely limited the Negro's right to vote. When the nation ratified the Fifteenth Amendment in 1870, legal challenges began working their way up through the federal courts. The first of these history-making cases tested the Enforcement Act of 1870. A Negro, Amzi Rainey, had tried to vote in a congressional election but had been threatened and assaulted. Rainey's attackers were indicted for violating the Enforcement Act. A federal circuit judge voided the indictment, holding that each state had the right to determine voting regulations for its citizens.

The Supreme Court found in a major 1875 case that the states also had the right to limit suffrage within their borders and that the right to vote was not a privilege or immunity of United States citizenship. In 1881, however, the Supreme Court did determine that state law could not limit voting to whites. In spite of that finding, a Kentucky court decided in 1884 that a state could limit the right to vote to white men.

The Supreme Court decided in two other significant cases of 1876 that the Fifteenth Amendment failed to confer the right to vote on Negroes. The majority ruled that it only guaranteed them freedom from discrimination by the states on account of race, color or previous condition of servitude, *while voting.*

Yet the court upheld the Negro's right to vote in a congressional election, ruling that Congress was empowered to protect voting rights in federal elections. The court's position was clear: southern states were barred from turning away Negro voters on the basis of race, color or previous condition of servitude. But the South was aided in its opposition to Negro voting by the court's strict adherence to the principles of states' rights in the enforcement of the Fourteenth and Fifteenth Amendments.

Another case, the 1895 appeal of *Gibson* v. *Mississippi,* marked the first appearance of a Negro lawyer before the Supreme Court. Among the Gibson attorneys was Cornelius J. Jones. The case involved the exclusion of Negroes from jury duty. The court ruled that the Negroes had failed to prove that the exclusion was due to racial bias. Hence a new rule of law developed: Negroes must establish by court evidence that their exclusion was racially motivated.

"SEPARATE BUT EQUAL" LEGALIZED

The wall of segregation was reinforced in 1896 when the Supreme Court heard the case of *Plessy* v. *Ferguson.* Louisiana had passed a law in 1890 requiring all railroad companies carrying passengers to provide "separate but equal" accommodations. It also provided that no persons could occupy seats in coaches except those assigned on the basis of color. Plessy, however, who was said to be one-eighth African and seven-eighths Caucasian by descent, took a seat in the coach for white passengers to test the state law. When requested to move to the Negro coach, he refused. A policeman evicted and arrested him for violation of the 1890 statute. Plessy filed suit, questioning the act's constitutionality and reasonableness, but was overruled. Then he petitioned the Louisiana supreme court for a writ of prohibition against the lower court judge, John Ferguson. The court denied his plea but heard his case on a writ of error.

The crusading novelist Albion W. Tourgee, "attorney for the segregated," as he was called, defended Plessy. He referred to the case in

---

RECORD, CASE No. 15,248.

SUPREME COURT OF THE UNITED STATES.

OCTOBER TERM, 1893.

TERM No., 880.

HOMER ADOLPH PLESSY, PLAINTIFF IN ERROR,

vs.

J. H. FERGUSON, JUDGE OF SECTION "A," CRIMINAL DISTRICT COURT FOR THE PARISH OF ORLEANS.

IN ERROR TO THE SUPREME COURT OF THE STATE OF LOUISIANA.

INDEX.

---

these words: "A discrimination intended to humiliate or degrade one race in order to promote the pride of ascendancy in another is not made a 'police regulation' by insisting that one will not be entirely happy unless the other is shut out of his presence. . . . This act is intended to 'keep the Negro in his place.' "

The fact that the law exempted Negro nurses, Tourgee argued, "shows the real evil lies not in the color of the skin but in the relation the colored person sustains to the white. If he is dependent it may be endured; if he is not, his presence is insufferable." The lawyer summed up the defense in one sentence: "Instead of being intended to promote the general comfort and moral well being, this act is plainly and evidently intended to promote the happiness of one class by asserting its supremacy and the inferiority of another class."

Justice Henry Billings Brown wrote the U.S. Supreme Court's opinion. And Justice John Marshall Harlan wrote another of his lonely dissents. The court decided that "separate but equal" accommodations did not deny protection to either race and was thus in harmony with the Thirteenth and Fourteenth Amendments. "A statute which implies merely a legal distinction between the white and colored races," Justice Brown ruled, "has no tendency to destroy the legal equality of the two races, or to reestablish a state of involuntary servitude."

Justice Brown dismissed Tourgee's contention that "the enforced separation of the two races stamps the colored race with a badge of inferiority." He reasoned that "if this be so, it is not by reason of anything found in the act, but solely because the colored race chooses to put that construction upon it. . . . The argument also assumes that social prejudices may be overcome by legislation and that equal rights cannot be secured to the Negro except by an enforced commingling of the two races. We cannot accept this proposition."

In place of this "coercion," Justice Brown offered his own proposition: "If the two races are to meet upon terms of social equality, it must be the result of natural affinities, a mutual appreciation of each other's merits, and a voluntary consent of individuals. Legislation is powerless to eradicate racial instincts," he added, "for to attempt to do so can only result in accentuating the difficulties of the present situation. If the civil and political rights of both races be equal, one cannot be inferior to the other civically or politically. If one race be inferior to the other socially, the Constitution of the United States cannot put them on the same plane."

The court had ruled that segregation was "within the competency of the state legislatures in the exercise of their police power," citing precedents to support this doctrine. Six cases had concerned school segregation rulings in the lower courts. In the seventh case to be cited, the Supreme Court had upheld a state law requiring separate coaches for the races on railroads. The court had in turn cited the precedent in *Hall* v. *DeCuir,* where it found that a law requiring integration interfered with interstate commerce.

Just as had happened in the earlier Civil Rights Cases, the dissent of Justice Harlan eventually eclipsed the ruling of the court's majority. He found that "separate but equal" placed upon Negroes "a badge of servitude wholly inconsistent with the civil freedom and the equality before the law established by the Constitution." The law of the land, Justice Harlan insisted, singles out "no superior, dominant, ruling class of citizens. There is no caste here. Our Constitution is color blind, and neither knows nor tolerates classes among citizens."

STATE ACTION AGAINST NEGRO SUFFRAGE

As late as 1879, southern white conservatives, hopeful of increasing their political alliances with Negroes, vocally opposed black disfranchisement. These were mainly the old Confederate leaders, however, still unmindful that the poor whites had more real power than the conservatives thought.

In the last two decades of the nineteenth century, many of the southern states discarded their Reconstruction constitutions guaranteeing free suffrage, because in their view those laws had been unfairly forced upon them by the radical Republicans. They substituted almost identical new constitutions, but added such clauses as the poll tax and the "grandfather clause." The latter provided that for a period of years after the constitution was adopted persons who had voted prior to 1861, their descendants, or those who had served in the wars, would be granted permanent registration without taxes or other requirements.

A new legal method—the poll tax—had been devised by the states to discourage the Negro from voting. It required payment of the tax in order to qualify for the ballot. The state assumed that Negroes would either not pay the tax or would fail to keep their receipts.

Mississippi found still other means of blocking Negroes from voting. In 1890 they outnumbered whites by more than 200,000 in this state. The black majority could have controlled elections in thirty-nine of the seventy-five counties. When a constitutional convention met in Jackson in 1890, it included 134 white delegates and one Negro, in contrast to the Reconstruction convention. This convention adopted its new legal framework for the state without submitting it to the voters. It provided that petty crimes would disqualify a voter and required a two-dollar poll tax as a voting prerequisite. The Mississippi constitution also specified that all voters be able to read any section of the state constitution, understand it and give a reasonable interpretation of it. This proviso was the well-known "understanding" clause. The literacy test was to be graded by the election managers who sought to disqualify as many Negroes as possible. Although the test could also serve to weed out illiterate whites, it was seldom used for that purpose.

The number of voters declined immediately after passage of the Mississippi act. Among the 116,000 Mississippians who had cast votes in the 1888 election were 30,000 Negroes. Four years later the total number of voters dropped to 77,000, only 8,000 of whom were Negroes. One of the constitutional convention's committees reported: "The white people only are capable of conducting and maintaining the government." The Negro population, "even if its people were educated, being wholly unequal to such great responsibility," should not vote. This committee urged repeal of the Fifteenth Amendment, "whereby such restrictions and limitations may be put upon Negro suffrage."

The Supreme Court ruled in the 1898 case of *Williams* v. *Mississippi* that these state laws did not violate the United States Constitution, since they did not discriminate between the races. It upheld such devices, saying that "it has not been shown that their actual administration is evil but only that evil is possible under them." This ruling naturally encouraged other states to follow Mississippi's lead in legalizing Jim Crow. As late as 1937 the poll tax law was tested and upheld by the Supreme Court.

Additional methods of keeping Negro voters from the polls also succeeded: polling places were set up in areas far from colored neighborhoods; election officials moved voting booths from place to place without notice; ballot boxes were stuffed to ensure a majority of white Democratic votes. Sometimes candidates resorted to bribery and false promises to secure votes. At other times officials mapped election districts into "gerrymanders" to reduce Negro voting power. This practice, still followed in some areas, allowed politicians to draw the boundaries of legislative districts to include or exclude certain party members, income groups or races, in order to ensure favorable election results. Sometimes a boundary line would be extended to an incredible distance to include a candidate's home, thereby making the area "his" district.

The effect of these evasive moves was clear. As Henry W. Grady, the influential editor of the Atlanta *Constitution* put it in 1890: "The Negro as a political force has dropped out of serious consideration."

South Carolina held a convention in 1896 to revise its constitution. Only six of the 160 delegates were black, even though the race outnumbered the state's whites by 225,000 in 1890. Since blacks were a majority in twenty-six of the thirty-five counties, the whites had already taken steps to curtail their power. An 1882 registration law had authorized the governor to name a state supervisor of registration for each county. Voters had to appear before him on a given date to be certified for the next election. The device had cut down the Negro vote as intended; it had also lowered the white vote. During the convention the white delegates asserted that blacks were too ignorant to vote. One of the six black delegates replied: "Why is the Negro ignorant? Is it not your fault? Was there not a law on the books in 1831 making it a crime for a Negro to learn to read and write?" The white delegates did not answer. The constitution which the convention wrote—and which was, as in Mississippi, adopted without a popular vote—called for a literacy test and a voucher that all taxes were paid as a condition of voting.

The Alabama Democratic Party platform declared that after thirty years of using all means to qualify the Negro to vote, it was obvious that "as a race he was incapable of self-government and the intelligent exercise of the power of voting."

North Carolina had passed the County Government Act in 1876, under which the legislature named the justices of the peace in each county, instead of having them chosen by local elections.

The justices of the peace, in turn, chose the county commissioners. This very effectively took power out of local hands and gave citizens no way of recalling or changing unfair administrations.

Thus, by various methods, the southern states deprived Negroes of the right to vote and to hold office. Although South Carolina's Negro population numbered more than 600,000 in 1896, fewer than 3,000 voted. That year Louisiana registered 130,000 Negroes for the election, but only 5,000 of them qualified by 1900. The Negro vote was estimated to have been cut in half in South Carolina, and to a fourth in Mississippi.

When the Virginia convention debated the issue of eliminating Negroes from the polls, State Senator Carter Glass declared openly: "Discrimination! Why, that is precisely what we propose. That, exactly, is what this convention was elected for: to discriminate to the very extremity of permissible action under the limitations of the federal Constitution, with a view to the elimination of every Negro voter who can be gotten rid of, legally, without materially impairing the numerical strength of the white electorate."

The white primary was yet another means of disfranchising black voters. By devising various means of preventing Negroes from taking part in the nomination of party candidates, the Democrats, who now had control of southern politics, assured themselves of no interference caused by the black vote. For all practical purposes the South would now be governed by a conservative, one-party system. Thus, through the "political process" the Democrats rebounded as the white party of the South, and the Republicans were driven out.

ORGANIZED TERROR

As early as 1867, white terrorist groups had sprung up in several locations in the South. They were known as the Knights of the White Camelia, the Jayhawkers or the Ku Klux Klan. Early membership was composed largely of young Confederate veterans seeking excitement. They found it when they brought terror tactics to bear on Negroes who did not conform to the old southern image. They also terrorized those whites (carpetbaggers and scalawags) who helped the Negro along to social and political freedom.

Under its grand wizard, former Confederate General Nathan Bedford Forrest, the Ku Klux Klan became more powerful and expanded its campaign of violence and terror in local areas. Their means of frightening Negroes became a familiar pattern. The mildest form of coercion was a menacing warning scrawled on paper decorated with a skull and crossbones. More severe punishment could follow: a whipping, banishment from home, even hanging.

The knight of the Klan became the "regulator" in some states. He established a code of "proper conduct" for colored people, which was intended to "keep them in their place." The influence of the Klan spread quickly through the South. Its members had one central mission: to frighten Negroes into readopting the submissive folkways of their days in slavery.

The Klan's grand wizard declared in 1869 that the organization was disbanded. The statement was a hoax to lull the North into complacency, and Klan operations continued undisturbed. The Reconstruction governments proved unable to cope with the Klan's tactics.

Finally, in May of 1870, Congress passed the Enforcement Act. This was the first of three "Force Acts" empowering the President to break up the underground organizations. It also ensured Negro voting rights. In other words, this was Congress' attempt to enforce the Fifteenth Amendment. The Third Force Act was known as the Ku Klux Klan Act because its intent left no doubt as to which organization it meant to subdue.

Enforcement of these laws was in the hands of the South's military rulers, so application was not uniform across the South. For example, in Mississippi, one of the most terror-ridden states, there were arrests and indictments but no convictions. In all, there were over seven thousand cases tried throughout the whole country, with fourteen hundred persons convicted. This was a very small percentage of the numbers of Klansmen and others involved in terrorism. President Grant estimated that in certain counties of South Carolina over two-thirds of the male population

Thomas Nast's cartoon depicting Negroes being terrified by the KKK and the White League.

were armed participants in the reign of terror. Neither he nor his deputies, however, made serious attempts to implement the laws. In 1883 the Force Acts expired; they were not renewed.

The Klan's power grew in the following decade in inverse proportion to waning Negro power. Repeated protests were lodged against lynching and violence toward Negroes during the 1880's. Each month, however, the reports of hangings, burnings, savagery and brutality mounted. Many Negroes—their lives at stake—remained silent. Even so, mass and individual protests were commonplace in many areas. An Arkansas clergyman, the Rev. E. Malcolm Argyle, wrote in 1892 that Negroes "all over the states are being lynched upon the slightest provo-cation; some being strung up to telegraph poles, others burnt at the stake and still others being shot like dogs." He described how a convention of Negroes had met to draft a protest to the governor deploring these outrages. The same year Frederick Douglass, accompanied by the dynamic Negro leader Mary Church Terrell, sought and secured an audience with President Harrison. The two urged him to end the mob violence, but he took no action.

Toward the end of the nineteenth century the Klan had achieved its goals: Negroes held few offices and seldom voted, and most spent their lives in patterns tragically close to those of bondage. White supremacy had triumphed in the South.

CHAPTER THREE

The Legacy of Reconstruction— Negro Participation in Politics and Labor

THE postwar Republican Party was clearly the champion of the black's right to vote and to achieve full citizenship. The attitudes of the Democrats in Congress were usually less favorable. For this reason, more and more Negroes gave their political allegiance to the Republican Party. A minority of blacks throughout the country did support the Democrats, however. Some of them were closely bound to white employers as barbers, house servants, coachmen, artisans, etc. They shared the interests of the master class and voted as their employers did—either from sympathy or from fear. Other more politically conscious Negroes saw few reasons to remain loyal to the Republican Party. It was doing nothing for them.

Since 1868 the Republican Party had been threatened with a split, nationally. That year the National Union Republican Party had nominated Ulysses S. Grant, a popular war hero but a weak political leader. Grant had been at one time a staunch conservative, but now he actively supported the party platform sympathetic to Reconstruction activities. His victory in 1868 re-

sulted in part from the votes of thousands of newly enfranchised Negroes.

The Republican Party continued to pledge support to the Negro: the party needed his vote. As time passed, however, it became apparent that the Republicans were only paying lip service to the cause. The Grant administration typified this attitude. While in office, Grant did very little to help the blacks, despite the promises of his party.

Congress authorized President Grant to suppress violence and proclaim martial law if southern state officials could not carry out Reconstruction. The President issued a proclamation on the new laws, but did little to enforce them. General Philip H. Sheridan reported from New Orleans in 1868 that official records showed that 1,884 persons had been killed or wounded in his command area. Six parishes had also been the scene of "frightful massacres and terrorism."

Throughout the South former slaveholders sought to evade the three new constitutional amendments and the laws protecting civil rights. They met with success, as a rule. Then, in May of 1872, the General Amnesty Act pardoned Confederate officers and soldiers. With passage of the Amnesty Act, southern antagonisms began to melt. The ex-Confederates could vote again.

Grant was reelected in 1872 primarily because of lack of unity in both the Democratic Party and his own. He was a moderate who, because of his record in the war, stood as a symbol of the Union. Most northerners favored Grant, and he captured the Negro vote again.

Not all Negro leaders wished to cast a bloc vote for the Republicans, however. A Cincinnati high school principal and civic leader, Peter Clark, pledged his support to the joint Democratic–Liberal Republican ticket in 1872, opposing Grant's reelection. Thereafter, except in 1878, when he ran for Ohio school commissioner on the Workingmen's Party ticket, Clark urged his followers to vote Democrat. Years later he explained his position:

"I have never thought it wise for the colored vote to be concentrated in one party," he insisted, "thus antagonizing the other great party, and tempting it to do against us as Republicans what it would have hesitated to do against us as Negroes. Whenever colored men find themselves in

GEORGE T. DOWNING

accord with Democrats in local or national issues they should vote with them, and thus disarm much of the malevolence that is born of political rather than racial antagonism."

A Rhode Island Negro, George T. Downing, preached the same doctrine on the East Coast. He debated this issue with Frederick Douglass at the Colored National Labor Convention in 1869. Downing defended a divided Negro vote, "because I believe it will be better to have more than one party anxious, concerned and cherishing the hope that at least a part of that vote may be obtained; because division would result in an increased support from all quarters."

THE END OF THE RADICAL REPUBLICANS

The old liberal Republican leadership was indeed passing. In its place, new men like Roscoe Conkling, John A. Bingham and George S. Boutwell appeared. Conkling had served as a congressman from New York from 1859 to 1863 and from 1865 to 1867. Then he moved over to the Senate, where he became a leader of the liberal Radical Republicans. A staunch advocate of equality, he once remarked: "Whenever I see

PETER H. CLARK

a black man, I always feel that I am with a friend." Bingham of Ohio, the father of the Fourteenth Amendment, believed in "equality of rights for all." He ruled out color as a basis for any legal distinction. Congressman Boutwell of Massachusetts, primary author of the Fifteenth Amendment, would allow no distinction in the rights and privileges of men. Without the right to vote, he contended, the Negro "is secure in nothing."

These men, nonetheless, lacked the unbending idealism of Sumner and Stephens. Their party had guided the nation through civil war. Now they thought the emphasis should shift to peace and conciliation. At this time notices were appearing in the South warning the freedmen to look out for themselves. With the return of the old social structure, their status was in their own hands. Reconstruction idealism crumbled. The Supreme Court's rulings, together with a federal "hands-off" policy toward the states and private enterprise, combined to sway the northern statesmen toward a new, more pliant policy for the South.

The Democrats would finally triumph in the South because the Republicans could not cope with racism, the economic crises of Reconstruction, the piling up of state debts and the necessity of imposing higher taxes. Banks and corporations went bankrupt. Finances were chaotic.

In the midst of these problems, southerners greatly resented their northern overseers for their views on Negro political and civic life. Some northerners had little sympathy for southern problems, knowing that the southern class system only undermined Reconstruction gains. Most northern politicians, however, were concerned with their own regions and were apathetic toward the problems of the rest of the country.

In the presidential campaign of 1876, the Republican nominee, Rutherford B. Hayes, could depend on neither the pro-Union support given Grant nor the big business vote. The Negro vote was no longer large enough to help him. The Republicans, recently so powerful, now could claim only to be evenly matched with the Democrats, and on election day the popular vote was split almost equally between the two parties.

The electoral vote, however, reflected the growing power of the Democrats, which was aided by the reinstated southern leaders. The southern Democrats agreed to throw their electoral votes behind Hayes after he had promised to withdraw the last of the federal troops from the South. In this way the Republicans won the presidency. The congressional elections, however, gave the Democrats control, spelling the end of the Reconstruction Congresses. Now the federal picture was approaching that of the southern states—a change from liberal Republicanism to conservatism, accompanied by apathy toward civil-rights issues.

When President Hayes took office, he made several trips to the South. His speeches assured Negroes that their rights would be safer in southern white hands than in the control of the federal government. It became clear this was not true when the last of the federal troops were removed from the South in 1877. With no federal intervention to support their policies, the liberal Reconstruction state governments collapsed. Programs to ensure Negro participation in government stopped abruptly. In Louisiana, the last southern state to lose its military overseers, church bells rang out and cannons were fired in celebration. The "Solid South" had entered an era of one-party rule which was to last for perhaps a century. Negroes, now powerless again, responded in the only way possible—by trying to get along with whites as best they could.

The next Republican victory was President James A. Garfield's, in 1880. He had courted the southern Independents—largely the poor white and most anti-Negro element—because their vote now replaced the Negro vote in the South. Garfield knew he could not win the southern Democrats to his side, for by this time the Democrats were gaining some national cohesiveness. The southern Independents' power was even more threatening to Negroes than was that of the southern Democrats.

After only six months in office President Garfield was assassinated. Vice President Chester A. Arthur succeeded Garfield, and, although he was in some ways a good President, he could not unify his party. In an effort to oust southern Democratic rule, Arthur supported the Independents.

But the Independents were aligned against the Negroes, so Arthur lost any black Republican support he might have had.

Northern Negroes broke with the Republican Party. Southern Negroes fortunate enough to remain politically active turned away from the party, too. Many of them considered this only a temporary move. A Negro editor from Tennessee, Edwin F. Horn, wrote in 1877, "Though hampered by circumstances, we are yet for the party of Lincoln, Grant, and Sherman."

REPUBLICAN DISAFFECTION AND FURTHER DEMOCRATIC GAINS

A splinter group of Pennsylvania Negroes led by Robert Purvis and William Still broke away from the Republicans in 1883 to form the Colored Independent Party. Frederick Douglass, still an acknowledged leader, did not condemn the split. "Follow no party blindly," he advised. "If the Republican Party cannot stand a demand for justice and fair play, it ought to go down."

WILLIAM STILL

ROBERT PURVIS

The Republican governor of Massachusetts, Benjamin Butler, named the first Negro judge in the North. The former Union general appointed George L. Ruffin to the bench in 1883. Born in Richmond in 1834, Ruffin went to Boston where he later gained a seat in the legislature. Judge Ruffin formed the Massachusetts Colored League in 1885 and served as its president. He issued a statement that the Republican Party of that day was no longer the same party it had been in the time of his friend Charles Sumner. He suggested that Negroes support the party that offered the most to them.

A third voice joined in the cry for independence. "Give us a new party," demanded T. Thomas Fortune of the *New York Age*. He denounced "the infamous barter and treachery—the effeminate, the juvenile, the nerveless policy pursued by Mr. R. B. Hayes. . . . We do not ask the corrupt Republican Party for sympathy," Fortune stormed. "We shun it with loathing and contempt! Sympathy indeed!" He insisted in 1886 that the Negro's goal should be "race first; then party."

GEORGE L. RUFFIN

In 1884 Grover Cleveland became the first Democrat since pre-Civil War days to occupy the White House. Though Cleveland had come to the presidency from the governor's office in New York, he reflected little of the northern racial outlook. He favored giving back to the southern states the captured flags of the Confederacy. Such a protest arose that this transfer had to be delayed. Pushed by southern Democrats courting the Negro vote, however, President Cleveland did name Negroes to some federal offices in the South.

Several Negro leaders became avid Cleveland supporters at this time. "We are neither manly nor politic in clinging to the hem of the garments of the Republican Party," insisted one of them, T. McCants Stewart. He pointed to the liberalism of the Democratic Party in 1884, citing appointment of forty Negroes to public office. And James G. Matthews, president of the Colored Citizens State Democratic and Independent Organization, maintained that year that all men were equal before the law.

The Chagrin Club of Colored Citizens organized as a Democratic affiliate in 1889. "If, as I

insist," C. H. Lansing, Jr., told the club, "the Democratic Party has been a cooperating and a contributing force to bring about this most desirable condition, I am sure that, with me, you will applaud its liberality and agree that it deserves the consideration of continued support."

By 1888, though, Benjamin Harrison had regained the Presidency for the Republicans. Once again Negroes were appointed to public office, if only as a means of appeasing the entire race. But the Negro reaction was just what Harrison wanted. Fortune stopped attacking the Republicans. "Let the good work proceed," he wrote. "Turn the southern Democratic rascals out." Other Negro newspapers went on record as Harrison supporters. Negroes seemed eager to rejoin the party. Frederick Douglass even praised some of the President's white Democratic appointees as a tribute to Harrison's impartiality.

But the white southern conservatives were still at work, and on issues of great and far-reaching importance to Negroes neither Republicans nor Democrats came to the black man's aid. Congress defeated all civil-rights measures, including the Lodge bill for federal supervision of elections.

In rural areas, for a brief and hopeful time, one alternative appeared for the disaffected Republican Negro—a political alliance with the white farmer.

POPULISTS AND THE NEGRO

Small farmers across the country were being taken for granted by business interests. Their oppressors were the northern industrialists, the railroads and the large landowning corporations. The farmers' plight was compounded by a severe agricultural depression during the eighties and nineties, caused partly by a cycle of bad weather and poor crops. This took its toll of small farmers, tenant farmers and sharecroppers.

Many Negroes fell into the last category. Some also owned small tracts of land, but all felt the effects of the economic depression. These various groups combined forces in the late 1880's with the remnants of the Readjusters, the old

Greenback Party, and a few independent groups. They called themselves the People's Party but soon became the "Populists." They first met formally in 1891 in Cincinnati, where they adopted a platform calling for the coinage of silver in a set ratio with gold ("free silver"), the secret ballot and governmental reforms.

The Populist movement sprang from the West —especially Texas and Kansas, where farmers were particularly hurt by the depression. As the protesting farmers united and watched their influence spread throughout the southern states, the realization dawned that all poor farmers— black and white—should join together. Thus the Southern Alliance and the Colored Alliance, both farm groups, combined forces in the South.

The first group of Negro tenant farmers had formed a bloc in 1886 when a bearded white Baptist missionary called them together to organize the Colored Alliance in Houston County, Texas. Other groups locked arms with them throughout the South. Soon the Alliance was a thriving organization of over one million members. The white Southern Alliance boasted a membership in 1890 of about three million. The two groups met together for the first time that year in Ocala, Florida, where they mapped out a program of united action. The headlines of the Atlanta *Constitution* announced the amazing news story of the integrated convention: "Black and white will unite in stamping out sectionalism. The Colored Alliance in Ocala is ready to join a third party which will lead to the welfare of the farmer."

The Alliances set up cooperatives and exchanges for their members to use in buying supplies and selling their crops. The Colored Alliance had such exchanges in Houston, New Orleans, Norfolk, Charleston and Mobile. To other Americans, these cooperative efforts foretold socialism. They feared the end of the free enterprise system. But none of these joint marketing ventures ever became a real threat to the country's capitalism, which flourished under the Republican administration's laissez-faire, or "hands-off," policy towards business.

The Southern Alliance became very powerful politically, if not financially. They attacked Democratic leadership, and demanded that candidates pledge themselves to the platform written at the Ocala convention. In the 1890 elections they claimed four governors, forty-four congressmen, one senator and control of eight state legislatures. They thus hoped to gain control of the Democratic Party in the South (although actually the reverse was happening), while in the rest of the country the farm groups were joining with labor to form their own third party. This was the greatest threat the Democratic and Republican Parties have ever faced.

A call went out for a second conference in Cincinnati in 1891. It would consider forming a third national political party with a platform demanding national reforms. The conference met on May 19 with fourteen hundred delegates from the Northern Alliance, Southern Alliance, Colored Alliance, Knights of Labor and the Union Labor Party. The southern delegates tried to segregate the Colored Alliance by proposing that the conference adopt the unit rule: each organization would meet separately and be allowed one vote. The proposal was overwhelmingly defeated. No separate seating arrangement occurred during the conference. The southern whites also opposed the third-party idea, hoping to make approaches to the Democrats. The Negro delegates supported the third-party plan.

In the meantime, the 1890 convention of the People's Party in Kansas had named a Topeka Negro, the Rev. Benjamin Foster, its candidate for state auditor. This Populist move prompted Kansas' black Republicans to demand that one of their number be placed on the ballot to run against Foster. The cry went unheeded by the Republican leaders. Although Foster lost, he drew a large Negro vote to the polls. Even in defeat he ran six thousand votes ahead of his ticket. Foster, who had studied at Fisk and at the Chicago Theological Seminary, won the respect of both races in the Topeka area. He remained an active Populist, both as a candidate and as a campaigner.

Other states soon followed Kansas' example in appealing directly to the Negro vote. Arkansas Populists nominated another Negro minister, the Rev. I. Glopsey, for Congress. They resolved in their platform of 1892 "to elevate the downtrodden irrespective of color."

NORRIS WRIGHT CUNEY

Texas, where both the Colored Alliance and Southern Alliance flourished, offered a different set of circumstances on the third-party issue. The leading Negro Republican, Norris Wright Cuney, had labored to keep his hold on the party. When the Populists formed in Texas, many Negroes declined to shift their support away from Cuney. A number of Negroes, however, were dismayed with the Republican power structure. One such man was John B. Rayner.

A native of North Carolina, Rayner was the son of a white plantation owner and a slave woman. After the Civil War, his father arranged for him to attend private school. Rayner pursued a teaching career and later was ordained a Baptist minister. He moved to Texas, where he taught school and dabbled in Republican politics. Then, when the third party formed in Texas, Rayner became an organizer. He traveled throughout the cities, campaigning on behalf of the Populists and forming "Colored Populists Clubs." When the 1894 state convention met, he served on the platform committee. The next two years he sat on the Texas Populists' executive committee. Rayner traveled through nineteen counties during the 1896 campaign, supporting the premise that only the Populist Party held

opportunity for Negroes. The election was hotly contested: Texas Democrats opposed a fusion of Republicans and Populists. Though the Democrats won—by a slim margin—they owed their victory to fraudulent election returns. This defeat, however, marked the rapid decline of populism in Texas.

WHITE BACKLASH

The advent of the Populists in the South, the Republican hopes for a comeback and the split in white Democratic strength made the Negro vote a pivotal factor. It also crystallized the issue of the Negro's role in politics.

South Carolina furnished an example of the racial tensions that accompanied the Populist movement. "Pitchfork Ben" Tillman, who ran successfully for governor in 1890, had received a large share of the Negro vote, including ballots of the Colored Alliance. After the election Tillman changed his stance and became a bitter racist. He tried to pass a bill to provide for separate railroad coaches for the two races—an objective attained when *Plessy* v. *Ferguson* was decided in 1896. He also called for a constitutional convention in South Carolina to deprive Negroes of their voting rights. The legislature turned down his suggestion, but he had set the stage for such action at a later date.

The southern "black belt" had already glimpsed the threat of Negro political control. The cloud of danger became even more ominous to the white South with formation of a third party devoted to uplifting the social and economic underdogs of both races. The conservative whites redoubled their efforts to achieve supremacy by coercing Negro employees (that is, threatening to fire them if they voted for the Populists). Some marched their colored field hands to the ballot box and forced them to vote for the Democratic ticket. In other cases, Negro ballots would be counted for the "Party of the South" whether they voted or not. Often Democratic majorities exceeded the voting rolls for entire counties—thanks to such instances of ballot-box stuffing.

Negro votes were much sought after by the Populists. The most outstanding bid for Negro

TOM WATSON

support was issued by Tom Watson of Georgia. Watson won a seat in Congress in 1890, running on the Alliance platform. He was the first southern Congressman to embrace Populist tenets and, therefore, one of the movement's acknowledged leaders. Watson sought to build a bridge between the races which would include political as well as economic ties. He envisioned a united front to advance the lower classes of both races.

The Negroes responded to Tom Watson and his speeches. They came in large numbers to hear him speak at rallies. The Georgia Congressman used a favorite device at such gatherings—that of making white men take an oath to defend Negro rights. The period's foremost historian, C. Vann Woodward, submits that never before or since have the South's two races been as close as they were during Tom Watson's early years with the Populists.

Negroes encountered more threats of violence during the Populist revolt of the 1890's than they had met during all the Reconstruction years. Nevertheless, they still lent their support to the new party.

Negro speakers who campaigned for Watson did so at the risk of their lives. Even so, a Negro minister, the Rev. H. S. Doyle, proved the most effective and zealous worker in Watson's camp. Doyle made sixty-three speeches on Watson's behalf in the 1892 campaign, stumping Georgia's Tenth District and appealing to Negro voters. Toward the end of the campaign, while he was speaking at Thomaston, Doyle was threatened by a white lynch mob. He fled to Watson, who installed him on his private grounds. Watson then issued a call for help to farmers in the surrounding area. All that night men rode into the town from neighboring villages.

In time, nearly two thousand armed Watson supporters gathered to protect the Negro. One of these men was the Populist sheriff of McDuffie County. Watson and Doyle held a meeting on the courthouse steps in which the House member said: "We are determined in this free country that the humblest white or black man that wants to talk our doctrine shall do it, and the man doesn't live who shall touch a hair of his head, without fighting every man in the People's Party." The farmers stayed on guard for two nights to protect the Negro minister from further violence.

"Mr. Watson was held almost as a savior by the Negroes," Doyle remarked after the incident. "The poor ignorant men and women, who so long had been oppressed, were anxious even to touch Mr. Watson's hand, and were often a source of inconvenience to him in their anxiety to see and shake hands with him, and even to touch him."

The resentment of white Democrats grew greater with the Doyle incident in Thomaston, however. Later, when Doyle and Watson shared a platform in Davisboro, a bullet intended for Doyle hit a white man in the back and killed him. On another occasion, a Negro man who had spoken on behalf of the Populists was later sought at his home in Dalton, dragged out and murdered. Five black Populists were shot down at Rukersville while voting. Their white slayers claimed to have been their owners during the days of slavery.

One account estimates that fifteen Negroes were murdered in Georgia during the state elections of 1892. These slayings—combined with threats and other acts of violence—were hardly sparked by Democratic victory fever alone. The white supremacists, aroused to bitter hatred, saw a chance to control the election. But they also saw a way to put the Negro down once and for all: simply remove his right to vote. South Carolina passed the law in 1895 which Ben Tillman had championed earlier. It struck down Negro voting rights and inspired other states to do the same.

DEFEAT OF POPULISM

The Populists had succeeded in their attempts to unify their own white and Negro followers. In so doing, however, they had fanned the flames of racial hatred. Southern conservatives joined the racist fringe out of fear of a return to Reconstruction and what they called "Negro domination." The Populist Party's 1892 platform declared that the Civil War was over and "that every passion and resentment which grew out of it must die with it; and that we must be in fact, as we are in name, one united brotherhood of freemen."

The Populists supported William Jennings Bryan for President in 1896; Tom Watson was his running mate. The party platform espoused Watson's thesis of equality, denouncing lynch law and the Ku Klux Klan and demanding justice for the Negro. It called for many needed reforms, such as the Australian or secret ballot and an income tax. While the campaigners raged over the "free silver" issue, however, the Negro question lurked in the background of many southern minds. If there had been a secret ballot, the Democratic Populist ticket might have gained broader support. But Tom Watson's ideas of equality and justice had little effect on the ever more anti-Negro Southland.

Although the Republicans won the election, many of the Populist reforms became the law of the land within a decade. The Negro, whom the Populists had brought out of political obscurity following Reconstruction, nevertheless suffered more severely from the rise of the People's Party than he had during thirty previous years of freedom.

The final blow occurred in 1904. Tom Watson not only deserted his former Negro allies, but he became a bitter and antagonistic foe of the colored race as well. A biographer contends

that Watson probably turned on the Negro for the sake of passing his Populist reforms. Watson, who ran for President as a Populist in 1904, did not then speak out directly against the Negro. He did, however, sanction Hoke Smith's platform when the latter ran for governor of Georgia that year. And one of Smith's planks called for repeal of Negro voting rights. Watson's reversal was complete. He began to speak of the blacks as a "hideous, ominous, national menace." The Georgian admitted that "if there is any human creature I do not understand it is the southern Negro." His shift in views toward the Negro was a disheartening sign of further rancor in the agrarian politics of the South.

Southern white Populists were enthusiastic supporters of black disfranchisement in the 1890's. As Negroes lost their civil rights, the Democrats concluded their absorption of the Populist remnants. Republican efforts to cooperate with Populists in order to overthrow the Democrats in certain southern regions were somewhat successful in 1892, less so in 1894, and by 1896 had disappeared altogether. Republicans, who favored big business, had nothing in common nationally with the Populists save a common antagonism toward the Democratic Party, Moreover, the southern Republican Party was too fragmented to solidify, and their takeover during Reconstruction had earned them the everlasting enmity of the Democrats.

NEGROES IN THE AMERICAN LABOR MOVEMENT

Like the farmer, the laborer suffered at the hands of the big businessman. The American labor movement as it is known today had its beginnings in the postwar period. It developed from a growing self-awareness among workers which brought recognition of their common problems.

The war had encouraged industrial expansion. Stepped-up production, however, led to increased use of machines, and machines threatened to replace workers. This was the fear brought about by the industrial revolution. Despite the use of machines to cut costs, moreover, management exploited workers. Children were hired at extremely low wages and were forced to work long hours. The new waves of immigrants coming from Europe constituted a competitive source of cheap labor, as did the recently freed slaves.

With the immigrants came new social ideas. In Europe many workers were organizing to secure their rights. The new Americans were telling the story of a European "socialist idealism." Workers in the United States were encouraged to organize for their own protection. They reasoned that only through organization could they be heard; out of this climate two new groups emerged.

The early labor union movements, black and white, paralleled each other. Both were involved in politics before establishing firm foundations in areas directly concerned with labor.

Sporadic attempts to organize unions followed the Civil War. One of the most significant of these efforts, William Sylvis' white National Labor Union, was formed in 1866 with the futile aim of unifying many of the small organizations which had sprung up. So many interests had to

be served that labor issues soon gave way to more central, political, goals. Even agitation for the most basic political reforms could not hold the group together, however, and it disbanded in 1872 after an unsuccessful attempt to gain the presidential nomination on the Democratic ticket.

Negro labor leaders, who were not represented by any element of the union movement, met in 1869 to form their own National Labor Union. Isaac Myers, its first president, promised to establish a coordinating unit between southern and northern black workers. This organization, the first to unify black workers, did not long remain an active force in Negro life. Like its white counterpart, the colored labor union went into politics in 1872. Influenced by Frederick Douglass, Myers and his followers supported the Republican presidential candidate. In dissipating its energies, the union lost strength. Its demise came in 1874, when Douglass, editor of the union's newspaper, New Era, wrote a scathing attack on unionism entitled "The Folly, Tyranny and Wickedness of Labor Unions."

THE KNIGHTS OF LABOR

The Knights of Labor was founded in 1869 as a secret movement because its members feared reprisals from employers. With their membership open to Negroes and whites, foreigners and native born, Protestants and Catholics, the Knights became a widespread workers' movement. They abandoned secrecy in 1878.

Led by Terence V. Powderly, the Knights stood for fairer wages, an eight-hour day and the abolition of child labor. They also fought for arbitration with management, but employers were so hostile that the Knights' efforts procured little result.

By 1886 membership had grown to seven hundred thousand. A radical socialist element had come into the union, involving members in many strikes and boycotts. But with union members gaining cohesiveness under the forceful leadership of Powderly, employers were forced to recognize the strength and the voice of the union.

The Knights' constitution made no racial dis-

TERENCE V. POWDERLY

tinctions among its members, and, in fact, from the first they encouraged Negro membership. The movement's slogan warned that "an injury to one is the concern of all." The Richmond *Dispatch* also noted that the Knights recognized "no line of race, creed, politics, or color." Negroes joined the order in large numbers. There were thirteen assemblies of Negroes in Richmond alone by 1885. The Knights mounted an open defense of the ideal of brotherhood by their locals—a move which strengthened their organization and brought about fair treatment of Negroes. But the Knights' decline came rapidly, following a dispute between the order's leaders over the use of political action to improve labor's status.

PROTESTS AND STRIKES

New labor openings appeared with the settling of the West and the effort to run railroad lines from coast to coast. The need for workers produced a search for all the cheap labor available. Usually this meant Negro and immigrant workers—those unskilled laborers who were forced to accept the lowest wages because their lack of training offered them no choice. Naturally

the workers who had previously held these jobs resented being replaced by the new groups. This was the source of much prejudice on the part of the working class against Negroes, Orientals and "foreigners." In the South the feeling against Negroes went deeper.

Southern industry met proposals to hire Negroes with the following objections. First, it was said that white and Negro workers would not work together. Second, the industrialists contended, Negroes could not stand the monotony of the mill or the foundry. Some managers also insisted that Negroes would work only until they received a small amount of money, then leave their work to spend their earnings. To disprove these arguments, Negroes took jobs on probation. Their performances proved the objections unsound.

In many instances, white workers balked at working with Negroes. Such action by skilled laborers often closed the door of opportunity to the Negro worker. White workers at times walked off the job when Negroes joined their work force. Some fifty strikes occurred between 1882 and 1900 to protest the hiring of Negro workers. Eleven times white strikers prevailed and forced Negroes out. In thirty-nine cases, however, the protests failed.

Negroes also wielded the tools of protest in the 1890's to oppose laws which substituted segregation for slavery. When southern cities segregated their streetcars, Negroes organized boycotts. Such protests occurred in Atlanta in 1894 and in New Orleans, Mobile and Houston. The efforts were poorly organized and lasted only a short time. Yet the companies lost thousands of dollars, and Negroes learned the value of cooperation against this form of oppression. The states modified their laws and adopted a special seating arrangement on public transport. This was one defeat for Booker Washington's advice that citizenship rights should await economic progress and personal achievement.

Strikes were common in the 1890's as workers fought to gain higher wages and better working conditions. A cotton pickers' strike occurred in Texas in 1891 and spread to other states through the Colored Alliance. The Negro farmers struck by agreeing not to pick cotton for less than one dollar and their board per hundred pounds. Groups in Memphis and Charleston had reduced the price of cotton picking to a "very low standard," according to the Rev. R. M. Humphrey, superintendent of the Colored Alliance.

Negro laborers now planned a strike on the St. Louis levee. Four steamers arrived in April 1892, and the longshoremen refused to unload them. Tying up the traffic at the loading areas, they demanded that the owners pay union wages. The workers, all Negroes, were completely organized. The unsuccessful strike lasted only a few days. A similar incident occurred in 1898 when Negro longshoremen struck for higher wages at Galveston, Texas. They also protested against the use of strike-breakers.

The most memorable strike of the 1890's was the Pullman strike, which began at the Pullman factory in Illinois. Colored porters had worked with this company since Pullman cars were first used in 1867. Porters had become institutionalized as a part of the sleeping car, as B. R. Brazeal relates in his The Brotherhood of Sleeping Car Porters. "The porter created a large portion of the company's good will," Brazeal points out, "for a passenger upon the completion of his trip usually recalled not only the mechanical comforts of the sleeping car, but the porter's cheerful service."

The porters took no active part in the strike. They were mere pawns in the struggle. Most of the strikers belonged to the American Railway Union, headed by Eugene V. Debs, who later ran three times for the Presidency on the Socialist ticket. The railway union could have had many Negro members, but it followed an anti-Negro policy and refused to admit Negro porters or other nonwhite train workers. Management—in this case the Railway Managers Association—spoke for more than forty railroads. The union decided to strike in 1894 unless it was recognized and conditions were improved. The managers held that contracts must be fulfilled. The strike spread to twenty-seven states and territories.

When employees of the Chicago stockyards struck in sympathy with the union leaders, management used Poles and Negroes as strike-breakers. They were regarded as "scabs." Defined by the union convention, the term means a man who works in place of a man who strikes. Yet the black Pullman employees were refused union membership as porters while the railway union welcomed the white workers' membership. Negroes then formed an anti-strike railway union. "The colored men went to work out of revenge for treatment received at the hands of the American Railway Union," the Chicago Herald of July 17, 1894, reported. The white workers' union opposed this move and burnt a Negro in effigy.

The American Railway Union ordered a boycott of Pullman which was effective in Chicago. The federal courts issued injunctions at the urging of the Justice Department. Since the strike cut off mail delivery, President Cleveland was forced to send in troops to preserve order. A reign of terror began. Debs and six others were arrested, charged with contempt of court and sentenced, but were released in the last days of 1895. While the Supreme Court upheld Debs' conviction and the legality of the injunction by a unanimous vote, its interpretation of the Interstate Commerce Act and the Sherman Anti-Trust Act provided a means of breaking strikes and boycotts. But this was only a temporary expedient. President Cleveland named an investigating committee which condemned the Pullman Company and the Railway Managers Association while exonerating the American Railway Union. But the union—facing opposition from both the Pullman Company and the Railway Managers Association—folded after this strike.

The Pullman Company then barred its service workers, conductors and porters from joining the organized labor movement. The "Big Four" railroad brotherhoods—formed between 1860 and 1893—excluded Negro workers from their membership. These unions would remain segregated for nearly another fifty years.

CHAPTER FOUR

Achievements despite Separation— A Black World Apart

ALTHOUGH the hopes implicit in emancipation and Reconstruction never materialized, their importance in our history should not be minimized. Freedmen were prepared for neither, and the suddenness with which they were forced to cope with freedom, independence and government is one of the tragedies history must record. Given those circumstances, our black ancestors performed magnificently in a time characterized by historians as the nation's bleakest era.

Socially, the new hope and energy which emancipation and Reconstruction gave the black people enabled them to expand their horizons. New opportunities beckoned, and the Negro was quick to respond. Two areas in which the freedmen made great progress, and laid foundations for a century of achievement, were education and religion.

PROGRESS IN EDUCATION

The following statistics demonstrate the great desire of the black people for education. The national rate of Negro illiteracy in 1870 was over 81 per cent. That figure had fallen to 70 per cent by 1880 and to 57 per cent by 1890. As striking as the figures for elementary education are those for higher education. Prior to 1876 only 314 Negroes held college and professional degrees. In the next sixteen years, however,

blacks earned thirty-seven hundred degrees. This remarkable progress grew out of efforts within the home and by the schools—despite their shortcomings—and from the determination of individuals to improve their lot.

The country's outstanding universities educated few Negroes before the mid-twentieth century. Some of these schools refused to admit Negroes; others whose policies were more liberal had few black applicants. Yale was the first university to award a Doctor of Philosophy degree to a Negro scholar; this was to Edward A. Bouchet in 1876.

The first Morrill Act of 1862 granted federal aid to several Negro colleges. Alcorn Agricultural and Mechanical College of Mississippi secured the first grant in 1871. The next year two other schools, Virginia State College at Petersburg and the Normal, Agricultural and Mechanical College of South Carolina, also received federal aid. Kentucky State Industrial College at Frankfort won a grant under the Morrill Act in 1889.

The second Morrill Act of 1890 marked the first participation of all-Negro land-grant colleges in the federal aid program. The law provided for the funds to be divided on the basis of population. Eighteen schools benefited from this act in the next six years. In view of the southern efforts to undercut Negro education, the aid program proved vital. The grants helped qualify large numbers as voters and productive citizens who otherwise would have been held down by new local, prejudicial (Jim Crow), laws which were now replacing the federal Reconstruction Acts. Progress in education was the Negro's strongest weapon in his struggle for equality.

Northern liberal teachers continued to devote themselves to developing Negro private schools in the South. The northern churches' missionary boards supported these, since Negro students could seldom afford to pay for their education. Despite local opposition, these dedicated men and women remained in the southern states, where they often were the only source of schooling for the newly emancipated children and adults. The majority of the educators had been abolitionists and worked with the missionary's zeal. Most of the various local freedmen's aid societies were church-funded extensions of the abolitionist movement, remaining in existence until the late nineteenth and early twentieth centuries.

Philanthropists—among whom Daniel Hand was a shining example—were eager to improve southern schooling. Hand set up a one million dollar fund in 1888, which was later increased by half. The Daniel Hand Educational Fund provided that the interest "shall be used for the purpose of educating needy and indigent colored people of African descent, residing, or who may hereafter reside, in the slave states of the United States."

Some southern leaders joined the cause of education. The Southern Education Board was formed to unite southerners and northerners in this common effort. The first president of the Board, Robert Ogden of Philadelphia, also sat as chairman of the board of trustees at Hampton Institute. Such activities lent a strong impetus to the Negro's scholarly advancement.

George Peabody's gift of one million dollars in 1867 (later more than doubled) set up the first foundation for southern education. The Peabody Education Fund sought to promote "intellectual, moral or industrial education among the

Many Negro schools placed great emphasis on practical training for their students.

GEORGE PEABODY   ROBERT C. OGDEN

Negro children filled the schools as quickly as they were opened.

young of the more destitute portions of the southern and southwestern states of our Union." Distributed on a basis of need and opportunity for usefulness, the Fund gave a much-needed boost to public schools throughout the South. The aid from the Fund was given to southern schools in general—not directly to Negro education.

Another agency for the advancement of Negro education, the John F. Slater Fund, also began with a gift of one million dollars from its founder, in 1882. In bestowing the gift, Slater said he intended to uplift "the lately emancipated population of the southern states, and their posterity." The Fund's major concern was supporting manual training, so that youths might learn "trades and other occupations."

One young Negro helped by this fund was W. E. B. Du Bois. He won a scholarship for foreign study in Berlin. He wrote former President Rutherford B. Hayes, then administrator of the Slater Fund, asking for a scholarship. "I have so far gained my education," he said, "by teaching in the South, giving small lectures in the North, working in hotels, laundries, etc., and by various scholarships and the charity of friends. I have no money or property myself and am an orphan. I respectfully ask that I be sent to Europe to pursue my work in the continental universities."

On the award of this scholarship, Du Bois expressed his "sincerest gratitude" to Daniel Colt Gilman, who had succeeded Hayes as head of the Slater Fund. His words of thanks included a prophecy: "I shall, believe me, ever strive that these efforts shall not be wholly without results . . . ."

THE ORGANIZED NEGRO CHURCH

Reconstruction left a strong impact on the Negro churches. It broadened both their organization and their membership.

The Methodist Episcopal Church had formed northern and southern divisions. Northern Negro members stayed in their regional church, and, at first, southern Negroes remained in the southern branch. Gradually there came a further division in the South.

The General Conference of the Methodist Episcopal Church South, meeting in 1866, provided for separate Negro congregations, districts and conferences. With approval of the church bishops, a general Negro conference group was formed. The 1866 meeting also worked out plans to transfer all property held by the older Methodist conference to the newly organized Negro group.

When the Methodist Episcopal Church South met in general conference in 1870, it reported that five annual conferences had formed for colored members. The delegates voted to form a Negro general conference. Thus, the General Conference of the Colored Methodist Episcopal Church convened later that year in Jackson, Tennessee. It elected its first bishops, the Rev. William H. Miles and the Rev. Richard H. Vanderhorst. A new name for the organization, the Colored Methodist Episcopal Church in America, was accepted unanimously. After the death of Bishop Vanderhorst, the church met in general conference in 1873 to elect three more bishops. These were Bishops L. H. Holsey, J. A. Beebe and Isaac Lane.

It was the Negro Baptists, however, who experienced the greatest denominational growth after the Civil War. Wherever a dominant personality took the leadership, a local congregation would spring up. No outside control served to limit the independence of these churches. They enjoyed complete freedom of worship. The Baptists entered communities where Negroes had not been able to form their own churches in the past. Baptist associations and conventions were organized as these groups began to feel the need for cooperation. The Negro Baptists of North Carolina held the first state convention in 1866. The next year Baptists in Alabama, Virginia and other states did the same.

Several of the black Baptist leaders of this period became very influential in the church and in the larger community as well. One such man was Richard Henry Boyd, the son of a white Texas planter and a slave woman. Boyd is known for founding a company in 1896 which still remains a prominent black business, the National Baptist Publishing House in Nashville. Spirited evangelists John Jasper and Charles T. Walker

L. H. HOLSEY

This Methodist Episcopal Church and other churches like it throughout the rural South provided their members with a strong sense of unity.

A visit from the minister provided moral support for many poor families.

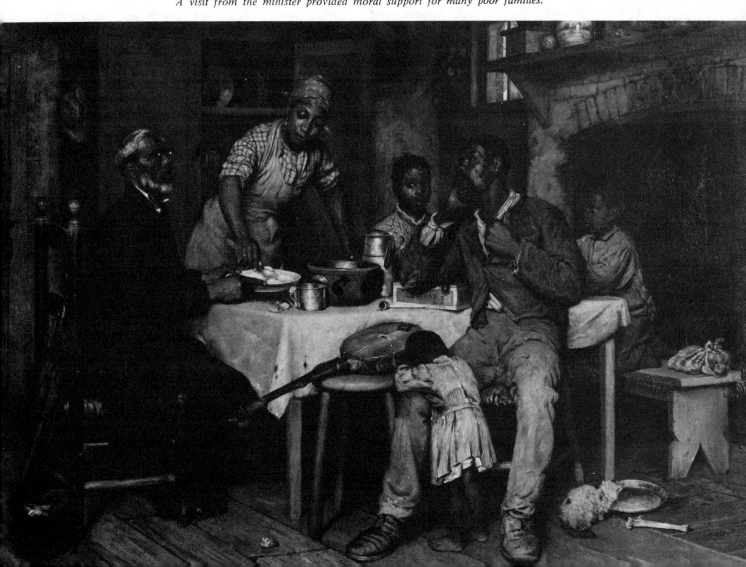

were among the nation's best-known preachers. Walker, whose sermons were also acclaimed in Europe, founded a Young Men's Christian Association in Augusta, edited a newspaper and was active in Georgia's Republican politics. Dr. Harvey Johnson, the son of slaves, built a very large congregation at Union Baptist Church in Baltimore. Johnson devoted much of his time to community service, helping Negro lawyers win admission to the Maryland bar and colored teachers gain entrance into the school system.

The African Methodist Episcopal Church expanded its work greatly as a result of the Civil War. Before the war, many of its South Carolina ministers, among them Daniel A. Payne and Morris Brown, were forced to leave the state. South Carolina forbade them to preach, so they moved North. Many others, however, remained to preach to their people in secret. The war's end opened new fields for the exiled, itinerant ministers. They went South under the leadership of Bishop Alexander W. Wayman "to seek their brethren."

When the General Conference of the African Methodist Episcopal Church met in 1868, it increased the number of bishops to seven by electing Bishops James A. Shorter, Thomas M. D. Ward and John M. Brown. A large gathering of ministers from the Deep South attended the conference in Washington, D.C. Membership grew so rapidly in that area that in 1872 a general conference committee reported that "our territory is greatly enlarged, our numbers augmented, and we rejoice in a united and vigorous denomination spreading its potent influence through every department of our national government."

The African Methodist Episcopal Zion Church (it approved the "Zion" in 1848) began to grow in 1863. In that year Bishop Joseph J. Clinton sent ministers to Florida and North Carolina. Large memberships soon appeared in these states and in Louisiana and Alabama. By 1880 the church had formed fifteen annual conferences in the South.

At this time other Negro church groups were forming and merging, although they attracted fewer members than those churches already named. Negroes in the Primitive Baptist Churches met in Columbia, Tennessee in 1865 to organize the Colored Primitive Baptists in America. The African Union First Colored Methodist Protestant Church of America resulted from an 1866 merger of the African Union Church and the First Colored Methodist Protestant Church. The General Assembly of the Cumberland Presbyterian Church legally set up the Colored Cumberland Presbyterian Church in 1869. None of these small sects, however active, could compete with the Baptists or African Methodist Episcopal Zionists in influence or membership. Most of the great black church leaders came from the larger churches—in some cases from traditionally "white" churches.

A Negro Roman Catholic priest-educator who made an immense contribution to American intellectual life was Father Patrick Healy. Born in Georgia, Father Healy was the son of a Connecticut sea captain and a black bondswoman whom the captain had freed and married. A member of the Society of Jesus, known as the Jesuits, Father Healy accepted the chair of philosophy at Georgetown University in 1866. Two years later he was appointed prefect of studies and began gradually to assume some of the duties of the president, because of the chief administrator's ill health. In 1873 Healy was elected president of Georgetown University, a post which he held until 1882.

Father Healy had a strong interest in forging high academic standards for the university. For this reason he chose to continue to function as prefect of studies while serving as president, thereby contributing much to the excellence for which the school is known today. A measure of the esteem in which his colleagues held him was shown when, against his will, they insisted upon naming the principal building on the Georgetown campus the Healy Building in his honor.

An important advance for black people came in 1875 when Father Healy's brother, James Augustine Healy, was named the first Negro Catholic bishop in the United States. He presided over the diocese of Maine and New Hampshire for twenty-five years. He was also honored by being named an assistant to the papal throne, an ecclesiastical office ranking just below that of cardinal.

JAMES AUGUSTINE HEALY

RICHARD HENRY BOYD

ALEXANDER W. WAYMAN

HARVEY JOHNSON

MUSICAL PERFORMERS AND COMPOSERS

The emergence of Negro entertainers really began at about this time, with touring musical troupes. Often these were family units like the Hyers sisters and the Luca family—Alexander C. Luca and his wife, sons and sister-in-law. The elder Luca, born in Connecticut in 1805, left the shoemaking trade for a career in music. He studied in New Haven while directing a Congregational Church choir. His family shared his talents, and they formed a small concert company. The Luca family made its debut at the New York anniversary meeting of the American Anti-Slavery Society in 1853. They traveled through New England and the Midwest, later joining with a white troupe, the Hutchinson family. With Alexander Luca as director, the two families presented joint concerts with tremendous success.

Hutchinson wrote in later years of those concerts "in the cruel days of the prejudiced past." He insisted that "in all our concertizing for 35 years, we never formed an alliance with any musical people with whom we fraternized more pleasantly, and loved so well, and who evinced so much real genuine talent in their profession, daily talk and conversation." The Lucas' white partner recalled that despite "the bitter prejudice of our audiences against us all for daring thus publicly to associate together, they cheered our combined efforts with loud applause and frequent encores."

Soon after the Civil War Charles Hicks formed the first successful all-Negro company, the *Georgia Minstrels*. It was a popular *Georgia Minstrel Show*. It was a very popular and lively show which toured successfully for many seasons. Managers and artists came and went, but the Georgia Minstrels kept their identity for over twenty years. Many famous entertainers got their start with this show, including the great character actor Sam Lucas.

After he left the Georgia Minstrels, Lucas went on a musical tour of England. When he returned he joined the Sam T. Jack *Creole Show*. It had made its debut in 1891 and later performed at the World's Fair. The show starred sixteen girls, with Lucas playing the comedian. This was a typical minstrel show routine, and the material parodied the southern Negro. Comedy at the expense of various national and ethnic groups was also extremely popular in the 1880's and 1890's.

Other productions satirizing Negro life followed Jack's show: *The Octoroons* and *Oriental America*, both in the 1890's. Each featured stereotyped comedians who exaggerated the whites' misconception of the Negro: he was travestied as an irresponsible, happy-go-lucky, wide-grinning creature who laughed loudly, rolled his eyes, danced, played the banjo, ate watermelon, sang Stephen Foster songs, and kept his audience in hysterical laughter through liberal use of slapstick comedy.

The princes of Negro comedy, Bert Williams and George Walker, appeared on stage in *The Gold Bug* in 1896. With two girl dancers, they made the Negro cakewalk famous. They worked together again in *Senegambian Carnival*. Both men starred in the famous Williams and

BERT WILLIAMS AND GEORGE WALKER

ANNA HYERS

EMMA HYERS

A. C. LUCA, SR.

C. O. LUCA

A. C. LUCA, JR.

J. W. LUCA

Wednesday Evening, Feb. 28th, 1872.

TO COMMENCE AT 8 O'CLOCK P. M.

OPERA HOUSE!

Grand Luca Concert.

OLMSTEAD LUCA

— THE —

Celebrated Black Pianist,

(Just returned from Europe after an absence of ten years,) has the
pleasure of announcing a

CONCERT!

— ASSISTED BY —

Madame A. A. Luca,
Contralto.

Mr. A. A. Luca,
Tenor and Violinist.

PROGRAMME.

PART I.

1. OVERTURE—"Tancredi," .... ROSSINI
   VIOLIN AND PIANOFORTE.
2. SONG—Good bye Sweetheart, ... HATTON
   MR. A. A. LUCA.
3. PIANOFORTE SOLO—"Le Reveil Du Lion," (Op. 115) .... KONTSKI
   OLMSTEAD LUCA.
4. TWO PART SONG—"The Wish," .... MENDELSSOHN
   MADAME LUCA & A. A. LUCA.
5. PIANOFORTE SOLO—Polka de Concert .... O. LUCA
   OLMSTEAD LUCA.
6. DUETT—Bridge of Sighs, ... WHITE
   MESSRS. A. A. & O. LUCA.

PART II.

7. AMILEE WALTZES. .... LANNER
   VIOLIN AND PIANOFORTE.
8. ROMANZA—"O can it be," .... MATTEI
   MR. A. A. LUCA.
9. PIANOFORTE SOLO—Sonata Patheticque, (Op. 13) .... BEETHOVEN
   OLMSTEAD LUCA.
10. DUETTINO—"I live and love thee," .... CAMPANA
    MADAME LUCA & MR. A. A. LUCA.
11. PIANOFORTE SOLO—"Andante & Rondo Capriccioso," (Op. 14). MENDELSSOHN
    OLMSTEAD LUCA.
12. DUETT—"What I live for," ....
    MESSRS. A. A. & O. LUCA.

☞ The Grand Pianoforte used on the occasion is from WM. KNABE & CO.,
kindly furnished by Mr. JOHN SELTZER & CO.

PRICES OF ADMISSION:

Reserved Seats, 75 Cts.   Unreserved Seats, 50 Cts.

Tickets to be obtained at the Music Store of JOHN SELTZER & Co.

Nevins & Myers Printers, 74 North High Street, Columbus, Ohio.

THE GREATEST MUSICAL PHENOMENA OF THE AGE!

THE FAMOUS CALIFORNIA VOCALISTS,

THE

HYERS SISTERS!

(COLORED.)

MISS ANNA MADAH HYERS .... Soprano

AND

MISS EMMA LOUISE HYERS .... Contralto and Tenore

ASSISTED BY

MR. WALLACE KING .... Tenor

AND

MR. JOHN LUCA .... Baritone

AND THE GIFTED PIANIST,

A. C. TAYLOR.

These young ladies (as will be seen from criticisms annexed)
have created a great sensation wherever they have appeared; and,
it being the intention of their father (who accompanies them) to
take them to Europe to perfect them in their art, he has been
induced, at the request of numerous friends, to make a tour
through the principal cities of America, to afford the musical
public and those anxious to hear these truly wonderful artists of
the colored race an opportunity of hearing them, and judging
for themselves. The music they sing is always of the highest
order, and their selections are from the most difficult and classical pieces that have been sung by the most accomplished artists.

Mr. WALLACE KING (tenor) possesses a fine voice of splendid
quality and great compass, which he uses with marked skill,
and is especially adapted to music of dramatic character.

Mr. JOHN LUCA (baritone) is also the possessor of a splendid
voice, and sings in admirable style, both in songs and concerted
music.

Mr. A. C. TAYLOR (pianist and accompanist). This gifted artist, besides being an excellent accompanist, is also a solo-player
of great promise. He has had the honor of playing before the
most critical audiences of New York and Boston; and it is predicted by our leading musicians he will rank with the first pian-
ists of the day.

Walker shows, then Williams performed on his own. In "The Comic Side of Trouble," an article Williams wrote for *American Magazine,* he contended that the Negro, despite adversity, was always a real optimist to whom laughter and joy came easily. When he could not laugh at life, Williams pointed out, the Negro sang. Bert Williams was a brilliant comedian, and one of the first Negroes to become a star in the theatrical world.

Scores of Negro singers made their public debuts during the postwar decades. Among them was a very famous prima donna of this era, Madame Marie Selika (in real life Mrs. Sampson Williams), who had chosen her stage name out of admiration for the heroine of Meyerbeer's *L'Africaine.* A patron discovered her remarkable coloratura soprano voice in 1879. In Boston the range of her voice inspired high acclaim. While touring in Europe she drew large crowds to concerts in Paris and Berlin.

Other Negroes showed musical gifts far above the average. One was the many-talented Henry F. Williams, a violinist, cornetist and composer. Williams played in the famous Jubilee Orchestra of Boston as well as the Gilmore Band. He composed *Lauriette,* a popular song of the day, *Parisian Waltzes,* which enhanced his musical reputation, and *I Would I'd Never Met Thee.* A remarkable Boston musician, Frederick Elliot Lewis, performed on the concert stage as a pianist, organist and violinist. Another brilliant Negro pianist, Samuel W. Jamison, had come to Boston from Washington, D.C., to study at the New England Conservatory. He gave recitals at Parker Memorial Hall during 1875 and 1876, demonstrating great talent at the keyboard.

An extremely versatile musician, Justin Holland, performed on the guitar and flute. Born in Virginia's Norfolk County, Holland enjoyed the words and music of an old song book as a small child. He moved to Boston to continue his studies. There he became interested in the guitar. Holland then studied at Oberlin College and moved to Cleveland four years later, where he gave guitar lessons.

Holland's published works totaled more than three hundred pieces of music. His arrangements of popular songs of that time, such as *Home Sweet Home,* were widely used. Many of his own compositions and medleys were also published for performance, and in addition he wrote *Holland's Comprehensive Method for the Guitar,* described by the *United States Musical Review* as "the most thorough, explicit, progressive, agreeable, and satisfactory [new method] in this country or in Europe."

Thomas Green Bethune, known as "Blind Tom," was the most famous Negro pianist of this period. He had a talent for music that caused others to marvel. Any piece he heard he could play from memory on the piano. His repertoire included more than seven thousand pieces.

"There is music in all things," a contemporary of his was quoted as saying, "but Blind Tom is the temple wherein music dwells. He is a sort of doorkeeper besides; and when he opens the portals, music seems to issue forth to waken the soul to ecstasy."

Born in Georgia in 1844, the blind child developed a musical interest at the age of two. When he was four, he was allowed access to the piano in his master's home. He became so accomplished that he was often asked to perform for his master and for guests. Later his master hired him out to entertain others, and Blind Tom's reputation grew. Despite his lack of formal training, Bethune became one of the greatest performers of his day.

An impressed observer reported that Tom "has played in almost every important city in the United States and in a great many of the smaller towns, in Paris, and in most of the principal cities of England and Scotland. Those who have observed him closely, and attempted to investigate him, pronounce him a 'living miracle' unparalleled, uncomprehensible, such as has not been seen before, and probably will never be seen again."

The critics put Blind Tom to numerous tests as a virtuoso, but he always managed to emerge triumphant. As one such musical authority recalled: ". . . whether in improvisations, or performances of compositions of Thalberg, Gottschalk, Verdi and others; in fact, under every form of musical examination and the experiments are too numerous to mention or enumerate—he showed a power and capacity among the most

HENRY F. WILLIAMS

FREDERICK ELLIOT LEWIS

BLIND TOM

JUSTIN HOLLAND

wonderful phenomena recorded in musical history."

The Colored Opera Company opened in 1872 in Washington, D.C. The next year it presented Jules Eichberg's *The Doctor of Alcantara* in both Washington and Philadelphia. A critic for the *Washington Chronicle* praised the singers highly, declaring that their dramatic and vocal skills "were quite as natural as [those of] many who appear in German and French opera." The *Philadelphia Inquirer* reviewer went even further in his praise. "The singing," he wrote, "is really unsurpassed by the finest choruses in the best companies."

Other Negro musical companies also prospered during this period—among them the Progressive Musical Union of Boston and the Philharmonic Society of New Orleans. They drew musicians from almost every large center of Negro population. In cities like Boston, Philadelphia, Detroit and New York, Negroes excelled as dance performers as well. New Orleans—the seat of French opera in the United States—employed groups of Negro dancers, singers and instrumentalists for its productions.

Pianist-composer Basile Barés, born in New Orleans in 1846, studied piano under Eugène Prévost, director of the French Opera House Orchestra. He performed in France in 1867. His first dance compositions were published two years later.

Another New Orleans pianist, Eugene Macarty, greatly impressed the French ambassador to the United States, who arranged for him to study at the Imperial Conservatory in Paris. Macarty also composed music and had a fine baritone voice.

The English Negro composer Samuel Coleridge-Taylor may be cited together with outstanding American Negroes. Though a foreigner, he maintained close artistic ties with the United States.

His *Hiawatha* made Coleridge-Taylor famous. He taught violin at the Croyden Conservatory of Music and composed waltzes, symphonic and choral works, and piano pieces and folk songs. The Englishman came to Washington in 1903 to direct a two-hundred-voice chorus—the Samuel Coleridge-Taylor Society, which had been named in his honor.

SAMUEL COLERIDGE-TAYLOR

One of the great Negro minstrels and song writers, James Bland, composed in the tradition of Stephen Foster. When Bland was fourteen, he had begun to perform at dinners and weddings as a minstrel show entertainer in Washington, D.C., where his family had moved when his father received an appointment to a federal office. The young musician was always more interested in music—particularly in playing the banjo—than in his studies, although he used his talent to support himself while he attended Howard University. One of his most popular tunes—*Carry Me Back to Old Virginny*—has delighted Americans through the years. Other Bland compositions, *In the Evening by the Moonlight* and *Oh, Dem Golden Slippers*, are so familiar they are sometimes considered folk songs.

Bland toured Europe, performing on the stage. But theatrical agents exploited him as they did Foster, because no copyright law then assured composers of royalties for the exclusive use of their songs. He died penniless and forgotten, although his songs will always be remembered.

CARRY ME BACK TO OLD VIRGINNY.

SONG AND CHORUS.

Words and Music by

JAMES BLAND.

Author of "The Old Homestead," "In the morning by the bright light," &c., &c.

Copyright, 1878, J. F. Perry & Co. 1,463—3.

SONGS FROM SLAVERY

Many northern whites who went to the South during and after the Civil War were enthralled by the beauty and variety of Negro songs. In 1867 the first collection of these folk songs was published under the title *Slave Songs of the United States*. In the same year Thomas Wentworth Higginson, the abolitionist turned Union officer, published songs he had heard his Negro troops sing. The interest generated by the study, performance and analysis of these songs spread throughout the United States and Europe.

In his study of American folklore, Richard Dorson says, "In terms of cultural history, *Slave Songs* erected a bridge from the obscure subculture of Negro folk music to the broad daylight of American civilization. This was to prove a two-way bridge, for the interest of the white public infected Negro singers and scholars."

The interest persists today; many artists and scholars continue the study of this unique musical form. Fisk University became a center for studies of Negro folk music in the late 1860's, when a chorus specializing in these songs began to give concerts. The Jubilee Singers quickly grew famous, even though several of the singers had initially balked at the idea of singing "plantation melodies."

When Fisk faced a postwar financial crisis, the university decided to send the singers on a northern fund-raising tour. The group performed in the White House for President Grant as well as in New England, the East and the Midwest. The Jubilee Singers did much toward popularizing the folk songs and spirituals in the northern cities. On a second northern tour, when they sang *The Battle Hymn of the Republic* at the World's Peace Jubilee in Boston, the chorus brought twenty thousand persons to their feet, with ladies waving handkerchiefs and men throwing their hats into the air. Later, the Fisk group sailed to England and sang spirituals before Queen Victoria and members of Parliament. The tour continued through Europe and was overwhelmingly successful.

The Jubilee Singers' concert tours raised $150,000, with which Jubilee Hall, a residence hall for women, was erected in 1875. Fisk still celebrates October 6, the day these singers set out on their first tour, as "Jubilee Day."

Later, from the Fisk campus, W. E. B. Du Bois would write:

> To me Jubilee Hall seemed ever made of the songs themselves, and its bricks were red with the blood and dust of toil. Out of them rose . . . bursts of wonderful melody, full of the voices of my brothers and sisters, full of the voices of the past.

The Fisk Jubilee Singers.

PAINTERS AND SCULPTORS

Two Negro artists—a man and a woman—left their imprint on American art in the years following the Civil War. They were Edward M. Bannister and Edmonia Lewis, both northerners born prior to the war. Bannister, a native of Canada, moved to Boston in his early years, then to Providence, Rhode Island. Bannister's first commissioned work was "The Ship Outward Bound." Then the Centennial Exhibition in Philadelphia in 1876 displayed his prize-winning painting "Under the Oaks." The Rhode Island School of Design has exhibited various Bannister paintings in its possession.

The sculptress Edmonia Lewis was a contemporary of Bannister's. She studied at Oberlin College, leaving there in 1860 for Boston. There she opened a studio while continuing her studies in clay modeling and sculpture. She made a medallion of the head of John Brown and a bust of Colonel Robert Gould Shaw in 1864. With funds from the sale of copies of the Shaw bust, Miss Lewis sailed to Europe, spending most of her time in Rome, where she continued her work. Her marble sculpture titled "Forever Free" was shipped to the United States for an exhibition in 1868. She completed a bust of Wendell Phillips in 1871 and later a bust of Longfellow for Harvard College. After her return to the United States, commissions came to Miss Lewis in large numbers. She exhibited several of her works in the Centennial Exhibition of 1876. Her "Death of Cleopatra" drew great acclaim from critics.

Another artist, Robert M. Douglas, Jr., of Philadelphia, possessed extraordinary skill and versatility. To support himself he operated a successful sign and ornamental painting business. But his greatest interest was in the painting of portraits.

Douglas made lithographs of William Lloyd Garrison and other well-known men of his time. He was a delegate to abolitionist conventions and, as a result, was refused a passport to visit England. The *North Star* said, before his death in 1887, that he was "an artist of skill and promise." The *Emancipator* described Douglas as "a disciple of Sully from whom . . . he has received the highest commendations."

EDMONIA LEWIS

EDWARD M. BANNISTER

INVENTORS

Congressman George W. Murray of South Carolina suggested during Reconstruction that the government print a list of ninety inventions patented by Negroes. His advice was ignored; this has complicated the task of pinpointing Negro inventions prior to the twentieth cenury. Even so, historians can trace a number of Negroes who broke new ground in the technology of this era.

The most valuable invention was made in the shoemaking industry. The president of the United Shoe Machinery Company of Boston, Sidney W. Winslow, maintained that his business success was due to his buying the patent on an invention by J. E. Matzeliger. Born in Dutch Guiana in 1852, Matzeliger came to Philadelphia to serve as a shoemaker's apprentice. He invented a shoe-lasting machine which outdated other mechanisms in use. It held the shoe on the last by a grip, drove nails into place, and delivered the finished shoe in an operation lasting less than a minute. Failing in his effort to form his own stock company, Matzeliger was forced to sell his invention. The device revolutionized the shoe industry and made United Shoe Company the largest shoe manufacturer of the day. The Matzeliger principle spread throughout the New England shoemaking districts, reducing shoe costs, raising workers' wages and greatly improving shoe quality and speed of production.

A pioneer engineer and inventor in New York, Lew H. Latimer, worked with both Alexander Graham Bell and Thomas Edison. He assisted Edison in 1878 and joined the General Electric Company engineering staff two years later. Latimer made the drawings for Bell's first telephone.

Two other Negro inventors, Elijah McCoy and Granville T. Woods, also served American industry. McCoy patented an automatic lubricating cup for machines in 1872. He secured patents in later years for fifty-seven inventions, most of which are in general use in lubricating machinery today. Woods worked mainly with electricity, the telephone and telegraph. He also invented a steam boiler furnace, an amusement apparatus, an incubator and automatic air brakes. He discovered a means to trans-mit telegrams between moving trains, and invented several important electrical devices for railways. General Electric, Westinghouse Air Brake Company and the Bell Telephone Company all bought patents from him.

These inventors—and other creative geniuses like them—proved what progress Negroes could make as individuals if granted the opportunity.

JOHN JONES: NEGRO LEADER

An early crusader for civil rights, John Jones was one of Chicago's most successful Negro businessmen. Born in North Carolina in 1816, his home a station on the Underground Railroad, Jones befriended both Frederick Douglass and John Brown. Jones entered a Chicago tailoring business in 1841, later erecting a four-story building as a business venture. He waged a one-man war against Chicago's discriminatory laws and saw their repeal in 1865. He entered politics, becoming a Cook County commissioner in 1874 and later the first Negro on the Chicago board of education. He donated much of his wealth to charity during his lifetime.

JOHN JONES

GRANVILLE T. WOODS

ELIJAH McCOY

J. E. MATZELIGER

LEWIS H. LATIMER

PAUL LAURENCE DUNBAR

A famous literary artist of the day, Paul Laurence Dunbar, had been singled out early in his short life by Frederick Douglass as "the most promising young colored man in America." Born in Dayton, Ohio, in 1872, Dunbar attended the city's public schools and edited his high school's newspaper. After graduating, the only work he could find was an elevator operator's job which paid him four dollars a week.

Dunbar received his first public attention when a high school teacher asked him to deliver an address of welcome to the Western Association of Writers meeting in Dayton in 1892. Dunbar delivered the welcome in metrical form, to the delight of his audience. He hastened back to his work, but the next day Dr. James Brander Matthews sought him out. Dr. Matthews questioned him about his life and secured copies of his poems. Dunbar's first volume of poems, *Oak and Ivy,* was published in 1893.

Frederick Douglass soon arranged for the young poet to read his works in a special ceremony. When Douglass died, Dunbar wrote a poem in memoriam. The last stanza reads:

PAUL LAURENCE DUNBAR

Ah, Douglass, thou hast passed beyond the shore,
  But still thy voice is ringing o'er the gale!
Thou'st taught thy race how high her hopes may soar,
  And bade her seek the heights and not to fail.
She will not fail, she heeds thy stirring cry.
  She knows thy guardian spirit will be nigh.
  And rising from beneath the chast'ning rod,
  She stretches out her bleeding hands to God.

Two of Dunbar's friends agreed to support the publication of his poems while allowing him to maintain ownership of the work. This agreement led to publication of *Majors and Minors,* which sold a thousand copies in 1895. *Harper's Weekly* published a favorable review of the book. His *Lyrics of Lowly Life* appeared in 1896.

Dunbar's life came to a tragic end when he was only thirty-four, but he left a legacy in lyric verse which will not be forgotten. His idiom was to America—black and white—what Robert Burns' was to the Scots. He ranks with James Whitcomb Riley, the Hoosier poet who wrote in the dialect of the Indiana farmer.

ECONOMIC ADVANCEMENT

Black workers, too, were making noteworthy gains. Negroes continued to seek jobs in new fields, and by 1890 the census showed 57.7 per cent of the Negro population gainfully employed. Most of those working—about 88 per cent—had farm or domestic help jobs. Farming, fishing and mining employed 57 per cent of the Negro work force. Nearly another third were engaged in domestic or personal service. Roughly 6 per cent toiled in mechanical and manufacturing industries. Another 5 per cent worked in trade and transport fields. A meager 1 per cent were listed as "professionals."

By 1900 a few notable shifts had taken place in these work categories. Those in agricultural jobs dropped four points to 53.7 per cent. Domestic and personal services remained at 33 per cent. Fractional gains appeared in the other job columns. The trend toward a greater spread of job skills reflected the progress in training many Negroes had made by the turn of the century.

A sizeable number of imaginative Negroes entered various small business ventures and took the lead in gaining cooperation to form larger firms. The small-scale establishments included

WHEN MALINDY SINGS

BY

PAUL LAURE[NCE]
DUNBAR

ILLUSTRATED W[ITH]
PHOTOGRAPHS BY [THE]
HAMPTON INSTITU[TE]
CAMERA CLUB

DECORATIONS BY
MARGARET
ARMSTRONG

Candle-Lightin' Time

by

Paul Laurence Dunbar

Illustrated with [photographs]
by the
Hampton In[stitute]

HOWDY HONEY HOWDY

BY

[PAUL] LAURENCE DUNBAR

Illustrated with photographs

BY

LEIGH RICHMOND MINER

Lyrics of Lowly Life

By

Paul Laurence Dunbar

With

An Introduction by W. D. Howells

POEMS OF CABIN AND FIELD

BY

PAUL LAWRENCE DUNBAR

ILLUSTRATED WITH PHOTOGRAPHS
BY THE
HAMPTON INSTITUTE
CAMERA CLUB
AND DECORATIONS BY
ALICE MORSE

DODD MEAD & COMPANY
NEW YORK MDCCCCIV

Majors and Minors:

::: POEMS :::

BY

PAUL LAWRENCE DUNBAR.

grocery stores, barber shops, restaurants and funeral homes. Large businesses were few, since the Negro businessman had little capital and investors persisted in regarding him as a poor credit risk.

A field in which Negroes had prospered, even in the pre-Civil War days, was that of food preparation and private catering. A New Englander, George T. Downing, began his catering services with a small business in Rhode Island; as his reputation and prosperity grew, he began to cater for many important functions on the East Coast, including those at the Capitol in Washington. Another outstanding caterer was Charles S. Smiley, a successful Chicago businessman. Much of Mr. Smiley's popularity was due to his versatility; when asked to cater a wedding, he would not only prepare the wedding cake and other food but would offer to arrange for the delivery of the wedding invitations, floral arrangements for the church, guards for the wedding gifts, and extra ushers.

Late in the Reconstruction era, Negroes also began to establish banking houses. The Rev.

W. W. Browne headed the first great effort of the Negro to organize a bank—an effort resulting in the formation of the Savings Bank of the Grand Fountain of the United Order of True Reformers, in Richmond. The bank opened in April 1899, with $100,000 in capital. Eleven years later the bank had greatly increased its capital and had opened thirty-two new branches. In Washington, D.C., Negroes opened the Capital Savings Bank. Organized in 1888, this venture was an immediate success. It survived the panic of 1893, paying every obligation on demand, and stayed in business until 1904. Two years after the founding of the Capital Savings Bank, another small private bank came into existence. This one, the Alabama Penny Savings and Loan Corporation, opened its doors for the first time on October 15, 1890, with two thousand dollars in capital. The bank was on such a limited budget that for the first few months of its operation the officers received no salaries. Eventually the Penny Savings and Loan Corporation began to prosper, and in the panic of 1893, while the white First National Bank had to close

Although farming had lost some of its appeal, Negroes working the land remained a familiar sight in the South.

The True Reformers Savings Bank, the first to be founded by a Negro.

The Capital Savings Bank.

W. W. Browne, founder of the True Reformers Savings Bank.

Treasurer and Manager
Chelsea Restaurant Company, Inc.
1308 Sansom Street
Philadelphia

H. FRANKLYN HALL

AUTHOR and INVENTOR
OF THE
"KITCHEN KING"

The Greatest Invention of the Age.

An Authority on all Cuisine and Culinary matters.

THE SOUTHERN CAFE
MEALS AT ALL HOURS

10 and 15 cts.

Miss S Warren, Proprietress

1037 BAINBRIDGE STREET

BUSINESS MEN S
LUNCH ROOM AND RESTAURANT
Good Quick Service
Townes & Sons, prop.
1304 SANSOM STREET

E. C. DAWKINS

Fine Groceries

Delicatessen

TEAS AND COFFEES...... AND WHAT ....YOU EAT

N. W. Cor. Watts & Poplar Sts.

Philadelphia

Advertisements such as these, which appeared in a Negro journal, attest to the success of Negroes in the catering and restaurant businesses.

its doors, the Negro bank remained open and solvent.

Some twenty-eight banks were founded by Negroes between 1889 and 1900. Most were short-lived; none survives today. Negro fraternal orders, benefit societies and churches wielded a vital influence in these undertakings. They wanted depositories for their funds, and felt that the establishment of Negro banks for that purpose would benefit the entire Negro community.

The Negro insurance firms were also a product of the fraternal organizations. B. L. Jordan, a member of the True Reformers, founded the United Aid and Insurance Company of Richmond, which had a membership of 21,500 and branches in all cities of Virginia as well as in some other states. Another successful insurance firm was the North Carolina Mutual Life Insurance Company, which was formed in Durham in 1898. Also founded in 1898 was Samuel W. Rutherford's National Benefit Life Insurance Company. It expanded rapidly, and ranked as one of the most prosperous Negro companies during the first years of the twentieth century. However, like so many banks and insurance companies across the country, it failed to survive the Great Depression.

NEGRO BUSINESS LEADERS

During the late 1800's, Negroes made steady progress in the world of business. Stories of those who achieved success in their fields became more and more common.

In Boston, J. H. Lewis opened his own tailoring firm, beginning with a working capital of one hundred dollars. By 1896 his firm had begun to gross $150,000 annually.

W. Q. Atwood, of Saginaw, Michigan, owned and operated a lumber business valued at $100,000. Both a civic leader and businessman, Mr. Atwood gained the respect and friendship of most of the people in his community. He was appointed the only Negro member of Saginaw's board of trade.

In 1871 Samuel Harris of Williamsburg, Virginia, went into business with a total capital of seventy dollars. By 1896 his firm had a gross annual income of $55,000, and he owned much real estate in areas near Richmond, Norfolk and Newport News.

Warren C. Coleman, born a slave, first went into business as a dealer in rags, boxes and iron scrap. Eventually he, too, moved into the field of real estate and accumulated an estate estimated at $100,000. At the peak of his career he served as vice-president and then president of the North Carolina Industrial Association, a group formed to promote industry among Negroes.

These men represent but a few of the many Negroes who were successful in business. By 1900 achievement in the field was so great that Booker T. Washington issued a plea for successful businessmen to unite in a national organization. His plea was answered with the formation of the National Negro Business League.

In late August of 1900, more than four hundred Negroes from thirty-four states met in Boston to form the league. Dr. Washington was elected president, and T. Thomas Fortune was made chairman of the executive committee. The *Boston Transcript* observed of the meeting: "Here were men who understood that the only sure basis of progress is economic." By the time the 1905 convention of the league was held in New York City, more than three hundred local leagues operated under the banner of the national organization.

The business leaders who started these firms and supported these organizations blazed new trails in Negro life. Their ambition and success gave added hope to Negro people as they moved upwards from slavery.

THE NEGRO PROFESSIONAL

Like the businessmen and laborers, many Negro professionals believed that the opportunities for progress would be greater in the large urban centers, especially in those cities with a high percentage of nonwhite residents. Although prejudice against the Negro doctor or lawyer was often in evidence, particularly in his exclusion from the majority of the white professional societies or associations of his city, the contributions of men like Dr. Daniel Hale Williams did much to combat such prejudice.

W. Q. ATWOOD

J. H. LEWIS

SAMUEL HARRIS

WARREN C. COLEMAN

DANIEL HALE WILLIAMS

A graduate of Chicago Medical College, Dr. Williams remained in that city to establish his own practice. He helped in the founding of Provident Hospital, the first interracial hospital in the nation. In 1893, his operation on James Cornish, victim of a knife wound, made medical history: it marked the first time that successful surgery had been performed on the human heart. The techniques used in the operation were studied by physicians throughout the country. In recognition of his skill, Dr. Williams was offered a position on the staff of Freedmen's Hospital in Washington, D.C. While in Washington, Dr. Williams not only established a training school for nurses but helped to launch the Medico-Chirurgical Society of the District of Columbia, an association of Negro physicians, all of whom were excluded from the white medical society and medical association of the District of Columbia.

The first Negro elected to the American College of Surgeons, Dr. Williams received many honors before his death in 1931. In 1956 his accomplishments were commemorated by the United States Treasury Department in its sale of savings bonds.

Among the Negro physicians who gained recognition for their skill were several women: Dr. Hallie Tanner Johnson, the first certified female doctor to practice in Alabama, Dr. Caroline Anderson of Philadelphia, and Dr. Alice McKane, founder of a Savannah nursing school.

Further professional gains were made through the success of many of the Negroes who entered the field of law. In Chicago, Edward Morris not only conducted a successful law practice but served two terms in the state legislature and was appointed to the Republican state central committee. F. L. Barnet served as the first Negro assistant state's attorney, and men like these, through their skill, their confidence and their perseverance, helped to open the door to future generations of able and dedicated Negro professionals.

CHAPTER FIVE

Implications of Black Inferiority— The One-sided Issue

THE last decade of the nineteenth century, the "Gay Nineties," had witnessed heated debate over the alleged inferiority of the Negro. But as the task of reuniting North and South advanced, the new issue of nationalism pushed the race issue aside. This hardly eased the plight of the Negro or that other underdog, the foreign-born immigrant. Neither law nor custom was on their side. They remained second-class citizens at the turn of the century, despite signs of measured progress. In order to lessen the chance of racial conflict, the southern states declared, contacts between black and white would be restricted. Racial separation would be enforced in travel, theaters, restaurants, churches, schools, industry, and in political and social structures.

A more subtle and cunning racial barrier arose in the North. Negroes could not buy or rent houses outside the areas generally understood to be reserved for them. The masses of Negroes accepted these restrictions. Even when they could afford homes in white sections, few were willing to "rock the boat." Yet a minority, resentful of these limitations upon their rights, watched for chances to attack them. They noted cynically that the real estate codes failed to ban

the foolish, the uncultured, the dishonest. The only yardstick was a man's color.

Other disheartening events were occurring in the meantime on the voting front. In 1880 Congress had forbidden the military to oversee elections in the South. Three years later, Congressman Henry Tucker of Virginia filed a House bill "to repeal all statutes relating to supervisors of elections and special deputies, and for other purposes." It passed Congress the following year and President Cleveland signed it into law. The Tucker Act nullified major sections of the Enforcement Acts, thus stamping out what remained of Negro voting rights in the South, with the tacit acceptance of Congress. The Tucker Act notified the southern states, in effect, that their obstacle courses for Negro voters—their poll taxes, property taxes, literacy tests and grandfather clauses —would stand unchallenged.

Presidents Hayes and Arthur had failed to enforce the Civil Rights Act of 1875, either by word or by deed. Nor did their attorneys general. The Supreme Court voided the law in 1883.

In his first presidential message, Benjamin Harrison agreed that Negroes had been deprived of their rights and urged Congress to pass a law guaranteeing "a free exercise of the right of suffrage and every civil right under the Constitution and laws of the United States." But by 1890, the election laws were defunct. The "Force Bill," which sought to revive them, did not get the support of Congress, despite the efforts of Senator Henry Cabot Lodge of Massachusetts. Senators from the South and the West united to defeat the bill as part of a bargain to gain support for "free silver," a major issue in the nineties.

Notwithstanding these severe setbacks, Negroes inched forward toward self-reliance. Their illiteracy rate dropped from 80 per cent in 1870 to 57 per cent in 1890—thanks to a school program which sent many from primary grades through some higher training. This sort of training boosted the ranks of Negro "professional-service" types to thirty-four thousand by 1890. A growing number of Negroes were also buying homes. Some 235,000 Negroes owned homes free of debt by 1890, and by 1900 that figure rose to more than 295,000. Hence, in Negro communities across the nation, an increasing number were entering the "solid citizen" circles of the middle class.

THE CONCEPT OF NEGRO INFERIORITY

The belief in Negro inferiority held sway during Reconstruction and in its aftermath despite the growing Negro American middle class. This concept arose prior to the South's segregation laws and served to justify them. It held that Negroes were a different breed of mankind, biologically inferior to whites. Many Europeans shared this belief. They partitioned Africa, with "the white man's burden" as their rationale. When they colonized the Dark Continent, they sought to place the African natives under "proper supervision." The editor of the *Atlantic Monthly* viewed the Europeans' credo as one ripe for plucking by white southerners. "If the stronger and cleverer race is free to impose its will upon 'new-caught sullen peoples' on the other side of the globe," he asked, "why not in South Carolina and Mississippi?" This school of thought—an extension of the "master race" doctrine of the Confederacy—found a class of eager disciples in the solid South.

HENRY WARD BEECHER

Although many abolitionists worked hard to win freedom for the Negroes, most were not interested in them socially. Negroes remained less than equal, even when possessing full political and civil rights for a few short years after the Civil War. Then new writers appeared on the southern scene to further undermine Negro progress, inflaming passions with the prewar doctrine of inferiority.

The great Henry Ward Beecher, staunch supporter of emancipation, was once asked what plans the abolitionists had for absorbing Negroes into the American mainstream after freedom. Beecher, in reply, stated that Negroes could certainly not be expected to perform in the same manner as their white counterparts—implying inherent inferiority.

Earlier in the nineteenth century, Samuel G. Morton and Josiah Nott had turned to physiological studies in an attempt to prove the Negro an inferior race. So did others seeking to justify racism in the last half of the century. They purported to use scientific methods—anthropology, biology and ethnology—to influence American thought. They subjected Negroes to physical and mental tests, measuring the head and brain. They examined differences in anatomy, then made their reports. But the studies were based on inconclusive data. They reflected the biases of the testers more than actual scientific findings. Often the discourses would begin with mention of the "well-known" racial differences, alerting the educated reader to the researchers' prejudices.

One of these latter-day propagandists, Hinton R. Helper of North Carolina, issued an anti-Negro tirade entitled *Nojoque* in 1867. The color white was to Helper "a thing of life, health, and beauty." Black was "a symbol of ugliness, disease, and death." Helper's thesis left no one doubting where he stood. "We should so far yield to the evident designs and purposes of Providence," he wrote, "as to be both willing and anxious to see the negroes, like the Indians and all other effete and dingy-hued races, gradually exterminated from the face of the whole earth."

John Van Evrie expressed the same view the following year in his *White Supremacy and Negro Subordination*. The inferior Negro could not be uplifted, he said, and he conjectured that education would be harmful because it would develop the cranium and give the Negro "a broad forehead and small cerebellum," thereby affecting his center of gravity and interfering with his capacity to stand erect or to walk.

The influential editor of the Atlanta *Constitution,* Henry W. Grady, also believed firmly in Negro inferiority. "The supremacy of the white race of the South," he told an audience in Dallas in 1887, "must be maintained forever, and the domination of the Negro race resisted at all points and at all hazards—because the white race is the superior race."

In Frederick L. Hoffman's 1894 study, *Vital Statistics and the Negro,* the author suggested a new way to document Negro inferiority through statistics. "What else but a high rate of mortality and low degree of morality," he asked, "could be the result of such tendencies of a race wholly unprepared for the intensity of the struggle for life. . . . On the strength of the facts that are here brought together [in this report], I cannot but repeat that the differences are physical and permanent."

Such "scientific studies" served one purpose— to keep the Negro a social subordinate. During the late nineteenth century and even into the twentieth century, Jim Crow was thus brought

NOJOQUE;

A QUESTION FOR A CONTINENT.

BY

HINTON ROWAN HELPER,

OF NORTH CAROLINA,

AUTHOR OF "THE IMPENDING CRISIS OF THE SOUTH."

How natural has it been to assume that the motive of those who have protested against the extension of Slavery was an unnatural sympathy with the negro, instead of what it always has really been—concern for the welfare of the White Man.
SEWARD.

Deep-rooted prejudices entertained by the whites; ten thousand recollections by the blacks, of the injuries they have sustained; new provocations; the real distinctions which Nature has made, and many other circumstances, will divide us into parties, and produce convulsions, which will probably never end but in the extermination of the one or the other race.
JEFFERSON.

And thou, too, Ethiopia! against thee 'also will I unsheathe my sword.
ZEPHANIAH.

NEW YORK:
George W. Carleton & Co., Publishers.
LONDON: S. LOW, SON & CO.
MDCCCLXVII.

into the scientific field to "prove" racial inferiority. Countless experiments by unbiased researchers later proved these findings false.

SOCIAL DARWINISM AND ITS EFFECTS

The man most responsible for applying Charles Darwin's findings in biological evolution to the realm of human society was Herbert Spencer. He was a famous and very influential person. An English engineer turned writer and self-made philosopher, Spencer had developed his own theory of evolution, independent of Darwin. He saw evolution as a force unifying the universe, and believed that a single principle governs all of nature. He drew from Darwin's theories that which would be consistent with his own, and did much to popularize evolutionary theory, explaining, expanding and reinterpreting Darwin's work in social terms. He believed strongly that the various human races were evidence of the evolution of one superior and dominant race, with the others like stair-steps beneath it.

Spencer was extremely influential among sociologists in this country. One of his best-known disciples was William Graham Sumner. Sumner and Spencer were also concerned with broad economic theories and were thoroughly opposed to any kind of social reform (welfare laws, labor regulations, charitable institutions). Their thinking, which was not inconsistent with the dominant policies of that era, not only condemned blacks to an innately inferior place in the world order but also condemned any attempts of theirs or others which might help them to rise. Sumner once said, "A man may curse his fate because he was born of an inferior race."

Darwin died before he could finish his studies. Although he had made some speculations on the human species, his major interest was in animals. The far-fetched theories which went by the name of "Social Darwinism" had little bearing on the discoveries and writings of that scientist.

It would take great determination and many years before the pseudo-scientific teachings which "proved" Negro inferiority could be refuted.

A young German-Jewish anthropologist at Clark University, Franz Boas, entered the dispute shortly after coming to this country in the 1880's. His report "Human Faculty As Determined by Race," was read before the American Association for the Advancement of Science in 1891. It sought to dispel the false concepts advanced by the Social Darwinists.

Throughout his life Boas continued to assert his theories that all races are equal and that biological differences are meaningless in determining differentiation among peoples. His arguments were logical and scientific, and he would not even address himself to theories lacking a rational basis. He was very active and influential in the scientific community until his death in 1942. His work caused one historian of race theories, Thomas Gossett, to observe, "It is possible that Boas did more to combat race prejudice than any other person in history."

Such damage had been done before Boas' time,

however, and had spread out and filtered down to such a vast extent, that it seemed irreparable. Most people, incapable of grasping the writings of Spencer, Sumner or Boas, preferred to start with their own prejudices and take from these scientists' writings that which made them feel comfortable, without regard to a thorough understanding of the principles involved.

With such "scientific" evidence as Spencer's and Sumner's at their disposal, white supremacists were hardly impressed with contradictory data.

Well into the twentieth century, in fact, the popular magazines—*Harper's, McClure's, Scribner's, Atlantic Monthly* and the *Century*—opened their pages to unfavorable portrayals of the Negro. In the stories, cartoons, poems and travelogues, Negroes were painted as lazy, improvident, humorous, happy-go-lucky, ignorant and immoral. American readers, accepting the views of such trustworthy journals, saw little need for action on programs to achieve racial equality.

Many American writers were most prolific in writing books disparaging the Negro's abilities, reinforcing the public's image of the Negro as a bestial ignoramus. One such author, Thomas Dixon, wrote *The Leopard's Spots: A Romance of the White Man's Burden* and *The Clansman: An Historical Romance of the Ku Klux Klan.* These novels glorified white supremacy at a time when Negro voting and industrial participation were big issues. Charles Carroll made a more extreme presentation in his books *The Negro: A Beast or in the Image of God?* and *The Tempter of Eve: Or the Criminality of Man's Political and Religious Equality with the Negro and the Amalgamation to Which These Crimes Inevitably Lead.* Carroll's first book theorized that the Negro was created before Adam and was not of the human species. This view agreed with others developed before the Civil War. The second book depicted Eve as a Negro woman who "betrayed" the human race in the Garden of Eden. The amalgamation of races, Carroll wrote, "damned millions upon millions of souls." Upon such theology as this, a set of erroneous beliefs concerning Negro Americans took firm root. Read by both North and South, this literature intimated that the Negro was undesirable as a voter and as a social equal.

Caricatures such as this print were a common affront to the race. Even more blatant, but no less insulting, were the books decrying the Negro and assuming the superiority of the white. Thomas Dixon's The Leopard's Spots *is an example of this. Another, Charles Carroll's* The Negro: A Beast or in the Image of God? *was answered by the book* Is the Negro a Beast? *by William G. Schell, who joined with many others to refute white supremacist ideas.*

Can the Ethiopian change his skin or the leopard his spots?

THE
LEOPARD'S SPOTS

A ROMANCE OF THE WHITE
MAN'S BURDEN — 1865–1900

BY

THOMAS DIXON, JR.

ILLUSTRATED BY C. D. WILLIAMS

NEW YORK
DOUBLEDAY, PAGE & CO.
1902

IS THE NEGRO A BEAST?

A REPLY TO
CHAS. CARROLL'S BOOK
ENTITLED
"THE NEGRO A BEAST."

Proving that the Negro is Human from Biblical, Scientific, and Historical Standpoints.

BY

WM. G. SCHELL,

Author of "Biblical Trace of the Church," "The Better Testament," "The Ordinances of the New Testament," etc.

MOUNDSVILLE, W. VA., U. S. A.
GOSPEL TRUMPET PUBLISHING COMPANY.
1901.

THE SOCIAL GOSPEL AND THE NEGRO

Like Social Darwinism the Social Gospel was a post-Civil War philosophy whose concepts swayed American thought on the Negro rights issue. The Social Gospel began with the rise of the nation's labor organizations. Labor claimed that the church—especially the Protestant groups—sympathized more with capitalists than with workingmen. This caused some liberal churchmen to revise their doctrines on social and economic questions in the light of Christ's teachings.

Four prominent preachers of the Social Gospel bear recalling. The four—George D. Herron, Josiah Strong, Lyman Abbott and Washington Gladden, all Congregationalists—wrote and studied the life and work of Christ with the intent of applying His principles to postwar society. But they failed to include Negro rights in their range of democratic ideals. "Men are beginning to see," Herron said in *The New Redemp-*

WASHINGTON GLADDEN

THE NEW REDEMPTION.

A Call to the Church to Reconstruct Society According to the Gospel of Christ.

BY

GEORGE D. HERRON,

The E. D. Rand Professor of Applied Christianity in Iowa College.
Author of "The Larger Christ," "The Message of Jesus to Men of Wealth," "A Plea for the Gospel," and "The Call of the Cross."

"Whoever does not assume unconditionally the might of goodness in the world, and its ultimate victory; whoever starts from moral unbelief, not only cannot lead in human affairs, but must follow with reluctant steps. We live indeed in the kingdoms of the redemption, and no more in the kingdoms of this world."—Rothe, *Theologische Ethik.*

NEW YORK: 46 East 14th Street.
THOMAS Y. CROWELL & COMPANY.
BOSTON: 100 Purchase Street.

tion, "that the welfare of each is the responsibility of all, and the welfare of all the responsibility of each." And Gladden covered nearly every aspect of American life in his *Ruling Ideas of the Present Age*; but he, like Herron, seemed unaware of the Negro's plight. Gladden insisted that the Christian doctrine of equality among men was well established. But this noble intention was a far cry from reality. At times, latent racism crept into the discussion. "Whether the extinction of inferior races before the advancing Anglo-Saxon seems to the reader sad or otherwise," Josiah Strong observed, "it certainly appears probable." Lyman Abbott had opposed the Lodge bill of 1890. "The Negro problem," he said, "must be worked out by the Negroes and the white man of the South, with the aid of the North, not by the North or the Federal Government over the heads of the white man." The Protestant involvement in the Social Gospel failed to protest Jim Crow. It merely ignored his presence. In so doing, it appeared to sanction the caste system.

Negroes noted the discrepancy between philosophical postures assumed by men like Gladden and the facts of segregated life. The National Association of Colored Men, for instance, needled the Social Gospel preachers in its founding statement in 1896:

> We aim at nothing unattainable, nothing Utopian, not what the society of the future is seeking, but merely what other citizens of this civilization are now enjoying. . . . We are not frightened at the Mumbo-Jumbo of so-called social equality. . . . We know that under the existing conditions of American society the same laws which apply to our other fellow-citizens apply equally to us. We recognize the universal law that no man or race gets more social or political preferment than he fights for and can maintain.

One gleans from this statement a Negro awareness of being passed over in this period of "reawakening" and a desire to protest such omission. But it was futile to hope for social justice where the intellectual atmosphere had been poisoned by prejudice and half-truths. In every area of life—social, political and economic, even legal—the Negro was rebuffed at every turn.

INFRINGEMENTS OF CIVIL RIGHTS

In these unjust times men often took the law into their own hands, punishing suspects of crimes as they saw fit. All legal rights were denied the accused, and this "mob justice" often resulted in cruel punishments and lynchings. Although a Tuskeegee study showed that in many years more whites than Negroes were lynched, and that lynchings took place in both North and South, this barbaric practice came to be directed almost entirely toward Negroes and practiced almost exclusively in the South. It was used effectively to intimidate whole black populations to such an extent that they were fearful of defending themselves. This was one way southern Negroes were "kept in their place"; it reinforced the new Jim Crow laws and voting restrictions.

When Negroes in Florida provided themselves with guns and ammunition to protect a prisoner threatened with lynching, the *Afro-American Sentinel* praised their action. "Let colored men everywhere imitate the brave example of those at Key West," the *Sentinel* suggested, "and lynching will become rare."

Northern Negroes protested just as actively when whites violated due process of law or denied them equal treatment. "It is a question of whether men shall be protected by law or be left to the mercy of cyclones of anarchy and bloodshed," Frederick Douglass declared in 1883. "It is whether the Government or the mob shall rule the land; whether the promises solemnly made to us in the Constitution shall be manfully kept or meanly and flagrantly broken."

Negroes met in conventions in the South to protest with direct action against threats to their civil rights. The letter of a Negro minister, the Rev. E. Malcolm Argyle of Arkansas, to the *Christian Recorder* described conditions there in the 1890's.

"It is evident that the white people have no further use for the Negro," Argyle wrote. "He is being worse treated now than at any time since the surrender. The white press of the South seems to be subsidized by this lawless element; the white pulpit seems to condone lynching."

The Afro-American League, one of several self-defense groups, appeared in a number of states. T. Thomas Fortune, editor of the *New York Age*, became its leading spirit. A league convention with 140 delegates from twenty-three states met in Chicago in 1890. The league had become a clearinghouse for Negro groups and mass protests. It insisted upon trials by judge and jury, resistance by legal and reasonable means to mobs and lynching and an end to racial barriers. The Afro-American League regrouped in 1898 as the National Afro-American League, but failed to function effectively beyond its meetings.

A mass meeting of Negroes convened in New York City in 1892, eliciting this comment from *Harper's Weekly*:

> We recommend that the [Negro] race in the South maintain their trust in God, but we also recommend that they unite for mutual protection; that they seek to bring to their support and into public expression the opinion of that part of the white people of the South who are disgusted and who feel compromised by the lawless elements among them. . . . We urge organization; we urge agitation; we urge the prosecution of every peaceful remedy; but we also advise our brethren to protect to the extent of their ability their defenseless fellows charged with crimes against the lynchers and midnight marauders, who are also brutal outlaws, and we advise our brethren to let it be known that endurance has a limit, and that patience under some conditions may cease to be a virtue.

The mass meeting in New York had broken into an uproar when Fortune had read a long list of outrages against Negroes. "What are you going to do about it?" Fortune demanded. A multitude of voices united in shouting back, "Fight!" For a few minutes chaos reigned. Then, despite Fortune's effort to stop him, former Congressman John R. Lynch of Mississippi managed to quiet the crowd. The gathering finally formed a committee to address the President, asking him to urge Congress to right the wrongs against the nation's Negroes.

Protest took other forms. When the Negro members of the Georgia legislature were expelled, they decried this action on the floor of the house. The outspoken Henry MacNeal Turner rose to deliver a withering address. "It is extraordinary," he told the white lawmakers, "that a race such as yours, professing gallantry, chivalry, education and superiority, living in a land where chimes call child and sire to the church of God, a land where Bibles are read and Gospel truths are spoken, and where courts of justice are presumed to exist, that with all these advantages on your side, you can make war upon the defenseless black man."

The warnings failed to deter the racists—then or in the years to come. When the National Association of Colored Men met in Detroit in 1896 its patience was nearly exhausted. It decided to send a document to Congress in the form of an address. While the group looked for "no superiority over others," the message said, "we emphatically deny the assumption of superior rights by others over us." The signers also warned of "the opening of the militant period of our race in this country," and added: "Our calm and deliberate advice is for every member of the race henceforth to employ every weapon of every kind of warfare legitimately and courageously in the demand of every right."

Du Bois noted in 1899 that it was hard to find an intelligent Negro at the turn of the century who did not belong to several distinctly Negro religious, business or social groups. These groups—some of which grew to a national scale—helped provide an outlet for Negro creativity at a time when white America did very little to encourage it.

MARY CHURCH TERRELL

In 1896 the National Association of Colored Women was formed, with Mary Church Terrell as its first president. The association's motto, "Lifting As We Climb," was well chosen. The organizers of this group must have realized that the decades ahead would see great progress. They founded homes for orphans, hospitals, and many other social agencies which benefited thousands of disadvantaged people. These women were also politically active and were influential in the fight for woman suffrage. They did much to encourage political education among black people and endorsed the concept of change through cooperative action.

THE DEATH OF FREDERICK DOUGLASS

When Frederick Douglass died on February 22, 1895, America lost one of its most active and renowned leaders in the struggle for equal rights. Born a slave, the twenty-one-year-old Douglass expressed his love of freedom by fleeing from his master and escaping to New York.

Once free, Douglass became an active abolition-ist. For the rest of his life he remained an outspoken and eloquent champion of human and civil rights.

As adviser to President Lincoln, Douglass was instrumental in rallying and recruiting Negro soldiers for the Union army. It was his wish that black men share with whites "the danger and honor of upholding the government." At the war's end, he rejoiced in emancipation and was happy to see the beginnings of the participation of colored citizens in the life promised them by the Union. Until the day of his death, Douglass advocated political action and education as the means to a truly free life for all men and women, regardless of color.

His sudden death was sad news for the country. Thousands paid him tribute, many of them paying their last respects at the Metropolitan African Episcopal Church in Washington, D.C., and later at the city hall in Rochester, New York.

The death of Frederick Douglass, who had once been a slave and who had exemplified what the free black man could become, left a great void in the leadership of all Americans who sought equality.

JOSEPH C. PRICE

Joseph C. Price, the bridge in Negro leadership between Douglass and Booker T. Washington, was born in North Carolina in 1854. The son of a slave father and free mother, Price assumed the free status of his mother. He studied at Lowell Normal School at New Bern, North Carolina, and taught there for four years. Later he entered Shaw University, then transferred to Lincoln University in Pennsylvania, where he graduated in 1879 at the head of his class. Price took a graduate degree from the theological department in 1881, distinguishing himself as an outstanding orator.

Price founded Livingstone College, sponsored by the African Methodist Episcopal Zion Church, and served as its president. Here he became known as a man of eloquence and force—the "Lion of the Lyceum." His church had sent him to the general conference of 1880 at Montgomery, Alabama, where he had proved his skill as a

JOSEPH C. PRICE

debater of matchless eloquence. He gained even greater distinction as an orator when he attended the Methodist Ecumenical Conference in London in 1881. While in England and in Europe, Price collected $10,000 toward the purchase of the grounds and buildings of Livingstone College.

The Zion Church elected Price chairman of its board of commissioners for the organic union of the A.M.E. and A.M.E. Zion Churches. He also headed a delegation of Negroes who met with President Garfield during his brief term in the White House. Price's travels took him as far west as California in lecturing campaigns, raising funds for his college. His career was cut short by his untimely death in 1894. If Joseph Price had lived, many historians contend that he would have ranked with Booker T. Washington as a great Negro leader and orator.

BOOKER T. WASHINGTON

In the year that the long-time Negro leader Frederick Douglass died, a young educator—the principal of Tuskegee Institute in Alabama—was espousing a philosophy of education contradictory to that of Douglass. The year was 1895,

BOOKER T. WASHINGTON

a time when there were many crosscurrents of opinion regarding the Negro's status in America. Because of his innovative work at Tuskegee, Booker T. Washington gained an unusual amount of attention in the press.

A native of Virginia, Washington had been born into slavery in 1858 or 1859; he wasn't sure which. "I know nothing of my ancestry beyond my mother," he later wrote. With fifty cents in his pocket, he made his way to Hampton Institute in 1872, in search of an education. The principal at Hampton, Samuel C. Armstrong, taught his pupils that their labor would be rewarded if they worked honestly, accurately and intelligently. Armstrong believed that the South's future lay "in a vigorous attempt to lift the colored race by a practical education that would fit them for life." These ideas formed the basis of Washington's plans for a school of practical living. After graduating from Hampton and teaching for a short time, Washington was called to Tuskegee in 1881 to help found a teachers' college.

Washington fused practical and academic training in the new educational methods which he introduced. To the Tuskegee educator, the goal of schooling was to solve problems. He believed the southern whites would lend support to the education of former slaves if they felt it was in the interests of the South. He argued that the white man would need to remain in the gutter himself if he insisted on holding blacks there.

THE "ATLANTA COMPROMISE"

Washington gave an epic speech in September of 1895 when he addressed the Cotton States and International Exposition at Atlanta. It spotlighted him as an acknowledged spokesman for the Negro people. His ideas were so phrased as to harmonize with the prevailing southern thought of his time. His conciliatory theme, his emphasis upon work and the earning of citizenship privileges rather than upon agitation for them, ensured not only his position of leadership but his role as go-between and interpreter for the two races. He achieved the stature of a national politician in his intermediary role, advising Presidents on Negro appointments and influencing the distribution of northern philanthropy.

Governor Bullock of Georgia introduced Washington in Atlanta with the comment: "We have with us today a representative of Negro enterprise and Negro civilization." As Basil Mathews described the scene, "There was a remarkable figure, tall, bony, straight as a Sioux Chief, high forehead, straight nose, heavy jaws and strong determined manner. . . . His voice rang out clear and true and he paused impressively as he made his point."

Washington called for Negroes to stay in the South, acquire property and improve themselves through self-help. "Cast down your bucket," he urged his race. "Cast it down in making friends in every manly way of the people of all races by whom we are surrounded." The Negro, he observed, was then one-third of the South's population—a fact which the Exposition recognized in espousing biracial friendship. Washington spoke from experience, for he had built Tuskegee Institute in this way. He had constructed a sawmill to produce lumber and a kiln to bake bricks. Students worked at such non-academic enterprises, and Washington watched approvingly as they learned the dignity of labor. He had convened the first annual farmers' conference at Tuskegee in 1892 and then had set up farm extension courses. He counseled acquiescence by "the most patient, faithful, law-abiding and unresentful people that the world had seen." He anticipated the "separate but equal" doctrine and spelled out his philosophy for living with it.

RUFUS B. BULLOCK

When Dr. Washington finished his address, he later recalled, Governor Bullock rushed across the stage and shook his hand, and others did the same. The newspapers took up the chorus, both in the South and in the North. Telegrams and letters of congratulations poured in from all parts of the country to "the progressive Negro educator," as Washington was described in the Atlanta *Constitution*.

"Your words cannot fail to delight and encourage all who wish well for your race," President Grover Cleveland wrote Washington after reading a copy of his address. "If our colored fellow-citizens do not from your utterances gather new hope and form new determinations to gain every valuable advantage offered them by their citizenship, it will be strange indeed."

This overwhelming acceptance stemmed from the confusing racial issues which troubled Americans. Washington offered everyone a simple answer. Whites were delighted to hear the famous black spokesman espouse a doctrine which did not actually contradict that of white supremacy, even though it implied that blacks might catch up with whites one day. But that point was in the vague future; if anything, Washington's attitude reinforced Social Darwinism.

At first Negroes, too, praised Dr. Washington's ideas, but later some felt he had failed to speak out forcefully enough for what they termed the "rights" of their race. Some feared that what Washington proposed was something very close to second-class citizenship.

"This 'Atlanta Compromise,'" said W. E. B. Du Bois, "is by all odds the most notable thing in Mr. Washington's career." He wrote in the *New York Age* that the speech might have been the basis of a North-South settlement, but the southern laws of separation prevented any such accord. Even so, the address made Washington a popular man in America—one sought as a speaker and as an adviser to philanthropists planning to endow Negro education and welfare programs. Washington saw no compromise or surrender in his words. For years he had championed industrial education, and he would continue to do so.

Washington elaborated on his Atlanta speech in 1896 when he accepted an honorary degree from Harvard University—the first Negro to receive that honor. His remarks in Cambridge stressed the interdependence of whites and Negroes in America and their need for cooperation and mutual respect. He found the condition of the Negro deplorable, but needing change from within. The change should be gradual, and its wake should not disturb the rest of American society.

"During the next half century and more," Washington told his Harvard listeners, "my race must continue passing through the severe American crucible. We are to be tested in our patience, our forbearance, our perseverance, our power to endure wrong, to withstand temptations, to economize, to acquire and use skill and our ability to compete, to succeed in commerce. . . . This is the passport to all that is best in the life of the Republic, and the Negro must possess it, or be debarred."

To Booker Washington the exercise of political rights was "a matter of natural growth, not an overnight, gourd-vine affair." But he did not believe that the Negro should cease voting. The nonwhite, he said, should "proceed from the possession of property, intelligence and high character for the full recognition of his political rights." Had Washington's conditions applied to all voters, white and Negro, his argument would have carried more weight. While he did advocate that the tests "should be made to apply with equal and exact justice to all races," he could not reasonably have expected the South, with its political climate of the 1890's, to honor this formula.

More aggressive Negro leaders, among them Du Bois, thought Washington had surrendered the ideals for which they had pressed their claims in years past. Thus, five months after Washington's Harvard speech, John Hope, the president of Morehouse College, answered with this retort: "If we are not striving for equality, in heaven's name, for what are we living? I regard it as cowardly and dishonest for any of our colored men to tell white people or colored people that we are not struggling for equality. If money, education and honesty will not bring to me as much privilege, as much equality as they bring to any American citizen, then they are to me a curse and not a blessing. . . . Yes, my friends, I want equality, nothing less.

"Now, catch your breath," President Hope warned, "for I am going to use an adjective: I am going to say we demand *social* equality. In this Republic we shall be less than freemen, if we have a whit less than that which thrift, education and honor afford other freemen. . . . Why build a wall to keep me out? I am no wild beast, nor am I an unclean thing.

"Rise, Brothers!" the Morehouse official exhorted. "Come let us possess this land. Never say: 'Let well enough alone.' Cease to console yourselves with adages that numb the moral sense. Be discontented. Be dissatisfied."

Another southern educator had raised his voice. His cry, however, was a protest against

JOHN HOPE

complacency and acceptance of existing conditions. John Hope's voice was a contrast to Washington's. Few whites wanted to hear Dr. Hope's message, and Washington continued to be the black spokesman most acceptable to the white establishment. In this capacity Washington was a kind of diplomat, moving between the white and black worlds, accepting that separateness in all of his actions and teachings. He became perhaps too closely identified with the misguided racial policies of his time, instead of being appreciated solely as an educator and counselor. His unchallenged leadership exemplifies the dominance of a certain closed-minded element in both white and black society at the turn of the century.

CHAPTER SIX

American Expansionism— Negroes Serve Their Country at Home and Abroad

IN the latter half of the nineteenth century the United States felt itself becoming a world power. The industrial revolution, coupled with the freedom with which the government allowed big business to develop and to use the country's vast natural resources, made America wealthy. The great lands to the west lay unexplored—a huge source of further expansion and riches. The country's potential seemed limitless.

This was truly the land of plenty of which all citizens might partake. But free participation was still limited for the country's Negroes. They were deprived of equal opportunities after Reconstruction's end. The few black citizens who did manage to join the mainstream of American life were often found in the military service. Thus they served America's needs in the most direct way, although the country seldom offered their race even the basic rights of citizenship.

NEGROES IN THE MILITARY AND NAVAL ACADEMIES

As a result of their service in the Civil War and of Reconstruction's new opportunities, Negroes were named to the Military Academy at West Point and the Naval Academy at Annapolis. The first Negro to enter West Point, James W. Smith of South Carolina, was admitted in 1870. Life at the academy was not easy for Smith, nor for the few other Negroes who received appointments there in those years. In 1873 Henry Ossian Flipper came there—and was the first Negro cadet to graduate. In his memoirs of his days at West Point, Flipper's examples of the prejudice shown toward him by the white cadets point up how difficult the first young black appointees' years must have been. In the end, Flipper was admired for his abilities, but that respect had been dearly earned. Not until the 1960's would black cadets at West Point be treated by their white fellow students with complete equality.

Upon Flipper's graduation, *Harper's Weekly* wrote: "The only colored cadet will not only graduate at the coming June commencement, but his character, requirements, and standing on the merit roll are such as will insure his graduation among the highest of his class."

Flipper entered the regular army as a second lieutenant of the 10th Cavalry Regiment, then spent many years fighting in the Indian wars. After a court-martial at Fort Davis, Texas, in 1881, Flipper received a discharge. Until his death, however, he maintained that the charge on which he was convicted—carelessness in handling funds—resulted from the prejudice of the white officers. Flipper pursued a career as a civil and mining engineer in Arizona, Mexico and Venezuela for over thirty years. The first of his race to gain distinction in engineering, Flipper also became an expert in Southwestern folklore and history.

The second Negro graduate of West Point, John H. Alexander, was assigned as a second lieutenant in 1887 to Fort Robinson in Nebraska. He served at Fort Washaki in Wyoming and Fort Duchesne in Utah before his death of a heart attack in 1894. At the time of his fatal seizure he was a military instructor at Wilberforce University. Alexander was permanently honored in military circles, a fort in Virginia having been named for him.

Colonel Charles Young was the third Negro West Point graduate. On receiving his commission in 1889, Young reported to the 10th Cavalry, serving in Cuba and Mexico.

The experiences of these cadets and officers reveal the obstacles which faced Negro men seeking advancement in the nation's military establishment. Although the three just cited served with loyalty and courage, it was not until 1936 that a fourth Negro graduated from West Point. Even at that late date, Cadet Benjamin O. Davis, Jr., faced a lonely and unhappy first year at the Military Academy. But by the time he graduated, near the top of his class, he was one of the most respected men in the corps.

HENRY OSSIAN FLIPPER

No Negroes graduated from the U.S. Naval Academy during Reconstruction. Not only was admission there even more selective than at West Point, but graduation was also a few degrees more difficult. Three Negroes attended Annapolis in the seventies, but it was not until 1936 that another colored youth entered the academy. In 1949 Wesley A. Brown was the first of his race to graduate from Annapolis.

One reason for the decline of Negro admissions to the academies after Reconstruction is obvious: the southern Negroes in Congress who had sponsored the Negro cadets were removed from politics, one by one. Their twentieth-century successors, members of the "lily white" southern bloc in Congress, proved unwilling to provide the necessary sponsorship for Negro applicants.

NEGROES HELP TO WIN THE WEST

After the Civil War, six units of Negro soldiers remained in army uniform. The army later consolidated them into four units—the 9th and 10th Cavalry and the 24th and 25th Infantry. The units were manned by ex-slaves, freemen who had been soldiers, and by other volunteers.

JOHN H. ALEXANDER

CHARLES YOUNG

RUNNING THE GAUNTLET.
SPECIAL COURSE FOR COLORED CADETS AT WEST POINT.

They were commanded by white officers from West Point who were assigned to these units. Many were eager for this duty and built their reputations in such commands. The white officers often turned out to be efficient commanders such as Colonel John J. Pershing, known as "Black Jack" because of the men under his command. Each regiment had a chaplain, whose duties included instructing the men.

A typical unit, the 9th Cavalry, had formed in New Orleans during 1866-67. Non-commissioned officers were scarce. Only one man could write well enough to serve as a sergeant, but transfers and volunteering soon remedied these weaknesses. Two years later, three units of the 9th Cavalry went into battle against the Indians at Horsehead Hills, Texas. This regiment fought in sixty battles with the Indians between 1868 and 1890. The soldiers also built forts along the Rio Grande and in Indian territory. Once the forts were completed, white soldiers occupied them. The Negro soldiers then moved on as advance construction teams.

The 25th Infantry or "Black Battalion," as it was called, had also formed in New Orleans, in 1869. The army restationed it in Texas a year later. It remained there for the next ten years before moving to the frontier Department of Dakota.

All of the Negro regiments engaged in fighting Indians and served as border patrols along the western frontier. Both white and Negro settlers in the West often depended on the bravery and courage of these Negro troops, who guarded the pioneers prior to their settlement in new territory.

The Indian territory was also being invaded by white settlers, despite Presidents Hayes' and Arthur's proclamations to the contrary. The Indians had begun to fight back in 1876, refusing to remain on the reservations provided by the Treaty of 1868. They attacked whites invading their land, notably in the Yellowstone country. The Indian leader Sitting Bull fought with little skill. But he, along with Crazy Horse, Crow King and Rain-in-the-Face, was an aggressive leader of 4,000 Sioux, Cheyennes, Arapahoes and other tribes armed with rifles and a fierce determination to preserve their land.

The troops rode their horses hard on the plains from Arizona to the Dakotas. In so doing, they earned a place in works of art and literature and in western folklore. Frederic Remington often used the 9th and 10th Cavalry as subjects of his paintings. One such scene is "Captain Dodge's Colored Troops to the Rescue." A soldier of the 9th Cavalry wrote a favorite ditty of the plains fighting:

> The Ninth marched out with splendid cheer,
>   The Badlands to explore,
> With Colonel Henry at their head
>   They never feared the foe;
> So on they rode from Christmas eve
>   Till dawn of Christmas day:
> The Redskins heard the Ninth was near
>   And fled in great dismay.

Books and motion pictures have portrayed the life of the desperado Billy the Kid. It is a little-known fact that when he was caught in Lincoln, Nebraska, his hideout was surrounded by Negro troops.

Remington's painting "Leaving the Canyon" depicts black soldiers out West.

A company of black soldiers in 1883.

A squadron of the 9th Cavalry on maneuvers during the Indian wars.

At least fourteen Negro soldiers showed outstanding valor during this period. General Benjamin Butler, who had been a liberal senator from Massachusetts, praised these soldiers of the 9th Cavalry—winners of Medals of Honor—"for good conduct in the field against the Indians and for soldierly bearing exhibiting to all comers instances of the best qualities of America's cavalry." General Wesley Merritt, who commanded these Negro soldiers in the West, said of them: "I have always found the colored race as represented in the Army obedient, intelligent and zealous in the discharge of duty, brave in battle, easily disciplined and most efficient in the care of their horses, arms and equipment."

Black soldiers often fought unruly cowboys, and many lost their lives in the settlement of the West. Today they lie buried there, unnamed and unsung. "The bones of Negro soldiers," it was once said, "whiten the plains or are buried beneath them from the Concho country and Panhandle of Texas to the North British provinces."

NEGRO COWBOYS AND WESTERNERS

Some Negroes had lived in the western states when they were territories prior to the Civil War. However, the great migrations of both free men and former slaves began after the war.

Fascinating stories are told of individual Negro cowboys—"bad men as well as good ones." They were seldom described in literature and films as folk heroes, yet they took an active part in the opening of the West and should be included among the famed westerners. They rode horses, roped cattle and performed in the rodeos. During the three decades after the Civil War, thousands of Negro cowboys came out of northern Texas and other ex-Confederate states into the cattle country. Here they fought the Indians, trapped and tamed wild horses and sat in the saddle on watch for marauders. Others became cattle rustlers. It has been estimated that between 1868 and 1895 "fully 35,000 men went up the trail with herds—about one-third were Negroes and Mexicans."

In *The Negro Cowboys,* Philip Durham and Everett L. Jones noted that "a typical trail crew had among its eight cowboys two or three Negroes. Its boss was almost certain to be white, although a few Negroes led crews up the trail. When nationality or color is mentioned in accounts of the trail drives, far more Negroes than Mexicans are identified."

The black westerners naturally filled roles other than that of the cowhand. Some worked as cooks, some as bronco-busters to break in the wild horses, some as wranglers to care for the horses on long drives.

Negroes joined the thousands who poured into the Colorado mining area in search of wealth. Some also mined gold and silver in Wyoming, Montana and Idaho—either as individuals or in corporations. In one such arrangement, Negroes from Georgia worked a mine in the Greenwood Valley of California's Eldorado County. Some Negroes—like Lewis Walker in Idaho—ran their own mining businesses. George Parker, one of the original prospectors in Silver City, New Mexico, helped plan the settlement of that city. And James Williams, a mining operator, temporarily left his mine to open a Sacramento restaurant. Negro miners in Colorado met racial opposition and moved on to other frontiers. Many drifted from one mine to another. One Negro in Southern California discovered a rich gold mine, sold portions of it, and worked some of it. He left for Sacramento in a short time with $100,000 in his hands, lost it, and committed suicide. Such were the up-and-down fortunes of western life which Negroes had come to share.

"WHITE MAN'S BURDEN"

The United States watched Africa with mixed feelings at the turn of the century. The nations of Europe were carving out colonies and spheres of influence throughout the Dark Continent. Refusing to intervene in Africa, the United States referred to the Monroe Doctrine to fend off any European ventures in Latin America. When British Guiana and Venezuela squabbled over their boundaries, Secretary of State Richard Olney warned the British government to stay out of the dispute. "Today the United States is practically sovereign in this continent," Olney said. "Its infinite resources combined with its isolated position render it master of the situation and practically invulnerable as against any or all other powers." This statement spelled out Washington's position clearly: while the United States would not rival other powers seeking to expand their empires in Africa, neither would it tolerate them as rivals in its "sphere of influence"—the Americas. For throughout Latin America, Yankee industry and Yankee dollars were at stake. So, as imperialism triumphed in Africa and the Middle and Far East, the poet Rudyard Kipling trumpeted its guiding philosophy—the "White Man's Burden":

> Take up the White Man's Burden—
>   Send forth the best ye breed—
> Go bind your sons to exile
>   To serve your captives' need;
> To wait in heavy harness,
>   On fluttering folk and wild—
> Your new-caught sullen people,
>   Half-devil and half-child.
>
> Take up the White Man's Burden—
>   Ye dare not stoop to less—
> Nor call too loud on Freedom
>   To cloak your weariness.
> By all ye will or whisper,
>   By all ye leave or do,
> The silent sullen peoples
>   Shall weigh your God and you.

France and Germany soon took up the chorus. "The superior races have a right as regards inferior races," the Frenchman Jules Ferry wrote. "They have a right because they have a duty. They have a duty of civilizing inferior races." Such doctrines also made headway in the United States.

CUBAN OPPRESSION

Reports of Spanish army outrages and repressions against the Cuban people reached the United States just before President McKinley's election. The Cubans—one-third of whom were nonwhite—periodically revolted against this treatment. They formed an "Army of Liberation" to overthrow the Spaniards. Americans sympathized with the insurgents, scarcely aware of the large number of African descendants among them. One news account from Havana ironically noted: "Nearly all the leaders and fighters in the Cuban Army of Liberation are men, who if in South Carolina, Mississippi, or Louisiana, would

be made to ride in the 'Jim Crow Cars,' and would be denied the right to occupy a private residence on Beacon Street in Boston."

A ten-year war (1868-1878) between Spaniards and Cuban rebels had threatened to involve the United States earlier. At that time, fifty American sailors on the *Virginius* perished when the Spanish boarded the ship near Santiago Bay. The incident caused great alarm, since the *Virginius* was carrying arms to the insurgents.

Later, President Cleveland sent General Fitzhugh Lee, nephew of General Robert E. Lee, to Cuba as consul general. When McKinley entered the White House, he retained Lee in Havana, even though Lee was known to side with the Spanish.

Congressman George H. White was among the Negroes seeking belligerent rights for Cuba, which sanctions President Cleveland declined to grant. While the insurgents had America's sympathies in their struggles, he said, they had formed no government in Cuba for Washington to recognize. Hence the State Department would pursue a neutral policy.

Though aware that the Cuban struggle pitted Afro-Cuban people against Spanish tyranny, some Negro Americans still supported the Cleveland-McKinley policy.

The Cleveland *Gazette* stated early in 1898: "Very assuredly every intelligent and loyal black man who feels the least personal concern for his surroundings will not only desire a peaceful settlement of the difficulties, but will in case of an actual break between Spain and our government feel himself duty bound to lend all aid, encouragement and support to his government, and if need be offer himself in vindication of the national defense."

Despite their basic preference for peace and tranquillity, however, it was inevitable that American Negroes would be sympathetic to the oppressed Cubans. American tempers were especially aroused by the Spanish treatment of General Antonio Maceo. The black Cuban general led his Negro and mulatto guerillas in attacks on the Spanish, ambushed small parties of soldiers, burned mills and terrorized the enemy. After a short period of success in assaulting Spanish lines and defending his own camps, Maceo was

ANTONIO MACEO

invited to a peace parley. Upon his arrival, Spanish infantrymen pressed forward and shot him. Maceo's friends buried him in a secret grave and later erected a monument to his memory. The incident recalled the martyrdom of Haiti's black liberator, Toussaint L'Ouverture, who died in prison after French troops dishonored a flag of truce.

The Spanish government sent Cuba a new governor-general in 1896, General Valeriano Weyler. He earned the nickname "Butcher" by his ruthlessness; he put thousands in concentration camps to break the Cubans' contact with rebel bands. The camps were places of suffering, disease and death. It was the heyday of sensational newspaper reportage, or "yellow journalism," in America. Daily newspaper stories of Weyler's brutality incited the American public to a war fever.

After much adverse worldwide publicity, the Spanish withdrew "Butcher" Weyler and published a decree of autonomy for Cuba. The decree failed to satisfy the Cuban patriots, and they protested. But Consul General Fitzhugh Lee denounced these protests and warned that the United States might need to send warships to Cuba. Lee was concerned about the vast sums Americans had invested in Cuban sugar plantations, mills, mines and railroads—all imperiled by the guerilla warfare.

THE SPANISH-AMERICAN WAR

The battleship *Maine* steamed into Havana in late January of 1898. The Spanish navy received it with courtesy. Then, on the night of February 15, the *Maine* was blown up and 260 officers and crew died. Twenty-two Negro sailors were among the dead. The Americans immediately charged sabotage. Both Spain and the United States investigated the explosion. The Spanish reported that the tragedy was due to internal causes. The Americans found that the blast had originated from a submarine mine which triggered a partial explosion of two or more of the ship's forward magazines.

The war cry "Remember the *Maine*" rang out across the United States. Congress hurriedly voted a war fund of $50 million and three weeks later added $39 million more to the appropriation. President McKinley reported the situation to Congress on April 11, the anniversary of Lexington and Concord. Congress declared on April 19 that a state of war existed and that "the people of the island of Cuba are, and of right ought to be free and independent." The lawmakers disclaimed any "sovereignty, jurisdiction, or control over said island except for the pacification thereof." When that peace-making task was completed, Congress agreed, the United States would "leave the government and control of the island to its people."

NEGRO TROOPS AND OFFICERS

The *Maine* crisis found the United States militarily unprepared. When war began on April 21, the regular army was less than thirty thousand strong. The Negro regiments—the 24th and 25th

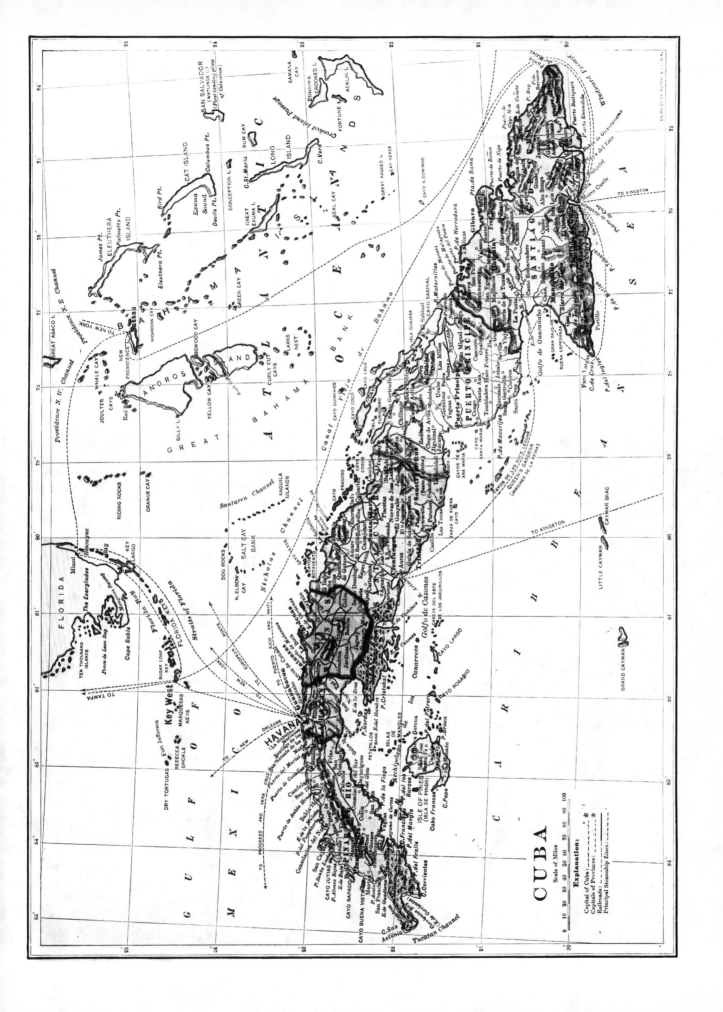

CUBA

Scale of Miles

0 10 20 30 40 50 60 70 80 90 100

Explanation:

Capital of Cuba: ⊛
Capitals of Provinces: ⊙
Railroads: ─────
Principal Steamship Lines: ─ ─ ─

Infantry and the 9th and 10th Cavalry—remained intact. Congress authorized the President to call for 200,000 volunteers. His appeal was answered by 182,000 enlisted men, among whom were thousands of Negroes.

New units formed to bolster the existing Negro regiments. These volunteer troops manned light regiments: the 3rd North Carolina Regiment, the 9th Ohio Regiment, the 23rd Kansas Regiment, the 6th Virginia Regiment and the 7th, 8th, 9th and 10th United States Volunteers. The volunteers served in state regiments formed around National Guard units. In all, sixteen Negro regiments—some at full strength and some undermanned—fought in the Spanish-American War. All the volunteer units except the Alabama regiment had some Negro officers. The Ohio in-

fantry battalion led by Major Charles Young fought under an all-Negro officer cadre.

Several Negro officers received direct commissions. Governor Wolcott of Massachusetts issued the first of these to Captain William J. Williams and Lieutenants William Herbert Jackson and George Braxton. The three officers were assigned to "L" Company of the 6th Massachusetts Regiment. It became the first Negro company attached to a white regiment. "L" Company, organized in 1782 from the Bucks of America, was the oldest Negro military unit. It formed the base of the 54th Massachusetts Infantry Volunteers of Civil War fame.

During the Spanish-American War, Charles Young rose from second lieutenant of the 10th Cavalry to major in the 9th Ohio Regiment. John

The destruction of the battleship Maine.

A black infantry unit "marching for Cuba" in 1898.

THE NEGRO SOLDIERS IN ACTION

The first Negro American to die for the United States during the war was Elijah B. Tunnell, a black cook on the *U.S.S. Winslow*. The *Winslow* had been disabled by gunfire in the harbor of Cardenas. After the attack, the *Wilmington* tried to tow the *Winslow* beyond the range of the Spanish batteries. Tunnell left his work below the deck to help fasten a towline. A shell exploded over the workers, killing Tunnell and three others. Many other demonstrations of black valor were to follow.

When the destruction of the *Maine* occurred, the 25th Infantry Regiment was stationed at Fort Missoula, Montana. It received orders to move into the Department of the South when the war began. Then it was transported first to Key West, Florida, and later to Chickamauga Park, Georgia. When it arrived there on May 15, 1898, thousands of civilians—some of whom had never seen Negro soldiers before—came to wish the troops

A black cavalry unit in Cuba.

R. Lynch, former Mississippi Congressman, was made a major. Other rising colored officers included Colonel James H. Young of the 3rd North Carolina Negro Volunteer Regiment and Colonel John R. Marshall, commander of the 8th Illinois Regiment. Colonel Marshall, the first Negro to attain this rank, was the son of slaves and had studied at Hampton Institute.

These Negro officers found most of their contacts with white officers and enlisted men unpleasant. A Texas regiment of white soldiers once refused to accept their pay checks from Major John R. Lynch. When General Stanton read the report of this incident, he sent a dispatch to the commanding paymaster stating that Major Lynch had been commissioned by the President of the United States and that "the troops must take their pay from him or go without pay." President McKinley later approved this dispatch. It was reported that the President had agreed to promote a Negro officer to the rank of brigadier general, but the war ended before this could be accomplished.

ELIJAH B. TUNNELL

The torpedo boat Winslow, *upon which Elijah Tunnell met his death.*

well. The regiment boarded the transport *Concho* for Cuba, landing there on June 22. After mustering the units, the regiment marched into the Cuban jungle for the fighting front. The Negro infantrymen proved their valor in the battles of Las Guasimas, El Caney and San Juan Hill. They joined with white troops at Guasimas to drive the Spaniards from their positions on higher ground. At El Caney and San Juan, these "smoked Yankees" mounted magnificent assaults. Then they marched with white regiments against the city of Santiago de Cuba. Battling at their side were the "Rough Riders" of the 1st Volunteer Cavalry. The unit's executive officer, Lieutenant Colonel Theodore Roosevelt, had resigned his post as undersecretary of the navy to accept the army commission.

The "Rough Riders" were suddenly fired upon as they advanced through wooded country. Spanish forces lay concealed in an improvised fort on San Juan Hill. The "Rough Riders" returned the fire and tried to push on, but the Spanish volleys took their toll in lives. Two Negro units—the 9th Cavalry on the left and the 10th Cavalry supporting the center—moved into the fray. The 10th Cavalry, rushing forward at double-quick time, demolished the fort with a Hotchkiss gun. Then the "Rough Riders," aided by Negro troops, routed the Spaniards and continued their march. An Associated Press eyewitness claimed that had it not been for the Negro cavalry the "Rough Riders" would have been exterminated.

Negro units helped the "Rough Riders" rout the Spaniards at San Juan Hill.

Corporal Brown, a Negro soldier, was killed at his Hotchkiss gun while shelling the Spanish fort.

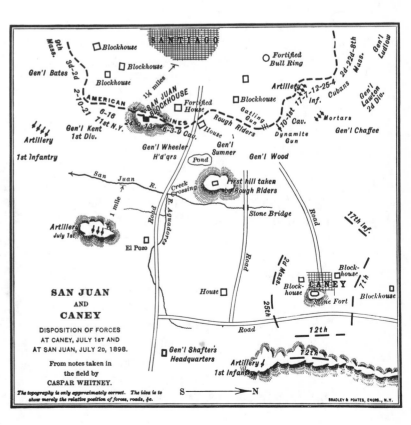

SANTIAGO

9th Mass.

□ *Blockhouse*

○ *Fortified Bull Ring*

Gen'l Ludlow

3d-2d

Gen'l Bates

□ *Blockhouse*

2d-22d-8th Mass.

□ *Blockhouse*

1¼ miles

SAN JUAN BLOCKHOUSE

Fortified House

□ *Blockhouse*

Artillery 17-7-12-25-4

Inf. Cubans

Gen'l Lawton 2d Div.

2-10-21

AMERICAN

6-16

71st N.Y.

LINES 9-13

Gatling Gun

Rough Riders

House

Cav.

Dynamite Gun

Gen'l Chaffee

↓↓↓ *Artillery*

Gen'l Kent 1st Div.

6-3-9 Cav.

↑↑↑ *Mortars*

1st Infantry

Gen'l Wheeler H'd'qrs

Gen'l Sumner

Gen'l Wood

San Juan R.

Pond

Creek Crossing

First hill taken by Rough Riders

1 mile

R. R. Aguadora

Road

Stone Bridge

Road

17th Inf.

Artillery July 1st

El Pozo □

2d Mass.

Block-house

Block-house

CANEY

□ Block-house

7th

Road

SAN JUAN AND CANEY

House □

25th

Stone Fort

□ Blockhouse

DISPOSITION OF FORCES AT CANEY, JULY 1st AND AT SAN JUAN, JULY 2D, 1898.

From notes taken in the field by CASPAR WHITNEY.

Road

12th

Gen'l Shafter's Headquarters

Artillery 1st Infantry

72d

The topography is only approximately correct. The idea is to show merely the relative position of forces, roads, &c.

S ——→ N

BRADLEY & POATES, ENGRS., N.Y.

When the Negro troops reached El Caney, another incident placed them in the spotlight. The battle there opened at dawn and lasted until dark. The Spanish were entrenched on a hill about a blockhouse. The American forces—including the 24th and 25th Infantry—stormed these positions. With other troops wavering before the withering Spanish fire, the Negro soldiers maintained their charge, although with broken ranks each man pushed ahead almost for himself. The first man to enter the blockhouse, a Negro private of "H" Company named T. C. Butler, took possession of the Spanish flag. Before delivering it to the American commander he tore off a piece of the flag to keep as evidence of his feat.

At San Juan Hill, the gallantry shown by the 9th and 10th Cavalry brought glory to their units. For eleven days after the truce at San Juan, the 25th Infantry dug trenches. Knowing the dangers of open field fighting, they worked feverishly day and night, moving from trench to trench. As soon as the black troops finished their work, white troops occupied the trenches. When the news came of the Spanish army's surrender at Santiago, the 25th Infantry stood within a thousand yards of the city—closer than any other regiment.

Members of all the black regiments fought with valor. Five of them received the Congressional Medal of Honor, and an estimated one hundred were commissioned as officers during the war.

When Colonel Theodore Roosevelt bid farewell to his troops, he took the opportunity to laud the Negro soldiers who fought alongside his "Rough Riders." "Now, I want to say just a word more," he said, "to some of the men I see standing around not of your number; I refer to the colored regiments who occupied the right and left flanks of us at Guasimas, the 9th and 10th Cavalry regiments. The Spaniards called them 'Smoked Yankees,' but we found them to be an excellent breed of Yankees. I am sure that I speak the sentiments of officers and men in this assemblage when I say that between you and the other cavalry regiments there exists a tie which we trust will never be broken."

A later article by Colonel Roosevelt, which appeared in *Scribner's* magazine, claimed that Negro soldiers only fought well under white officers. When their white leaders were killed or disabled, the Negro sergeants were allegedly unable to handle their men. Roosevelt wrote that about twenty Negro infantrymen in his command weakened under fire at San Juan Hill and started to the rear. Thereupon, Roosevelt said, he drew his revolver and ordered them to return to their ranks and go forward. The *Scribner's* article was challenged by several Negro veterans of the battle, among whom was Sergeant Preston Holliday.

Sergeant Holliday answered the Roosevelt article in the *New York Age* in 1899. He recounted an incident in which a Negro sergeant led his men to the front. When they reached San Juan, he wrote, few companies were in order; most were badly mixed. He asserted that Colonel Roosevelt erred in saying his command included

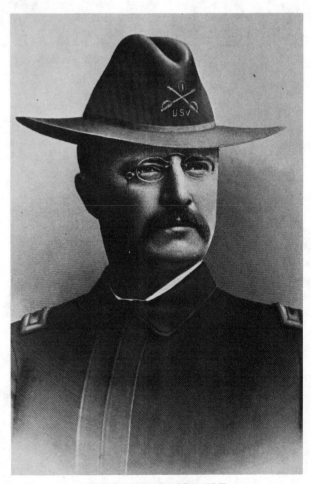

THEODORE ROOSEVELT

Troop C of the 9th Cavalry played a major role in the successful charge at San Juan Hill.

When the news came of the Spanish army's surrender at Santiago, the 25th Infantry stood closer to the city than did any other regiment—within a thousand yards.

some black infantrymen—for all Negro troops in the command were cavalrymen. When the call came for men to carry the wounded to the rear, Holliday recalled, a few Negro soldiers volunteered. Lieutenant Fleming of the 10th Cavalry ordered them to the rear. Colonel Roosevelt, seeing the men but not knowing their orders, drew his revolver, as he said. But Lieutenant Fleming later assured him that the men were acting under his orders.

"Everyone who saw the incident knew that the Colonel was mistaken about our men trying to shirk duty," Sergeant Holliday maintained, "but we all knew that he could not allow any heavy defection from his command, so no one thought ill of the matter." The sergeant remembered that Roosevelt came to apologize the next day for threatening to shoot some of the Negro cavalrymen. "He had seen his mistake," Holliday said, "and found them to be far different from what he supposed."

The *New York Journal* waxed eloquent in its version of the Negro's fighting at San Juan Hill: "Side by side with Roosevelt's men they fought— these black men. Scarce used to freedom themselves, they are dying that Cuba may be free. . . . The Rough Riders and the Black Regiment! In these two commands is an epitome of almost our whole national character."

An ex-Confederate cavalryman, General Joe Wheeler, commenting on the battle of Santiago, wrote: "The reports of all their commanders unite in commending the Negro soldiers." He concluded that they "returned from Cuba's bloodstained fields covered with glory." While the war lasted but four months, the Negroes who participated were able to take considerable pride in their important contributions to the American victory. Seven Negroes received Medals of Honor for their outstanding valor in the Spanish-American War. Five were members of the 10th Cavalry and two were navy men.

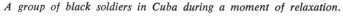

A group of black soldiers in Cuba during a moment of relaxation.

EMILIO AGUINALDO

PUERTO RICO, THE PHILIPPINES AND HAWAII

Spain's military setbacks in the Caribbean left other islands in American hands. The Americans invaded Puerto Rico and controlled the island after two weeks. In the Philippines, the rebel leader Aguinaldo had led a revolt against the Spaniards, agreeing to cooperate with the Americans in the attacks. The joint effort ended Spanish rule in most of the Philippine Islands. Hostilities soon ceased, and peace commissioners were authorized to meet in Paris.

President McKinley proclaimed that the Americans had come to the Philippines "not as invaders or as conquerors but as friends." The Filipinos, like the Cubans, had expected to gain their independence; however, the treaty that ended the war simply took their country out of Spanish hands and placed it under American control. Throughout the country small bands of Filipinos began to rebel. Isolated but unpleasant

incidents between American and Filipino soldiers soon grew into island-wide armed conflict. For two years American soldiers, both Negro and white, were to battle the rebels, while at home many Americans began to question the justice of the position of the United States in the Philippines.

The Filipinos fought bravely, but without comparable weapons and ammunition they were no match for the Americans. Their leader, Aguinaldo, was forced into hiding in the mountains. Captured in 1901, he issued a plea to his followers to stop fighting. In spite of the plea and Aguinaldo's own oath of allegiance to the United States, however, resistance in the islands continued for some time. Frustration and anger on both sides resulted in the use of methods of retaliation which horrified American civilians. One American brigadier general, "Hell-Roaring" Jake Smith, was court-martialed for his brutal treatment of the Filipinos. It was revealed that he had been indirectly responsible for the shooting of prisoners without trial and that he had issued an order to "kill everything over ten" on the island of Samar. Peace was finally restored in 1902.

Insurgents attacking a U.S. barracks in Manila.

At the Paris Peace Conference, Spain had ceded her possessions in the West Indies, the Philippines and Guam to the United States. After debating the issue of annexing Cuba and the Philippines, Congress chose to adopt the Platt amendment which made Cuba a protectorate. A naval base was opened at Guantanamo. The last American forces left the island in May of 1902, and Cuba became an independent republic. The Filipinos were declared "citizens of the Philippine Islands," thus entitling them to United States protection. The President appointed Judge William Howard Taft to be their first civil governor. The Philippines finally gained full independence in 1946.

At about this time the United States also began to value the Hawaiian Islands for their sugar and other tropical products. Queen Liliuokalani granted American ships the exclusive right to use Pearl Harbor in 1887. When, six years later, President Harrison presented the Senate with a proposal to annex Hawaii, it refused to give its consent. When President McKinley again proposed the treaty, however, Congress approved, and the Hawaiian Islands became a territorial possession in 1900.

IMPERIALISM AND THE COLORED PEOPLES

The Spanish-American War brought under United States control large populations of non-white persons. The more than three thousand Philippine Islands included roughly eight million Malays, Chinese and persons of mixed Negro ancestry, but only a few more than 14,000 whites. Puerto Rico—which was kept as a territory—added a million more inhabitants. Of these, about one-third were Negroes. Many others classed themselves as "mixed." In the Hawaiian Islands, white, Negro, Chinese, Japanese, Polynesian and mixed peoples dwelled together. The United States undertook a colonial burden at this point. It entered upon a new path in its history, abandoning its policy of isolation and taking up the "White Man's Burden" in the western world.

A year after the Paris Peace Conference, the Philippine Act of 1902 gave the Filipinos the right to elect members to the House of Representatives. All males of twenty-three or older who had held public office, possessed property or paid taxes gained the right to vote—if they could read, speak or write in English or Spanish. These standards—which were more objective than those for Negroes in many states—gave the Philippines a semblance of democracy.

Since the Clayton-Bulwer Treaty of 1850 between Britain and the United States, Washington had been studying an inter-ocean canal project proposed for a narrow strip of land in Central America. Colombia gave a concession to a French company led by Ferdinand de Lesseps, the builder of the Suez Canal. But the plan failed, and the company disposed of its rights for $40 million. The Hay-Pauncefote Treaty of 1901, another London-Washington pact, permitted a canal to be built for the use of all nations. Another treaty in 1903 granted the United States a ninety-nine-year lease of a six-mile strip of land across the Isthmus of Panama. The United States agreed to pay $10 million and an annual rental fee of $250,000, beginning nine years after the date of the agreement. When the plan was presented to Colombia, however, its senate refused to ratify the treaty. Still the United States pursued its interests there.

A rapid succession of events took place in the isthmus area. A revolution occurred while American marines patrolled the area. The Colombian secessionists set up the Republic of Panama, which the United States soon recognized. Washington signed a treaty with the new government in 1903, granting a ten-mile strip for a canal route. Thus the Panama route triumphed over one suggested for Nicaragua, and Panama subsequently became a sort of United States chattel itself.

The new imperialism tightened racial tensions in the United States. For now the United States faced a dilemma not unlike those facing the nations of Europe in Africa and the Asian subcontinent. Anti-imperialist leagues sprang up to oppose the colonial trend across the nation. Both the Democratic and Republican Parties stood divided over the issue. Within each party, imperialism was defended and denounced. Republican Senator Albert Beveridge insisted that self-government should be confined only to those

Negroes contributed much of the labor during the building of the Panama Canal.

nations "who are capable of self-government."
Beveridge clearly considered the newly acquired
territories incapable. Though an expansionist,
Theodore Roosevelt disagreed. He regarded the
islands as an "Achilles heel" for the United
States. These same divisions appeared among the
Democrats. Many whites and Negroes vocally
opposed the Spanish treaty because of its colonial
commitment for the future.

"It is a sorry, though true, fact," Lewis H.
Douglass (son of Frederick Douglass) lamented,
"that whatever this government controls, injustice
to dark races prevails. . . . It is hypocrisy of the
most sickening kind to try to make us believe that
the killing of Filipinos is for the purpose of good
government and to give protection to life, liberty,
and pursuit of happiness."

Negro Americans repeatedly raised this issue.
They could not imagine the noble-sounding plans
for colored Filipinos coming to fruition—not
while they themselves were denied equal citizenship on the United States mainland. A group in
Boston even proposed to raise a private army to
quietly move into the Philippines and aid the in-
surrectionists.

The United States acquired its Spanish-speak-
ing territories with different means from those
used by the European imperialists. Instead of
annexing and acquiring colonies, American ex-
pansionists penetrated the island societies through
loans and investments for buying raw products.
These efforts—accompanied by educational aid
and material improvements in the islands—gave
birth to the catch phrase of anti-Americanism:
"Dollar Diplomacy."

LEWIS H. DOUGLASS

But whether through territorial expansion or
business investment, imperialism proved more
than the United States had bargained for. The
New York World expressed the general sentiment
of the country in 1899 in a discouraging reply to
Rudyard Kipling:

> We've taken up the white man's burden
>   Of ebony and brown;
> Now will you kindly tell us, Rudyard,
>   How we may put it down?

CHAPTER SEVEN

Black Protest and Pride— Reaction to Sanctioned Discrimination

EVERY former Confederate state had disfranchised the Negro citizen by 1910. In fact, between 1890 and 1910 eight of these states had adopted constitutional amendments that limited the Negro's vote. The rest of the South took equally effective measures toward that end.

By this time northerners generally thought it unwise to force Negro suffrage on the South. Many saw voting practices as a state problem which outside interference would only make worse. Conditions could not have become much worse, however, for the Negro vote had nearly vanished from the South. Federal and state courts had held that the states' rights to control voting had limits—namely the prohibitions of the Fifteenth Amendment. Mississippi, South Carolina and Louisiana still passed discriminatory laws during the 1890's. The other Deep South states enacted similar statutes in the next few years: North Carolina in 1900, Alabama and Virginia in 1901, Georgia in 1908 and Alabama once again in 1910. All sought to remove the Negro vote by means of the law.

Another development which helped remove Negroes from southern politics was the "white primary." It kept them from entering the party nominating process. Party registrars raised this new barrier by tacit agreement with other white officials. Since the choice of Democratic candidates took place in a virtual one-party region, it was tantamount to election. The system proved so effective that an Atlanta *Constitution* writer could state in 1907: "We already had the Negro eliminated from politics by the white primary." A small number of Negroes still managed to vote in the primaries of a few states. Where no contrary laws existed—as in Florida, North Carolina and Tennessee—voting was regarded as the privilege of a select Negro group. But from 1910 to 1920, the white primary solidified in most of the South as a device to sidestep the Constitution.

Some legislators from the various districts clamored for laws barring all persons of African blood from entering the United States and achieving citizenship. They also favored a ban on Negro advancement to certain jobs they considered "desirable for white men." Their special venom, however, was reserved for Negro education. Certain lawmakers threatened to cut all funds to black colleges. Florida and Kentucky went so far as to pass laws making it a crime for a white person to teach a Negro.

Most white churches finally joined in the movement to degrade the Negro in political, economic and social life. The noted clergyman Lyman Abbott, who had spent earlier years working for political, social and economic reforms, now sought to justify segregation through theology.

In this way, the "Christians" in both North and South could avoid services which forced them to break bread with Negroes, whom Abbott and others claimed God had created as their social inferiors. Churches in which Negroes had previously worshipped side by side with whites now formed separate congregations. They usually set up an inadequate system of makeshift religious institutions for Negroes. White bishops, tiring of a ministry to Negro members, acquiesced in the racial schism. Soon a demand arose for complete separation—not just within the church edifice, but in the management of all church affairs.

The racial wall posed as many problems as it supposedly solved. Few white pastors were eager to serve Negroes in their special places of worship. Whites also thought it "impracticable" to elevate Negroes to positions of trust in mixed churches. While many white churchmen in the· North disliked contact with Negroes, they balked at losing control of black membership rolls, as had the southern churches after the Civil War. These mixed feelings blocked a move to unify the Methodist churches. Some northern Methodists held out for at least a "separate but equal" status for their Negro affiliates. But the Methodist Episcopal Church South accepted Negro communicants only on the understanding that they should not be treated as equals of white members. The two church branches finally united under a compromise plan. The Southern branch agreed to include Negroes if church authority would be decentralized through a regional conference system.

Social agencies which undertook the work the churches never performed faced the same problem. For years the Young Men's Christian Association and the Young Women's Christian Association maintained separate black branches in the South. For a long time after the Civil War, racial prejudice was not powerful enough to exclude Negroes in the North from occasional use of the "Y's." But racial bigotry was on the increase. In these centers, too, when Negroes began to increase in number a color line was drawn. The northern "Y's" compromised by building separate centers in the cities for Negro youths and boarders. Even as segregated structures, the "Y's" served a useful hotel function. But they failed to lend the needed social uplift so vital to Negroes of this era.

NEGRO PARTICIPATION IN POLITICS

In the light of the evils of the age, the obvious question becomes that of assessing the activities of the governments—federal, state and local— with regard to black problems. The period was marked by many inconsistencies in federal and state racial outlook. Some of the southern states turned increasingly to strengthening legal contrivances to nullify the effects of the federal government's Reconstruction Amendments. In many cases they enjoyed the support of the courts in their discriminatory actions. At other times, however, the courts became the real champions of black rights. The civil-rights records of the Presidents of the period—William McKinley and Theodore Roosevelt—are uneven. A surprising sanctioning of some forms of discrimination appeared during their administrations, coupled with reasonably steady increases in black appointments to important public offices.

In efforts to save their party's power, Republicans continued to court any remaining southern Negro voters. When William McKinley sought the votes of southern delegates in 1895, his campaign manager rented a house in Thomasville, Georgia, to which the state's federal officeholders and convention members of both races were invited. McKinley and his party visited Savannah State College, where an old Negro ally, Richard R. Wright, Sr., was president. Such relationships were common. The Negroes traditionally voted Republican, and whites who sought control of the party wooed their support.

Negro newspapers took up the discussion of Negro rights and blazoned the story to their readers. One such paper, the *Afro-American Sentinel*, was published in Nebraska, home state of McKinley's opponent, the Democrat William Jennings Bryan. The Omaha newspaper took up Bryan's banner, pointing to his support for a congressional bill to aid Negro education in the South. Although the measure failed to pass, its sponsor acknowledged a debt to Bryan for his assistance in a letter published in the *Afro-American Sentinel*. These endorsements helped the Bryan ticket gain greater Negro backing than previous Democratic tickets had received. Aided by the heavy Negro voting, Bryan eventually managed to carry New York by over a thousand votes.

The southern bloc began to wield a strong influence in the Democratic Party by the 1890's. It had backed free coinage of silver and cheered for the cause of the farmers. Through the Populists' endorsement of Bryan, the South tightened its grip on the Democrats.

The hopeful Bryan campaigned in many states, and by the time that the 1896 election returns were in, Bryan had carried all the former slave states except Delaware, Maryland, Kentucky and West Virginia. He also captured many of the western states. But McKinley won the Midwest, New England, the mid-Atlantic and the remaining western states, and won the election.

JUDSON W. LYONS

McKINLEY'S ADMINISTRATION

Negroes—like other Americans—were keenly interested in McKinley's new appointments. T. Thomas Fortune had lashed out at the Republican Party's failure to name qualified Negroes to federal offices in the past. The new President revealed his intentions when he chose Judson W. Lyons, a Negro, as postmaster of Augusta, Georgia. Certain congressmen, representatives of the white South, promptly objected. The Savannah press raised such an uproar that Lyons withdrew his name, accepting the job of registrar of the treasury instead. President McKinley failed to bow to such opposition, however. He named other Negroes to federal offices in the South. When he chose a Negro as postmaster for Hogansville, Georgia, another storm erupted. The white community rented a store to replace the post office. A white man collected the mail and carried it to the store, where a white woman distributed it. On the way home one night, the Negro postmaster was ambushed, but he survived three bullet wounds.

RICHARD R. WRIGHT, SR.

News reports of the incident caused a strong public reaction across the nation. Georgia's Governor Atkinson denounced the attack. But he chided McKinley, whom he termed an accessory to the crime, for having appointed the Negro against community opposition. Senator A. O. Bacon of Georgia added that the President should name Negroes to local posts only where the whites approved.

Dr. Clarence A. Bacote of Atlanta University, a student of the Negro in Georgia, noted that McKinley made more Negro appointments in Georgia than had all earlier Presidents combined. During his tenure, McKinley named about seventy Negroes to federal posts—twice the number of any of his predecessors. McKinley did, nonetheless, tolerate segregation of the Negro masses in order to reunite North and South.

"It will be my constant aim," McKinley said, "to do nothing, and permit nothing to be done that will arrest or disturb this growing sentiment of unity and cooperation, this revival of esteem and affiliation which now animates so many thousands in both old antagonistic sections, but I shall cheerfully do everything possible to promote and increase it."

Six months after his second term began, President McKinley died at the hands of an assassin. He was greeting visitors to the American Exposition in Buffalo when a Polish anarchist, Leon F. Czolgosz, shot and mortally wounded him. A Negro waiter, J. B. Parker, seized Czolgosz and held him until police arrested him. McKinley died September 14, 1901. Negroes joined with other grief-stricken Americans in holding memorial services for their President.

ROOSEVELT'S ADMINISTRATION

McKinley's successor, the wealthy New Yorker Theodore Roosevelt, showed as much ambivalence and spontaneity in his dealings with Negroes as he did in his conduct of the other affairs of the presidency. Writing in 1907, towards the end of Roosevelt's seven-year term in office, Professor Kelley Miller of Howard University found Roosevelt's relations with the Negro to have been "marked by an almost whimsical alternation of good and bad impressions." Miller described his

J. B. PARKER

contemporary as "a man of instantaneous impulse . . . unhampered by the tedium of logical coherence or consistency of procedure."

Theodore Roosevelt's mother was a product of the Old South; his father had been a Union sympathizer in the Civil War. "Teddy," the rugged outdoor adventurer, spent his boyhood in the Dakotas and developed an easy acceptance of all kinds of people from his military contacts in Cuba and his political alliances in New York.

Not long after assuming office in 1901, after McKinley's assassination, the new President shocked and offended many white southerners by inviting Booker T. Washington to dine with him at the White House. The southern press attacked the action bitterly. "When Mr. Roosevelt sits down to dinner with a Negro," the New Orleans *Times Democrat* angrily commented, "he declares that a Negro is a social equal of the white man." Another New Orleans daily denounced the invitation as "a studied insult to the South." Said a Memphis paper: "No southern woman with proper self-respect would now accept an invitation to the White House." The criticism annoyed the President. He quickly offered the retort that he would invite Dr. Washington as often as he pleased.

Roosevelt never asked the Tuskegee educator to return, however, and later said that "it was a mistake" to have invited him in the first place. But throughout his White House occupancy Roosevelt continued to seek Dr. Washington's advice before appointing Negroes to public office. During his administration nearly fourteen thousand Negroes entered the federal civil service, most with public approval. Many of Roosevelt's appointments continued to incense the South.

When the President appointed Dr. William D. Crum to the post of collector of the port of Charleston, South Carolina, many white southerners thought he had made a serious mistake. President Harrison had previously named Dr. Crum to a postmaster vacancy, but when the protests had surpassed what was expected, he had withdrawn the nomination. Roosevelt stood his ground. He kept Crum in office by interim appointments until the Senate finally granted its grudging approval.

Critics screamed again when Roosevelt reappointed Mrs. Minnie Cox to the postmaster job in Indianola, Mississippi, which she had held in the Harrison and McKinley administrations. The furor of the local whites this time forced her resignation as a safety measure. Roosevelt answered them by shutting down the post office. The South rose up to condemn the President's action, and some northerners joined them; but Roosevelt would not be intimidated. He maintained that the choice of public officials without regard to race was in line with his "Square Deal," the phrase for the Republican President's program. Negro leaders came to his defense. Bishop W. B. Derrick said the President had opened the door of hope to the Negro. Other Negroes in both the North and the South echoed his praise. Roosevelt later reflected on his Negro appointments and the southern reaction they provoked as follows:

> It may be that it would have been better . . . not to have [had] Booker Washington at dinner. It may be that it would have been better not to have originally nominated Crum for the Charleston electorship. Personally, I think I was right in both instances, but even if I was wrong, to say the South's attitude is explained by these two acts is to say that the South is in a condition of chronic, violent hysteria.

FURTHER ACCEPTANCE OF DISCRIMINATION

Prejudice and discrimination were certainly not confined to the South. During nearly every period of history in this country, the South's prejudice has taken forms more obvious and overt than the North's. The subtle, and often more hypocritical, signs of discrimination within the so-called "liberal" and "open" areas and institutions of the country has been just as hateful. At some time, but particularly in the late nineteenth and early twentieth centuries, every group which was not "white Anglo-Saxon Protestant" has been relegated to second-class status in some way, and has been subjected to discriminatory tactics.

One group of Americans harassed most cruelly by others were the Indians. In 1881 Helen Hunt Jackson wrote a commentary on the American Indian, entitled *A Century of Dishonor,* in which she revealed previously undisclosed facts on the treatment of Indians during the nineteenth century. Heedless of the public outcry raised by the book, Congress passed the Dawes Act in 1887. This legislation opened many Indian reservations to settlement, including more than a million acres in Oklahoma. At the blast of a bugle, thousands

W. B. DERRICK

An anti-Chinese riot in the streets of Seattle, Washington.

of whites and Negroes who had assembled to await the signal pressed forward on foot, on horseback and in wagons across the border to claim choice land.

Scholarly estimates of the early Indian population vary greatly and can provide only approximate figures. Anthropologists surmise that at the time of Columbus' arrival there were well over one million Indians—some scholars guess as many as ten to fifteen million—on the land. By the turn of the twentieth century there were under 250,000 Indians left.

Orientals—the Chinese, in particular—also suffered from repressive laws and violence. Labor conventions adopted resolutions against the entry of Chinese workers into the labor market. A New Orleans convention of Negroes joined in opposing use of Chinese labor in Louisiana. Resent-

ment against the Chinese stemmed from their low-wage toil during construction of the transcontinental railroads. It grew to fever pitch, exploding into anti-Chinese riots in the 1890's. The decade saw a corresponding rise in anti-Catholicism and anti-Semitism.

The common bond of discrimination sometimes promoted friendly relations between Negro and immigrant workers and cooperation among their labor leaders. As increasing numbers of Negroes flocked to the industrial centers, however, ill feeling toward them developed in New York, Boston, Philadelphia and other large eastern cities.

The familiar cry, "Back to Africa with the Negroes," echoed with Slavic, Polish, Hungarian, Greek, Russian and Lithuanian accents. The major source of friction was that the immigrants and the Negroes were often competing for the same menial occupations: members of both groups became porters, dock hands, waiters, barbers, cooks, maids and domestic workers. A keen rivalry formed between the two "have not" groups, sometimes erupting into violent clashes.

One of the worst race riots occurred in Detroit. Most members of the attacking group were reported to be "Americanized" Poles and other recent immigrants. Despite conflicts of this sort, Irish groups in a number of northern cities allied themselves with Negro voters in defeating Ku Klux Klan candidates for office. Jewish groups, themselves at times victims of discrimination, also often were allied with Negro voters.

A savage anti-Negro riot in Wilmington, North Carolina, shocked the nation in 1898. The press reported "two dreadful days and nights in the clutch of a bloody revolution." Once again, in 1899, riots exploded in Washington, North Carolina, and in Greenwood, Mississippi. Similar outbreaks occurred in Springfield, Ohio, and in Statesboro, Georgia, in 1904, and in Greensburg, Indiana, and Atlanta, Georgia, in 1906. That was also the year that the famous Brownsville affair shook south Texas. Still another race riot took place in Springfield, Illinois, in 1908.

THE BROWNSVILLE AFFAIR

An incident occurred in Brownsville, Texas, in mid-August of 1906, which stirred the nation's Negroes and in which President Roosevelt became a key figure. Three companies, "B," "C" and "D" of the 25th Infantry Regiment, had been sent to Brownsville to relieve a battalion of the 16th Infantry. The withdrawing unit of white troops had engaged in a clash with civilians as a result of repeated misunderstandings. The townspeople resented the presence of soldiers generally, and when they learned that black troops would replace the white troops, resentment ran high. To make matters worse, according to historian Lawrence Hugh Cook, the men of the 25th Infantry had been involved in some affrays prior to stationing at Brownsville, which had resulted in deaths and injuries.

The city mounted a protest, and a near-riot took place on August 14. One person was killed;

two others were wounded. Local citizens accused the Negro infantrymen of starting the riot and "shooting up the town." Some of the soldiers— veterans of three or four enlistments in the regular army—were arrested and criticized severely for the "conspiracy of silence" that enveloped Fort Brown. For when the Army Department and the unit's own officers asked for the names of the men implicated in the shooting, no one spoke out. The soldiers were then given discharges without honor en masse, without the benefit of hearings, by order of the President.

The White House and the army found themselves deluged by protests from white and Negro groups demanding that the order of dismissal be rescinded. The *New York Age* called the executive order "merely another sacrifice offered by the President upon the altar of Southern race prejudice."

The *Washington Post* also questioned the White House move. "While the President's power to discharge a soldier cannot be questioned," the *Post* stated, "it is not conferred for purposes of punishment." The Secretary of War withheld the presidential order for thirty-six hours while he contacted Roosevelt by cable in Panama. When the President returned to Washington, he took no steps to rescind the order. Many of the dismissed soldiers had excellent records. It was later proved that a number took no part in the disorders.

A congressional champion of the soldiers' cause, Senator Joseph B. Foraker of Ohio, insisted that the soldiers were discharged without convincing proof of guilt or involvement. The evidence included an army inspector's report which stated that the soldiers had killed and wounded Brownsville's citizens. After studying the official reports, Senator Foraker said he could not agree with the President's action. He maintained that the findings failed to justify discharging whole companies of soldiers without honor. The Senator found the evidence "flimsy, unreliable, insufficient and untruthful." South Carolina's old Populist, "Pitchfork Ben" Tillman, used the occasion to castigate the President. He called the dismissal "an executive lynching." Senator Foraker offered a resolution calling upon the Secretary of War to send all information on "the

Brownsville affair" to the Senate. After lengthy debate, the Senate adopted the Foraker resolution.

President Roosevelt sent the Senate a message accusing the infantrymen of being the aggressors from start to finish. His language was vehement and almost abusive. "The evidence proves conclusively," the President wrote, "that a number of soldiers engaged in a deliberate and concerted attack as cold-blooded as it was cowardly, the purpose being to terrorize the community and to kill men, women and children in their homes, in their beds and on the street."

"If these men committed murder, as charged," Senator Foraker replied, "the punishment is inadequate." The Ohio lawmaker reflected on President Roosevelt's southern friends and relatives. "No one can say this had anything to do with his action in discharging the colored soldiers, but it was doubtless quite agreeable to him to see his fierce enemies suddenly become warm friends." Senator Foraker then reviewed the evidence in detail, pointing out its errors and discrepancies. At one point he summed up the military records of the discharged soldiers in these words: "Faithfully, uncomplainingly, with pride and devotion, they have performed all their duties and kept all their obligations. They ask no favors because they are Negroes, but only for justice because they are men."

Finally, President Roosevelt reacted to Foraker's steady criticism. He sanctioned the inquiry that the Senator had requested in a resolution. This investigation lasted more than a year. The committee majority reported in March of 1908 that members of the battalion had, in fact, done the shooting, but that it was not possible to identify the guilty soldiers. A minority report contended that the evidence was too flimsy to implicate all the soldiers. Senator Foraker sponsored a bill authorizing a military court in hope of approving any qualified soldier for re-enlistment. Congress passed the measure and the President signed it into law, but the effort failed to salvage all the soldiers' careers. The military court agreed with the earlier inquiries. It failed to find any testimony identifying any member of the infantry unit, "white or black," with the Brownsville fray. The tribunal qualified fourteen of the accused for

JOSEPH B. FORAKER

re-enlistment. Senator Foraker kept up his attack even after leaving the Senate. Some years later he said he believed not one particle of testimony pointing to the guilt of the regiment would ever be produced.

Brownsville was to remain a potent political issue for some time to come. In addition to the legislators, other whites protested the President's action. A Republican manufacturer of pneumatic tubes, named John Milholland, was a key figure working with Booker Washington in the fight for the soldiers' acquittal. Mary Church Terrell and Gilcrist Stewart of the Constitution League were among other prominent Negro leaders working to gain a reversal of the Roosevelt order. Two days after his retirement from the Senate in 1909, Senator Foraker received a silver loving cup from black citizens in appreciation of his service to the soldiers. A certain vindication of Senator Foraker's efforts remains to this day: no new facts have ever appeared to prove the soldiers' guilt in the affair.

LYNCHING AND CRIME

Thousands of Americans turned their attention at this time to the evils of lynching and other mob action against Negroes. Tuskegee records for the period 1889 to 1925 show that some 3,557 such incidents occurred across the nation. Of this total, 2,835 victims were Negroes and 722 were whites.

Ida B. Wells Barnett, a prominent black Chicago woman who crusaded tirelessly for anti-lynching laws, dispelled a popular myth through her revealing study of police records. Writing in the *Independent* in 1901, she showed that the majority of lynching cases were not linked with assaults or accusations of assaults upon women. She claimed that hundreds had died at the hands of lynch mobs for misdemeanors or minor offenses. About four-fifths of the atrocities occurring through "mob justice" took place in the South and mostly in isolated rural areas.

Among the lynching victims were fifty Negro women and eleven white women; only about 19 per cent of those lynched had been accused of assault. Lynchings decreased to less than a hundred in 1902, 1904, 1905, 1906 and 1907. But in

An NAACP anti-lynching poster.

1908, when the number of victims again rose to one hundred, many Americans demanded a federal anti-lynching law to preserve order, to end mob action and to restore the nation's good name throughout the world. State and local officials seemed powerless or unwilling to curb the mobs, thereby lending strength to the arguments of those favoring such a law.

Another evil, less publicized than lynching, was perpetrated in the South—with full legal sanctions. As the population and the amount of crime increased and as methods of law enforcement improved, the jails held a growing number of prisoners. An unmet demand for labor on the outside was growing at the same time. To meet the situation, an institution called the "convict-lease" system developed in several southern states.

The prisoners were forced to work on roads, railways, farms, plantations and mines. The employer paid for their maintenance, with a bonus

IDA B. WELLS BARNETT

going to the state for the convicts' services. The system was often abused; convicts received such poor treatment that a clamor arose for the states to abolish the program. Mississippi discarded its convict-lease system in 1895. Then Georgia did the same in 1909. Soon the other southern states followed their example. They replaced these programs, however, with a parole system which put prisoners under outside employers. Some states sent convicts to work in chain gangs. That is, the prisoners were shackled by chains to work under an armed overseer. Too often this system subjected them to conditions approaching slavery. Since black men comprised a large proportion of the prisoners in the places where the convict-lease system was used, many blacks suffered cruelly under it.

Prison statistics for the period are difficult to obtain and often inaccurate. It is still clear, however, that Negroes accounted for a much larger proportion of convicts than their numbers in the population would warrant. Statistical estimates vary widely. In *The American Negro: What He Was, What He Is, and What He May Become*, William H. Thomas claimed that Negroes comprised 75 per cent of the inmates of major prisons in 1901. Another sociologist, Charles H. McCord, placed the percentage much lower. In his study *The American Negro as Dependent, Defective and Delinquent*, McCord states that Negroes accounted for 32.6 per cent of the prison population in 1904, while they numbered only 12.1 per cent of the nation's citizenry.

While some observers interpreted the prison statistics as evidence that Negroes were more criminally inclined than whites, the figures by no means demonstrated a necessary connection between race and crime. For one thing, the prejudices of white arresting officers, judges and juries may well have been a factor in raising the number of Negro convictions: some might have had a tendency to arrest, accuse and convict blacks too hastily. Even so, the incidence of real black crime was certainly high. In reaching conclusions about race and crime in the late nineteenth and early twentieth centuries, however, it is necessary to take into account such social factors as the consequences of slavery, effects of migration from the farms to the cities,

limited job opportunities, poor schooling and the wretched home life which often results from poverty.

BLACK PROTEST

Many Negro groups rose in protest against the outrages perpetrated against their race. Blacks organized to protest the violence politically and in the press.

The National Afro-American Council of the United States called upon Negroes to observe June 2, 1899, as a day of fasting and prayer. The Council arranged for a special sunrise service on Sunday, June 4. The protest called attention to Jim Crow railroad cars, to persecution instead of justice in the courts, to arrests and jailings of the innocent on suspicion, and to the torturing and hanging of Negroes.

In an open letter to President McKinley in 1899, Massachusetts Negroes stated the core of the issue:

> We have suffered, sir. God knows how much we have suffered since your accession to office, . . . and you have seen our sufferings, witnessed from your high place our awful wrongs and miseries, and yet you have at no time and on no occasion opened your lips in our behalf. "Why?" we ask. "Is it because we are black and weak and despised? Are you silent because without any fault of our own we were enslaved and held for more than two centuries in cruel bondage for your forefathers? Is it because we bear the marks of those sad generations, generations of Anglo-Saxon brutality and weaknesses that you do not speak?"

At the height of the Statesboro riot, Fred P. Gordon, a New Yorker, wrote President Theodore Roosevelt asking that he send all the military power at his disposal to "arrest the leaders of the mob who should be punished for a crime which is a burning disgrace." The acting attorney general replied that the Justice Department "cannot, at the present time, take any action in the matter." This "hands off" policy prompted a flood of letters from Negroes across the nation.

Effective group protest, however, did not come until later. The futility of the earlier group action prompted many black authors to assert equality individually, through their writings. Black pride had its origins in the protest movements.

THE BIRTH OF BLACK PRIDE

A number of Negro history books came out in these decades. Two outstanding examples were George W. Williams' *History of the Negro Race in America from 1619 to 1880* (1883) and Edward A. Johnson's *A School History of the Negro Race in America from 1619 to 1890* (1891). Johnson dedicated his book "to the many thousand colored teachers in our country," pointing to "the sin of omission and commission on the part of white authors, most of whom seem to have written exclusively for white children, and studiously left out the many creditable deeds of the Negro." Johnson charged that these history texts implied that Negroes were inferior if they did not say it in so many words.

Four years earlier William T. Alexander had published his *History of the Colored Race in America*. Then, in 1902, W. H. Crogman issued his major work, *Progress of a Race*. Other notable books in the new Negro history movement included: *The Afro-American Encyclopaedia: Thoughts, Doings, and Sayings of the Race;* W. H. Councill's *Lamp of Wisdom or Race History Illuminated* (1898); C. T. Walker's *Appeal to Caesar* (1900); W. L. Hunter's *Jesus Christ Had Negro Blood in His Veins* (1901); Pauline Hopkins' *Primer of Facts Pertaining to the Early Greatness of the African Race* (1905); and Booker T. Washington's *Story of the Negro* (1909).

The Negro's first biographer, William J. Simmons, wrote *Men of Mark: Eminent, Progressive, and Rising* in 1891. The earliest work of its kind, it included pictures of the well-known leaders of his day. It is still considered a work of value. G. F. Richings, another Negro historian, published his *Evidences of Progress among Colored People* in 1897.

The American Negro Historical Society was founded in Philadelphia in 1897. It sought to collect "relics, literature and historical facts relative to the Negro race, illustrating their progress and development in this country." Meanwhile, John Edward Bruce and Arthur A. Schomburg were forming the Negro Society for Historical Research in Yonkers, New York. Bruce, a former Maryland slave, attended public school in the

ALEXANDER CRUMMELL

District of Columbia. He later became a writer and newspaper contributor. Bruce's book, *The Blood Red Record,* attacked lynching. Schomburg, a scholar of Puerto Rican descent, urged the study of Negro history as a defense against bigotry. He spent much of his life collecting and assembling Negro historical data.

During the 1890's intellectual groups laid heavy stress on folk culture. One such group, the Society for the Collection of Negro Folklore, formed in Boston in 1890. The editor of the *African Methodist Episcopal Church Review,* H. T. Kealing, also stressed the Negro's literary heritage. He advised the Negro author in 1898 "not to imitate white authors but to explore from the depths of his own being where lies unusual material that is to provide him a place among the great writers." The *Colored American Magazine* also called upon Negroes to summon their inner gifts of creativity. In 1900 it urged them to forge "the bonds of that racial brotherhood, which alone can enable a people to assert their racial rights as men."

When the American Negro Academy opened in 1897, its first president, Alexander Crummell, explained its unique purpose: "If we are fortunate to see, of a sudden, a clever mathematician of our class, a brilliant poet, a youthful but prominent scientist or philosopher let us rush forward, and hail his coming with no hesitant admiration, with no reluctant praise." The academy sought among other goals "to gather into archives valuable data and the works of Negro authors." It aimed its energies at aiding the "talented tenth" among Negroes.

Edward A. Johnson was one of the first scholars to place the Negro in context in American history.

A SCHOOL HISTORY

OF THE

Negro Race in America

FROM 1619 TO 1890

COMBINED WITH THE HISTORY OF THE
NEGRO SOLDIERS IN THE SPANISH-AMERICAN
WAR, ALSO A SHORT SKETCH OF LIBERIA

BY

EDWARD A. JOHNSON, LL.B.

Author of "Light Ahead for the Negro" and "The Negro Almanac and Statistics'

———

REVISED EDITION, 1911

ISAAC GOLDMANN Co., Printers, 200-204 William Street, New York

PROGRESS OF A RACE

..OR..

THE REMARKABLE ADVANCEMENT OF THE AFRO-AMERICAN NEGRO

From the Bondage of Slavery, Ignorance and Poverty
to the Freedom of Citizenship, Intelligence,
Affluence, Honor and Trust

BY

H. F. KLETZING, A. M.,

AND

W. H. CROGMAN, A. M.,

Professor in Clark University, Atlanta, Ga., Author of "Talks for the Times."

ॐ ॐ

WITH AN INTRODUCTION

BY

BOOKER T. WASHINGTON,

Principal of Tuskegee Normal and Industrial Institute, Tuskegee, Alabama.

ॐ ॐ

PUBLISHED BY

J. L. NICHOLS & CO.

Atlanta, Ga.   Naperville, Ill.   Toronto, Ont.

(To whom all communications must be addressed.)

1898

☞ AGENTS WANTED.

W. H. Crogman was one of the early writers on the history of his race.

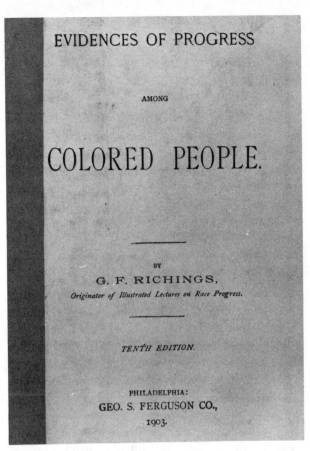

EVIDENCES OF PROGRESS

AMONG

COLORED PEOPLE.

BY
G. F. RICHINGS,
Originator of Illustrated Lectures on Race Progress.

TENTH EDITION.

PHILADELPHIA:
GEO. S. FERGUSON CO.,
1903.

Another early work on the Negro was written by G. F. Richings.

The Afro-American Encyclopaedia *also recorded the Negro's role in American history.*

Afro-American Encyclopaedia;

OR, THE

THOUGHTS, DOINGS, AND SAYINGS OF THE RACE,

———— EMBRACING ————

Addresses, Lectures, Biographical Sketches, Sermons,
Poems, Names of Universities, Colleges, Seminaries,
Newspapers, Books, and a History of the Denomi-
nations, giving the Numerical Strength of Each.
In fact, it teaches every subject of interest
to the colored people, as discussed by
more than one hundred of their
wisest and best men and women.

ILLUSTRATED WITH BEAUTIFUL HALF-TONE ENGRAVINGS.

Compiled and Arranged by James T. Haley.

SOLD BY SUBSCRIPTION EXCLUSIVELY.

No man has a right to bring up his children without surrounding them with good books
if he has the means to buy them. A library is one of the necessities of life. A book is
better for weariness than sleep; better for cheerfulness than wine; it is often a better physician than a doctor, and a better preacher than a minister.—*Beecher.*

NASHVILLE, TENN.:
HALEY & FLORIDA.
1895.

THE BLACK PRESS

The Negro press included among its ranks some members of this talented elite. T. Thomas Fortune, the editor of the *New York Age*, was the best known. Fortune had contributed articles to the New York *Sun* and the Chicago *Times Herald,* both white dailies. His *New York Age* was regarded as the organ of the Negro leadership and was read across the nation. The editors of the Negro newspapers crusaded against discrimination and strongly supported racial equality and voting rights. When fifty of the black editors met in the Afro-American Press Association gathering in 1890, they protested the mistreatment of Negroes under the South's new Jim Crow laws. They predicted that the laws would "perpetuate the undemocratic infamy of minority and caste rule."

While disorder had persisted, the Negro press had thrived. By 1890 the number of publications totaled 154. The outstanding city papers included: the *New Era*, founded in 1870 in the nation's capital; the *Progressive American*, a New York weekly started in 1871; the Washington *Bee* (1879); the Cleveland *Gazette* (1883); the Philadelphia *Tribune* (1884); the Savannah *Tribune* (1885); the *New York Age* (1887); and the *Afro-American* (1892), founded in Baltimore.

The boldest of the new papers was Monroe Trotter's *Guardian,* first published in Boston in 1901. Unlike the older black newspapers, with their more conservative approach and parochial reportage, the *Guardian* spoke out aggressively on national issues. Soon other outspoken writers were airing their views in their own papers. Robert S. Abbott began editing the *Defender* in Chicago in 1905 as a handbill, which he distributed himself. The paper kept up a reputation for leadership; Negroes across the nation turned to it for guidance and even for legal assistance, and the *Defender* continued to champion their cause. The *Pittsburgh Courier* came under the dynamic hand of editor Robert L. Vann in 1912, two years after its founding.

The first Negro magazine, the *Colored American Magazine*, made its appearance in 1900 and lasted for six years. Its prime mover, Walter W. Wallace, lacked literary talent but had the ambition to create and publish a magazine for Negro readers. By informing readers of important issues, by mobilizing opinion, by giving advice and even by simply showing concern, the Negro press became the chief instrument in the unification of the black community and in that community's growth in influence and power.

These black publications spoke for and to the Negro, voicing his hopes, aspirations and protests. They reflected his historic, civic, cultural and social concerns. The editors of the various black big city newspapers, however, sometimes faced a curious dilemma. Two aims of most newspapers often conflict, namely, that of voicing a needed point of view on current events, and that of selling newspapers. Sometimes protest sells; at other times it does not. The *Chicago Defender* serves as a good example of the vicissitudes which confronted the black press.

Edward T. Clayton in *The Negro Politician* and James Q. Wilson in *Negro Politics* express differing views on the *Defender*. Clayton emphasizes the paper's steadfast race consciousness and social contributions. He states that the *Defender*'s columns "enticed, pleaded, challenged, promised and shamed the southern Negro into migrating north with such editorial compulsion that the paper was finally banned in many southern areas."

The motivation in protest may well have been economic, however. For, according to Wilson, writing in 1960, while the *Defender*'s editor "focused attention on race issues and visualized the paper as a crusading—and lucrative—enterprise," for his nephew, who took over the editing later, "the paper has been both less lucrative and less crusading."

In the early twentieth century, Dr. Robert R. Moton of Tuskegee wrote sadly of the predominance of crime reporting in the Negro newspapers. But crime was what the readers seemed to want, explained an officer of the *Defender* in Wilson's book. "You can't write about segregation and discrimination every day. People get a surfeit of it. People get tired of it. You have to stay away from the constant note of protest, protest, protest. . . . But it's hard to do, because the Negro press was born out of protest."

EARLY WRITINGS OF DU BOIS

The failure of federal officials to aid in protecting the civil rights of Negroes led many gifted writers to protest in books, pamphlets, articles and newspaper editorials. Heading the list at the beginning of the twentieth century was W. E. B. Du Bois. While trained in history at Harvard and Berlin Universities, Du Bois emerged as more than a historian.

After his *Suppression of the African Slave Trade to the United States of America* appeared in 1896, he left Wilberforce University to accept a job as assistant instructor in sociology at the University of Pennsylvania. There he wrote *The Philadelphia Negro: A Social Study*, which the university published in 1899. Du Bois later submitted articles to the *Atlantic Monthly, World's Work* and *Dial*. He was planning to start a Negro magazine when the editors of *McClure's* asked him in 1900 to furnish material for a book. The young scholar proposed a broad study of the Negro problem in the United States, based on his research at Atlanta University. The publishers were interested in a smaller work. Du Bois then assembled his published and unpublished essays which he issued in book form in 1903 as *The Souls of Black Folk: Essays and Sketches*. This book has seen twenty-four editions to date.

Reviewers varied widely in their opinions of the Du Bois volume. "This book is dangerous for the Negro to read," a Tennessee newspaper editor wrote, "for it will only excite discontent and fill his imagination with things that do not exist or things that should not bear upon his mind." But the New York *Commercial Advertiser* disagreed. "At a time when race prejudice has suddenly taken on an aggravated form," it said, "when almost every day witnesses a new onthrust in some unexpected quarter, a volume of this sort, written by a Negro with unwavering faith in the inherent possibilities of his race, cannot be otherwise than wholesome and inspiring." It was in this volume that Du Bois uttered a famous phrase: "The problem of the Twentieth Century is the problem of the color line."

The Du Bois book fed a growing controversy by its pointed criticism of Booker Washington and his school of thought. "I sought to make a frank evaluation of Booker T. Washington," Du Bois said many years later. "As I read that statement now . . . I am satisfied with it. I see no word that I would change." Du Bois resented the "adjustment and submission" of Washington's philosophy. He bridled at the Tuskegee educator's downgrading of voting rights, his scorn for Negro colleges, his habit of blaming Negroes for their plight rather than laying the blame on whites. And he had little use for "the Tuskegee Machine." With many others, Du Bois believed that without Washington's approval funds would not flow to the Negro schools. Nor would white politicians venture to appoint Negroes to public office without a nod from Washington. He called Washington "the political referee in all federal appointments or action taken with reference to the Negro."

Du Bois had dreamed of publishing a "Negro journal" in 1901 that would reflect "a new race consciousness to the world." He conceived of the magazine as "a high-class journal" appealing to "intelligent Negroes." He realized this dream in 1905 when he launched the *Moon Illustrated Weekly* with his savings—$1,200. Du Bois served as editor-in-chief while remaining at his teaching duties in Atlanta. The *Moon*, Du Bois later said, was "a precursor of the *Crisis*," the house organ he later edited for the National Association for the Advancement of Colored People. The *Moon*, with its circulation ranging from 250 to 500, folded after a brief life. Other Negro journals of the day—*Alexander's Magazine*, the *Colored American Magazine* and the *Voice of the Negro* —shared its fate. When the *Moon* failed, Du Bois turned to a second magazine, the *Horizon*, editing it until 1910, when he assumed editing duties on the *Crisis*.

CHAPTER EIGHT

Protest and Affirmative Action— First Movements toward Black Unity

THE opening decades of the twentieth century saw a half-dozen national organizations form to promote black progress. Among these were the Negro Independent Movement, the National Association for the Advancement of Colored People, the Equal Rights League, the National Urban League and the National Negro Business League. While these organizations were developing, the National Association of Colored Women continued its program to further the cause of racial equality.

All these group efforts were sorely needed. In some states the anti-Negro forces proved so strong that black citizens fled from their homes in large numbers. When Negroes tried to vote, mobs drove them from the polls. Lynchings occurred, triggered by the slightest affront. Many families were reduced to virtual peonage as the hooded vigilantes ran rampant through the southern countryside, threatening and committing violence wherever they were resisted.

To make the situation more perplexing, many who spoke to and for the Negroes advised them to accept the turn of events philosophically.

Dr. Du Bois, on the other hand, held the position that Negroes could not be conciliatory and follow this advice when they were denied education; driven from their churches; barred from hotels, theaters and public places; refused decent jobs; forced to the bottom of the wage scale; compelled to pay the highest rent for the poorest homes; banned from buying property in decent neighborhoods; ridiculed in the press, on the political platform and on the stage; disfranchised; taxed without representation; denied the right to choose their friends or to be chosen by them; deprived by custom and law of protection for their women and robbed of justice in the courts.

Booker Washington called together a group in New York in 1904. The financier Andrew Carnegie paid the bill. This Carnegie Hall Conference set up a Committee of Twelve for the Advancement of the Interests of the Negro Race. The panel published several pamphlets on self-help and related topics. The conference itself adopted resolutions advising Negroes to remain in the South. It proposed that education should include trade schools and colleges, that Negroes should vote and be assured of protection while voting, and that they should sue when denied public accommodations.

THE NIAGARA MOVEMENT

It was during these stormy times that W. E. B. Du Bois issued a call from Atlanta for a 1905 summer conference. As envisioned by Du Bois, the meeting would achieve three goals. It would (1) oppose firmly the trend toward strangling honest criticism, manipulating public opinion, and amassing political power through graft and influence peddling; (2) organize the nation's most articulate Negroes as a pressure group which would insist on manhood rights, job opportunity and spiritual freedom; and (3) set up a journal to sway public opinion on the race issue.

The conference—a gathering of twenty-nine persons—met near Niagara Falls, Ontario, from June 11 to 13. It was to have met in Buffalo, but it changed sites when racial barriers prevented the delegates from using hotel accommodations in the New York port city. The conferees, all Negro professional men, became known as members of the Niagara Movement. At the outset Du Bois urged the session to confine its agenda to principles. One of the movement's first actions was to publish a statement Du Bois had written in 1904. Printed in scroll form, this *Credo* soon appeared on the walls of many Negro homes.

Some conferees expressed personal support for Booker Washington's philosophy of conciliation. J. Max Barber later reported in the *Voice of the Negro,* however, that Washington's name was mentioned only twice during the sessions. Recalling the Niagara Movement, James Weldon Johnson said that it divided Negroes into two camps— a breach which remained for many years. Gunnar Myrdal made the same point in *An American Dilemma.* In his opinion the movement revealed "two types of Negro strategy, one stressing accommodation and the other raising the Negro protest against recent reactionary development."

The Du Bois group drew up a "declaration of principles" which began by citing Negro progress from 1895 to 1905. The statement singled out for praise "the increase of intelligence, the buying of property, the checking of crime, the uplift in home life, the advance in literature and art, and the demonstration of constructive and executive ability in the conduct of great religious, economic and educational institutions."

The declaration also protested a wide range of inequities—obstacles to Negro voting, civil rights, job opportunities, schooling, jury participation, labor union membership and advancement in the armed services. It also decried the practice of importing Negroes to work only during emergencies. The conferees parted company with Booker Washington by noting the value of agitation against Jim Crow in all forms. But the movement did acknowledge the help of white friends in the quest for equality. The declaration ended by spelling out the responsibilities Negroes should assume as citizens in a democratic society.

"And while we are demanding, and ought to demand, and will continue to demand the rights enumerated above," the members stated, "God forbid that we should ever forget to urge corresponding duties upon our people. . . ." Among these duties, the Niagara Movement underscored "the duty to vote, . . . to respect the rights of others, . . . to work, . . . to obey the laws, . . . to be clean and orderly, . . . to send our children to school, . . . to respect ourselves, even as we respect others."

Du Bois acknowledged later that "the Niagara Movement raised a furor of the most disconcerting criticism." He was accused of envying Washington, whom he lauded as "a great leader." A leading New York journal, the *Outlook,* dismissed the movement as "a whim" and insisted that Dr. Washington and his followers were the Negro's true leaders.

The Niagara Movement's local branches increased membership but slightly—from the original 29 to 150 in the first year. This corroborated Du Bois' concept of the group as "the thoughtful, the dignified, and the very best class of Negroes." He was not trying to form a mass movement, but a cadre of the black elite.

While Du Bois did not regard himself as a leader, he pushed ahead with his Niagara Movement program. As he explained it, "Having put my hand to the plow, I had to go on." Thus, a second Niagara conference met at Harpers Ferry, West Virginia—the scene of John Brown's martyrdom. Du Bois intended the sessions to reconsecrate "ourselves, our honor, our property to the final emancipation of the race which John Brown died to make free." They met at Storer

College, with more than a hundred prominent Negroes in attendance. One conferee, Richard T. Greener, was looked upon as a member of the rival camp. John Hope, president of Atlanta University, served among the conference leaders. He sat as chairman of the committee on education. A New Haven attorney, George W. Crawford, chaired the civil-rights panel.

The Harpers Ferry conference urged full manhood suffrage and protested all discrimination. While the delegates denied a belief in violence, they paid tribute to John Brown and to the ideal for which he died.

The Niagara Movement grew steadily despite the frowns of Booker Washington, T. Thomas Fortune and their allies. Fortune tried to revive the National Afro-American Council, with Bishop Alexander Walters of the African Methodist Episcopal Zion Church as president. Dr. Washington broke with the interracial Constitution League, which New York industrialist John Milholland had founded in 1904, because of differences in strategy. Milholland favored reducing the House seats in Congress of those states which barred Negroes from voting. The Tuskegee leader's hostility to the plan prompted Milholland to join the Niagara group.

The Niagara Movement held its third conference in Boston's Faneuil Hall in 1907. Some wished to meet again at Storer College, but the college was not available because the school found its budget cut by the state of West Virginia after the 1906 meeting. Attendance dwindled at the Boston conference. The movement's treasury was nearly bankrupt. The delegates praised Senator Foraker and the Constitutional League for their part in the Brownsville affair protest. They criticized the Interstate Commerce Commission for upholding Jim Crow travel laws. Voters were urged to vote against Taft and other Republicans. The Niagara Movement endorsed the Democratic ticket. In that election, more Negroes voted against Taft than had voted against any previous Republican presidential candidate in history.

Du Bois' supporters held public meetings to aid the movement in New York, Cleveland, Minneapolis, Baltimore and Washington. When the Niagara Movement met for the fourth time at Oberlin, Ohio, in 1908, however, the old prob-

lems remained—sparse attendance and weak finances. The resolutions of the fourth conference attacked those who suppressed Negroes. They advised colored citizens to defend themselves against white mobs.

A fifth Niagara Movement conference gathered some fifty delegates and guests in Sea Isle City, New Jersey, in 1909. F. L. McGhee, head of the legal department, reported that he had failed to undertake the proposed legal work because funds were lacking. One resolution claimed that the group still furthered "spiritual unrest" and "sterner determination to be men at any cost." This was to be the last meeting of the Niagara Movement. The NAACP superseded the movement and was to surpass it both in service to the Negro and in significance to the nation.

The demise of the Niagara Movement occurred largely because of Du Bois' shortcomings as a leader. Colleagues described him as "aristocratic" and "an uncompromising advocate." Moreover, his decision to limit membership to middle class intellectuals doomed the movement almost from the start. "I was no natural leader of men," Du Bois admitted. He had been drawn from his scholarly work as an historian and social scientist at Atlanta University into a program of protest. "My career as a scientist," he recalled in later years, "was to be swallowed up in my role as master of propaganda." But the foundering Niagara Movement had won respect as well as biracial support by 1909.

MONROE TROTTER

The fiery militant William Monroe Trotter inherited much of his unbending spirit from his father, James Trotter, a Civil War veteran who had refused to accept the half-pay provided for Negro soldiers. The elder Trotter had also resigned from the Boston post office because of a promotion policy he considered discriminatory. When his son was born in 1872, James Trotter vowed to instill in him a dedication to equality.

Monroe Trotter graduated with honors from Harvard in 1895 to enter business as a real estate broker. Though he was deeply involved in the National Equal Rights League, his first love became the *Guardian,* a weekly newspaper he

W. E. B. DU BOIS

T. THOMAS FORTUNE

RICHARD T. GREENER

F. L. McGHEE

published jointly with George Washington Forbes, an Amherst College graduate of 1895. The *Guardian's* editorial fire was directed at what Trotter called "accommodation"—the approach embraced by Booker Washington.

Trotter and Forbes attended the Afro-American Council when it met in Louisville, Kentucky, in 1903. During Dr. Washington's address, they tried without avail to gain recognition from T. Thomas Fortune, the council's chairman. Later, in July of that year, Washington was again the main speaker at a meeting in the African Methodist Episcopal Zion Church in Boston. Ignoring chairman William Lewis' attempts to maintain order, Trotter and two associates raised questions. A melee followed. Trotter was arrested and served a month in jail for his part in what became known as "the Boston riot."

Working through others, Washington tried to divide Forbes and Trotter with the help of a rival newspaper, the *Colored Citizen*. But Trotter's imprisonment proved a major reason for Du Bois' decision to call together the Niagara Movement. Differences later arose between Du Bois and Trotter which led Trotter to form the National Independent Political League. The League developed branches in the Midwest and soon rivaled the National Association for the Advancement of Colored People in influence. Trotter had failed to join the infant NAACP in 1909 and had used the *Guardian* as a forum to attack it. He would not compromise his stand against racial discrimination. The flag over the *Guardian's* editorial page proclaimed Trotter's slogan: "Segregation for Colored Is the Real Permanent Degradation in the U.S.A.—Fight It."

THE NATIONAL ASSOCIATION FOR THE ADVANCEMENT OF COLORED PEOPLE

Rioting and lynching—the twin terrors of racism in the early 1900's—led to the founding of the NAACP. Rioting had spread to the North as well as the South. One such disorder broke out in the city of Abraham Lincoln's birth, Springfield, Illinois, in 1908. White mobs roamed the Springfield streets for two days in August, killing and wounding Negroes, wrecking homes and causing many to leave the city. White homes,

MARY WHITE OVINGTON

marked by white handkerchiefs, were not molested.

The nation's newspapers and magazines carried banner headlines over their news accounts of the racial turmoil. "The notoriety of Springfield's evil resorts has been widespread," the Chicago *Daily News* asserted. A section of Springfield adjoining the Negro ghetto was blamed for fomenting the riot.

Fearing that such rioting might flare up elsewhere, Mary White Ovington and William English Walling met to take preventive measures. Miss Ovington, a young white graduate of Radcliffe College, had worked in Brooklyn as a social worker. The New York *Evening Post* assigned her to cover the Niagara Movement's Harpers Ferry meeting in 1906. She returned to New York deeply moved by what she had heard. The young social worker moved into an apartment in a Negro section, where she planned to work with Negro people. She vowed that she would give all her strength and ability "to the problem of securing for the American Negro those rights and privileges into which every white American is born."

A leading publicist, William English Walling assessed the riots in an article for the *Independent* entitled "Race War in the North." He called for a strong citizens' group to work with blacks to achieve equality. Walling told of the Springfield riot and then observed: "Either the spirit of the abolitionists, of Lincoln and Lovejoy must be revived and we must come to treat the Negro on a plane of absolute political and social equality, or Vardaman and Tillman will soon have transferred the race war to the North."

After reading this article, Mary White Ovington began exchanging letters with its author. The correspondence led to a 1909 meeting with Walling and Dr. Henry Moskowitz. They agreed with Miss Ovington to issue a call for a national conference to form a new group. The grandson of William Lloyd Garrison, the *Evening Post*'s president Oswald Garrison Villard, was asked to draft a message urging "the believers in democracy to join a national conference for the discussion of present evils, the voicing of protests, and the renewal of the struggle for civil and political liberty."

Fifty-three persons of both races signed the Villard statement, and the conference opened on May 31. Five major demands surfaced during the conference: to ensure voting rights, to ban "white only" policies in public accommodations, to promote free labor relations, to urge a school program that would not educate youths as "servants and underlings" and to require equal justice under law. The gathering planned for a second meeting and adjourned with the comment that the association was "a new alliance between experienced social workers and reformers in touch on the one hand with scientific philanthropy and on the other with the struggling mass of laborers of all kinds, whose condition and need know no color lines."

Mary White Ovington described the early days of the NAACP in a book she wrote in 1914:

> We have had five conferences since 1909 but I doubt whether any have been so full of questioning surprise, amounting swiftly to enthusiasm, on the part of the white people in attendance. These men and women engaged in religious, social and educational work, for the first time met the Negro who demands, not a pittance, but his full rights in the commonwealth. The Association had twenty-four branches in 1913, but had expanded to fifty branches within another year.

The "Second Conference," which met in New York in 1910, set up a formal structure for the NAACP. It elected as president Moorfield Storey, a Boston attorney who had served as Senator Charles Sumner's secretary. Other officers chosen

JESSIE FAUSET

were Walling (chairman of the executive committee), John E. Milholland (treasurer), Villard (disbursing treasurer), Frances Blascoer (secretary), and Du Bois (director of publicity and research). Most of the all-Negro membership of the Niagara Movement merged with the biracial NAACP.

The first edition of the *Crisis* appeared in November 1910. The magazine took its name from James Russell Lowell's poem "The Present Crisis":

> Then it is the brave man chooses, while the coward stands aside
> Doubting in his spirit, till his Lord is crucified.

Du Bois edited the *Crisis,* assisted by Mary Dunlop Maclean and Jessie Fauset, the managing editors. The magazine was devoted to "the highest ideals of American democracy, and . . . reasonable but earnest and persistent attempts to gain these rights and realize these ideals." It aimed "to set forth those facts and arguments which show the danger of race prejudice, particularly as manifested today toward colored people."

In its opening editorial, the *Crisis* spoke out eloquently in behalf of racial equality. "Catholicity and tolerance, reason and forbearance can today make the world-old dream of human brotherhood approach realization," the editors asserted, "while bigotry and prejudice . . . and force can repeat the awful history of the contact of nations and groups in the past. We strive for this higher and broader vision of Peace and Good Will."

OSWALD GARRISON VILLARD   MOORFIELD STOREY

Representatives to the Fourth Annual Conference of the National Association for the Advancement of Colored People.

EUGENE KINCKLE JONES

GEORGE E. HAYNES

While the *Crisis'* first edition was limited to one thousand copies, within a year its circulation grew to two thousand readers and continued to rise. The magazine singled out achieving Negroes as examples to other blacks.

The *Crisis'* opinion-molding role was but one phase of NAACP activity. The association formed a legal committee, organized protests and, unlike the Niagara Movement, appealed for a massive membership across the nation.

THE NATIONAL URBAN LEAGUE

The influx of Negroes to northern cities during this period aroused a keen interest among urban social workers. Several groups already existed in 1905 to improve the living and working conditions of New York Negroes. One such unit, the Committee for Improving Industrial Conditions of Negroes in New York City, worked closely with Dr. George E. Haynes, a sociologist studying the Negro community. The National League for the Protection of Colored Women and a third group included many who were aiding Dr. Haynes.

Among the leaders were Hollingsworth Wood, William H. Baldwin, Frances Kellor, William J. Schieffelin, A. S. Frissel, Fred R. Moore and Dr. Eugene Roberts. These committees functioned separately, however, until 1911, when their merger formed the National League on Urban Conditions among Negroes, with Dr. Haynes as executive secretary. Later the name was changed to the National Urban League.

When Dr. Haynes resigned in 1911 to accept a professorship in sociology at Fisk University, Eugene Kinckle Jones became the League's field secretary. He had graduated from Cornell University and taught high school in Louisville, Kentucky. Dr. Haynes later returned to serve as educational secretary for the League. Professor E. R. A. Seligman of Columbia University was the League's first chairman. "With the consolidation of three bodies committed to constructive social work among Negroes," an early League survey predicted, "a new epoch opens in the effective consideration of this phase of the American city problem."

The Urban League's program, according to a 1912 report, relied on biracial accord to better city life for the Negro. It filled a number of needs. The League sought to organize skilled and unskilled workers into associations to promote their welfare and efficiency. It also opened a vocational bureau or labor exchange. This bureau worked with charitable and job-placement agencies to find employment for Negroes, guided them into training programs to suit their abilities, and tried to develop appreciation of Negro labor among employers.

Urban League branches opened in more than forty cities under Eugene Kinckle Jones' leadership. Other independent groups soon joined the Urban League as affiliates. The League assisted youths training for social work careers. The League's reports did a great deal to focus attention on the need for jobs and training for Negroes.

BLACK PRIDE AND POWER

The recognition and pride which black Americans now began to feel was reflected in several specific ways. In 1914 the NAACP instituted the Arthur B. Spingarn Medal, to be awarded each year to the Negro American with the highest achievement in any field of human endeavor. The first recipient of the Spingarn Medal, Professor Ernest Just of Howard University, earned the award in 1915, for his outstanding biological research. Major Charles Young was the Medal's second recipient, followed by Harry T. Burleigh, and, in 1918, by William S. Braithwaite.

A number of other events and organizations singled out Negro progress during this era. Howard University's board of trustees authorized the Moorland Foundation Library of Negro Life and History. Carter G. Woodson established the Association for the Study of Negro Life and History in 1915 in the District of Columbia. Dr. Woodson issued the first edition of the *Journal of Negro History* in 1916. The Julius Rosenwald Fund, established in 1917, expanded school construction in the South. It has been estimated that the fund assisted over five thousand schools.

THE JOURNAL

OF

NEGRO HISTORY

CARTER G. WOODSON
EDITOR

VOLUME I

1916

THE ASSOCIATION FOR THE STUDY OF NEGRO LIFE
AND HISTORY, Inc.
LANCASTER, PA., AND WASHINGTON, D. C.
1916

The first issue of the Journal of Negro History.

Black Americans now began to wield power in the press and in the political arena. Many leaned toward pressure group activities.

Negroes returned to politics in many states and began to develop some political sophistication. The old-line politicians, figuring conspicuously in Republican conventions, had been corralling the Negroes and delivering more than a million votes. In return, they placed Negroes in federal patronage jobs. But Negroes began to clamor for issues rather than offices. They wanted to know what the candidates had achieved—or would pledge themselves to achieve—for racial equality and justice.

Predictions about the Negro vote in the northern and border states grew uncertain. In response to this growing independence among Negro voters, a new sort of politician appeared. A number of Negroes gained seats in the state legislatures of Massachusetts, New York, Missouri, New Jersey, Pennsylvania, West Virginia, Ohio, Indiana and Illinois. Voters also chose Negroes as spokesmen in the city councils of New York, Baltimore and Chicago. The constant influx of Negro voters to the North soon produced a new idea: the possibility of electing Negroes from the city districts to Congress.

CARTER G. WOODSON

The Arthur B. Spingarn Medal.

ERNEST JUST   HARRY T. BURLEIGH

WHITE INTERPRETATION OF BOOKER T. WASHINGTON

Some whites continued to insist that Negro leaders themselves favored racial separation in civic and social areas. There may have been a bit of truth in this. Some Negroes pretended to accept white views in order to curry favor. Too often, moreover, when Negroes complained of the hardships of segregation, the system's white defenders would cite Booker Washington as an outstanding Negro whose career and teachings seemed to support the system.

Actually, the Tuskegee educator believed in the helpful contact of the races. In an article in the *New Republic* in 1915 (the year of his death), Washington forcefully characterized segregation as unjust because it invited unjust measures. He believed it incapable of producing good "because practically every thoughtful Negro resents its injustice and doubts its sincerity. . . . Any race adjustment based on injustice," he said, "finally defeats itself. The Civil War is the best illustration of what results where it is attempted to make wrong right or seem to be right." He warned against the effect of segregation on both races.

"It is inconsistent," he noted, "that the Negro is segregated from his white neighbor, but that white businessmen are not prevented from doing business in Negro neighborhoods. There has been no case of segregation of Negroes in the United States that has not widened the breach between the two races. Wherever a form of segregation exists, it will be found that it has been administered in such a way as to embitter the Negro and harm more or less the moral fiber of the white man. That the Negro does not express this constant sense of wrong is no proof that he does not feel it."

At its worst, therefore, segregation left the Negroes in a morbid state of mind, with feelings of despair mingled with those of revenge. They watched their former white friends retreating when racists taunted them as "nigger lovers." Some Negroes thought seriously of turning to their enemies at this point. Many felt that the attitudes of southern whites toward the Negro were caused by the attachment of most Negroes to the northern ideal, still hated by some southerners.

With a change in the political ties of the Negro, many politicians proclaimed that a new day would dawn for race relations in the South.

SOUTHERN CHANGE

Some of the most encouraging signs for the Negro appeared at this time in the South. It nearly escaped the nation's notice that the South, too, could produce white persons of vision—students of history and politics—well enough informed to know where prejudice was destined to lead the South. They realized that repression of the Negro would inevitably rebound on the white man. History had taught them that the oppressor loses his moral sense and vigor in the long run: that the entwining social, economic and political forces he weaves together eventually form the fabric of his self-destruction. These enlightened whites hoped to stop the course of prejudice and repression before it was too late. In short, primarily with the interests of the white man at heart, these leaders of "the new South" had come to appreciate the force of Booker Washington's wisdom: "I will let no man drag me down so low as to make me hate him."

Those who had refused to treat the Negro as a man had their troubles using him merely as an instrument. For the first time in southern history, the thoughtful whites believed that politicians like Ben Tillman, Hoke Smith, Cole Blease and James K. Vardaman had actually befuddled the country. For generations these white southern spokesmen had ridden into office on a worn-out slogan—"Down with the Negro"—appealing to the prejudices of their constituents and actually doing very little for the betterment of their lives.

A few members of the South's educated aristocracy launched the drive toward reform. Their weapon was publicity. After much academic discussion, the first proposals for racial cooperation took form in the Southern Sociological Congress. Mrs. Anne Russell Cole founded this group and Governor Ben W. Hooper of Tennessee formally inaugurated it in Nashville in 1912. All members of the group did not agree on the best way to promote racial harmony. There was much debate over what should or should not be done to aid the Negro. But the congress set up a committee on race problems which included whites and Negroes. Among the Negro panelists were Dr. H. B. Frissell and Dr. George W. Hubbard. The Southern Sociological Congress also initiated the formation of the University Commission on Race Questions. It consisted of educators of ten southern state universities. While the Sociological Congress permitted Negroes to join its membership and to address meetings, they were not granted a major role in managing the congress' affairs. Nor did the group select Negro speakers known to differ from Booker Washington in attitude.

This policy caused some Negroes to doubt the group's sincerity, even though the movement was never aimed specifically at solving the race problem. It was formed with a program "to study and improve social, civic and economic conditions in the South, to make the South better by promoting brotherhood and to enlist the entire South in a crusade of social health and righteousness." To fulfill these noble goals, the leaders of the movement knew that the cooperation of whites and Negroes was necessary. They took the Negro's problems seriously and made a concerted effort to cooperate in solving them, realizing that the welfare of the whole South was at stake.

The southern reformers were aware that they could not accomplish everything at once, but reasoned that they could still do much good by directing attention to a few urgent needs. Their movement attacked mob violence and backed schooling programs for Negroes. By appealing to college-trained men to sway public opinion on behalf of such reforms, they managed to sow two basic thoughts among them: that lynching Negroes also brutalized the whites, and that the mentally undeveloped worker was an economic handicap to the nation.

The reformers carefully avoided alienating their racist brethren, thus losing the confidence of militant blacks. Yet there resulted a somewhat greater respect for the Negro, a wider interest in industrial schooling and a renewed attack on the practice of lynching; but the movement failed to obtain dramatic results. This surprised almost no one, for the group lacked confidence, and it had tackled a monumental task with meager funds. It did, nevertheless, make inroads in intangible

ways: its message began to prick the conscience of the South.

THE KU KLUX KLAN AND RELATED GROUPS

The mild influence of the southern reform effort, already progressing along racial lines, was further diluted by the revival of hard-core racist organizations like the Ku Klux Klan. Other lunatic fringe groups sprang up to foment turmoil. These included the Women's League for White Supremacy, the White America Society and the National Association for the Preservation of the White Race.

The Ku Klux Klan was revived in the South in 1915. From a small nucleus, the band of racists grew to a boasted 100,000 allied against Negroes, Jews, Catholics, Orientals and foreign-born Americans. Its strength came in large part from the enthusiastic backing of many church-going citizens. Self-righteous Klansmen often took the law into their own hands.

The Klan was a notoriously racist organization, which sought to make the United States a pure Anglo-Saxon society free from "the encroachment and invasion of alien people of whatever clime or color." Two other super-nationalist groups, the Patrollers and the Bloody Shirts, shared the aims of the Klan.

The Clansman, a 1905 novel which denigrated the Negro's role during Reconstruction, was made into a very popular motion picture in 1915, entitled *The Birth of a Nation.* In the film the Ku Klux Klan was extolled, and the white South's bloody rise to power after Reconstruction was idealized. The film influenced a far wider audience than the NAACP or Urban League's publications could hope to reach, and was a setback to the cause for which the new organizations stood.

Significant attempts to counter these racist attitudes began with a biracial group known as the Amenia Conference, which met in 1916 for this purpose. It hoped to foster a more just and democratic society. The gathering convened on the estate of Joel E. Spingarn, president of Columbia University and an active member of the NAACP. Delegates to the Amenia Conference came from various sections of the

The Ku Klux Klan stages a ceremony to receive candidates for membership.

The Amenia Conference met in 1916 to discuss ways to counter growing racist attitudes.

ROBERT R. MOTON

nation and reflected a cross section of views. They resolved to bring about complete freedom for all citizens, but stressed that it would never come "without organization and without a practical working understanding among the leaders of the colored race." The conferees, among whom were some of the most important blacks in the country, were in accord on the importance of voting, the value of education and the necessity for a speedy end to lynching. With this much agreed upon, the gathering adjourned and did not meet again.

The Commission on Interracial Cooperation was formed in 1919. The gathering at Blue Ridge, North Carolina, included President Robert R. Moton of Tuskegee Institute and Methodist Bishop Robert E. Jones. The Commission strove to lessen racial tensions while holding to the tradition of "separate but equal." The southern reformers also trained their spotlight of publicity on the excesses of the Ku Klux Klan. As World War I became the issue of primary concern to the nation, however, the commission quietly drifted from the scene.

THE AMERICAN FEDERATION OF LABOR

In championing the causes of black social, political and civil rights, the new organizations did not forget the black laborer, whose cause had been lost in the one organization which had at first promised him the most help. The American Federation of Labor became in this period the most powerful organization of workers the country had yet known—a crucial factor in the lives of members and nonmembers alike.

It had been formed in 1881 by some discontented members of the Knights of Labor. Whereas the organizing principle of the Knights had been to unionize all workers in a given industry, the AFL sought to organize only skilled laborers, within their respective crafts. The AFL coaxed members away from the Knights by direct recruitment and five years after its inception could claim 150,000 members. Fifteen years later it had dwarfed the Knights, boasting well over a million members to the Knights' membership of 100,000.

Inspired by the Knights' old concept of the solidarity of all workers regardless of race, the Federation at first had had an ideal of integration. Samuel Gompers, the AFL's founder and long-time president, shaped the organization's early membership policy. An immigrant Jew, Gompers maintained that "the attempt to draw the line at nationalities would prove not only injurious but dangerous and in any event is absolutely wrong." In principle the Federation adhered to Gompers' credo: "The working people must unite and organize, irrespective of creed, color, sex, nationality or politics."

From the first Gompers had verbalized the conviction that unionization was a necessary factor in the black man's struggle for economic betterment. Gompers insisted, moreover, that organization with blacks was also in the ultimate best interests of white workers. The more power labor wielded the better, and the fewer unorganized black workers available for lower wages or for management's use as strikebreakers was also for the better.

Despite the AFL's rhetoric of racial unity, it became apparent rather early that this philosophy would severely hamper the Federation's expansion. A craft union seeks to keep wages high and jobs plentiful by limiting in so far as possible the numbers of workers possessing the skill. Industrial unions, on the other hand, like those which had formed the Knights' membership (and later those in the CIO) are primarily concerned with the force which large numbers of workers in all phases of the industrial operation can bring to bear on management. In a sense, therefore, it is "natural" that one type of union—the craft union—would seek to practice some form of discrimination. The black man, as usual, became the first target.

The swift decline of the AFL's racial idealism is dramatically illustrated by the fate of the International Association of Machinists. When this union applied for AFL affiliation in 1890, the Federation rejected it because of a clause in its constitution which explicitly excluded Negroes from membership. Five years later, however, the machinists were admitted through the simple expedient of removing the color bar from their constitution and transferring it to their ritual—thereby maintaining the old discriminatory policy.

Once the machinists had been admitted and the rule on racial non-exclusion broken, even unions with color bars in their constitutions were admitted. For the AFL executive council had only as much authority in these matters as its constituent unions were willing to concede. Craft autonomy had already become a sacred AFL principle, with the various unions growing more and more reluctant to censure each other's membership policies.

Writing in 1902, W. E. B. Du Bois gave a conservative estimate of the strength of organized labor as 1,200,000 workers. Of these, 41,000 were black. Du Bois named forty-three unions which lacked even one Negro member in any of their locals. Many of these expressly discriminated in ritual or constitution. Others claimed lack of black applicants or black workers in the trade. In the case of many of these unions, however, Negroes were barred from apprenticeships or other methods of learning the trade.

The racial attitude of the AFL officials became that of allowing its affiliates to discriminate, while "working from within" to eliminate

SAMUEL GOMPERS

prejudice. While retaining the goal of the solidarity of all workers, Gompers had yielded grudgingly to the temper of his times. The prevailing racial philosophy of the day, "separate but equal," became the rule for discriminating unions too. Until integrated solidarity could become a reality, the AFL encouraged blacks to form their own unions in those areas or trades in which they were not accepted by the white unionists. When Negroes were not admitted to a union belonging to the AFL, the AFL organized them into affiliated "federal" unions or separate local unions. Where central bodies refused to receive Negro delegates, the executive council of the AFL could charter separate central unions.

In theory the AFL executive council would serve as the "international" for the Negro locals or federals. In practice, however, the black affiliates were usually relegated to the guidance of the national union having jurisdiction in the field—exclusion from which was the only reason these separate unions existed in the first place! The assistance the blacks might expect in contract negotiation and grievance settlement was minimal.

Both the NAACP and the Urban League attacked the AFL's practices in their early years. Their growing membership and power enabled them to exert pressure and forced the AFL to come to terms with its own hypocrisy, but the Federation did little about it.

In 1910 the AFL made a formal statement denouncing racial bias and invited both Negroes and Orientals to join the Federation locals. This was repeated in 1913, but these statements still were not matched with non-discriminatory behavior within each member union. Negroes did begin to join the unions in increasing numbers, swelling the ranks of the exclusively black federals and locals.

Nine nationals—most of them tied to the railroad industry—still formally discriminated against Negroes in 1913. These unions wielded so much power in the AFL that they could continue in their prejudicial ways with impunity for many years to come.

The AFL conventions of 1916, 1917 and 1918 discussed the problems confronting Negro laborers. Having decided that the black work force should be organized, however, the AFL set up no machinery to put this policy into effect. A committee which spoke for many Negro unionists did send a letter to the AFL's annual meeting in 1918. It quoted President Gompers' remarks that Negro workers were welcome in the ranks, and made four basic demands: (1) the press should be given the AFL's published statement of welcome to Negroes; (2) the Federation should hire qualified Negro organizers; (3) cooperation among Negro unions should be encouraged; and (4) the AFL should take a more enlightened outlook on the issue of Negro workers. The letter was referred to a committee. A few days later, the panel reported that the AFL viewed with pleasure the new concern Negroes were showing for union organizing. It also offered a rather empty declaration that President Gompers should give special attention to organizing Negro workers. The AFL unanimously adopted this report—a token gesture at best.

Several more meaningful resolutions passed in 1919 when the AFL met in Atlantic City. One presented a non-discrimination policy. Another urged the AFL to study the application of a typical Negro union group for an international charter. The AFL also pressed those internationals with Negro workers to issue charters for Negro unions. Another resolution proposed that the AFL appoint Negro organizers, since white organizers often fared poorly in dealing with Negro workers.

When the National Urban League convened in Detroit in 1919, it adopted a resolution on organized labor. The League said:

> We believe that Negroes should begin to think more and more in terms of labor-group movements, so as ultimately to reap the benefit of thinking in unison. To this end we advise Negroes to organize with white men whenever conditions are favorable. When this is not possible, they should band together to bargain with employers and with organized labor alike. With America and the whole world in labor turmoil, we urge white and black men, capital and labor, to be fair and patient with each other while a just solution is being worked out.

Organized labor's most important action during this era occurred at the AFL's fortieth convention in 1920. The delegates, meeting in Montreal, heard Negro unionists present a strong case for equal treatment. Since the American Negro had fought in World War I for the freedom of all peoples, they declared, surely the Negro himself should not be denied this freedom. The American labor movement, the Negro spokesmen insisted, ought to recognize him and grant him full rights of participation. This set of resolutions was signed by railroad unionists from Arkansas, Ohio, Pennsylvania, Tennessee and Texas.

Discrimination was to continue, nevertheless. Three decades later labor historians Sterling Spero and Abram Harris counted nine AFL affiliates which had the color line in their constitutions and two more which discriminated in their rituals. By 1944 economist Herbert R. Northrup found only four AFL affiliates among the unions specifically excluding Negroes by constitution or ritual. In *Organized Labor and the Negro,* however, Northrup noted that six other AFL affiliates usually refused admittance to Negroes by "tacit consent," and nine others were cited which accepted black members only into Jim Crow auxiliaries.

Negro cotton pickers worked in the fields just as their parents had done under slavery.

BLACK LABOR MIGRATION

Ever since slavery had been outlawed, the white South had been seeking new methods to return the Negro to the fields. Labor contracts offered little income to Negroes; but with the dearth of job openings, they had few alternatives. Many signed on the white man's terms and became serfs on the soil of the South. The labor contracts varied with the state laws, but they had one aim in common: to exploit the Negro as a farm hand where he was vitally needed.

Those first adventurous black farmers who traveled North to find jobs wrote back urging others to join them. These new migrants failed to fill the demand, so industrialists sent labor agents to recruit wherever they could find workers. They found the Mississippi Valley a most favorable section from which to lure the needed manpower. All along the lower Mississippi region, floods had caused great suffering. Usually, Negroes in the delta area were hit hardest. Many welcomed a chance to go to a safer, more congenial, part of the country. The boll weevil, which had ravaged the Gulf States' cotton crop for years, was another factor serving to persuade

Negroes to leave the area. In short, when the North sounded its call for help, Negroes were ready to go—especially when they heard news of the higher wages.

Aware that the South was on the verge of losing the labor it had so long exploited, the section's employers viewed the Negro exodus as a calamity. They quickly took steps to slow and, if possible, to stop the movement. First they tried emotional appeals, telling Negroes of the horrors of the North—especially the hard winters. But when the Negroes received letters from friends who were easily braving these hardships, a new argument was needed. The southern states moved to handicap the labor recruiters by requiring them to have costly licenses. Then special ordinances barred the northern agents from inducing Negroes to leave. The recruiters were finally driven out of the South; yet this move also proved futile. The recruiters found the mails almost as reliable a means of reaching prospective migrants as was direct contact. The white employers next sought to halt the Negroes themselves. The migrants were driven from railway stations, taken from trains and jailed on false charges—anything to delay or to prevent their departure.

The exodus continued, however, and while the southern whites exhibited mixed feelings toward the Negro migration, the blacks themselves entertained dual attitudes. Advertisements for black laborers were carried in many northern Negro newspapers which were sent South. The *Pittsburgh Courier* and the *Chicago Defender* both joined the crusade to bring their black brothers to northern soil and away from the peonage of the South. Some Negroes in positions of leadership in the North foresaw the problems that would grow out of the massive migration and tried to exert their influence over southern Negroes to remain where they were. Their actions were of little consequence, however, for the promises of jobs and the fantasies of the golden opportunities in the North were too great for many of the downtrodden southern blacks to resist.

While many Negroes migrated with hopes of earning a decent living, they also were attracted by the prospect of educating their children, protecting their families from insult and enjoying the fruits of their labor. They recalled the days when Negroes wielded political and civic power. The dream of once again becoming masters of their own fates compelled many to leave the South.

URBAN RIOTS

Many Negroes who moved to the North encountered bitter rivalry with the radical white laboring element. Negroes touched off riots in Chester, Youngstown and East St. Louis merely by accepting the jobs offered them. Long harassed by white workers in East St. Louis, Negroes finally became the objects of a racial onslaught in July of 1917. The militia had been sent to maintain order, but members of the white mob took the law into their own hands and drove Negroes into their congested quarters.

Some 125 blacks fell in the massacre. In East St. Louis—just as in the South—the courts meted out a questionable form of justice. Though the whites were the aggressors in the riot, the courts inflicted heavier punishment on the Negroes. One black received a sentence of life imprisonment. He was later acquitted. Ten other

Negroes were given fourteen-year prison terms. By contrast, four white men received fourteen-to-fifteen-year sentences. Five others were placed behind bars for five years, and eleven were jailed for less than a year. The court fined eighteen whites and acquitted seventeen others. Ten thousand New York Negroes paraded to protest lynchings and mob violence in July of 1919.

These outbreaks served to verify the southern employers' warnings that the North would remove its welcome mat when Negroes arrived in masses. Some farsighted Negroes observed that the non-white prosperity in the factories was only temporary. They predicted that the war's end would reopen the old immigration pattern and force Negroes from their new jobs. Others shrugged off this argument, reasoning that the death toll of the population in Europe would prevent a large flow of immigrants to America. Despite racial conflicts, they urged Negroes to move North in ever greater numbers.

Without doubt, urban conditions influenced the health and mortality rate of the Negro masses. More often than not, they lived "across the tracks" or along the banks of rivers and streams on the outskirts of cities and towns. Many dwelled in alleys, along narrow streets and in unpaved slum areas where garbage collection and police and fire protection fell far below standard. Landlords seldom painted these dilapidated old buildings or patched their leaky roofs or repaired their thin sidings. Rooms remained damp and often overcrowded. Despite such wretched conditions, the landlords demanded exorbitant rent—thereby encouraging crowding.

A minority of Negroes escaped the worst slums. They managed to keep their homes repaired, and tried to upgrade sanitary conditions for themselves and their families. But the great mass of Negroes could not afford to relieve their housing plight. Nor could they enter other areas of the city where desirable housing existed— even if they could afford the price.

Those Negroes seeking to buy homes in desirable white residential sections were often warned not to move into them. If they did, they faced having their new homes stoned or bombed. Cases of this sort occurred frequently in Kansas City, Baltimore, Philadelphia and Chicago. In

The Chicago Defender

WORLD'S GREATEST WEEKLY

VOL. XI. NO. 1. SATURDAY CHICAGO, JANUARY 1, 1916 SATURDAY PRICE 5 CENTS

LATEST NEWS
If You See It In
The Defender It's So

HOME
EDITION

COLORED WOMEN LEAD MUSKOGEE RIOT

Oklahoma Mob Put to Rout by Negro Vigilants

THE NATIONAL BAPTIST DISPUTE

Morris Claims That Boyd Is Ducking Issue—Both Can't Be Right, and Some One Will Soon Be Forced to Back Down.

WHAT WILL PUBLIC DO?

By E. P. Johnson, Special Correspondent.

Nashville, Tenn., Dec. 31.—There has been a great deal of curiosity throughout the country since my last news as to just how the issue of defense that the Rev. R. H. Boyd would take in his fight to recapture the National Baptist Convention from the church of the National Publishing Board.

PRISONERS DISPLAY RARE GENIUS

Columbus, O., Dec. 31.—H. W. Crosh, serving life sentence from Fayette county for second degree murder, has made a stage with several mechanically operated figures...

GEORGE C. RAMSEY RECEIVES APPOINTMENT

By Wm. D. Edwards.

San Diego, Calif., Dec. 31.—Mr. George C. Ramsey of this city has been appointed sanitary inspector of the 19th exposition.

DETROIT FIGHTS "BIRTH OF A NATION."

Detroit, Mich., Dec. 31.—The second week of the fight against the passage of an ordinance to prohibit "The Birth of a Nation" and kindred plays has developed a strong and patriotic sentiment in favor of the ordinance.

NATIONAL EQUAL RIGHTS CONVENTION

Representative Citizens from All States of the Union Gather and Plans Means to Combat the Curse of Race Prejudice in the United States.

HON. BRYSON GUNNER PRESIDES

SCHOOL TEACHER STABBED TO DEATH

Body Found in Log Near Station, Clothes and Valuables Missing. Two Suspects Arrested.

Aberdeen, Miss., Dec. 31.—The body of Mrs. Effie R. Fowler was found Dec. 21 in a lot near the stable which is in the rear of her home.

GENEALOGY OF TUS-KEGEE'S NEW HEAD

Son of African Chief Who Was an American Slave Imported from Africa in the Age of Iron Fetters, Becomes Leader of 12,00,000 People.

THE CENTURY'S TRANSFORMATION.

From the Soul and Spirit of His Sires This Noble Man Offers Leadership from Economic Fetters to Industrial Independence—The Joseph of His Race.

By Wm. E. Eary.

Hampton, Va., Dec. 31.—About the year 1810 there was a fierce battle between two of the stronger tribes on the west coast of Africa.

DEMOCRATS ADVANCE EMPLOYES.

Several Notified of Change in Different Departments—Race Held Back for Three Years, Given Chance as Election Draws Near.

ST. LOUIS CITIZENS GIVE FREELY.

Nearly Seventy Thousand Dollars Pledged in Ten Days for the Y. M. C. A. Building.

St. Louis, Mo., Dec. 31.—This city set a pace when the race donated nearly seventy thousand dollars in the campaign fund for a Y. M. C. A. building.

MRS. HORN ATTEMPTS SUICIDE.

(Special to Chicago Defender.)

174 W. Penn street, shot and seriously wounded herself Monday night in a fit of despondency.

OLDEST MAN IN UNITED STATES DIES.

Washington, Dec. 31.—Isaac Cartwright is dead at his home in this city at the age of 119 years.

GOV. WILLIS SLATED FOR G. O. P. CONVENTION

Ohio Abounds with Great Possibilities in the National Convention, as Heretofore Her Claim Has Been First for Presidents.

A WISE CHOICE.

ATTORNEY SCRUTCHIN MAKES STRONG PLEA

Strange Case May Go to Supreme Court—All Concerned Are White Except Noted Lawyer—Eight Thousand Dollars at Stake.

Bemidji, Minn., Dec. 31.—A case that is probably the first of its kind in the state of Minnesota.

CHARLES SCRUTCHIN

Able lawyer of the race who make a strong plea in a strange case now before Minnesota courts.

AARON WILLIS LOSES HIS MIND.

Runs Amuck Until Shot by Neighbor to Keep Him from Killing Someone.

Aberdeen, Miss., Dec. 31.—Aaron Willis lost his mind last Sunday night.

DRIVES CITY AUTO TRUCK.

Aberdeen, Miss., Dec. 31.—This city boasts of being the only city in the south that has a race man driving an automobile fire truck.

YORUBA PEOPLE RE-SISTED HOUSE TAX IN WEST AFRICA

England Forced the "Natives" of Nigeria to Pay House and Land Taxes, But Germany Broke Up the Suggestions—Win at Mass Meeting.

(Special to Chicago Defender.)

THE DEFENDER SPIRIT DID THE WORK IN MUSKOGEE

Dear Mr. Abbott:

Muskogee, Okla., Dec. 27, 1915.

You no doubt by this time have heard the news of what we did in saving this city from a lynching bee.

NOTED LATIN TEACHER DEAD.

Prof. Gregory, Oldest Graduate of Howard University, Dies—Was Close Friend of Frederick Douglass.

Washington, D. C., Dec. 31.—Professor James Monroe Gregory, for twenty-five years professor of Latin at Howard University and the oldest graduate of that institution, died Dec. 21 at Baltimore, Md., at the residence of his daughter.

MOUND BAYOU IN BAD STRAIGHTS.

Present Financial Difficulties and Nearness of Crops Causes City to Send for Aid—Mayors Man to Help.

Mound Bayou, Miss., Dec. 31.—Word comes that this community is threatened with grave embarrassment due to the financial difficulties of Isaiah T. Montgomery.

PASSAVANT HOSPITAL FUND RECEIVES VALUABLE AID

Jacksonville, Ill., Dec. 31.—The widow of Mr. Frank Mallory and Laura Allen in behalf of the Passavant hospital fund deserve great praise.

MRS. ELLA DAY DIES.

Minneapolis, Minn., Dec. 31.—The recent death of Mrs. Ella Day was the passing away of one of the pioneers of the city and the end of a long and useful career.

ART CLUB HOLDS EXHIBITION

Montgomery, Ala., Dec. 31.—The Alpha Art Club, which is composed of twelve of the most promising women of the race, held an exhibit note Dec. 18 and it was well attended.

MINISTER GETS TRIP HOME

ALABAMA PENNY SAVINGS BANK CLO

Montgomery, Ala., Dec. 31.—The Penny Savings Bank, a pioneer institution of Birmingham, open its doors today.

MAX HALL GIVEN RESPONSIBLE POSITION

Oakland, Cal., Dec. 31.—Pacific has again paid high tribute to another race man in the selection of Max Hall.

CITY EMPLOYEE COMMITS SUICIDE

Race Men and Women Determined to Prevent Lynching of Two of Their Race, Fire on Mob and Send Them Scampering in All Directions.

McCRAY, EYEWITNESS, TELLS STORY

Leaders of Race at Muskogee, Okla., Give Notice That Illicit Relations Between White Men and Race Women Must Cease—Form Vigilant Committee to Force Justice

ROSCOE CONKLING BRUCE ON WITNESS STAND

Washington, D. C., Dec. 31.—The mandamus proceedings instituted by D. R. Bruce Evans against the Board of Education.

BENNING OWNS TURKEY RANCH

Nebraska Farmer Making Good Raising Poultry.

Lincoln, Neb., Dec. 31.—Phillip Benning of Cherry County, near here, is one of the best known farmers in the state.

CLOTHES WORN BY ABRAHAM LINCOLN GIVEN HIGH VALUE

EVANSTON WHITE CLERKS TOO IMPORTANT

MRS. BELL ENJOYS MINNESOTA CLIMATE

The Negro press sought to keep black readers informed on current racial topics.

fact, efforts to ward off Negro home buyers resulted in race riots in Tulsa, East St. Louis, Chester, Knoxville, Washington and Chicago during the migration of 1916-1918 and its aftermath. In these cases, white mobs acted in the absence of "the law." Some observers contended that Negro districts were burned for reasons other than reprisal. They thought the arsonists hoped to force the Negroes into even less liveable quarters to clear the path for business expansion. Some Negroes later lost their property as the result of special ordinances. The city statutes required rebuilding on such an expansive standard as to force people to sell their prized land and try to find their housing elsewhere.

The bigotry behind the housing and labor riots, and a number of less sensational incidents, caused the NAACP and Urban League to step up their programs. Financed by private philanthropy, the leaders of these organizations worked diligently toward the goals of equality and justice. Conferences, educational programs, publications and repeated assertions of pressure on government, politics, labor, business and education slowly chipped away at massive prejudice. The Urban League sought to improve the labor and housing conditions in the cities, while NAACP's major thrust was through the courts of law.

CHAPTER NINE

Defeat at Home, Victory Abroad— Negroes Fight in the Courts and on the Battlefields

THE American battle cry, "make the world safe for democracy," had a hollow ring for most Negroes as the nation entered World War I. To them "the American way of life" meant second-class citizenship. In the South, educated Negro professionals and businessmen were not allowed to remain in their towns if they did not "know their place." Many moved North. Those who remained in the South prospered— some even cast ballots—as long as they bowed to the region's customs. A reformist writer, Ray Stannard Baker, tells of a man opposed to Negro voting who, nonetheless, said of a Negro banker: "He's a sensible Negro. I went with him myself when he registered. He ought to vote." The right to vote thus became a privilege enjoyed by the select and compliant few. Other civil rights were "bestowed" on blacks in the same way.

THE SUPREME COURT ON THE BRINK OF SOCIAL JUSTICE

To fight discrimination, Negroes did have recourse to the law and the bench, but often with limited effectiveness. Many northern city dwellers were able to base their demands on state civil-rights acts. These laws protected the individual against discrimination in the use of theaters, hotels, railroads, steamboats and the like. Southern Negroes, denied those basic rights guaranteed by the United States Constitution, brought suits to the courts with less success. Although the litigation often ended in awarding nominal damages to the individual who had suffered the discrimination, basic alterations of the laws to end such discrimination in the future were few.

(18,721.)

SUPREME COURT OF THE UNITED STATES.

OCTOBER TERM, 1902.

No. 493.

JACKSON W. GILES, APPELLANT,

vs.

E. JEFF HARRIS, WILLIAM A. GUNTER, JR., AND
CHARLES B. TEASLEY, BOARD OF REGISTRARS OF
MONTGOMERY COUNTY, ALABAMA.

APPEAL FROM THE CIRCUIT COURT OF THE UNITED STATES FOR
THE MIDDLE DISTRICT OF ALABAMA.

INDEX.

A famous case on voting rights, *Giles* v. *Harris,* reached the Supreme Court on appeal in 1903. In 1901 Alabama had adopted a clause in its constitution framed to restrict the franchise and aimed chiefly at Negroes. The privilege of voting in Alabama was declared restricted to persons with either an education and regular employment or a war record (his own or an ancestor's), property worth $300 and an understanding of the duties of citizenship. Moreover, the new registration procedures were very complicated and difficult to supervise.

William Giles had been a registered voter for twenty years when the constitution was changed. He sued the state of Alabama on his own behalf and that of five million other disfranchised Negroes. When the case reached the Supreme Court on appeal from a federal circuit court, Justice Oliver Wendell Holmes could not find a basis for judicial relief. In a series of elaborate phrases and legal sophistry unusual for the high court, Holmes said virtually nothing about the real issue—the state constitution's violation of the principles embodied in the Fifteenth Amendment, which had given blacks the vote in 1870. In 1904 a second Giles suit reached the Supreme Court. Holmes' original decision had included a suggestion that Giles might win an award for damages by suing the offending voting registrars —for while the system itself was taken to be legal, the possibility was conceded that it might have functioned improperly in Giles' case. The Alabama courts threw out the suit; the Supreme Court did the same.

The Giles case represented a continuation of the weak civil-rights concern of the high court marked most clearly by the earlier Plessy case, and progress in the next few decades was to continue to be very uneven. Two cases which reached the Supreme Court, both entitled *Bailey* v. *Alabama* and both involving the same plaintiff, were to break new ground. The cases challenged the so-called "contract system" of labor and involved an illiterate Alabama Negro, Lonzo Bailey, who had "contracted" to work on a farm for twelve months at a pay rate of $12 per month. He accepted an advance of $15, then worked for nearly a month before quitting. When he left his job, Bailey refused to return the advance to his employer. Under Alabama law, a worker who entered a contract with the intent of defrauding his employer was criminally liable. Bailey claimed he had had no such intention, but he had no way to prove his innocence. When his employer brought him to court, he was not allowed to testify in his own defense (a custom which affected most southern Negroes). The court found Bailey guilty and sentenced him to 136 days at hard labor.

When the case reached the Supreme Court in 1908 Justice Holmes again delivered the majority opinion, implicitly upholding the legality of the contract system by stating that the matter really did not come under the high court's jurisdiction. Justice Harlan dissented, apparently fully aware that the state was depriving Bailey of his rights. Harlan was of the opinion that the Supreme Court should speak out on the contract system and settle the matter.

(21,790.)

SUPREME COURT OF THE UNITED STATES.

OCTOBER TERM, 1909.

No. 564.

ALONZO BAILEY, PLAINTIFF IN ERROR,

vs.

THE STATE OF ALABAMA.

IN ERROR TO THE SUPREME COURT OF THE STATE OF ALABAMA.

Three years later the suit reached the Supreme Court again, through the efforts of Booker T. Washington and others who financed the costly litigation. Some new justices were on the bench, and this time the court declared the Alabama law, which had denied Bailey the right to attest to his own innocence, to be unconstitutional. In delivering the majority opinion, Justice Charles Evans Hughes finally reached the core of the issue. Slavery had been outlawed, and yet the very "essence of peonage is compulsory service in payment of a debt." While the very consistent Mr. Justice Holmes dissented, the majority of the court finally declared in 1911 that since the states were forbidden to impose a system of slavery directly, it was also illegal to contrive to do it indirectly.

Two years after the second Bailey decision the court's position regressed in *Butts* v. *Merchants' and Miners' Transportation Company*. The Civil Rights Act of 1875 forbidding discrimination in public places and conveyances against "persons within the jurisdiction of the United States" had been very severely weakened long before. What was left of the act fell before the Supreme Court in 1913 when Mrs. Emma Butts, a Negro woman, sued a steamship company for denying her equal accommodations with white passengers. Because most of the 1875 Civil Rights Act had already been declared unconstitutional, the court ruled the entire statute unconstitutional. Thus the court would not prohibit segregation in travel on the high seas.

The Supreme Court rendered another key decision involving civil rights to public transportation in 1914. The case of *McCabe* v. *Atchison,*

CHARLES EVANS HUGHES

Topeka & Santa Fe Railroad concerned interstate commerce and involved four Oklahoma Negroes who protested a state law which deprived them of the rights guaranteed interstate passengers using common carriers. The NAACP considered involvement in this particular issue, but withdrew its support upon a close examination of the merits of the case. The Supreme Court disagreed with one of the lower court's conclusions that separate sleeping, dining and chair cars did not violate the Fourteenth Amendment, since they were luxury conveniences and the demand for them by Negroes was limited. Justice Hughes stated that the constitutional rights to equal protection of the laws "does not depend upon the number of persons who may be discriminated against." But the court upheld the lower court's decree favoring the railway. It concluded that the Negro plaintiffs' case was too vague, and technically groundless. Once again, the Negro had to start from the beginning and bring new suits.

THE NAACP AND CIVIL RIGHTS

From the beginning of the NAACP in 1909, its legal redress committee had assumed an active role in the courts. NAACP attorneys won a very auspicious Supreme Court decision in 1915. A prominent New York attorney, Arthur B. Spingarn, led the biracial staff of lawyers. The committee first tackled the discriminatory voting laws and practices in effect throughout the South. It directed its attack on the Oklahoma grandfather clause, which restricted Negro voters to a handful of descendants of antebellum free blacks. The Supreme Court agreed with the NAACP challenge in 1915 by ruling the grandfather clause unconstitutional. In *Guinn* v. *United States* it found that, while states could set up literacy standards, this clause violated the Fifteenth Amendment. The legal victory over the Oklahoma statute—achieved in the NAACP's first test case taken before the Supreme Court— paved the way for other assaults on Jim Crow laws.

Another legal battle financed by the NAACP and private donations was the 1917 case of *Buchanan* v. *Warley*. It dealt with city ordinances seeking to segregate Negroes in residential districts. Such measures, it had been argued, preserve the purity of the races, maintain the public peace and prevent the depreciation of property. The court conceded the seriousness of the situation. It admitted the right of a state to make race distinction in public accommodations on a "separate but equal" basis, but would not sanction complete denial of access to Negroes. It held that a law to prevent sale of property to a person because of his race oversteps the state's police power. It directly violates the fundamental rule embodied in the Fourteenth Amendment preventing state interference with property rights except by due process of law.

Negro frustration over the court battles was heightened by the fact that many Negroes were making valuable and selfless contributions to the same society and government that denied them their basic constitutional rights.

MATTHEW HENSON—FIRST MAN AT THE NORTH POLE

Matthew Alexander Henson discovered the North Pole with Admiral Robert Edwin Peary on April 6, 1909. Henson was born in Charles County, Maryland, in 1866. Little is known of Henson's boyhood, except that he lived and worked on a farm. He ran away from home as a youth and hiked to Washington, D.C., where he found a job as a porter in Steinmetz's hat store. One day Lieutenant Robert Peary visited the store to buy a hat. He studied Henson for a while, noting the careful way he arranged the hats on the shelves after dusting each one. Peary was looking for a valet to accompany him on an expedition into Nicaragua. Henson accepted Peary's offer of employment and was soon accompanying Peary on a mission in the Nicaraguan jungles.

When Peary and Henson returned to the United States, it was decided that the explorer would attempt to reach the North Pole. Others had attempted this feat, but the severe weather and frozen state of the Arctic region always doomed their missions. Men from several nations had died in quest of the North Pole. Peary asked Henson to make the trip with him because he saw in him the qualities needed for the ordeal. They made seven expeditions. Each one brought severe hardship, but the two persevered. Henson developed into a good dog-team driver and a skillful hunter. Twice he saved Peary's life. He thus advanced from a personal companion to a most essential aide.

As Peary and Henson moved northward by dog sleds, and the time for the polar dash neared, the admiral chose four Eskimos to join them. When the team neared the Pole, Peary became disabled and could not continue. He stopped and sent Henson on to make observations and compute the remaining distance. Henson went forward to gather the needed scientific data. Some forty-five minutes later, the four Eskimos appeared at the Pole with Peary on the sled. Peary checked Henson's figures and found them correct. Together—black man, white man and four Eskimos—they raised the Stars and Stripes, placing it "on top of the world." Peary as leader of the expedition received the credit for this marvelous feat. But Henson, it must be remembered, shared his pains and his agony and stood with him at the Pole—actually the first man to reach it.

The state of Maryland has honored Henson with a bronze memorial in its State House at Annapolis, unveiled and dedicated in 1961.

NEGRO BRAVERY IN THE MEXICAN WAR

The Mexican government underwent a series of coups during the early 1900's. Pancho Villa, a Mexican revolutionary with a loyal following, took over the government. When President Carranza invited American engineers to operate abandoned mines in northern Mexico in 1916, Villa's band shot and killed the Americans at Santa Ysabel. Villa also raided Texan and New Mexican towns. When his band killed seventeen Americans in Columbus, New Mexico, President Wilson called out 150,000 militiamen and placed them along the Mexican border. General John J. Pershing was ordered to pursue Villa into Mexico with 15,000 men.

"Black Jack" Pershing relied heavily on the Negro troops under his command. At the outset of their expedition, the Negro soldiers formed

MATTHEW HENSON

part of a flying column commanded by a Colonel Dodd. They rode for days over hills and valleys, ate in their saddles and slept little while they searched for Villa and his band. It was reported that General Funston chose the 10th Cavalry for this campaign because of his confidence in their physical endurance. The Negro units rode into ambushes and fought with courage. When troops of Companies "C" and "K" were attacked at Carrizal on June 21, 1916, they showed bravery and endurance. Though far outnumbered, they dismounted and charged the Mexicans, routed them and killed their commander. Some seventeen of these troops died in the fray, and twenty-three were taken prisoner by the Mexicans.

One memorable moment during the battle of Carrizal revealed the valor of Peter Bigstaff, a Negro soldier. He fought at the side of his white commander, Lieutenant Adair. When the officer's revolver would not fire, Bigstaff gave him another and they fought on. Finally Adair fell, mortally wounded. He urged his Negro comrade to leave the scene of battle to save his life. Bigstaff refused to leave. He lifted the lieutenant's body from the water where it lay and placed it against a tree. Then he returned to the battle.

The release of American troops taken prisoner and the signing of an agreement led to the army's withdrawal from Mexican soil. The experience gained by the Negro soldiers who had fought in Mexico would stand them in good stead as the United States moved into World War I.

WORLD WAR I BRINGS PROSPERITY

The world plunged rather unexpectedly into a universal struggle in 1914. Archduke Francis Ferdinand, heir-presumptive to the Austro-Hungarian throne, was assassinated on June 28 in Sarajevo, then the capital of Bosnia. Blaming the Serbs for this crime, the Austrian government sent Serbia an ultimatum demanding that the offenders be brought to trial by a tribunal in which Austria should be represented. Serbia refused to yield to this and other Austrian demands and won Russian support. Germany upheld Austria, fearing that if such an act passed unpunished it would threaten the crowned heads of all Europe. Germany contended that the Russian army's mobilization was really a declaration of war against her. She declared war on Russia on August 1 and on France two days later. In the meantime, France declared war on Germany. England resented German violation of Belgian neutrality. Accordingly, the British Empire entered the war against Germany and Austria, the Central Powers. When Germany showed such disregard of her treaty obligations as to invade neutral Belgium, moreover, Kaiser Wilhelm lost the sympathy of other European and American nations, most of whom eventually joined the Allies in the fight to curb the power of Germany.

While in sympathy with the struggle against autocracy, the United States did not regard the sinking of its neutral ships and interference with its commerce sufficient cause for entering the war. America had begun an unprecedented period of business prosperity, supplying wartime goods for the belligerent countries. Many struggling industries suddenly received an unusual impetus. New enterprises sprang up rapidly. Persons used to eking out a meager living multiplied their wealth almost overnight by timely investments.

The nation's prosperity brought on a new day for the laboring man, and these good times also aided the Negro. The large influx of immigrant labor which reached American shores each year was promptly blocked by the war. As a result, the domestic supply of workers soon proved too scarce to meet demand. The northern and western industrial centers raised wages to attract more laborers. The manpower needs of the munitions makers and other war production industries were so great that the white labor market would not suffice. Departing from time-honored custom in the North, the needy employers began to bid for Negro workers in the South. When skilled Negroes sought jobs, they found them. Even unskilled Negro workmen were hired by the hard-pressed industries.

Eventually, however, the pressures of the war began to be felt more than the prosperity, and the United States prepared for its own entry into the conflict.

THE NEGRO ENTERS WORLD WAR I

When Congress declared that a state of war existed with Germany on April 6, 1917, a new epoch opened in the history of the American Negro. Though most citizens thought that the German war machine should be destroyed, few were anxious to be transported to the bloody battlefront of Europe. Men had to be converted to the war effort. Some German sympathizers approached Negroes in hopes of persuading them against the war effort. A few Negroes voiced pro-German leanings. Many more insisted that before Negroes joined the fight in behalf of the oppressed of Europe, they should enjoy a few of the privileges of democracy at home.

Those who expected the Negro to prove disloyal to the United States, however, had misjudged him. Many American Negroes loved their

Recruits such as these from Illinois turned out in large numbers to serve their country.

native soil and would have died readily in its defense. They had clung to the hope that white citizens would one day embrace the ideals of democracy for all men.

Some whites urged the government not to recruit Negroes. These same spokesmen had been ready to brand Negroes with suspicion and to prosecute them for disloyalty. Looking to the future, moreover, these whites thought it unwise to train Negroes in the arts of war. Men who have waded through blood to victory, they reasoned, would be less easily intimidated. And they would be more militant in dealing with the insults and outrages legalized and practiced in backward districts. These arguments failed to sway the War Department, however. Blacks, indeed, donned their "doughboy" uniforms in slightly higher ratios than did their white countrymen. For they comprised approximately 9.4 per cent of the population during the war and approximately 9.6 per cent of the total number of registrants under the Selective Service Act throughout the duration of the war. A higher percentage of Negro-to-white registrants were actually accepted for service: about 36 per cent of the Negroes and 25 per cent of white registrants were taken. According to Ulysses Lee, historian of Negro troop employment in the Second World War, more than 400,000 black Americans served in World War I. Among them were thirteen hundred commissioned officers, nine field clerks and fifteen army nurses.

Neither France nor Great Britain hesitated to use black troops in Europe. A force of 208,000 Senegalese helped to repel the Germans on the Ourcq and the Marne. Another 30,000 Congolese and about 20,000 Negroes from the British West Indies also fought at the Allied front.

When the United States finally decided to induct Negroes for the American Expeditionary Forces (AEF), some federal officials sought to restrict their role. Many Negroes had to register at separate induction centers to avoid being mixed with white troops. At first the War Department failed to provide for training Negro officers. Some southern congressmen urged that Negroes be confined to stevedore regiments, where they would labor under white officers. Negro leaders vehemently protested against any such arrangement. They charged the War Department with conscripting Negroes for labor alone. Although the secretary of war assured them that nothing of the sort was planned, most Negro draftees were sent to service supply regiments. No less than three-fourths of the 200,000 Negroes sent to France were reduced to army laborers. Neither the marine corps nor the coast guard accepted Negroes as enlistees. About ten thousand Negroes enlisted in the navy, and most of these served as messmen.

While there were several excellent and ultimately well-honored black combat units in the army, most American Negro troops found themselves engaged in the service supply divisions abroad. Negro units encamped at the English and French ports and at depots like Givres. Millions of dollars worth of American goods were handled by twenty-five thousand men—passing through vast warehouse corridors to begin a 140-mile trip over interior railroad lines to the front. Negroes unloaded the transports, prepared the trains to carry supplies to the interior and built depots for storing them. When American forces found hills and forests in their path, the labor battalions built roads from the port of entry to the front. They also buried the dead, salvaged war materiel and detonated explosives scattered over France by the enemy.

NEGRO OFFICERS

Blacks were told diplomatically that they would be drafted to fight in the ranks as other soldiers. But at first the War Department was not sure that the army could use nonwhites as officers. The students and faculty of Howard University launched a nationwide campaign to force a new policy. The Central Committee of Negro College Men demanded a training camp in which well-educated Negroes could qualify as officers. All Negro colleges of consequence as well as many citizens of both races promoted this plan, with the result that the War Department was obliged to restudy the question. After some indecision, the Wilson administration established a segregated camp to train Negro officers in June of 1917. The training site was Fort Des Moines, Iowa.

Many wondered how the Fort Des Moines experiment would work out. They also wondered whether the army would actually commission a large number of Negro officers. Both questions were answered by October 15, 1917. On that date, 639 of the 1,200 officer candidates received commissions. It was the largest single group of Negroes ever to win the rank of second lieutenant. It was believed that the Wilson administration granted Negro demands for officers in order to gain their support for the war. But the army hardly welcomed the move. Its handling of the case of one high-ranking Negro officer revealed its leanings.

Colonel Charles Young, a Negro graduate of West Point, became the highest ranking Negro officer of the war. He was confident and persistent in his efforts toward excellence and toward commanding the respect of his men. When white troops once refused to salute him as an army officer, Young stripped off his coat and made them salute the buttons. He later served as a professor of military science and tactics at Wilberforce University.

At the outbreak of the Spanish-American War, Young had been assigned to the 9th Ohio Regiment and had participated in the Cuban action. After the war he had served overseas as a military attaché, then was assigned to the 10th Cavalry, commanding a squadron in Mexico in 1915. Early in World War I, Colonel Young was retired with a physical disability, but vigorously protested his retirement. To prove his stamina he made a dramatic ride by horseback from his Ohio home to Washington, D.C., but to no avail. The army would not assign him to active duty.

Later, however, and before the war ended, he was recalled into the army and trained recruits

During World War I, Negro recruits were sent to segregated training camps such as Camp Gordon, Georgia.

Segregation was the rule—even in the Red Cross waiting room.

in Illinois. After the war he was transferred to Liberia to help organize that country's army. On vacation in Lagos, Nigeria, he contracted a severe fever from which he never recovered. He died there in 1922 and was buried with full honors in Arlington National Cemetery.

Negro officers often suffered discrimination, especially those men in the 92nd Division, the unit in which most of the Negroes trained at Fort Des Moines served. Many regarded the division's commanding general, Charles C. Ballou, as unfit. Surrounded by biased white officers, Ballou shaped his policy accordingly. In a famous incident at Camp Funston, Kansas, General Ballou issued an order insisting that the men of his division not raise the "colored question" and stir up racial antagonism when a black sergeant was not admitted to a theater. While Ballou had the theater owner prosecuted, he also ordered his men not to go where they were not welcome. What caused real bitterness among Negroes, however, was the General's feeling that the success of the division depended on the good will of the white public.

Wherever Negro officers were stationed, moreover, a systematic effort was made to get rid of them. Their superiors brought them before efficiency boards as soon as possible in the hope of speeding their retirement or assignment to labor battalions. The same thing happened in all-Negro regiments. Such was the case in the New York 15th Infantry where the white commander engineered the transfer of all Negro officers after retiring a few for inefficiency. Many senior officers openly stated that they preferred that white officers be sent to their regiments.

COMPLAINTS AGAINST BLACK OFFICERS

To rid their staffs of black officers, many commanders filed grave complaints against them. They often charged the Negroes with cowardice under fire. This was the lot of four officers in the 368th Regiment who were later lauded for their bravery. They received orders at the French front to advance and then to withdraw. They obeyed the orders. Their troops were actually unprepared to attack, lacking maps, hand grenades, adequate ammunition and artillery support. The army's

high command had no intention of sending these troops "over the top," orders from headquarters later revealed. In the first phase of this offensive, the Negro troops were reserved as combat liaison units between the United States 77th Division and the French Chasseurs à Pieds. These ill-equipped troops were sent into battle against orders, though, as part of the zero-hour assault. The white officer in charge of leading the attack was nowhere to be found during the engagement. Nor was the battalion commander, Major Max A. Elser, near enough to the front to be reached. As a result, two companies of the 2nd Battalion became badly disorganized. After he charged the unit's four Negro officers with inefficiency, Major Elser was promoted to lieutenant colonel. A later probe ordered by Secretary of War Newton D. Baker, however, showed that Elser had gone to the rear as soon as the fire had become intense. This inquiry also cleared the Negro officers of all blame. Secretary Baker took the occasion to praise these and other Negro soldiers for their valor at the front.

Another white officer, Colonel Allan J. Greer, risked a court-martial in hopes of ridding the army of Negro officers. He wrote a letter to Senator Kenneth D. McKellar of Tennessee pointing out weaknesses he had observed in Negro officers. "Now that a reorganization of the army is in prospect," he told Senator McKellar, "I think I ought to bring a matter to your attention that is of vital importance, not only from a military point of view, but from that which all southerners have. I refer to the question of Negro officers and Negro troops."

While some high-ranking white officers like Colonel Greer tried to weed out Negro officers on grounds of inefficiency, the French had nothing but praise for the Negroes with whom they were brigaded. French officers often interceded to save a Negro officer from humiliation and dishonorable discharge. It was obvious to men like the French General Goybet that the Negro's only shortcoming as a soldier was his low morale— a condition caused by white racial bias.

The charges of general inefficiency among Negro troops proved baseless. The 370th Regiment of the 8th Illinois Division, a unit led by Negroes, helped to shatter this myth entirely.

Major Max Elser poses with the men under his command. They were praised for their valor at the front.

Its heroes won twenty-one American Distinguished Service Crosses, sixty-eight French Croix de Guerre and one Distinguished Service Medal. Another Negro regiment, the 369th, was under fire longer than any other United States unit. The entire regiment was honored with the Croix de Guerre, and 171 officers and enlisted men were also awarded the Legion of Honor Medal.

THE STATUS OF BLACK SOLDIERS IN FRANCE

While fighting in France to "make the world safe for democracy," Negro soldiers were subject to the social code of their white fellow soldiers. Emmett J. Scott, a Negro who served as a special assistant to the secretary of war, documents many examples of discrimination and prejudice toward black troops serving overseas. Negro troops were ordered to sail on the battleship *Virginia*. After they had gone aboard, however, the officer in charge removed them on grounds that no colored troops had ever traveled on board a United States battleship. Where it might have been necessary for officers of both races to eat and sleep in the same barracks, special arrangements were made. White officers were assigned to their own quarters, Negro officers to theirs. In preparing for a reception for General Pershing at one of the front-line camps, General Logan ordered all troops except Negroes to be ready for an arms inspection. Negro troops not at work were to remain in their quarters or tents.

The white commanders made every effort to keep Negro soldiers away from the French people. General James B. Erwin sought to reduce the Negro soldiers to the status of undesirables by issuing an order that Negroes should not associate with French women. The order was not obeyed, but the general tried to enforce it. Negro officers in school at Vannes accepted invitations to attend French-American charity dances. These dances charged an admission fee. Upon hearing of the dances, one of the commanders prohibited Negro attendance. He decreed that no officer of the 167th Brigade should be permitted to attend a dance when a fee was charged. White officers at the same school, however, were allowed to attend.

According to Scott, American army headquarters sought to extend a racial barrier throughout France in a document issued August 7, 1918. General Pershing's headquarters passed a memorandum entitled "Secret Information concerning Black Troops" to a French mission. It proclaimed that French officers in command of black Americans should have an understanding of the racial status assigned Negroes in the United States. The document branded Negroes a degenerate menace, tolerable only through the maintenance of an impassable gulf between the two races. The French were cautioned not to treat Negroes with familiarity or indulgence, as this would give affront to white Americans. The United States, the memo went on, feared that comradeship with French soldiers might stir the Negroes with undesirable aspirations on their return to the States. Only business and service associations between the races were possible, it said. The black, the directive added, was noted for his want of intelligence, lack of discretion and lack of civic and professional conscience.

The French army was then advised to prevent intimacy between French officers and black officers: to discourage its officers from eating with blacks, shaking their hands or seeking to talk or meet with them outside of the requirements of military service. The memo also asked the French not to commend the black American troops too highly in the presence of white Americans. Although it was all right to single out the good qualities and service of black Americans, it suggested, this should be done in moderate terms strictly in keeping with the "truth." The French did not accept the American view, but insisted on *"liberté, égalité, fraternité."* Whether in Champagne, the Argonne Forest or at Metz,

the Negro soldier distinguished himself. A score of Negroes, like Needham Roberts and Henry Johnson of the New York 15th Division, repelled a German raid in May of 1918, against almost overwhelming odds. These soldiers returned to their homes as heroes, decorated by France with the Croix de Guerre for their bravery in action.

The strain on race relations, however, continued. Finally, Secretary of War Newton D. Baker, in conjunction with President Wilson, asked President Robert R. Moton of Tuskegee to go abroad and make an investigation into the problems reported there. One commanding officer had complained of the high incidence of crime among his black troops. Upon checking the facts, however, Moton learned that out of a total force of over twelve thousand men only six had committed serious offenses. While in France, the Tuskegee president also spoke to the men, counseling them and reassuring them of the victory that would be theirs when they returned home to the new democracy they were fighting to create and to maintain.

NEEDHAM ROBERTS

Henry Johnson enjoys a hero's welcome upon his return from France, where he had received the Croix de Guerre for bravery.

AFTER THE WAR

"The problem of the twentieth century," W. E. B. Du Bois had prophetically written as early as 1903, "is the problem of the color-line, the relation of the darker to the lighter races of men in Asia and Africa, in America and the islands of the sea." This prediction in *The Souls of Black Folk* has particular application to the mood and temper of the period following World War I.

The war in Europe had been a broadening if brutal experience for black and white soldiers alike. Negroes, however, returned from France and England with new cynicism. They had risked their lives in "the war to end all wars"; yet the old order of prejudice and exclusion remained at home. Despite the loyalty shown by Negro soldiers, they were treated with contempt on returning to the South. The army uniform on a Negro created in the racist the same reaction as a red cape waved in the face of a bull. Negro soldiers clamoring for equality and justice were beaten, shot down, lynched—in general, terrorized. They had violated no law; yet the mobs reasoned that lynching a few Negroes would serve as an example to the rest. The violence would remind them of "their place."

The postwar hysteria finally reached the nation's capital itself. A number of white enlisted men had been antagonized by reports of Negro assaults on white women. Upon hearing a rumor that a marine's wife had been molested, they proceeded, on July 19, 1919, to the southwest section of Washington, where they assaulted several Negroes. The next day white soldiers and sailors joined with civilians to spread the terror. Negroes were pulled from autos and street cars and pummeled into unconsciousness. One was seized by a mob and beaten unmercifully, right in front of the White House. Other Negroes were shot and left to die in the streets.

The mob had misjudged the Negroes of Washington. After the whites tried to invade Negro areas the following day, the blacks took the offensive. The white mob wounded about three hundred Negroes one night; the next night Negroes were ready for the attack. This time the number of white wounded was much larger than the Negro casualty list. Four whites and two Negroes died in the fray.

A similar riot occurred in Chicago a few weeks later. The white population was incensed to the point of touching off a race war. This was the direct result of Negro migration to Chicago's industrial plants and their invasion of desirable residential districts. The first clash took place at a bathing beach, following upon bombings of homes bought during this period by Negroes. The black population fought back in Chicago, too. A number of whites died in the violence.

A serious riot had erupted two years earlier in Houston after the American Expeditionary Forces entered the war. Negro soldiers based in Texas had been insulted repeatedly by whites. The issue exploded on August 23, 1917, when over a hundred Negro soldiers marched into Houston armed with rifles. This demonstration followed a number of disputes with local patrolmen and military police. The morning after the riot it was announced that thirteen had died (including one Negro) and that nineteen were wounded (among them five Negro soldiers). These troops had been sent to guard government property at Camp Logan. The arrival of so many Negro troops alarmed some white citizens in Houston. Six hundred Negroes were there at the time, and more soldiers were expected. Some of the troops resented the segregation rules they had

to observe. Prior to the riot, white officers had been regarded as sympathetic to the Negro soldiers. Prohibitionists, however, concerned about soldiers drinking in the local saloons, fomented discord by encouraging a local newspaper to publish an editorial entitled "Remember Brownsville," which further inflamed tempers.

The mayor of Houston ordered an investigation of the riot and the incidents which led to it. The testimony and other data showed that the outbreak was due to several factors: problems of segregated transportation, mistreatment of Negro women by white police, poor ties between Negro military police and white civilian police, and retaliatory action of a small band of Negro soldiers.

Twenty-five such conflicts broke out in 1919. In a disorder occurring in Elaine, Arkansas, white men fired on a Negro church meeting. One white man was killed in the aftermath. Mobs of whites roamed the streets, killing and beating any Negroes they found. Several Negroes were arrested and another white killed. Finally, federal troops were called in to quell the outbreak. The accused Negroes were tried without the assistance of legal counsel and were found guilty after forty-five minutes. The NAACP took the case and entered an appeal to the Supreme Court, which reversed the decision and ordered a new trial.

The riots and other incidents caused by severe prejudice publicized the plight of the black man in America. Many whites became aware of its severity for the first time. Because of this the NAACP grew in militancy and in membership. Between 1917 and 1920 dues-paying members rose from 10,000 to nearly 90,000. NAACP branches formed everywhere. They multiplied from 80 in 1917 to 356 in 1920.

Black men and women had gone from frustration to hope and back to despair in their struggle for equality. The long period of rioting was a reaction to a seemingly hopeless situation. When it ended, the Negro American began to try once again to find realistic means of obtaining justice for himself and for his children.

CHAPTER TEN

Promises of the Twenties— Broken by Politics, Fulfilled through Black Pride

WHEN it was founded, the Republican Party had been led by men of the Charles Sumner mold who opposed slavery and who demanded freedom for all Americans. The Negro vote had been as vital in their view as the white vote. Thus Negro leaders like Frederick Douglass saw the party as a friend. Another wing of the party, however, included pragmatic politicians concerned with building Republican fortunes, in the South as well as in the North. Not long after the Civil War, the party began to take the Negro vote for granted as its own. When the black Populist elements began to contend with the white exclusionists in the South during the 1880's, the Cleveland Democrats saw a way to win the black vote by appointing Negroes to office.

It was at this point that the Republican Party began to lose the allegiance of the black voter, though it would be many years before the Democrats could claim it; neither party at this time was loyal enough to the Negro American's cause to earn his vote.

PRESIDENT TAFT AND THE NEGRO

While historians are forced to render an ambivalent judgment of Theodore Roosevelt's relations with Negroes, they are more certain with regard to the policies of his successor, William Howard Taft. Without a doubt, his administration helped perpetuate the prejudice so prevalent at that time. Taft outlined his approach in his inaugural address, hinting that in order to avoid national ill-will and the furtherance of sectionalism he would avoid naming Negroes to public office in the South. Taft later expressed his opinion of what he had accomplished for his party in the South in these words:

"What I have done in this line of recognition of the democracy of the South," he explained, "has been without sacrifice of any interest of my own party. I have appointed many Negroes to office and have given some of them . . . offices of essential dignity at Washington. What I have not done is to force them upon unwilling communities in the South itself."

ROBERT H. TERRELL

Taft did appoint many Negroes to public office in the North, where it was still sometimes difficult if safer politically. The key appointment of William H. Lewis to the post of assistant attorney general of the United States did prompt a howl from southern members of the American Bar Association. Attorney General George Wickersham came to Lewis' defense. Wickersham's forceful stand assured Lewis' confirmation by the Senate. Upon Attorney General James C. McReynold's advice, Taft renamed Judge Robert H. Terrell to the municipal bench in the District of Columbia. Despite efforts to quash the appointment, the President kept Terrell's name before the Senate until he was confirmed.

Both Negroes and whites alike, especially through such groups as the NAACP, continued to believe that some good could come from publicity, from agitation, from petitioning Congress and the state legislatures for a redress of grievances. In 1911, the National Independent Political League sponsored a two-day observance of the hundredth anniversary of the birth of Charles Sumner. At this time they drafted a

plea asking the President to enforce the Constitution. It asked Congress to halt the trend toward peonage and disfranchisement, to pass a federal anti-Jim Crow law for interstate passengers, to grant federal aid to education, to enact a national anti-lynching bill and to reinstate the soldiers discharged after the Brownsville riot.

The Democratic convention of 1912 heard a Negro, Reverdy C. Ransom, inveigh against Republican President Taft for failing to name Negroes to public office in the South.

PRESIDENT WILSON AND THE NEGRO

Woodrow Wilson, the Princeton University scholar running for President in 1912, made a strong appeal for Negro support. He wrote a letter to Bishop Alexander Walters during the campaign, saying that he hoped to see "justice done them in every matter; and not mere grudging justice, but executed with liberality and cordial good feeling." Tom Watson, the disillusioned Populist, attacked Wilson as a man "ravenously fond of the Negro." This was hardly the truth, however, for Wilson remained a conservative administrator throughout his life. As president of Princeton, the Virginian had not admitted Negroes as students. While campaigning for office, Wilson actively courted the Negro vote. "I want to assure them that should I become President of the United States," he wrote to Bishop Walters, "they may count upon me for absolute fair dealing and for everything by which I could assist in advancing the interests of their race in the United States." This promise helped swing the black vote to the Democratic Party.

Accounts in Negro newspapers show that larger numbers of Negroes voted the Democratic ticket than in previous elections. The shift came partly through the efforts of a national Negro league for Wilson, which issued an address to northern Negroes from its headquarters in Richmond. The league urged Negroes to break their alliance with the Republican Party. The National Independent Political League also appealed for nonwhite votes. It spent $52,000 in the effort. The *Crisis* added its weight to the Wilson support, asking why Negroes remained loyal to the Republican Party when Taft and Roosevelt, whom Negroes had supported, had deserted them. The editorial mentioned no Democratic commitment, however. Taft won the 1912 Republican nomination. Theodore Roosevelt came back from Africa to run as a third-party candidate. While most northern Negroes voted for Taft, Negro leaders estimated that some hundred thousand voted for Wilson.

After his election, Wilson received a proposal from Oswald Garrison Villard, urging him to name a national commission on race to conduct "a nonpartisan, scientific study of the status of the Negro in the life of the nation." At first Wilson listened to the proposal with sympathy. Shortly afterward, though, he decided against it and, without informing Villard, he charted a totally opposite course.

It was during Wilson's administration that segregation entered the federal service. The President had not ordered segregation, but he knew of it and sanctioned it. Wilson wrote to Oswald Garrison Villard that the change occurred with "the initiative and suggestion of the heads of departments." The separation of black and white began in the Post Office Department under Postmaster General Albert Burleson. It then spread to the Treasury Department and the Bureau of Engraving and Printing, with the approval of Secretary of the Treasury William McAdoo. The Navy Department, headed by Josephus Daniels, was next. Feelings became so intense among Negroes that, after a trip to the nation's capital, Booker Washington wrote to Villard, "I have never seen the colored people so discouraged and so bitter as they are at the present time."

In 1914 a delegation of Negroes headed by Monroe Trotter met with the President to protest the segregation in the federal government. Wilson's amazing statement to that group deserves quotation:

> The white people of the country, as well as I, wish to see the colored people progress, and admire the progress they have already made, and want to see them continue along independent lines. There is, however, a great prejudice against the colored people. . . . It will take one hundred years to eradicate this prejudice, and we must deal with it as practical men. Segregation is not humiliating but a benefit, and ought to be so regarded by you gentlemen. If your organization goes out and tells the colored people of the country that it is a humiliation, they will so regard it, but if you do not tell them so, and regard it as a benefit, they will regard it the same. The only harm will be if you cause them to think it is a humiliation.

Reactions to the Wilson policy soon poured in by letters and petitions—some signed by a few hundred persons and others, like Trotter's petitions, including up to 21,000 names. The protests were spearheaded by the NAACP and Trotter's National Independent Political League. Mass meetings were held to circulate more petitions and resolutions. The National Negro Press Association (serving 126 newspapers), the Crisis, and those daily newspapers with liberal editors gave news space to the protests. Villard reported late in 1913 that segregationists were taking a back seat as a result of these complaints. In fact, they were. But Negroes still faced lynchings, segregation in government offices, a freeze on promotions and the filing of a new flock of anti-Negro bills in Congress.

The Democratic administration took no steps to protect Negroes' civil rights, and the black vote in 1916 for the losing Republican candidate, Charles Evans Hughes, was probably more anti-Wilson than pro-Republican. Oddly enough, that year marked the first Republican effort to bar southern Negroes from its national convention. Wilson was reelected in 1916; his second term was dominated by the World War. Wilson was the force behind the founding of the League of Nations, forerunner of the United Nations. His idealistic foreign policy contrasted sharply with his domestic policy. Negroes could not forget that just as the Republicans had deserted them at the end of the nineteenth century, now the Democratic Party seemed unwilling to fulfill its pledge of loyalty.

The Republican national committee adopted a resolution at its 1920 convention to reduce representation from the South. That year the number of Negro delegates fell to twenty-seven. Just eight years earlier, a total of sixty-two Negroes had attended the convention. The party used another tactic to undermine Negro committeemen. It sponsored candidates for office on platforms opposed to any Negro role in politics. Negroes responded by running all-black slates for state offices in Kentucky, Texas and Virginia.

JOHN MITCHELL, JR.

They also ran a black ticket in Baltimore. One Virginia Negro candidate, John Mitchell, proposed that Negroes support local Democrats in all city and county contests.

When the nation adopted woman suffrage (the Nineteenth Amendment), white supremacists, most of whom had not been strong advocates of the Nineteenth Amendment, began to fear the voting power of Negro women. They promptly urged white women to join white men at the polls.

PRESIDENT HARDING AND THE NEGRO

In the national elections of 1920 the black vote went against Democratic candidate James Cox, because Negroes could not forget Wilson's administration. This helped sweep Warren G. Harding into the Presidency. He promised a "return to normalcy" under the Republicans. Governor Calvin Coolidge of Massachusetts became vice-president. One plank in the Republican platform that year reflected the NAACP's efforts. It urged Congress "to consider the most effective means to end lynching . . . which continues to be a terrible blot on our American civilization." Candidate Harding said in his acceptance speech: "I believe the federal government should stamp out lynching and remove that stain from the fair name of America."

The nation was so outraged by the lynching issue that Congress was asked to make the crime a federal offense. The NAACP, with James Weldon Johnson as its national secretary, launched a campaign to support such a law. Johnson met with President Harding on April 4, 1921. The Negro poet spoke of the "unrest among colored people and their dissatisfaction with conditions which allowed lynchings, disfranchisements, peonage and other forms of racial injustice." Johnson's eloquence swayed the President. Eight days later Harding asked Congress to wipe out "the stain of barbaric lynching from the banners of a free and orderly representative democracy." But this request failed to budge the Republican Congress. Neither did other White House messages in 1921 and 1922. The anti-lynching campaign had been sponsored by Senator Arthur Capper of Kansas and Congressman L. C. Dyer of Missouri. Johnson worked feverishly for two years, talking to members of Congress about the bill. The mail response aided his lobbying effort immensely. "The Dyer bill," Johnson said, "brought out the greatest concerted action I have yet seen the colored people take."

House debate on the bill lasted several weeks. Spectators—many of them Negroes—thronged the House galleries. Finally, on January 26, 1922, the House passed the Dyer bill by a 230-119 margin. The nation's Negroes were jubilant. The NAACP described the vote as "one of the most significant steps ever taken in the history of America." But the joy was short-lived. The Senate let the bill die in committee.

The NAACP expressed its dismay over the bill's defeat in "A Message to Colored Americans," issued in September of 1923. It urged Negroes to withhold support from both parties, since both were charged with killing the bill. The message predicted that "nothing will more quickly bring the old parties to a clear realization of their obligation to us and the nation than a vigorous third-party movement."

President Warren Harding, in the meantime, had lost his early zeal regarding anti-lynching legislation. His program offered little to aid the advancement of Negroes. The President made a highly publicized statement on race in October of 1921 when he spoke in Birmingham, Alabama, at Woodrow Wilson Park:

> Men of both races may well stand uncompromisingly against every suggestion of social equality. Indeed, it would be helpful to have the word "equality" eliminated from this consideration; to have it accepted on both sides that this is not a question of social equality, but a question of recognizing a fundamental, eternal and inescapable difference....
> Take the political aspect: I would say let the black man vote when he is fit to vote; prohibit the white man voting when he is unfit to vote. . . . On the other hand I would insist upon equal educational opportunity for both. . . . There must be such education among the colored people as will enable them to develop their own leaders, capable of understanding and sympathizing with such a differentiation between the races as I have suggested. . . . Racial amalgamation there cannot be. Partnership of the races in developing the highest aims of all humanity there must be if humanity is to achieve the ends which we have set for it.

Negroes were widely divided in their reaction to the speech. Howard's Kelley Miller said that this emphasis was "calculated in the long run to do the Negro as much harm as the Taney Doctrine. The Negro has no rights which the white man is bound to respect." Du Bois chided the President for his references to social equality. Others, however, including Robert R. Moton, Perry Howard, Henry Lincoln Johnson and Robert R. Church, commented favorably.

Weekly Negro newspapers all discussed the "social equality" issue in a searching manner. "The Negro," the Atlanta *Independent* asserted, "has never asked nor invited social equality. That has been the bugaboo of his enemies." The Richmond *Planet* declared: "There is every reason to believe that more amalgamation between the races is going on in the South and behind closed doors than in the Northland with its matrimonial publicity." The Houston *Informer* suggested that confusion between "social equality" and "social intermingling" was the real issue. "It is possible," the *Informer* observed, "for a man to be another's social equal, and then not his social companion."

KELLEY MILLER

The *Chicago Defender* had the last word. "The only comment which we wish to make about the divine command of the President to the races on social equality," the *Defender* said sardonically, "is to suggest that what he really meant was lawful amalgamation.... What they mean is no black woman shall have the right to bring her half-white child into court and force the white father to give that child the name it ought to have."

President Harding, beset by scandal in his cabinet, ignored the plight of Negro voters. Congressman George H. Tinkham of Massachusetts proposed that Congress investigate racial discrimination and reduce the congressional representation of states which did not protect the right to vote as provided in the Fourteenth Amendment. The speaker of the House did not support the bill, and it died in committee.

During the next few years some Negro leaders urged political independence from both major parties. The NAACP convention of 1923 advised Negroes to force "a new political emancipation." That year the taciturn Vice-President

Calvin Coolidge succeeded Harding, who had died in office. Coolidge said little, and he had a reputation as an honest man. Fewer lynchings and fewer race riots occurred while Coolidge served out the rest of Harding's term. Most Negroes voted for Coolidge in 1924. A smattering voted for Senator Robert M. LaFollette of Wisconsin, a third-party candidate.

THE KU KLUX KLAN

President Coolidge shared Negroes' wariness of the Ku Klux Klan. After its earliest southern revival it grew in the twenties (attacking Negroes, Jews, Catholics and foreigners alike), and reported five million members by 1924. The Klan's constitution declared that its purpose was "to unite white male persons, native-born Gentile citizens of the United States of America, who owe no allegiance of any nature to any foreign government, nation, institution, sect, ruler, person or people, whose morals are good, whose regulations and vocations are exemplary . . . to exemplify a practical benevolence; to shield the sanctity of the home and the chastity of womanhood; to maintain forever white supremacy."

As the years passed, the Klan planned to interpret its program as the needs of local communities required. The KKK leaders, in their white robes and with their crosses burning, could instill terror in Negroes without fear of the "law" in the South. Internal weaknesses and corruption, however, led to a temporary decline in Klan activities after 1925.

Republican failure to denounce the Klan in the party platforms of 1920, 1924 and 1928 caused more Negroes to leave the ranks. When Herbert Hoover allied himself with the "lily white" South after entering the White House in 1928, the Negro bolt to the Democrats was assured. Hoover failed to appoint Negroes to public office. He also antagonized Negroes by naming Judge John Parker to the United States Supreme Court. Parker called the black man's participation in politics "a source of evil and danger to both races." This statement may have been the Judge's undoing, for the Senate refused to confirm his appointment.

POSTWAR POLITICAL GAINS

The repeated failure of political promise for the Negro during the first two decades of the twentieth century did not represent defeat. Already the effects of these setbacks were stiffening the minds of thinking Negroes. The returning black war veterans, together with the postwar psychological emancipation, quickly fired black society with a new militancy of spirit and ideology.

The Negro migration to the North had instilled a new spirit in every city where black masses lived clustered together. An editorial in the *Crisis* late in 1919 breathed postwar militancy. "For three centuries we have suffered and [have been] cowed," the editors noted. "No race ever gave passive resistance and submission to evil longer, [or endured] more piteous trial. Today we raise the terrible weapon of self-defense. When the murderer comes, he shall no longer strike us in the back. When the lynchers gather, we too must gather armed. When the mob moves, we propose to meet it with bricks and clubs and guns."

The political benefits of the great Negro migration North were first reaped after World War I. There had been a few scattered Negro victories even before this. Oscar De Priest was elected alderman in Chicago in 1915. Two years later, Edward A. Johnson of Manhattan won a seat in the New York state assembly. Where Negroes showed their strength at the polls, the political party in control paid them heed. Their votes were often pivotal in Chicago, New York, Cleveland, Cincinnati and Philadelphia. In these cities, Negroes started appearing on city councils and boards of aldermen.

Then, in 1928, Oscar De Priest, a Republican, won a seat in Congress from Chicago's heavily Negro South Side. The Illinois congressman was the first of his race to sit in the House since Reconstruction. He was also the first Negro congressman from the North. De Priest served as the only Negro in Congress from 1929 until 1933. Arthur W. Mitchell, a Democrat, succeeded him in 1934. Two Negro lawyers were elected as Democrats to New York City judgeships in 1930.

OSCAR DE PRIEST

The success of increased cooperative action advanced the promise of a better future to hundreds of thousands of Negro Americans. Whereas the period following the Civil War had in many ways blocked the adjustment from slavery to freedom, this "Second Reconstruction" was an attempt to foster adjustment to the new economic, educational and social conditions created by World War I. The voice of the Negro was heard in journalism, literature, the theater, educational research and socio-political groups. Whether these new gains would really result in a better life for the Negro, in improved race relations and in a better total national environment remained to be seen.

INFLUENTIAL JOURNALS

Several magazines carried progressive thinking to black readers. *The Messenger*, a monthly published by A. Philip Randolph and Chandler Owen in New York, called for an aggressive organized labor movement. Randolph and Owens planned *The Messenger* as "a magazine of scientific radicalism." It scorned the patient leadership of Booker Washington and even rejected

Du Bois for not pressing vigorously enough. The editors opposed the Republican Party and openly criticized the Christian church. The magazine took a Russian Marxist line, stating that "under the Soviet system their [Negroes'] right to vote would be based upon their service and not upon race or color."

Another New York monthly, *Opportunity*, trod a more conservative path. Published by the National Urban League, it demanded a greater role for Negro labor in clear and certain terms. Charles S. Johnson, later a professor and president of Fisk University, became the editor of *Opportunity* in 1928. Under Johnson, the magazine was concerned with reviewing the Negro's talent in poetry, literature, art, sports and other fields. It fostered pride in Negro achievements, past and present. *Opportunity* sponsored contests to discover talented black writers and to publish their works. Prizes were offered to writers of short stories, poetry, plays, essays and personal sketches. For years the *Crisis* had relayed the NAACP's message to organize Negroes in all walks of life. Like *Opportunity*, it, too, held contests in art and literature.

CHARLES S. JOHNSON

THE NEW NEGRO

The concept of the New Negro may not have been original to the 1920's. Perhaps he had always lingered within the black masses. But wherever he showed himself—in Chicago, New York, St. Louis or Philadelphia—he appealed above all to the weary and downtrodden. Here, where the poets romanticized "blackness" and "brownness," the New Negro was at home. Gwendolyn Bennett envisioned one such image in these lines "To a Dark Girl":

I love you for your brownness,
And the rounded darkness of your breast;
I love you for the breaking sadness in your voice
And shadows where your wayward eye-lids rest.

Something of old forgotten queens
Lurks in the lithe abandon of your walk,
And something of the shackled slave
Sobs in the rhythm of your talk.

Lucian B. Watkins also sensed a new black awakening in the war's aftermath. He wrote in his sonnet "The New Negro":

Ah, he has sensed the truth—
Deep in his soul
He feels the manly majesty of power.

William Sexton, too, made poetic comment on the awaited renaissance in another poem entitled "The New Negro":

Out of the mist I see a new America—a land of
    ideals.
I hear the music of my fathers blended with the
    "Stars and Stripes Forever."
I am the crown of thorns. Tyranny must bear a
    thousand years—
I am the New Negro.

James D. Corrothers glimpsed another side of the New Negro—the political profile "At the Closed Gate of Justice":

To be a Negro in a day like this
Demands strange loyalty. We serve a flag
Which is to us white freedom's emphasis.
Ah! One must love when truth and justice lag,
To be a Negro in a day like this.

The fiery Claude McKay, in "If We Must Die," saw his New Negro with sword gleaming for battle:

Oh kinsmen! We must meet the common foe;
Though far outnumbered, let us still be brave,
And for their thousand blows deal one death blow!
What though before us lies the open grave?
Like men we'll face the murderous cowardly pack.
Pressed to the wall, dying, but—fighting back!

THE THEATER

The success of early Negro drama depended on its depiction of black culture as the audience wanted to visualize it. This was particularly true in musical comedy. Two Negro comedians, Bob Cole and J. Rosamond Johnson, performed in the first Negro musical, *A Trip to Coontown*. They also composed songs and lyrics for such shows as *Shoo Fly Regiment* (1906), *Rufus Rastus* (1905), *Shuffle Along* (1921) and *Chocolate Dandies* (1924). Mainstays in these plays included Noble Sissle and Eubie Blake, under contract to Warner Brothers; Miller and Lyles, later the stars of *Shuffle Along*; and Ernest Hogan, Florence Mills and Ethel Waters. These Negro casts performed at Worth's Museum at Sixth Avenue and 30th Street in Manhattan, as well as at the Lafayette and Lincoln Theaters, the traditional theatrical homes of the Harlem community.

As the Negro's role in society began to improve, his drama became both cause and effect of his own influence. It expanded into groups like the Ethiopian Art Theater in Chicago, the Krigwa Players in New York, and other companies in Washington, Philadelphia, Baltimore, Cleveland, Los Angeles, and in colleges throughout the nation.

Eugene O'Neill used Negro subjects in his early productions—*The Dreamy Kid* (1919), *The Emperor Jones* (1920) and *All God's Chillun Got Wings* (1924). David Belasco introduced Jules Bledsoe and Frank Wilson in *Lulu Belle* and *In Abraham's Bosom*. Bledsoe also appeared in Edna Ferber's *Show Boat* during 1927 and 1928. Wilson performed in Heyward's *Porgy*. A more elaborate production with an all-Negro cast, Marc Connelly's 1929 play *The Green Pastures* won a Pulitzer Prize.

Several Negro actors achieved fame for their work in the legitimate theater. Charles Gilpin appeared in *The Emperor Jones*. For his per-

RICHARD HARRISON

CHARLES GILPIN

CLAUDE McKAY

ETHEL WATERS

formance he won the Spingarn Medal, and the Drama League placed him among the ten people making the greatest stage contribution in 1920. Another Spingarn winner was Richard B. Harrison, who gave substance to *The Green Pastures* in the role of "De Lawd." Harrison first appeared on stage in 1889, and after a successful stage career taught dramatics at North Carolina College.

The many-talented Paul Robeson graduated from Rutgers University as a Phi Beta Kappa scholar and from Columbia Law School. For two years he played on Walter Camp's championship football team and was an All-American choice. Upon graduation, he decided to go into the theater rather than practice law. Robeson first appeared in *Taboo*, in 1922. Then in 1924 he succeeded Charles Gilpin in *The Emperor Jones*. But it was *Show Boat* which brought him into the international spotlight. The talented baritone toured with the London and Berlin productions.

CHARLES W. CHESNUTT

LITERATURE

Black authors caught up in the new spirit burned with its flames in their prose as well as in their poems. With the precedent of only two writers of consequence, Charles W. Chesnutt and Paul Laurence Dunbar, several noted Negro writers, including poets Claude McKay and Countee Cullen and novelist Walter White, emerged in the twenties.

McKay's *Harlem Shadows*, a volume of poetry published in 1922, included his well-known "If We Must Die" and "The Lynching." *Home to Harlem*, McKay's first novel, appeared in 1928. It relates the experiences of a Negro soldier who has returned from the war in France. With the publication of *Banjo* in 1929, McKay took his place among the nation's foremost authors.

Countee Cullen was only twenty-two when his first volume of poems was published in 1925. Cullen's verse had a special quality of gentle lyricism which was at its best when he dealt with the race problem. The result was a subtle protest. Cullen's volumes of verse included *Color*, *Copper Sun*, *The Black Christ* and *On These I Stand*.

COUNTEE CULLEN

Walter White, well known for his work as a national NAACP leader, wrote two novels. *The Fire in the Flint* appeared in 1924, and *Flight* was released two years later. The first work presented an account of the sufferings of southern Negroes. White's second novel portrayed as its heroine a woman who could "pass for white." Another White book, the 1929 work *Rope and Fagot: A Biography of Judge Lynch*, is one of the most vivid treatments of lynching ever published.

After Jean Toomer's only work, *Cane*, was published in 1923, William Stanley Braithwaite described him as "the very first artist of the race, who, with all an artist's passion and sympathy for life, its hurts, its sympathies, its desires, its joys, its defeats and strange yearnings, can write about the Negro without the surrender or compromise of the artist's vision . . . Jean Toomer is a bright star of a new day of the race in literature."

NEW RECOGNITION

The "Harlem Renaissance" proved that black creativity had come into its own. Now the serious Negro artist was praised by critics and the public, and both the white and the black communities—still quite separate—recognized the rich contribution he was making to American culture.

Alain Locke published his anthology of works by many Negro authors, *The New Negro*, in 1925. The same year the Arthur Schomburg Collection of Negro Literature was founded in Harlem. It gathered together books published over the years on Negro history, literature and art. The Carnegie Foundation bought this collection in 1926 and presented it to the New York Public Library. It has served since then as an important center of research on Negro history and culture. In 1926 the Harmon Foundation conferred the William E. Harmon Award for distinguished achievement among Negroes in seven categories: in literature to Countee Cullen; in fine arts to Palmer Hayden; in industry to C. C. Spaulding; in science to James C. Evans; in education to Virginia E. Randolph; in religious service to Max Yergan; and in race relations to W. W. Alexander.

Monroe N. Work completed *A Bibliography of the Negro in Africa and America* in 1928. The Phelps-Stokes Fund and the Carnegie Corporation aided his research. Work, the director of records and research at Tuskegee Institute, compiled a volume of 698 pages. It remains a valuable and scholarly source book.

Two noted sociological studies on the Negro appeared during this period. George E. Haynes published his *Negro at Work in New York*, and Sadie Tanner Mossell Alexander issued her *Standard of Living of 100 Negro Migrant Families in Philadelphia*. At the same time, Negro history volumes rolled off the presses in great numbers. Among these were Benjamin Brawley's *A Short History of the American Negro* (1919) and his *Social History of the American Negro* (1921). William Henry Ferris issued *The African Abroad* at this time, in two volumes. Carter G. Woodson's *History of the Negro Church* saw print in 1921, and *The Negro in Our History* (1922) was in four printings by 1927. In the meantime, Dr. Haynes released *The Negro at Work during World War I and during Reconstruction*, and Charles H. Wesley completed a pioneer volume on *Negro Labor in the United States: A Study in American Economic History*. James Weldon Johnson's *Black Manhattan* appeared in 1930, and *The Black Worker*, by Abram Harris and Sterling Spero, was published the following year.

The sum of the Negro's achievement at this time was far greater than at any previous time in American history. His pride in an emerging culture quickened his sense of racial integrity, and led to such proposals as those of the Pan-African Congresses and the Garvey movement. But whereas most people dream in spite of themselves, the black man had earned his vision through three hundred years of sacrifice.

THE PAN-AFRICAN CONGRESSES

The Pan-African Congress, founded in London in 1900, was inactive until after World War I. At the close of the war, however, Negro Americans agitated for a government policy on Africa. It was this which led to the revival of the London Congress. Dr. W. E. B. Du Bois, editor

SADIE T. M. ALEXANDER

ALAIN LOCKE

WALTER WHITE

MONROE WORK

of the NAACP's *Crisis,* sailed for Europe. He had failed in his attempt to meet with President Wilson. The closest person he could reach at the White House was Colonel Edward M. House, the President's adviser. Late in December of 1919 the Chicago *Tribune* carried a dispatch on the London meeting.

"An Ethiopian Utopia, to be fashioned out of the German colonies," the *Tribune* reported, "is the latest dream of leaders of the Negro race who are here at the invitation of the United States Government as part of the extensive entourage of the American peace delegation. Robert R. Moton, successor to the late Booker T. Washington as head of Tuskegee . . . and Dr. William E. B. Du Bois, editor of the *Crisis,* are promoting a Pan-African Conference to be held during the winter while the Peace Conference is in full blast. It is to embrace Negro leaders from America, Abyssinia, Liberia, Haiti, the French and British colonies, and other parts of the black world."

The *Tribune* dispatch said that Du Bois had presented a memorandum to President Wilson, laying out the scheme for self-determination in the former German colonies. "Dr. Du Bois' dream," the article stated, "is that the Peace Conference could form an internationalized Africa, to have as its basis the former German colonies with their 1,000,000 square miles and 12,500,000 population." According to the *Tribune*, the Du Bois plan also envisioned negotiation for decolonizing the Belgian Congo and the Portuguese colonies Angola and Mozambique.

"The Africa for the Africans," the dispatch added, "could be under the guidance of [an] international organization. The governing international commission should represent not simply governments, but modern culture, science, commerce, social reform and religious philanthropy. It must represent not simply the white world but the civilized Negro world."

Du Bois consulted French Prime Minister Clemenceau, who finally granted permission to hold a Pan-African Congress in Paris. It assembled fifty-seven delegates from fifteen countries (twelve Africans, sixteen American Negros, seven Frenchmen, one Englishman and twenty-one West Indians). The New York *Evening Globe* commented that "the first as-sembly of the kind in history . . . has for its object the drafting of an appeal to the Peace Conference to give the Negro race of Africa a chance to develop unhindered by other races."

The Congress asked for a Mandates Commission to draw up a code of law to govern the native Africans. The code would be similar to the proposed international code for labor. The Commission would also agree on principles of land, capital, labor and education. The Africans would take part in their government. The League of Nations would then name a permanent bureau to oversee the infant nations. "Whenever it is proven that African natives are not receiving just treatment at the hands of any state or that any state deliberately excludes its civilized citizens or subjects of Negro descent from its body politic and cultural," the Congress' report urged, "it shall be the duty of the League of Nations to bring the matter to the attention of the civilized world."

The second Pan-African Congress met in 1921 in Brussels. Du Bois, the Congress' secretary, had corresponded with delegates in many parts of the world. When the Brussels sessions convened more white persons were present than Negroes. The Congress passed resolutions criticizing Belgian administration of the Congo and asking for the creation of an international section of the League of Nations' labor bureau, to be charged with protecting native labor.

This Congress asked Du Bois and a committee to meet with League of Nations officials at Geneva. Dante Bellegarde of Haiti and others raised the African plan question once again and urged "that the League of Nations take a firm stand on the absolute equality of races, and that it suggest to the colonial powers connected with the League of Nations to form an international institute for the study of the Negro problem, and for the evolution and protection of the Negro race."

The third Pan-African Congress was to have met in Paris in 1923. It was postponed, however, and later assembled in Lisbon, Portugal. It restated the principles of an earlier resolution and added that the main objects of capital and labor should be "the welfare of the many rather than the enriching of the few."

Four years passed before the fourth Pan-African Congress met in New York in 1927. The meeting attracted 208 delegates from thirteen countries. Again the members adopted resolutions urging the Du Bois plan for Africa. The fifth Pan-African Congress did not meet until 1945. This gathering grew out of a meeting of the Trade Union Conference in London in 1944. The Congress assembled at Manchester, England, aided by the British Labour Party. A committee of the Congress obtained a hearing before the colonial section of the Fabian Society. Beyond the hearing, though, actual accomplishments were few. The Congress, which seemed a weak voice crying in the night, had demonstrated the need for native involvement in colonial government.

THE GARVEY MOVEMENT

Another development of the New Negro movement was begun by the black nationalist Marcus Garvey. He came from Jamaica in the British West Indies in 1916, preaching the doctrine of black unity and a return to Africa for the Negro race. He, too, dreamed of establishing a Pan-African government.

Garvey and his ideas stirred the black masses as nothing else had done. He gave Negroes a new sense of pride in their ancestry by stressing the military, political and artistic triumphs of their African heritage. He emphasized the beauty of blackness, telling of a black God and black Christ, a black Virgin Mary and black disciples. His weekly newspaper, the *Negro World*, dramatized these beliefs through graphic arts.

Garvey climaxed his career when his New York City followers in 1921 proclaimed him "Provisional President of Africa" at a public affair. In addition to this title, "President" Garvey was given a court and courtiers. A "Black Legion" formed, as well as "Black Cross" nurses. The nurses wore uniforms bearing decorative orders such as the Sublime Order of the Nile and the Distinguished Order of Ethiopia. Throughout the nation, Garveyites joined the Universal Negro Improvement Association. Garvey claimed a fol-

MARCUS GARVEY

lowing of millions, but a sober guess is that they were closer to half that number.

Garvey focused his attention on the international scene. He sent a delegation to the Versailles Peace Conference, asking that the German colonies be granted to his African government. When this gambit failed, Garvey warned the European governments that their stay in Africa would be brief. He urged Africans to overthrow their colonial rulers.

Garvey began commercial relations with Africa by organizing a steamship concern, the Black Star Line, which consisted of three ships—the vessels of his "back to Africa" dream. When the line folded his backers lost large sums of money. Garvey was convicted of using the mails to defraud. The court sentenced him to a five-year term in a federal prison in Atlanta. He was released through a Presidential pardon which Coolidge granted in 1927. Garvey died in 1940. The movement limped on for a while under less colorful leadership. From time to time the "back to Africa" idea has been revived, but without any real success.

CHAPTER ELEVEN

Depression and New Deal— The Black Factor in the National Economy

THE steady flow of migration between World War I and 1925 was reduced somewhat during the next ten years. Southern Negroes continued to desert the marginal farms and come to the northern cities. By 1923 nearly 500,000 Negroes had resettled in the North. When the Depression began in 1930, one Negro out of every five lived in the North.

The census of that year showed that over eleven million Negroes were scattered throughout the nation. Although most of them lived in the Black Belt of the cotton-growing states— they numbered more than 50 per cent of the population of the Mississippi Delta region—the Negro population of the Black Belt had been decreasing since 1900. The farming sections were rapidly losing Negro labor. The black workers flocked to the cities of the South in quest of higher wages and better schooling. The educational programs, it should be noted, owed much to northern philanthropy. The Negroes had found it impossible to prosper on the worn-out soil. Since they could not buy land in many places, they held it temporarily—and on terms of a stringent land lease which deprived them of most of their earnings. Many Negro farmers had to pay usurious interest rates. Only in exceptional cases could they succeed in maintaining themselves without loans from whites.

Once having moved to southern cities, however, the Negro farmers often moved on. For a number of years the so-called "talented tenth" of the race had lost many of its best members to the North. In the course of time the laboring element gradually found its way to the same centers.

OCCUPATIONAL SHIFTS

Though the majority of Negroes remained farmers, this occupation declined sharply. The figure plummeted from 55 per cent in 1910 to 44 per cent in 1920 to 36 per cent in 1930. The 1940 census showed that the Depression slowed this migration to the cities. But Negroes as a rule shunned the "back to the farm" movement that began during the darkest days of the Depression. By 1940 seven cities counted more than 100,000 Negroes each: New York, Chicago,

Philadelphia, Baltimore, Washington, New Orleans and Detroit.

As black labor deserted agriculture, it made new gains in mechanical industries. Since 1910 Negroes had found openings as steel, garment and automobile workers. Jobs also beckoned in glass factories, in brick and tile yards, in transit companies and in city government. Coal mining attracted many Negroes during this period as well. By 1920 about 8 per cent of the nation's bituminous miners were Negroes. Of these, almost 53 per cent mined in Alabama, 20 per cent in Kentucky and 20 per cent in West Virginia. While the actual number of Negro miners had doubled by 1930, their percentage of the total decreased slightly. But as industrial conditions improved more Negroes entered the mines, and by 1940 the government reported that the trend "is again upward."

The meat-packing industry also noted interesting changes. Four meat-packing plants in Omaha employed a Negro work force of 15 per cent in 1923. By 1930—with the number of laborers increased by half—Negroes accounted for less than 10 per cent of the workers. Under 1 per cent of the Negro employees worked in technical or office jobs or as foremen or skilled workers.

The rising numbers of whites applying for the same jobs in industry greatly increased the competition. Prejudice and lack of skills too often relegated the Negro workers to inferior positions or kept them from being hired. In addition, industry-sponsored training programs schooled whites only.

By 1930 the concentration of Negro workers in certain skilled trades had been broken. A sharp drop-off now appeared in the number of black seamstresses, firemen, machinists and millwrights. Statistics also show a decline in the number of Negro toolmakers and tobacco factory workers in this decade. Jobs in some of these crafts had decreased generally for all workers; the tapering off appeared due to increased use of machines to do the work.

The largest increase in black workers occurred in the building trades. Here the ranks of 150,000 Negroes rose to almost 181,000 between 1920 and 1930. Yet the highest rate of unemployment also occurred in this industry.

The steel industry showed a strong shift toward Negro workers. By 1937 they accounted for one-tenth of the labor in the iron and steel mills. While 62 per cent of the Negro steelworkers were employed in the South in 1910, by 1930 more than 71 per cent of them worked in the North. The southern foundries were losing their employees, who sought the more inviting wages and living conditions offered in the North.

NEGROES IN THE LABOR MOVEMENT

When the AFL met in Denver in 1921, several internationals still banned Negroes. Jordan W. Chambers, a Negro delegate, reminded the convention that it had ordered the word "white" stricken out of AFL constitutions. It had also decreed that the international officers meet with Negroes seeking membership. Chambers noted that only a few such conferences had been held and urged stronger action by the AFL. A motion to bar discriminating laws in organized labor, however, failed to win adoption.

The AFL, nevertheless, did order the internationals to confer with Negro unionists within ninety days. In the summer of 1921 the Negro Freight Handlers and Station Employees organized. Negroes also gained admission to other unions. These moves resulted from conferences in Washington and Toronto. The Brotherhood of Railway Carmen agreed to admit separate lodges of Negroes under the jurisdiction of the nearest white local. The AFL thus sanctioned a race barrier among workingmen, however noble the wording of its constitution. In some factories, despite union discrimination, Negro and white workers labored side by side. Such conditions were reported among the longshoremen, the garment workers, the candy makers, the stenographers and a few of the building-trades unions. When the international longshoremen's convention met in Buffalo in July of 1921, some eighty Negro delegates attended. Of these, sixty-five came from the North and fifteen from the South.

Unlike white workers, Negroes were not, as a rule, encouraged to organize. In view of the large part Negroes played in the nation's economic life, that oversight proved costly. AFL indifference led Negro labor to organize for itself, independent of white unionists. A number of national groups formed on such a basis. These included the International Order of Colored Locomotive Firemen, the National Order of Locomotive Firemen, and the Shopmen's Craft of the Railway Men's International and Benevolent Industrial Association. A National Federation of Railway Men also organized in 1921 in Birmingham, Alabama. Later that year in the same city Negro delegates met from fifteen states and twenty-six railroads. Among the gathering were labor spokesmen from 150 international trade unions. It should be remembered, however, that all of these Negro unions still had only "auxiliary" status in the AFL.

Radicalism made new inroads among Negro laborers, for the declarations of the Soviet labor congresses seemed to ring true on racial issues. The Industrial Workers of the World (the IWW), which had become the spokesman of the political left, boasted 100,000 Negroes on its rolls. The Fourth Congress of the Third Internationale, for instance, declared in 1922 that its purpose was "not simply the organization of the enslaved white workers of Europe and America, but equally the organization of the oppressed colored peoples of the World." And it vowed "to fight for . . . equality . . . with the white people . . . for equal wages and political and social rights."

The attraction of radicalism became noticeable in the American Negro Labor Congress of 1925. When the Congress met in Chicago in October, it attacked organized labor in unmistakably Marxist terms: "The failure of the American Federation of Labor officialdom, under pressure of race prejudice benefitting only the capitalists of the North and South, to stamp out race hatred in the unions, to organize Negro workers, and to build a solid front of the workers of both races against American capitalism, is a crime against the whole working class."

The Congress added that "if the unions of the American Federation of Labor, through ignorance and prejudice, fail in this duty to the American workers and continue a policy of exclusion in the face of the influx of Negro workers into industry, we Negro workers must organize our own unions as a powerful weapon with which to fight our way into the existing labor movement on a basis of full equality."

The American Negro Labor Congress was sponsored by the leftist Workers Party of America (which was later to affiliate with the African Blood Brotherhood). With its appeal on the basis of racial equality, there was little doubt that the group would gain a following among Negroes. If the conservative old-line labor unions would not accept the offer of cooperation, Negro labor would find its own way to organize. A. Philip Randolph demonstrated this by forming the Brotherhood of Sleeping Car Porters. In spite of opposition from the Pullman Company and apathy within the ranks of the porters, it became the most successful of the Negro unions. Within two years, most Pullman car porters were union members. The Pullman Company refused to recognize the union, however. It suggested an employee representation plan instead. The porters threatened a strike in 1928, but the Pullman Company averted it through concessions. The following year the porters won an AFL federal charter for their union.

A. PHILIP RANDOLPH

THE NEGRO PROFESSIONAL

A continually growing portion of educated Negroes entered business, draining top talent and industry from the Negro schools, churches and social agencies which had been the main repositories of Negro brain power heretofore. After this shift in objectives became clear, one could observe in each large Negro center a sizeable number rising to commanding positions in business life. The Negro had learned that one of his chief hopes was to develop economically from within.

The ranks of Negro professionals showed a marked increase between 1920 and 1930. The rate of upsurge here—69 per cent during the decade—more than doubled the 31 per cent increase of the 1910-1920 period. Negro technicians in chemistry and in metallurgy joined those fields at twice the rate of whites. Negro engineers also outpaced their white counterparts as newcomers to mining, electrical, civil and mechanical specialties. Fewer Negro physicians graduated from medical schools than in the previous decade, yet at the same time the number of Negro dentists grew. The numbers of librarians, social workers, artists and musicians also showed gains. The number of Negro actors increased by over 100 per cent, about the same growth rate that occurred among Negro college professors. Clergymen and lawyers also showed an upswing during the 1920's.

The Census Bureau reported in 1939 that Negroes operated nearly 30,000 retail stores, employed almost 43,000 workers and topped $71 million in sales. They ran restaurants, food stores, fuel and ice businesses, automobile sales shops, barber shops, and many other kinds of retail establishments.

The Negro cosmetic business was controlled largely by two women. Anne E. Malone of St. Louis manufactured Poro College Products, including the "Wonderful Hair Grower." Madame C. J. Walker of Indianapolis, whose hair straightener and cosmetic products built a large company, left a fortune to her heirs. Two other firms, Overton Hygienic Company of Chicago and Apex Company of Atlantic City, also conducted businesses with gross incomes in millions of dollars. The Depression had its effect on these companies, but losses here were not nearly so severe as those incurred by other Negro-owned businesses.

MADAME C. J. WALKER

THE DEPRESSION

During the terms of GOP Presidents Warren Harding and Calvin Coolidge, the United States enjoyed an unparalleled business boom. The automobile industry grew steadily. The radio rose in popularity. The new rayon manufacturing plants hired thousands of workers. Chain stores came into their own as farming production increased. Mining and manufacturing formed a firm base for national prosperity—or so it appeared to the Wall Street speculators. Borrowing on "margin" to finance new business ventures, they watched the inflated dollar rise in a dizzying spiral. Some economists issued dire warnings that the boom could not survive without government controls. But they went unheeded. Harding, Coolidge and Secretary of Commerce Herbert Hoover, who became President in 1929, believed in a market unfettered by regulation. Then, on October 29, 1929, came the stock market crash and the Great Depression. Businesses closed. Mines shut down. Banks failed. Workers were without jobs and without cash. The "chicken in every pot" which President Hoover had promised

A Negro owned and operated business in the South—a barber shop in Oxford, North Carolina.

before entering the White House became a grim joke to the hungry millions.

Negroes, some of whom had shared in the national prosperity of the Roaring Twenties, were the hardest hit. By 1934, 26 per cent were jobless, compared with 17 per cent unemployment among whites. Most attempts to organize labor proved futile. A. Philip Randolph and Chandler Owen had formed the National Association of Labor Unionism among Negroes in the twenties, only to see their efforts fail during the Depression's bleak years.

Farmers still suffered from the recession of 1920. The rising cost of manufactured goods worsened their plight. And the masses of American Negroes were still employed in farming. Both in the cities and on the farms, hundreds of thousands of families were reduced to living in crude shanty communities—"Hoovervilles," as the bitter, jobless masses called them.

Negro banks, in particular, met with disaster during the Depression. The Metropolitan Bank and Trust Company (Norfolk, Virginia), the Prudential Bank (Washington, D.C.), the Douglass National Bank (Chicago)—all closed their doors after the crash. When this happened it ensured the failure of other Negro financial ventures. The Victory Life Insurance Company—after doing business in fourteen states—reorganized but existed for only a short while longer. The National Benefit Life Insurance Company had operations in twenty-eight states. It failed in 1933. Lower wages and unemployment meant that people were not buying insurance.

Many Negroes were forced to live in crudely built shanties.

Negro workers suffered great setbacks in the Depression. The willingness of white workers to take jobs hitherto reserved for Negroes forced many black laborers onto public relief. In Chicago, Cleveland and St. Louis—the large industrial centers—Negroes accounted for up to 50 per cent of the jobless totals. At least 75 per cent of all Negro workers in Birmingham, Alabama—the steel-making center of the South—were out of work. Roughly 80 per cent of all Negro workers in St. Louis were either unemployed or in jobs far below their abilities. Mechanization, crop reduction and eviction were forces which combined against the Negro sharecroppers and tenant farmers. From an overall point of view the Depression was more severe for the Negro than for the white.

SHARECROPPING AND TENANT FARMING

As the Depression dragged on, the percentage of tenant farmers increased greatly. Yet among Negroes this shift was barely noticeable by the 1930's. The large proportion of Negro tenant farmers remained about the same for most of the period between 1900 and 1935.

Bigotry made the poor Negro farmer's lot even harder than that of the white southern sharecropper or tenant farmer. Unlike white farmers, Negroes had no access to the usual sources of credit. Thus, the landlord was expected to furnish seed and fertilizer as well as subsistence credit. In turn, the landlord received a share of the crop. He usually placed a lien upon the crop as security for the credit advanced to the sharecropper. Over the years the landlord's books invariably showed the tenants' increasing indebtedness. "Even when croppers and share tenants clear anything on the year's farming," one investigator noted, "they usually exhaust their resources within a few months and are destitute again at the beginning of the crop year." Thus the tenant farmers became virtual serfs in a system similar to medieval feudalism.

But by 1940 land ownership had risen among Negro farmers to 21 per cent; sharecropping was reduced by one-fourth. Establishing and maintaining credit remained a problem, even for the middle class farmer. Merchants were the main

Economic conditions forced Negroes back to the white man's fields.

sources of credit, at prices far above the market rate. Interest rates ran the gamut—sometimes soaring as high as 100 per cent.

Two added factors deeply disturbed Negro farmers. One was the shift of cotton culture to the Southwest—to Texas and New Mexico. Negroes who wanted to follow this path of migration were frustrated by Mexicans and southern whites who competed against them for the right to work the new plantation land. A second factor was farm mechanization. The use of tractors, the mechanical cotton picker and other farm machinery helped bar unskilled Negro labor. Farming with machinery had become skilled work. It was regarded as a white man's job. Just how much displacement occurred as a result of the machine cannot be ascertained, but it has been the basis of much speculation.

Farm land had fallen more and more under corporate control. A survey of forty-six southern counties in 1934 showed that corporations held one-tenth of the farm land.

Other factors slowed the advance of Negro farmers. Some seemed insurmountable, for example the indolence resulting from malnutrition and apathy due to the bleak life on the farm. In addition to the one-crop system, Negro workers were victimized by mob law and lynching and the old scourges of southern farming—seasonal labor and the boll weevil.

ROOSEVELT AND THE NEW DEAL

A dismal economic picture faced President Roosevelt as he took office on March 4, 1933. American industry in 1932 had operated at less than half its maximum volume of 1929. Total wages paid in 1932 were 60 per cent less than in 1929. American business had run a net loss of more than five billion dollars; well over twelve million Americans were jobless. In towns which relied upon industry, whole populaces were reduced to wards of society. But the President came into office with a cheerful resolution. "The only thing we have to fear is fear itself," he had said in his inaugural speech. By spring of 1933 Roosevelt had begun his series of morale-building radio addresses, his "fireside chats." He named Harold L. Ickes, the president of the Chicago NAACP, as secretary of the interior. Speaking to the Federal Council of Churches, Roosevelt recalled Lincoln's phrase "freedom to the free." Having earlier denounced lynching, the President told the NAACP: "No democracy can long survive which does not accept as fundamental to its very existence the recognition of the rights of its minorities." The President's wife Eleanor stood firmly behind her husband in this conviction. Mrs. Roosevelt devoted herself tirelessly to improving welfare and human rights programs.

During 1933 and 1934 the federal government abandoned its former laissez-faire philosophy toward business. Roosevelt embraced the economic theories of England's John Maynard Keynes. They required a planned economy— in these hard times, much more federal deficit spending. A host of federal agencies was created by Congress during Roosevelt's first months in office. This busy legislative period—known as "the one hundred days"—prepared to tackle the massive rebuilding task. Its programs included the Civil Works Administration (CWA), the Public Works Administration (PWA), the Civilian Conservation Corps (CCC) and the Works Projects Administration (WPA).

The Roosevelt program, called the New Deal, helped stem the tide of the Depression. Yet even the massive make-work projects under the WPA, which helped millions of families, ultimately failed to bring about a full national recovery, and huge federal debts were incurred to pay for these extensive measures of relief. All these programs were authorized under the National Recovery Act which created the National Recovery Administration (NRA). This agency drafted and acted as overseer for a series of codes to set market prices and limit commerce. When President Roosevelt asked Congress in 1935 to extend the emergency acts for two more years, it countered by granting only a ten month extension.

In the meantime, Congress was writing new social-reform laws. It passed the Social Security Act in 1935—two decades after the income tax was adopted. Though critics attacked such measures as "creeping socialism," these policies did help to stabilize the nation in its darkest hour. For more than one million needy Negroes the Roosevelt crash program was a welcome approach.

GOVERNMENT AID TO FARMERS

The sorely pressed farmers received some federal relief during the Depression, but the prospect of aid to Negro farmers raised a new issue. Congress had created the Federal Farm Board in 1929, but it had offered little help to Negro farms under the Hoover administration.

William S. Scarborough, president of Wilberforce University, was among several men appointed to a Negro commission established as an arm of the Federal Farm Board. Although these men conducted studies and made local investigations, no help was forthcoming to aid the plight of the Negro farmer.

Under the New Deal two new farm loan agencies were created, the Regional Agricultural Credit Corporation and the Federal Land Banks. But they aided few farmers of either race. The agencies did manage to relieve the South's credit system, though not on a large scale.

The Agriculture Department's county extension workers showed many Negro farmers how to improve their crop production as well as how to diversify their crops. Yet these agents—including some 416 Negroes in 1937-38—were far too few to achieve a large-scale solution to the black farmers' problems.

HAROLD L. ICKES

FRANKLIN D. ROOSEVELT

The Civilian Conservation Corps (CCC) attracted many young Negroes in search of employment.

The Agricultural Adjustment Administration (AAA) introduced federal production curbs to the farmer. It controlled crop harvests of wheat, corn, cotton, rice and tobacco, as well as livestock and other crops. Farmers were paid cash subsidies to restrict the acreage for their crops or to reduce their livestock. The AAA, seeking to reduce crop acreage, aimed at providing a controlled harvest at controlled price levels. The farmer was expected to benefit from this planned approach. Yet the AAA program scarcely helped the Negro farmer. Many tenants and farm laborers were made expendable by the acreage reduction. Though federal contracts with employers stated that tenants should not be laid off, evictions and displacements were commonplace. Thousands of Negro tenants became jobless. Many could not secure relief checks. Fraud and dishonesty also occurred in payment of parity checks. Tenants reported that they never received their checks. When the government made crop payments directly to farm workers, their status improved. But such justice seldom prevailed.

THE NEW DEAL AND DISCRIMINATION

The NRA, functioning under its Blue Eagle emblem since 1933, attracted criticism from many quarters. Some viewed it as a way for workers to enjoy an easy living without engaging in legitimate work. Others charged that it failed to improve the workers' lot; still others noted the widespread abuse of the NRA's code in the South, where the minimum wage scale was regarded as "too much money for Negroes." NRA relief measures did aid many thousands, but they were of little help in easing racial bigotry.

The adoption of codes under the National Recovery Administration promised better times, but they did not appear soon. Attempting a system of equality, the NRA divided all the nation's work force by jobs and geography. This regional and occupational quota system served unwittingly to remove many southern black workers from minimum-wage and maximum-hour statutes.

A united front of all Negro groups was proposed in mid-1933 by the Negro Industrial League. This unit had sought equal treatment of Negroes under the industrial codes. Under John W. Davis, its executive secretary, and Dr. Robert C. Weaver, its director of research, the League had advised the Roosevelt administration in keeping with its aim "to establish a group of fact finders in Washington to study the plans of the federal government for recovery and to seek to integrate the Negro into such plans." The Joint Committee on National Recovery formed in the fall of 1933 toward this end. It spoke for twenty-two national "member organizations."

The committee studied the announcements, press releases, proposed codes and executive orders which flowed daily from the National Recovery Administration. It appeared publicly before committees of Congress, filed protests and legal briefs, and fed news releases to the Negro press. The panel's careful checking paid off in one respect. The White House soon saw the ·NRA's effect on Negro workers. Dr. Clark Foreman was named the agency's adviser on Negro affairs as a result, and Dr. Weaver became his assistant.

An administrative order banned discrimination in the Works Progress Administration

ROBERT C. WEAVER

"on any ground whatsoever, such as race, religion or political affiliation." Forrester B. Washington of the Atlanta School of Social Work was named WPA adviser on Negro affairs. After seven months Alfred Edgar Smith succeeded him. Under both Washington and Smith this office dealt mainly with studies. At the time, over a hundred Negroes served in jobs at WPA headquarters in the District of Columbia. Other Negroes held supervisory posts on the WPA's field staffs.

The Farm Security Administration had already set up an office of race relations, headed by Joseph H. B. Evans, to promote racial integration of the federal farm-aid program. By late 1933 the Farm Credit Administration had opened its Negro relations section with Henry A. Hunt in charge. Cornelius King, a Louisianan, later succeeded him.

THE CONGRESS OF INDUSTRIAL ORGANIZATIONS

The Wagner Act of 1935 had set rules for collective bargaining, and the Fair Labor Standards Act of 1938 established wage guidelines. Both laws were regarded as major victories for the labor movement. A new leader had entered the labor scene in the meantime. The forceful John L. Lewis, president of the United Mine Workers, had formed the Congress of Industrial Organizations (CIO) in 1935.

The CIO began as a committee of the AFL. But it was an industrial union, not a craft union. It assembled the unskilled and semi-skilled under its wing.

When the AFL refused to pursue a more liberal recruiting policy, including seeking more unskilled laborers for unionization, Lewis and his newly formed committee pulled out of the predominantly craft union federation. Their activities were concentrated in areas where no unions existed, or where there were large numbers of unskilled workers who, although unionized, had no national affiliation. From the start, the policies of the CIO were nonrestrictive where Negroes were concerned. The garment workers, composed of two separate unions, had long included Negroes in their midst; the longshore-

men on the West Coast, headed by Harry Bridges, not only urged Negroes to be unionized but also made certain that no one was discriminated against because of race or color.

Only in the South was the Negro still forced to remain in all-black unions under CIO jurisdiction. This was due to the attitude of the southern laborer, who refused to fraternize with Negroes in unions. But even in the South the CIO organizers were eventually successful in breaking down some barriers, and the formation of its Committee to Abolish Racial Discrimination aided the CIO toward that end.

When Willard Townsend, president of the newly formed International Brotherhood of Redcaps, received permission for his union to enter the ranks of the CIO, he became the first black national officer in organized labor. Elected an international vice-president in 1940, Townsend became a motivating force behind complete integration in the labor movement. Townsend's administrative assistant, George L. P. Weaver, went to the CIO national headquarters to become permanent secretary of the Committee to Abolish Racial Discrimination.

GEORGE L. P. WEAVER

The National Labor Relations Board, an outgrowth of the Wagner Act, served further to eliminate discrimination among laborers because it protected the right to form unions in the many industries. Thus the United Auto Workers, an arm of the CIO, gained jurisdiction over the automobile industry in Detroit and was largely responsible for the inclusion of Negroes in jobs requiring skilled labor.

In some instances, however, Negroes were reluctant to join unions for fear of repercussions on their jobs. Many shared a distrust of the national unions based on past experience. The presence of Townsend on the national governing board of the CIO undoubtedly served as an inducement to other Negroes to join, as well as reassurance that the unions were acting in their behalf.

The initial involvement with the unions on the part of more skeptical members of the Negro working class soon convinced them that unionization meant job security and better wages. Furthermore, the open racial policies of the CIO motivated the AFL to place more pressure on some of its affiliates to drop their restrictions or face loss of membership in the national organization.

Between 1935 and 1945 Negro membership in the CIO rose from 180,000 to 1,250,000. Negroes also joined with whites in labor blocs like the Southern Tenant Farmers Union.

For the first time since the Populist movement of the 1890's, black and white linked arms in portions of the rural South, seeking unity for survival. But the Southern Tenant Farmers Union did not succeed in its efforts to force landowners to keep the tenants on the farms where most of the land had been placed in the nonproductive land bank. Instead, as union membership grew, the landowners became more determined to rid themselves of their sharecroppers and tenant farmers. The fact that Negroes had joined forces with poor whites further annoyed landowners. Therefore, the only advantage for Negroes in this new alliance was the hope of continued unity with their white counterparts. But even this failed when, like the Populists before them, the poor whites decided that a black alliance was detrimental to their cause.

BLACK LABOR GAINS

When the Joint Committee on National Recovery met at Howard University in 1935, it decided to found a National Negro Congress. A. Philip Randolph suggested its formation "not only to arouse and fire the brooding masses to action in their own defense, but to attack the forces of reaction that seek to throttle black America with increasing Jim Crowism, segregation and discrimination." The congress met in Chicago in 1936 to organize and name local councils. It held its last conference in 1940, when its leaders seemed bent on radicalism as a means of achieving racial justice. This radical ideology soon brought about the group's demise. The Southern Youth Congress was organized at Richmond in early 1937 and drew a large following. But by 1940 this group had also fallen into leftist hands and had folded.

In some areas, other kinds of tactics were used. St. Louis' local Urban League began a Jobs-for-Negroes campaign in 1931 which led to the boycott of a chain store. The movement spread to other cities. Pickets carried signs with the motto "Don't Buy Where You Can't Work" in front of white stores in Negro districts which refused to hire Negroes. The Rev. Adam Clayton Powell, Jr., led a series of such boycotts in Harlem. Their success made the young Baptist clergyman a political power in Harlem for years to come.

ADAM CLAYTON POWELL, JR.

EXPANDING JOB OPPORTUNITIES

In the spring of 1935 the Supreme Court ended the National Recovery Act, ruling that it violated the Constitution. The decision meant an expanded role for other New Deal agencies. They moved quickly to assume the NRA's program burdens and soon they oversaw such Depression statutes as the Wages and Hours Act. Both the Works Progress Administration and the Public Works Administration carried the majority of the responsibilities.

More than a million Negro breadwinners made their livelihood through WPA projects, according to federal estimates. For the first time, thousands of Negro women were employed in occupations other than domestic and farm work. Negro men, too, found new horizons in the job market. They worked in areas ranging from mural painting and stage set design to mapmaking and plastering. Negroes accounted for 39 per cent of all WPA personnel in South Carolina and Louisiana, 37 per cent in Georgia and 67 per cent in the District of Columbia.

The WPA organized a number of special projects requiring the talents of writers, musicians, artists, teachers and entertainers. The Negro Theater Project in New York, for instance, employed 232 theater workers in 1936. The Federal Music Project hired others. The Federal Writers Project gave several hundred Negroes a chance to develop their gifts in literature, history, art, music, drama and education. The Federal Art Project encouraged a number of Negro artists whose work is regarded as significant. Thousands of the Depression's victims also gained access to the projects' health, recreation and social centers.

Another New Deal thrust was aimed at Negro youth. Negro staff members sought to develop the special interests of the young. The National Youth Administration, a WPA subsidiary, helped thousands of Negro boys and girls to attend high school and college through its work program. Many out-of-school youths were aided through community centers, libraries and playgrounds. Two Negro educators, Dr. Mordecai W. Johnson and Dr. Mary McLeod Bethune, were made members of the NYA's national advisory committee. Dr. Bethune became director

MORDECAI W. JOHNSON

MARY McLEOD BETHUNE

of the division of Negro affairs; R. O'Hara Lanier served as her assistant.

The NYA believed in "learning to do by doing." It planned a vocational guidance and placement program, so that youth could be aided directly. Scholarships totaling more than $520,000 went to some 113 Negro colleges in 1937-38 alone. Roughly 63,000 Negro youths (ages 16 to 24) benefitted from the program. The NYA's enacting statute required fair distribution of funds without discrimination because of race.

The Civilian Conservation Corps (CCC) trained young Negroes and hired black educational advisers in its camps. At first, it was claimed, Negroes were not accepted in CCC camps in as high a proportion as whites. But as time went on this situation was largely remedied. The camps reported housing 40,000 Negro youths in 1936, as well as 25 medical officers and chaplains, 136 study advisers, 600 business managers and 1,400 chauffeurs. By 1940 the corps included roughly 300,000 Negroes.

A handful of other New Deal agencies also lent a hand to Negroes as well as to whites. The Home Owners' Loan Corporation loaned the funds to forestall mortgage foreclosures. The Federal Housing Authority assisted workers in modernizing their homes. The Reconstruction Finance Corporation granted loans to institutions. The Federal Security Agency also made valuable contributions to the advancement of citizen welfare.

WORKERS IN FEDERAL CIVIL SERVICE

The number of Negroes listed on the Civil Service Commission roster as federal employees from 1933 to 1938 was estimated to have risen from fifty thousand to eighty-two thousand.

In most cases prior to 1938, Negro workers were assigned to the sub-clerical levels as janitors, porters and messengers. This occurred even under the competitive Civil Service Commission ratings. Certain presidential patronage positions had been lost to them under new rulings, as any one of three top eligibles tested could be selected for a job. This became discriminatory when officials harbored racial prejudice. Some jobs were denied to Negroes by tradition or agreement. Such barriers worked as effectively as explicit orders.

Departmental racial segregation had been sanctioned by some federal officials. The humiliation felt by many Negro applicants resulted in a decline of black workers by 1930. The ratio of Negro bureaucrats was usually far below that expected. Many white workers voiced complaints when assigned to work under black supervisors. This attitude changed radically with the passage of time.

One method used by the government to bring about fair treatment of Negroes has been mentioned earlier: the naming of Negro advisers to federal agencies. This policy first appeared in the 1917 appointment of Dr. Emmett J. Scott as confidential adviser to the secretary of war on matters affecting the interests of Negro citizens. Scott had been secretary to Dr. Booker T. Washington at Tuskegee Institute. A second step was taken shortly afterward when Dr. George E. Haynes of Fisk University became director of Negro economics in the Department of Labor. The appointments of Drs. Foreman and Weaver were the first under the New Deal, and were the nucleus of a loose coalition of Negro

EMMETT J. SCOTT

advisers who became known as Roosevelt's "Black Cabinet." Others were later added to smooth over racial problems in agency programs. The value of these advisers remains open to dispute. Nonetheless, their very presence called attention to the roadblocks facing Negro workers.

Two other Negroes, James C. Carter of Georgia and Clifton R. Wharton of Massachusetts, served the Roosevelt administration in the consular and diplomatic service. Lester A. Walton represented the nation as minister to Liberia, and William C. George was the United States vice-consul there. Even so, the number of Negro diplomats had declined since Theodore Roosevelt's last term. Eleven Negroes had been foreign service envoys in 1908. By 1938, there were only three.

HOUSING AND RESETTLEMENT

Slums had proliferated in the nation's cities as a result of overcrowding. Low-cost housing projects built by the Public Works Administration relieved these conditions somewhat. The

CLIFTON R. WHARTON

A migrant worker's tailoring and cleaning shop.

plans for these developments called for Negro management staffs and reduced rentals. By 1936 some thirty-five major cities had opened low-rent housing projects for Negroes at a cost of $130,000,000. The building contracts aided the labor situation by granting jobs to skilled Negroes in proportion to their number in the 1930 census. Negro architects, builders and contractors were hired to plan and construct the housing projects. Dr. Robert C. Weaver helped oversee these policies as special assistant to the administrator of the Federal Housing Authority.

The South grudgingly accepted the federal outlook on hiring Negroes. Several rural resettlement projects were launched—at Bricks, North Carolina; Orangeburg, South Carolina; Tuskegee, Alabama; and in Phillips County, Arkansas —which hired qualified Negroes for the work force.

Other projects followed these early ones. By 1937, nine resettlement projects embraced roughly one thousand families at a cost exceeding $7,700,000. When the Tennessee Valley Authority (TVA) opened its model homes for workers at Norris Dam, it admitted that Negroes would be barred because "they did not fit into the program." Negroes were gradually hired on the project, however. Investigators later found that the pay scale was proportionately lower for Negroes than for whites. They also noted the poor conditions under which Negroes worked, and the discrimination in housing assignment.

GAINS AND LOSSES

Although Negro workers made some gains toward employment under the New Deal, many obstacles remained in their way.

Private industry's rehiring of Negroes taken off WPA rolls moved very slowly. Negroes were seldom able to find steady work with adequate pay. The National Urban League's annual report for 1936 stated that most Negroes who returned to private firms found work in the basic industries—rubber, packing, iron and steel and the railroads—but seldom did these industries hire more Negroes than had worked for them prior to the Depression.

As usual, a significant factor in Negro unemployment was the substitution of white for Negro labor. This trend jeopardized the jobs of Negro hotel workers, waiters, elevator operators and bellboys. Racist groups were organized with the sole purpose of driving Negroes from jobs regarded as desirable for white workers. Leaders of the Black Shirts and former members of the Ku Klux Klan made speeches declaring that they loathed Negroes "that held jobs of white men" and "who were usurping the white man's rightful place." Through the years, Negro workers found it harder to get jobs as well as to keep them. Discrimination, low wages, the barrier against skilled Negro workers and continued joblessness gave rise to the slogan black labor applied to itself, "Last hired, first fired."

CHAPTER TWELVE

World War II, Korea and Vietnam— The Military Integrates

SINCE the end of World War I, War Department policy had kept down the level of Negro enlistments in the armed forces. Until 1939, the regular army included only four Negro regiments —the 9th and 10th Cavalry and the 24th and 25th Infantry. Two quartermaster companies were added in 1939. A year later the army added Negro units in field artillery, antiaircraft, chemical warfare and engineering.

At the time, the regular army of 230,000 officers and enlisted men included only 4,450 Negroes. Of the five black officers, three were chaplains. Eleven warrant officers had volunteered for service, but army policy prevented their acceptance.

Prior to the outbreak of World War II, the navy counted 2,800 Negroes in its 116,000-man department—but not a single Negro officer. Many naval and military officials felt at the war's outset that, despite the Negro's earlier service record, he would make a poor soldier or sailor. But as the racist Adolf Hitler and his German blitzkrieg began methodically overrunning Europe in 1939, Negro leaders demanded, and got, a change in policy toward black enlistees.

SELECTIVE SERVICE AND THE NEGRO

Congress required in the Selective Service Act of 1940 that military training and service should be shared by young men of all races. No color discrimination would be permitted. The system of induction would be "fair and equitable." Selective service boards were formed to carry out the act. More than 1,800 Negroes served as members of local registrants' advisory boards, boards of appeal and medical advisory boards and as examining physicians and clerks. By September, 1941, nearly forty thousand Negroes had volunteered for army service and been inducted by selective service.

"Negroes have been notably a loyal and patriotic group," the first report of the Selective Service System stated. "One of their outstanding characteristics is the single-mindedness of their patriotism. They have no other country to which they owe or feel any allegiance. They have neither cultural nor economic ties with kindred in any other lands. Therefore they have built in

America a fine record of loyalty and willingness to support and defend their native land."

Colonel Campbell C. Johnson, a Negro, was named assistant to the director of selective service. Colonel Johnson had served as an officer during World War I and later had headed Howard University's ROTC program. A lawyer, he had also worked as executive secretary of the Washington Negro YMCA. He directed the racial relations division of the Selective Service System under General Lewis B. Hershey.

As more and more men were called up, the number of Negroes drafted rose steadily. The count increased from 2,069 in 1940 to over 103,000 in 1941 and nearly 371,000 in 1942. Before the end of 1943, nearly 102,000 Negroes were in the navy, 12,400 in the marine corps and 3,500 in the coast guard. The total number of Negro fighting men was about 920,000— with 850 serving in the officer ranks. Some 200,000 were deployed overseas.

CAMPBELL C. JOHNSON

SEGREGATION IN THE ARMED FORCES

The congressional attitude as expressed in the 1940 Selective Service Act brought strong pressure to bear on the War Department. The public had become increasingly aware of the common practice of segregation and discrimination in the armed forces.

Of the 140,000 enlisted men in the navy during 1940, only about 4,000 were Negroes. All of these were confined exclusively to cooking and meal service details. Immediately after the Japanese attack on Pearl Harbor, the number of Negroes accepted into the navy increased, although no change was made in their status: Negroes could still serve only as messmen. Ironically enough, a Negro navy messman was to become America's first hero of World War II.

Dorie Miller, a first-class messman on the *U.S.S. West Virginia*, received the Navy Cross from Admiral Chester W. Nimitz for valor displayed during the Japanese air attack on Pearl Harbor. The Negro seaman removed his wounded captain from the bridge and, although untrained as a gunner, returned to man an antiaircraft gun and to down four enemy planes. Miller was later reported among those missing when the *Liscombe Bay* was sunk in the Pacific with her entire crew.

Although his action at Pearl Harbor has been described as "perhaps the only American victory on that day," it resulted in little personal victory for Dorie Miller. When the *Liscombe Bay* went down, the young sailor still stood at his former rank.

The marine corps had long made a practice of excluding Negroes from their ranks. The same practice existed in the army tank, signal, engineer and artillery corps. After the appearance of Congressman Hamilton Fish's anti-bias clause in the 1940 Selective Service Act, stating that "there shall be no discrimination against any person on account of race or color," the marine corps began to admit its first Negroes. Then the War Department announced that it would accept Negroes as aviator trainees, and the officer candidate schools began to receive Negroes in unsegregated units.

DORIE MILLER

SEGREGATION REAFFIRMED

Within a month of the passage of the act, however, the War Department issued a statement which openly defied its directives by reaffirming the old pattern of segregated military units. The military's policy, it said, "is not to intermingle colored and white enlisted personnel in the same regimental organizations. This policy has been proved satisfactory over a long period of years and to make changes would produce situations destructive to morale and detrimental to preparations for national defense."

Servicemen of both races petitioned against the race barrier. Over a hundred thousand signed their names to a request to form voluntarily integrated units. The petitions were refused, however, and a dual registration system—one for blacks and one for whites—was introduced under the selective service in many states.

The same racial wall appeared in military recreation and social service programs. White officers reinforced these differences through orders and directives. As a result, the morale of both races suffered. Separate transportation carried soldiers from one camp to another—a new source of friction. Riots occurred in Louisiana,

Georgia and North Carolina. The humiliation which led to these outbreaks is described vividly in the following account.

> Nine of us, all colored soldiers, were on our way . . . to the hospital at Fort Huachuca, Arizona. After having been crowded like cattle in one coach from Alexandria, Louisiana, we arrived [but] had to wait for our train for about twelve hours. We went to the "colored" USO, slept overnight and returned . . . next morning—nine sick American soldiers. We could not purchase a cup of coffee at any place around the station. The only place that would serve us was the lunch room at the station. But we couldn't eat where the white people were eating. To do that would contaminate the very air of the place, so we had to go to the kitchen. . . . About 11:30 the same morning, about two dozen German prisoners of war came into the lunchroom with two guards. They entered the large room, sat at the table. Their meals were served them. They smoked and had a swell time. As we stood on the outside and saw what was going on, we could scarcely believe our own eyes. They were enemies of our country, people sworn to destroy all the so-called democratic governments of the world. . . . What are we fighting for?

Military segregation proved unusually difficult for northern Negro soldiers stationed in the South. These servicemen were insulted, arrested, beaten and injured, while the army took no measures to protect them. The ensuing tensions resulted in riots in several cities. The worst of these broke out in Detroit in 1943. President Roosevelt found it necessary to declare an emergency and sent federal troops to quell the disturbance. In 1945 a severe riot occurred at Camp Polk, Louisiana, where Negro servicemen had become outraged by displays of prejudice.

The public became aware of such incidents and registered a series of protests. They soon had the desired impact. The navy announced that it would plan an experiment in which the races would be integrated. A Negro crew was placed on board the *U.S.S. Mason* in February of 1944, and the plan was successful. In another test, a larger number of Negroes was added to a naval crew. The navy, convinced by the results, ended segregation of crews in July 1944. By August, twenty-five auxiliary ships were integrated, with Negroes accounting for 10 per cent of the crews. Secretary of the Navy James Forrestal took the final step in a February, 1946, circular.

"All restrictions governing the types of assignments for which Negro personnel are eligible are hereby lifted," the Forrestal letter declared. "In the utilization of housing, messing, and other facilities, no special provisions will be made for the accommodation of Negroes."

Still, segregation extended through all units of the army during World War II. Negroes served in all-black regiments in Europe. Both at home and abroad they felt the sting of racial bigotry. William H. Hastie, a Negro civilian aide to the secretary of war, resigned in disgust in January 1943. The War Department was hesitating at the time over its racial policy. Hastie informed Secretary of War Henry Stimson that he had "no alternate but to resign in protest and to give public expression to my views.

"I have believed," Hastie explained, "that there remain areas in which changes of racial policy should be made but will not be made in response to the advocacy within the Department but only as a result of strong and manifest public opinion. I have believed that some of these changes involve questions of sincerity and depth of our devotion to the basic issues of this war, and thus have an important bearing, both on the fighting spirit of our own people and upon our ability as a nation to maintain leadership in the struggle for a free world."

A year after Hastie's resignation from the War Department, Robert C. Weaver stepped down as chief of the minority group service of the War Production Board. Dr. Weaver had served as race relations officer in the Department of the Interior and as special assistant in the Federal Housing Administration.

The first Negro to be made a general in the army was Benjamin O. Davis, elevated to that rank in 1940. In 1944 his son, Benjamin O. Davis, Jr., West Point's fourth Negro graduate, was promoted to colonel. Colonel Davis had transferred to the army air corps in 1942, where he was named commander of the 99th Fighter Squadron at Tuskegee and then ordered to North Africa. He later served in the Italian war zone. Colonel Davis and eighty-eight of his pilots were awarded the Distinguished Flying Cross.

The navy began to admit Negroes into its officer corps in 1942. Bernard W. Robinson was the first of his race to be appointed an ensign.

WILLIAM H. HASTIE   BENJAMIN O. DAVIS, SR.   BENJAMIN O. DAVIS, JR.

Two members of the Negro crew of the U.S.S. Mason.

Negro women also enlisted in naval service as WAVES. Harriet Pickens and Frances Wills were commissioned as officers in 1944.

The navy, marines and coast guard actively recruited Negroes beginning in 1940, but units would still be segregated, even when new branches of the service and new kinds of duty opened up.

The navy launched the *Booker T. Washington* in 1942 with Captain Hugh Mulzac, a Negro, in command. Mulzac had attended the shipping board school in New York and served as second mate on ships engaged in transporting war materials during World War I. He passed the officers' examination in 1920, but Negroes were then denied ensign status. He remained a second mate. When his appointment finally came, he was told that his crew would all be Negro. Mulzac refused to accept under these conditions. His stand had its effect, and he was allowed to take the best men available, regardless of race.

Mulzac's pride in having won his post despite the prejudices which had held him back for so long is movingly revealed in his own words.

"Everything I ever was, stood for, fought for, dreamed of, came into focus that day," he said. "The concrete evidence of the achievement gives one's strivings legitimacy, proves that the ambitions were valid, the struggle worthwhile. Being prevented for those twenty-four years from doing the work for which I was trained had robbed life of its most essential meaning. Now at last I could use my training and capabilities fully. It was like being born anew."

SEGREGATION AND BLOOD BANKS

In the meantime, the American Red Cross defended its practice of maintaining two sets of stored blood—one for whites and one for Negroes. White patients were to receive blood from white donors only, and Negroes would receive only Negroes' donated blood. Ironically, a Negro doctor finally proved that blood does not differ according to race, and showed that the old blood storage system was senseless. Dr. Charles Drew, chief surgeon at Freedmen's Hospital in Washington, D.C., took leave to study blood plasma at the Columbia University Medical School. He found a way to preserve the plasma in blood banks for emergency use, a discovery of inestimable value in wartime. Dr. Drew organized a blood collection service for Great Britain and the United States which saved countless lives of both soldiers and civilians. Dr. Drew's methods are still used today.

With tragic irony, Dr. Drew's own death resulted when a "white" hospital refused to admit him for an emergency blood transfusion after he was injured in an automobile accident.

ENLISTMENTS GROW

By mid-1942, Negroes were graduating from the three-month officers' training schools at the rate of two hundred per month. Black officers quickly increased from five thousand to more than seventy-five hundred. The latter figure included a brigadier general and thirty-four colonels and lieutenant colonels.

Nearly seven hundred black physicians and dentists had been inducted into the military by 1945. Among these was Major Hildrus A. Poindexter, professor of bacteriology at Howard University Medical School. He received the Bronze Star for his work in reducing malaria in the Solomon Islands. The officers' corps also included 144 Negro chaplains in 1943. The army's schools trained both officers and enlisted men of all races in languages, medicine, technology, and mathematics. By the war's end, Negroes held responsible posts in almost every branch of the army.

In 1948 Secretary of Defense James Forrestal invited sixteen Negro leaders to meet with the heads of the military branches assigned to Negro recruitment and training. The meeting led to a new recognition of the Negro as a soldier.

A Defense Department aide, civilian assistant James C. Evans, oversaw racial policy in the army, navy, marines and air force. Hundreds of complaints crossed his desk for investigation, and in 1953 Evans received the Dorie Miller Foundation Award for his work. The Defense Department cited him in 1956 for "his outstanding contribution . . . in the field of racial relations."

JAMES C. EVANS

CHARLES DREW

Captain Hugh Mulzac (front row, third from right) poses with crew members after the Liberty Ship Booker T. Washington *completed its maiden voyage to England.*

WHITE HOUSE ACTION

President Roosevelt approached the race issue with promising decisiveness. His famous Executive Order 8802 had not only banned race bias in defense contracts but had authorized a Fair Employment Practices Committee to be named by the President. Roosevelt had been prodded by A. Philip Randolph, who threatened in 1941 to lead a march on Washington protesting discrimination. Unlike other protests, it was planned as an all-Negro move. During FEPC's first year, it investigated conditions in Los Angeles, Chicago, New York, Washington and Birmingham. At stake were policies in forty-nine industries, unions and defense training programs. Three of every four complaints involved discrimination against Negroes. Another 10 per cent involved bias against Jews. The rest dealt with other minorities. But the committee had no authority to go beyond persuasion, and its work was ineffective in achieving long-range results. President Roosevelt later signed a second executive order granting more sweeping powers. It created a second committee empowered to combat discrimination as well as to hold hearings. Foes in Congress cut its budget, however, and employers remained defiant.

THE TRUMAN EXECUTIVE ORDER

In the late 1940's Secretary of Defense George C. Marshall observed that Negroes improved in military effectiveness as the importance of their duties increased. His views buttressed the landmark Executive Order 9981 signed by President Truman in July of 1948. It declared that "there shall be equality and opportunity for all persons in the armed services without regard to race, color, religion or national origin" in order to maintain "the highest standards of democracy."

Truman also created the President's Committee on Equality of Treatment and Opportunity in the Armed Services "to examine the rules, procedures, and practices of the armed services in order to determine in what respect such rules, procedures and practices may be altered or improved with a view to carrying out the policy of this order."

The committee was headed by Charles Fahy of Georgia. Its seven members made extensive field trips and held more than forty hearings before issuing their report, *Freedom To Serve,* in 1950. It made several key observations and recommendations.

Among its specific suggestions, the committee urged the navy to give chief stewards the rank of chief petty officer. The navy did so. But it continued its separate recruitment policy until 1954. The marines ended their separate training units in 1949, the same year the air force opened all training and jobs to all servicemen.

The committee suggested a cautious approach in following up the Truman policy, "Reforms would be more readily accepted and make headway faster," It said, "if they represented decisions mutually agreed upon. Imposed decisions can be enforced by discipline, but joint decisions engage the loyalty of those who have concerted them."

Truman continued to champion civil-rights causes, even risking his political career by doing so.

In the meantime, the army had set up a three-man board of inquiry under Lieutenant General Alvan C. Gillem. After three months of study, the board found that the army was making efficient use of its Negroes in segregated units. It favored continuing the racial barriers until another war loomed. In that event, the Gillem panel suggested, the end objective would be use of all manpower "without regard to antecedents or race."

When the Fahy committee studied the Gillem report it described it as seeking "equal treatment and efficient utilization of manpower within a framework that foredoomed the realization of either." The statement was valid since, at the time, the army barred Negroes from 198 of its 490 job specialties. Negroes were not admitted to all army training schools, and Negro enrollment quotas existed in 21 of 106 courses.

The Fahy committee cooperated with the army in seeking to end such restrictions. By spring, 1950, the committee's recommendations had been adopted. But not until General Matthew Ridgway succeeded General Douglas MacArthur in the Korean War did the Defense

Department announce it. Meanwhile the cold war had hastened the erasure of the color line in the armed services. Secretary of Defense Robert A. Lovett could report by 1952 that "the army's policy to reduce the number of units composed of Negro troops and to assign all personnel on the basis of individual proficiencies and needs of the service made encouraging progress." Progress occurred so rapidly that the all-Negro companies were abolished ahead of the 1954 deadline. And Secretary of Defense Charles Wilson was able to state in his official report in 1956 that the changeover had moved forward "without untoward incident."

THE NAVY INTEGRATES

As noted above, Negroes were barred from any branch of the navy's general service. Nor could they become naval fighters or be schooled in the skilled trades taught in the navy, prior to World War II.

In 1942, however, the secretary of the navy announced that Negroes would be accepted as volunteers for general service in the navy, the coast guard and the marine corps. *A Guide to the Command of Negro Naval Personnel* was issued in 1944. It stated that individual performance, not race differences, would be the basis for navy employment. The navy then opened a training station, Camp Robert Small, at the Great Lakes Naval Training Station, as well as one at Hampton, Virginia, where Negroes were trained in many trades.

By the time Japan surrendered in 1945, the number of Negro naval officers had risen in one year from thirteen to sixty. The first Negro graduate of Annapolis, Ensign Wesley A. Brown, was granted his commission in 1949. Among the crew of the first atomic-powered submarine, *Nautilus*, eight of the ninety-nine enlisted men and twelve officers were Negroes.

A Negro marine unit of nine hundred men was formed in 1943 to train in artillery warfare, as well as in radio, electricity, accounting, carpentry and blacksmithing skills. The unit's success led to breaking a 116-year tradition against Negro marine enlistments. By late 1943 some eighty-five hundred Negroes wore marine uni-

WESLEY A. BROWN

forms. And that figure easily doubled within a year. In 1945 the corps commissioned its first Negro officer, Frederick Branch. After the battle for the island of Saipan, the marines' commanding general declared: "The Negro Marines are no longer on trial. They are Marines. *Period.*"

Negroes had served in the nation's coast guard for many years. When World War II began, the guard was expanded and some three hundred Negroes entered the service to train in seamanship, lifesaving and boat handling. A year later, three thousand Negroes had joined the coast guard. The guard's first Negro officer, Ensign Joseph C. Jenkins, was commissioned in 1942 and assigned as an engineering officer in Boston.

Between 1940 and 1941 thirty-one thousand Negroes served in the merchant marine, and soon many were commissioned officers. Four Negroes assumed command of the so-called Liberty Ships—troop transports and freighters of the merchant marine—during World War II: Captains Hugh Mulzac, Adrian T. Richardson, John Godfrey and Clifton Fostic.

Fourteen Liberty Ships were christened after black leaders. Four merchant marine ships were named for Negro naval heroes who lost their lives during the war.

Negro and white servicemen study together at the United States
Naval Training Station at Hampton, Virginia.

JOHN GODFREY

The John Hope was one of fourteen Liberty Ships named for Negro leaders.

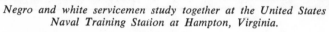

NEGRO ENGINEER AND OTHER SERVICE UNITS

The first Negro army troops landed at Dakar, Senegal, in the summer of 1942. They were the 41st Engineer Regiment, known as "the Swinging Engineers." The troops were to serve under an agreement with Liberia by which the United States was given the right to build, control, operate and defend airports in Liberia. The United States was to grant $1 million in lend-lease aid, undertake a road-building program and train a Liberian army. The engineers worked rapidly at their road-building task, despite the rainy season and the threat of malaria and other tropical diseases.

Negro engineers worked in Alaska to build the Alcan Highway, a sixteen-hundred-mile road connecting Alaska, Canada and the United States. Here they battled the elements—glaciers and temperatures well blow zero. The same Negro troops built superfortress bases in India and the Ledo Road from India to China over the Himalayas, where bad weather and malaria imperiled their progress. When these construction jobs were complete, the soldiers drove the trucks and loaded cargo, furnishing supplies for the armed forces.

More than 80 per cent of all the Negro enlistees were in army service units. They worked as truck drivers, ditch diggers, ambulance drivers, bridge and road builders, and stevedores. These support jobs were vital. The fighting forces could not have engaged in combat without their assistance. The support units also faced the danger of enemy attack—even if they weren't fighting in the front lines.

Hard-boiled General George Patton generously praised the work of the all-Negro 514th Quartermaster's Corps Company attached to the Third Army in Europe.

"The tasks which have been placed upon your shoulders during this history-making campaign," he said, "have been almost superhuman. You have rolled your trucks through mud and snow and sleet and rain. You have operated around the clock for days on end. You have fought side-by-side with the Infantry and rolled side-by-side with the Armor. But no matter what the obstacles, roll you must, and roll you did. You never failed me."

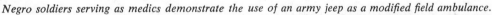

Negro soldiers serving as medics demonstrate the use of an army jeep as a modified field ambulance.

Negro soldiers of the U. S. Army engineer corps worked on the building of the Alcan Highway.

During the construction of roads in isolated regions of Liberia, the army engineer task force endured the discomforts of rain, insects and dense jungle.

T/5 William M. Thomas and Pfc. Joseph Jackson proudly display specially prepared "Easter eggs" for Hitler.

NEGRO COMBAT TROOPS

The Paris edition of the *Stars and Stripes* carried a story noting the presence of Negro infantrymen in the first line of defense. "Long contemplated," it reported, "the plan of mixing white and colored doughboys in fighting units was launched not as an experiment in race relations but as an answer both to the needs of the military situation and repeated requests by Negro service troops for an opportunity to get into the war as combat men."

Soldiers of the 93rd Infantry Division engaged in South Pacific jungle fighting alongside their white countrymen. Negro truck companies and engineering units took part in the storming of the Pacific islands from the Marianas to Okinawa. The result of employing Negro troops in integrated units—a tactic not used since the American Revolution—was to break down old arguments for racial barriers. A report from the 1st Infantry Division stated that "nothing but favorable reports have been received as to the performance and morale of these colored soldiers."

A branch of the black 92nd Infantry Division joined the Fifth Army in Italy in August of 1944. It remained in the front line for five weeks. The Negro troops, numbering 12,000, took heavy losses—330 killed, more than 2,000 wounded and 616 "missing in action."

The Battle of the Bulge, in December 1944, threatened to turn an expected Allied victory into defeat. The need for new front-line troops became critical. Negro soldiers were called as volunteer combat infantrymen.

Members of the 25th Combat Team, 93rd Division, were among the Negro ground troops used for combat in the Pacific theater.

This section of the 450th Antiaircraft Artillery Battalion was the first Negro antiaircraft outfit to see action overseas.

An early quota of two thousand was quickly filled and was raised to twenty-five hundred. When the final quota was reached, the relief units were sent to the front lines. They saw duty in key battles along the Rhine, advancing eastward and southward until the German Siegfried Line collapsed. During the bloody campaign, Negro units suffered heavy losses.

The 99th Fighter Squadron, the black unit in the air corps, flew more than five hundred combat missions for over three thousand sorties during its first year of service. The 99th Pursuit Squadron's pilots flew over Pantelleria until its surrender.

The 99th combined with three other squadrons in 1943 to form the 332nd Fighter Group under Colonel Benjamin O. Davis, Jr. The group began overseas duty in Italy in 1944 with bombing raids on German oil and coal supply targets.

The Negro pilots joined the Allied invading army in southern France and aided in driving the Germans from France. They later engaged with enemy planes over Austria and added to their list of achievements. The Davis group then flew to Greece to assist in the liberation of Athens. From Greece, the unit moved to cover the Balkans—especially Yugoslavia and Czechoslovakia. Wherever the 15th Air Force was stationed, the 332nd flew as escort. It struck against a number of German targets. The climax came with the air battle over Berlin in 1945.

AWARDS FOR MERIT

Colonel Davis was personally decorated for maneuvering his squadron so skillfully "that in spite of the large number of enemy fighters, the bomber formation suffered only a few losses." Shortly afterward, Colonel Davis received the Legion of Merit Award, the Silver Star for gallantry in combat, the Distinguished Flying Cross and the Air Medal with Four Oak Leaf Clusters. His all-Negro unit received the Distinguished Unit Citation in 1945 from President Truman.

One of the 92nd Infantry Division's officers received the Distinguished Service Cross with the following citation:

Shown at left is the Silver Star, center, the Legion of Merit, and right, the Distinguished Flying Cross.

Second Lieutenant Vernon J. Baker demonstrated outstanding courage and leadership in destroying enemy installations, personnel, and equipment during his company's attack against a strongly entrenched enemy in mountainous terrain. When his company was stopped by the concentrated fire from several machine-gun emplacements, he crawled to one position and destroyed it, killing three Germans. Continuing forward, he attacked an enemy observation post and killed its two occupants. With the aid of one of his men, Second Lieutenant Baker attacked two more machine-gun nests, killing or wounding the four enemy soldiers occupying these positions. He then covered the evacuation of the wounded personnel of his company by occupying an exposed position and drawing the enemy's fire. On the following night Second Lieutenant Baker voluntarily led a battalion advance through enemy mine fields and heavy fire toward the division objective. Second Lieutenant Baker's fighting spirit and daring leadership were an inspiration to his men, and exemplify the highest traditions of the armed forces.

Another division officer, Captain Charles F. Gandy of Washington, D.C., was ordered to deploy his company in reinforcement of another company on steep and treacherous mountain terrain. Captain Gandy "personally led his company out in broad daylight," his citation states, "and through further reconnaissance and by personal example and leadership, succeeded in getting his entire company across a canal with an abrupt twelve foot wall. This was accomplished in rain and under extremely heavy enemy fire."

"Halting the company at its intermediate objective," the report says, "Captain Gandy went forward alone to reconnoiter the route of the next movement. While engaged in this activity, he was mortally wounded by enemy machine-gun fire. His outstanding gallantry and leadership in combat exemplify the heroic tradition of the United States Army." For this action, Captain Charles F. Gandy was posthumously awarded the Silver Star.

Many Negro soldiers, like Master Sergeant Albert F. Williams, earned medals for less flamboyant acts of valor. Sergeant Williams' Legion of Merit citation recalled that "as a member of the advance detachment of an expeditionary force from April to June, 1942, he distinguished himself by his soldierly qualities, leadership, and dependability. Upon arrival on a strange continent, by his example of cheerfulness, confidence, energy, and industry he was a constant source of inspiration to his fellow soldiers and a tower of strength to his commanding officer. Sergeant Williams set the pace for all duties assigned. . . . He was largely responsible for building up an enviable reputation for our soldiers abroad and contributing materially toward the preliminary mission of the force."

Two Negro companies, the 311th and 539th, won citations for "outstanding performance in combat during the seizure of the Japanese-held islands of Saipan and Tinian in the Marianas.

The 969th Field Artillery Battalion received a Distinguished Unit Citation, along with the 101st Airborne Division and other attached units that formed the garrison which fought the epic battle of Bastogne. The citation describes their bravery:

These units distinguished themselves in combat against powerful and aggressive enemy forces composed of elements of eight German divisions during the period from December 18 to 27, 1944, by extraordinary heroism and gallantry in defense of the key communications center of Bastogne, Belgium.

Essential to a large-scale exploitation of this breakthrough into Belgium and northern Luxembourg

the enemy attempted to seize Bastogne by attacking constantly and savagely with the best of his armor and infantry. Without benefit of prepared defenses, facing almost overwhelming odds, and with very limited and fast-dwindling supplies, these units maintained a high combat morale and an impenetrable defense, despite extremely heavy bombing, intense artillery fire, and constant attacks from infantry and armor on all sides of their completely cut off and encircled position.

This masterful and grimly determined defense denied the enemy even momentary success in operation for which he paid dearly in men, materiel, and eventually morale. The outstanding courage and resourcefulness and undaunted determination of this gallant force is in keeping with the highest traditions of the service.

Foreign governments also awarded Negro American soldiers their medals for bravery. A South Carolinian, Macon H. Johnson, received the Order of the Soviet Union. France conferred its Croix de Guerre upon W. P. Terrell, Steve Rodriguez, Ernest A. Jenkins, George W. Edwards and Arthur Jackson. William W. Green, a Virginian, won the Yugoslav Partisan Medal for Heroism. And the United Kingdom honored Norman Day with the British Distinguished Service Medal.

Working with divisions at the front, the performance of Negro medics was particularly outstanding. The 428th Medical Battalion of the First Army carried over one million patients in their ambulances in evacuating wounded to rear areas.

Reviewing the combat record at a postwar press conference in Paris, General Dwight D. Eisenhower was asked to comment on the contribution Negro soldiers had made to the European Theater of Operations. He answered:

To start with, I would like to say this: That I do not differentiate among soldiers. I do not say white soldiers or Negro soldiers and I do not say American or British soldiers. To my mind, I have had a task in this war that makes me look upon soldiers as soldiers. Now, I have seen Negro soldiers in this war, and I have many reports on their work where they have rendered very valuable contributions and some of them with the greatest enthusiasm. In late November, when we were getting short of reinforcements, replacements, some 2,600 Negro soldiers volunteered for front-line service and they did good work. All my commanders reported that these volunteers did excellent work. But their major job has been in service of supply, engineer units, quartermaster units, ordnance units. There,

Lieuenant General George S. Patton, Jr., pins the Silver Star on Private Ernest A. Jenkins, a member of the quartermaster corps. Jenkins was cited for his assistance in the destruction of an enemy gun and the capture of fifteen German soldiers.

so far as I know and certainly as far as any officer reports, they have performed equally with every kind of ordnance battalion, quartermaster battalion, and engineer battalion. They have done their job and they have done the job given them.

KOREA

At the end of World War II, American and Soviet troops occupied Korea. When the United Nations General Assembly set up a commission to conduct elections by the Korean people, Russia refused to cooperate. The voting resulted in the adoption of a constitution and a democratic government in the southern section of Korea occupied by the Americans. A Soviet-controlled "People's Republic" was set up north of the 38th parallel which claimed possession of all Korea.

When North Korean soldiers attacked South Korean defenders on June 25, 1950, President Truman ordered American troops to defend the southern section as advance guards of a United Nations police force. Negroes and whites joined in this police action.

General Matthew Ridgway, commander of the U.S. Troops in Korea, oversaw the historic and long overdue integration of army units. While commander of the Eighth Army, General Ridgway voiced his strong endorsement of a fighting force unfettered by the bonds of racial discrimination.

"It was my conviction," he said, "that only in this way could we assure the sort of *esprit* a fighting army needs, where each soldier stands proudly on his own feet, knowing himself to be as good as the next fellow and better than the enemy."

By early 1951 Ridgway's personnel office had begun to assign excess Negro servicemen to understrength white units. The results, noted the chief of military history, were "highly gratifying on the whole." Two black soldiers, William Thompson and Cornelius Charlton, won the Medal of Honor for acts of heroism. Both soldiers were awarded the Medal posthumously. Negroes also served in uniform in Europe, the Near East, the Far East and North and West Africa in the post-World War II period.

The Korean front, the first true test of racially-

mixed units over a prolonged period, laid the foundation for equal opportunity programs in civilian society. The army officers' training schools, which had reopened in 1949, welcomed all qualified candidates. Negro officers henceforth would command white as well as Negro enlisted men. Assistant Secretary of Defense John A. Hannah summed up the spirit of the new policy in 1954.

"The obligations to defend our country and our beliefs," Dr. Hannah declared, "are borne equally by all of our citizens without regard to race or color or religion. It should be a real gratification to all thinking Americans to know that our Armed Forces are leading the way in demonstrating both at home and abroad that America provides opportunities for all of her people."

A truce was signed in 1953; South Korea was in need of rebuilding. Congress granted $200 million for this purpose. An American peace-keeping force—manned by officers and enlisted men of all races—remained in South Korea to oversee the rebuilding effort.

VIETNAM

The current war in Vietnam has demanded of the Negro in uniform greater sacrifices than has any other armed conflict in the nation's history. The early commitment to South Vietnam—a small band of special forces "advisers" dispatched in the early 1960's—has grown into an army of hundreds of thousands of Americans. By June of 1967, more than 50,000 black men had served in the Southeast Asian tropics, many of them never to return. *Time* magazine observed:

> The American Negro is winning—indeed has won —a black badge of courage that his nation must forever honor. That badge, interlaced with all the bright strands of personal bravery and professional skill that have marked their performance in battle, proclaims a truth that Americans had not yet learned about themselves before Vietnam: color has no place in war; merit is the only measure of the man.

Though the Negro represents but 11 per cent of the nation's population, nearly one-quarter of the American troops in Vietnam are black. These

In Korea, white and black men are seen fighting side by side under the command of Negro squad leader M. L. Cleveland.

Sergeant Elijah McLaughlin (left front) and Corporal Luther Anderson (right front) lead their squad of Negro, white and South Korean troops to a new position.

LAWRENCE JOEL

DONALD R. LONG

MILTON L. OLIVE, III

servicemen—among them Medal of Honor winners Milton L. Olive, III, Lawrence Joel and Donald R. Long—won the unstinting praise of General William C. Westmoreland, the South Carolina-born commander of U.S. troops.

"I have an intuitive feeling," General Westmoreland said, "that the Negro servicemen have a better understanding than the whites of what the war is about." Both private Olive and Sergeant Long, for instance, gave their lives to save fellow soldiers. Both threw themselves on live grenades during fierce battles with enemy guerillas. Specialist Joel, a medical corpsman who is the only living Negro Medal of Honor winner from Vietnam, risked his life to aid his unit's wounded men while seriously wounded himself.

Secretary of the Army Stanley Resor noted the soundness of the armed service's integration policy in mid-1968. "The policy of equal treatment and opportunity, besides being a just one,"

he said, "has paid dividends to the Army. Today we have fifty-five hundred Negro Army officers. Among infantry sergeants—the backbone of our combat forces in Vietnam—24 per cent are Negro."

In May 1971 the army promoted three black colonels, Roscoe E. Cartwright, Oliver W. Dillard and James F. Hamlet, to the rank of brigadier general. Samuel Lee Gravely, Jr., was the first black to be named an admiral in the United States Navy. Brigadier General Daniel "Chappie" James, of the air force, was named to the post of deputy assistant secretary of defense for public affairs. The first black generals in the military reserves and the National Guard are respectively Brigadier General Benjamin L. Hunton and Brigadier General Cunningham C. Bryant. Other high-ranking black officers are Lieutenant Colonel Frank E. Peterson, Jr., of the marines, and Commander Bobby C. Wilkes, of the coast guard.

CHAPTER THIRTEEN

Black Breakthrough—
Negro Gift to
"The Soulless World"

IT was April 10, 1947, when the indomitable Branch Rickey, general manager of the Brooklyn Dodgers, summoned Jackie Robinson to Ebbetts Field to become the first Negro player in major league baseball. The sturdy second baseman's trials during that first season and his eventual acceptance into the annals of baseball's immortals are today a slice of history known to every schoolboy, black or white. Therein lies the importance of Robinson and other "superstars" of the sports and entertainment worlds: Willie Mays, Sidney Poitier, Sammy Davis, Bill Russell, Wilt Chamberlain, Althea Gibson and hundreds of others. The Negro "breakthrough" had been long in coming, and the black man was ready when it came. While his ascent to the pinnacle of success has been most visible in the world of sports and on the stage, it has occurred in virtually every field of human endeavor. And he has left an imprint on the minds of younger Americans of every race.

Even before Jackie Robinson broke baseball's color line, fair-minded Americans of all races had been thrilled by Jesse Owens' stunning feat in 1936, when he won four Olympic gold medals in Berlin. If that showing did not thoroughly humiliate Adolf Hitler and his Nordic supremacists, then Joe Louis' ring performance in conquering the Germans' heavyweight pride, Max Schmeling, must have given them pause. Scores of other Negro athletes trained hard and tirelessly to win the title of champion during the 1940's, 1950's and 1960's—men like Sugar Ray Robinson, Jim Brown and Bob Gibson. By the 1960's, in fact, Negroes dominated the professional sports scene—a matter of some pride among black youths as well as their elders. Perhaps equally vital, the new openness in the sports world had a special meaning for white youths. Their sports idols, too, often had black skins.

EDUCATIONAL STATUS QUO

The rise of the Negro sports hero, beginning in the 1930's, had shown the nation what might be expected of him in other fields—all other things being equal. But other things were not equal, especially in education. The Negro had come a long way in athletics, where formal schooling mattered little. The same was true of such areas of the entertainment world as the popular-song market. Elsewhere, he was still handicapped by discrimination—even when the law was on his side. In 1950, while the "separate but equal" doctrine still prevailed in the schoolroom, one of every five southern Negro adults had less than six years of education. The proportion of white boys who graduated from high school was nearly three times as high as the Negro ratio. Yet in 1966—twelve years after the Plessy ruling had been outlawed—the facts of racial isolation in the public schools left the Negro as short-changed as before.

"When measured by that yardstick [segregation]," the U.S. Office of Education reported in 1966, "American public education remains largely unequal in most regions of the country, including all those where Negroes form any significant proportion of the population. . . . The great majority of American children attend schools that are largely segregated—that is, almost all of their fellow students are of the same racial background as they are."

The data on de facto school segregation, moreover, appeared as alarming in the cities of the North as in the South. In 1963 a Negro Presbyterian minister, the Rev. Milton A. Galamison, described them in vivid terms. "There are two school systems in New York City," Dr. Galamison said. "One is for the whites and for the sprinkling of Negroes who manage by design or grace to matriculate. The second school system is for the ghetto children and the disparity is grotesque."

Dr. Galamison, leader of a series of public school boycotts in the mid-1960's, blamed the sad state of education on the educators. He claimed they defended their own failings by a mechanism he called "ifism." The teachers, he said, would shake their heads sorrowfully and bemoan: "If only they were not from the South"; or "If they just had a different set of parents"; or "If they enjoyed higher-income homes"; or "If their home had a library." The student could change none of these conditions, however. Dr.

MILTON A. GALAMISON

Galamison insisted that the one logical condition for higher achievement was never mentioned: "children might learn if they are properly taught." He now serves on New York City's school board.

In spite of the educational lag, an impressive array of Negroes did rise to prominence in literature, art, music, theater and other creative fields during the post-Depression era.

WRITERS

The bitter memories of youth in the ghetto have often given birth to deeply moving works of literature. While using Negro themes, writers like Richard Wright, Langston Hughes and Ralph Ellison gave keen insights into the psychology of American race relations. In *Native Son* (1940) and in *Black Boy* (1945), Wright examined the pressures of racial hatred in both the South and the northern ghetto. Both works were chosen as book club selections. The versatile Hughes—poet, author, playwright and news columnist—saw his play *Mulatto* run a year on Broadway. His opera *The Barrier* has been heard often,

RICHARD WRIGHT

ANN PETRY

GWENDOLYN BROOKS

LANGSTON HUGHES

and his books have been translated into many languages. Hughes won the Spingarn Medal in 1960 for "the highest achievement of an American Negro." Ellison's first book, *Invisible Man*, earned him international fame. It also won the 1953 National Book Award over one of Hemingway's works.

Frank Yerby, a 1938 graduate of Fisk University, avoided racial themes in his popular novels. His first novel, *The Foxes of Harrow,* made the bestseller list in 1946. Almost every year since then, Yerby has published another successful novel.

Another Negro author, Willard Motley, used the same formula to win critical acclaim. Motley's poignant novel of an Italian boy's experiences in an American city, *Knock on Any Door,* and his treatment of the American melting pot, *Let No Man Write My Epitaph*, were adapted by Hollywood into great box office successes.

In 1952 James Baldwin's first novel *Go Tell It on the Mountain*, was published. Three years later his first collection of essays, *Notes of a Native Son*, appeared. It was, however, with the publication of *Nobody Knows My Name* in 1961 that Baldwin became the literary prophet of the civil-rights movement. *The Fire Next Time* warned of the racial holocaust of the mid-sixties in America's cities. His other highly acclaimed works include the novel *Another Country* and the Broadway play *Blues for Mister Charlie*. In 1968 Baldwin published another novel, *Tell Me How Long the Train's Been Gone.*

While in his nineties, W. E. B. Du Bois completed a literary trilogy, *The Black Flame*. This work, based on Du Bois' own earlier years as a radical scholar, related the experiences of a Negro teacher in the South. Toward the end of his life Du Bois joined the Communist Party and became an expatriate in Ghana, where he died in 1963. His *Autobiography*, published posthumously, incorporates many of his published writings, along with some new material, to make a fascinating chronicle of his long, productive life.

Two black women, Ann Petry and Gwendolyn Brooks, are very well known. Miss Petry's short stories first appeared in the *Amsterdam News* and the *Crisis*. After attending the University of Connecticut, she received a fellowship which enabled her to finish her first novel, *The Street*. It described the struggles of a Negro mother and her son in the slums of New York City. Miss Brooks began writing poetry during her youth in Chicago—first for her high school paper, then for the *Chicago Defender*. Her first volume of poetry, *A Street in Bronzeville*, won her the Pulitzer Prize in 1950. She also received the Poetry Workshop Award.

The well-known poet and playwright, LeRoi Jones, won praise in the early 1960's for *Dutchman* and for several one-act plays performed off-Broadway. The controversial Jones headed a drama workshop for Harlem youths, in 1965. This was the famous Black Arts Theater where his inflammatory play *Jello* was performed. By the late 1960's, most Negro writers had turned, like Jones, to the vibrant issues of black power in America.

MUSICIANS AND COMPOSERS

As in literature, so in music the gifts of the Negro American multiplied as the nation showed its appreciation as an audience. These talents

ADELE ADDISON

TODD DUNCAN

LEONTYNE PRICE

SHIRLEY VERRETT

WILLIAM WARFIELD

JOHN WORK

ranged from the raw beauty of the plantation music combo to the rich voices of concert and opera stars and the artistry of philharmonic performers. In the postwar period, Negroes thrived both as popular and classical musicians. During the 1950's, the names of Marian Anderson, Paul Robeson, Roland Hayes, Dorothy Maynor and Todd Duncan reigned preeminently. Miss Anderson moved on from a Philadelphia church choir to perform on concert stages throughout the world. She was the first of her race to sing at the Metropolitan Opera House (in 1955). Baritone Robert McFerrin followed her in the same year. The next year tenor George Shirley and soprano Mattiwilda Dobbs sang at the "Met." Gloria Davy sang there in 1957, and four years later the magnificent soprano Leontyne Price carved out lasting fame with her interpretation of Verdi's *Aïda*. Before Miss Anderson's Met debut, Dorothy Maynor had performed as guest soloist at a number of international music festivals in both Europe and America. Earlier, Todd Duncan, a Kentuckian educated at Butler and Columbia, had appeared as Tonio in a New York production of *Pagliacci*. George Gershwin had engaged Duncan and Ann Brown for the leading roles in *Porgy and Bess*. Other outstanding Negro vocalists of the postwar period include William Warfield, Adele Addison, Betty Allen, Camilla Williams and Lawrence Winters. Another addition to the ranks of Metropolitan Opera stars is Shirley Verrett, a mezzo-soprano who has had starring roles in the last few seasons.

William Grant Still ranks with the top modern American composers. *Darker America, Africa,* the *Afro-American Symphony* and *New Symphony in G Minor* are among his major compositions. Still used Negro themes in his opera *Blue Steel* and in later works.

Howard Swanson, the only American composer represented at the Edinburgh Festival of 1951, heard his *Short Symphony* performed there. The Cleveland Symphony Orchestra introduced Ulysses Kay's *Sinfonia in E*, while the Louisville Orchestra played his *Serenade for Orchestra*. The New York Philharmonic performed another Kay work, *Of New Horizons*. The music of Hale Smith, another Negro composer,

has also been in the repertoire of major symphony orchestras. Other noted Negro composers of the twentieth century are Will Marion Cook, R. Nathaniel Dett, Nora Holt, Florence B. Price, Camille Nickerson, John Work, Hall Johnson and Jester Hairston.

Dean Dixon, the first Negro conductor to win both national and international acclaim, showed early promise as a high school musician in Harlem. At the Harlem YMCA he formed a small symphony orchestra composed of whites and Negroes. While completing his studies at Columbia University, the young conductor was invited to lead the Chamber Orchestra of the League of Music Lovers at Town Hall. Later he was asked to fill in as a summer conductor of the NBC Symphony. He has served as conductor of symphonic groups in Europe, as well as conductor of the American Youth Symphony Orchestra. An outstanding Negro violinist and composer of Haitian melodies, Clarence Cameron White, has also served as an orchestra conductor.

A number of unusual Negro musicians made names for themselves as jazz and "pop" composers. Heading the list was W. C. Handy, who

DEAN DIXON

W. C. HANDY

BESSIE SMITH

played in dance bands yet sought constantly to acquire a formal musical education. Handy sold his first outstanding work, *Memphis Blues*, to a New York publisher for $50. It soon swept the country; "Boss" Crump in Memphis adopted it for use as a political theme song. Handy then published his famous *St. Louis Blues* and was more careful in protecting his copyright. It probably sold more copies than any other single piece of music composed by a Negro.

A leading blues singer, Bessie Smith had little training but won high acclaim from music critics. When she died in 1937, her recordings —over 150—assured her a permanent place among the immortals of jazz. Among other jazz artists whose names and performances will live on are Nat "King" Cole, Wes Montgomery, John Coltrane, Dinah Washington and Billie Holiday. The attractive songstress Lena Horne has been an outstanding figure in American entertainment. For many years she has been in great demand as an entertainer. Ella Fitzgerald's and the late Louis "Satchmo" Armstrong's popularity are also examples of this timeless appeal.

Duke Ellington, a popular composer and pianist, has created a number of jazz classics, among which are *Solitude, Mood Indigo* and *Sophisticated Lady*. One critic noted the unique way in which Ellington's melodies move against one another in rich counterpoint, with off-beat rhythms moving in and out of his works like woven thread. The composer received the Spingarn Medal in 1960.

Other distinguished jazz and pop artists— James Brown, "Cannonball" Adderley, Count Basie, Dizzy Gillespie, Lionel Hampton and others—have toured abroad as goodwill ambassadors of the American people. Their audiences far outnumber the concert-goers, of course, since their records have sold in the millions.

Such gospel singers as Mahalia Jackson and Clara Ward and folk-singers Josh White and Harry Belafonte built up loyal followings among Americans of all races, as have a wide variety of Negro jazz and "pop" music singers and instrumentalists. Heading the list would be: Nancy Wilson, Erroll Garner, Fats Waller, Ramsey Lewis, Quincy Jones, Miles Davis and Sarah Vaughan. Among the jazz avant garde are: Thelonius Monk, Charles Lloyd, Cecil Taylor, Archie Shepp, Ornette Coleman and Roland Kirk.

THE THEATER

The Federal Theater of the Depression gave Negroes with stage talent a chance for training which Bert Williams and George Walker, Charles Gilpin, J. Rosamond Johnson and Robert Cole had never enjoyed. World War II also helped create new attitudes toward Negroes, as playwrights examined the nation's race relations.

Shortly after the war ended, a procession of serious dramas starring Negroes appeared. Hilda Simms, a 1943 graduate of Hampton Institute, took the leading role in *Anna Lucasta*.

In 1940 Ethel Waters headed the cast of the musical *Cabin in the Sky*. Muriel Smith and Muriel Rahn starred in Oscar Hammerstein, II's, *Carmen Jones* when Billy Rose produced it in 1944. Todd Duncan and William Warfield played the male leads in Gershwin's *Porgy and Bess*.

Kenneth Spencer and Paul Robeson appeared

JOSH WHITE

CLARA WARD AND THE WARD SINGERS

PAUL ROBESON

in the Jerome Kern-Oscar Hammerstein, II, musical *Show Boat*, which popularized the song "Ol' Man River." Robeson's performance in *Othello* earned him a reputation as his race's foremost Shakespearean actor. He played the title role on Broadway and on the road.

Many plays with racial themes—such as *Native Son, Strange Fruit, St. Louis Woman* and *Run, Little Chillun*—also helped develop Negro acting talent.

The American Negro Theater, formed under the leadership of Frederick O'Neal in 1940, sought to help Negro actors find stage employment. At the time, few dramatic roles were open to Negroes. The group hoped to launch and build its own theater, but the goal was never reached. The Negro Actor's Guild of America also organized to assist Negro actors and to promote their welfare. While the Guild still exists, the crucial need for its functions has diminished somewhat as the theater world has removed its racial barriers. By the mid-1960's, for instance, Frederick O'Neal was heading Actors Equity Association, the stage performers' union, which vigilantly opposes racial bias.

The stunning success of Lorraine Hansberry's play *A Raisin in the Sun* was a landmark in racial drama. The all-Negro cast, headed by Sidney Poitier and Claudia McNeil, enjoyed a long run in New York and later starred in the film.

MOTION PICTURES, RADIO AND TELEVISION

Negroes had long resented the image of their race based on the stereotype portrayed by Negro actor Stepin Fetchit, who consistently played the witless lackey. The Negro press, the NAACP, and artists' groups had all protested against this Hollywood device. Exportation of such films and of films portraying the Negro as a dangerous villain had drawn criticism from abroad. Dr. Nnamdi Azikiwe, then a member of the Nigerian Assembly, wrote a resolution in 1949 urging a ban on "films which are derogatory and humiliating to the Negro race." *The Birth of a Nation* was probably the most offensive of the second category of such unfavorable films.

Another film genre, typified by the movie *Pinky*, sought to show the dilemma of the mu-

Lorraine Hansberry's moving play A Raisin in the Sun *starred Sidney Poitier and Claudia McNeil (right center) in both the stage and film version.*

latto. Though its theme was a great improvement over the blatantly racist themes of the earlier pictures, the film also reflected a prejudiced point of view.

During the past two decades the Negro-as-caricature films have disappeared from the mass market. New themes have appeared, and new names have star billing: Sidney Poitier, Ossie Davis, Ivan Dixon, Ruby Dee, Roscoe Lee Browne, Leonard Parker and Cicely Tyson, to name the more prominent. In 1966 Poitier won an Oscar for his acting in *Lilies of the Field*. *Shaft*, a new black detective movie, was produced in 1971 by MGM, starring a young black male model, Richard Roundtree. Gordon Parks, the creator of the photographically beautiful film *The Learning Tree*, also directed *Shaft*. Bill Cosby has come forth with his own motion picture, *Man and Boy*, as has Melvin Van Peebles with *Sweet Sweetback*.

Television, too, developed rapidly in its treatment of race in the late 1960's, although charges of "tokenism" still found their mark. Once again the inroads resulted from unrelenting pressure by the civil-rights movement combined with the economic realities of Negro buying power as it related to shows' sponsors. Negroes have taken their rightful place as television performers and as actors in commercials. Not only have the Negro "superstars" like Harry Belafonte and Sammy Davis, Jr., broken down resistance to black showmanship, but frequent guest appearances by Negroes on the adult "talk shows" have made these programs a forum for social reform. In the adventure series, too, actors Greg Morris (*Mission Impossible*) and Don Mitchell (*Ironside*) have won acceptance for the Negro in roles that would have been off-limits a few years earlier. Versatile actor-comedian Bill Cosby was awarded an Emmy in 1967 for his performance in *I Spy*. While the Negro still has some barriers to overcome in television, the response of the networks gives every reason for optimism, Even greater change has occurred in radio, due largely to the popularity of "soul music" in the nation's large cities. A number of radio stations in these Negro centers are owned and operated by black persons.

HARRY BELAFONTE

SAMMY DAVIS, JR.

BILL COSBY　　　　ARTHUR MITCHELL　　　　ALVIN AILEY

DANCERS

Change has also come about in Negro dance artistry. The tap dance routines displayed to perfection by Bill Robinson and the buck-and-wing patterns of Florence Mills and Josephine Baker gave way during the 1940's to creative dancing as developed by Katherine Dunham. Miss Dunham visited Haiti, Jamaica, Martinique and Trinidad on a Rosenwald Fellowship in order to study these islands' dances, rhythms and costuming. She and her dance company performed on the concert stage and in Hollywood and were associated with the Moscow Art Theater. The Dunham group has given concerts in over fifty countries.

"For my part," Miss Dunham says, "I am satisfied to have been at the base of the awakening of the American Negro to the fact that he had roots somewhere else, and to have presented dark-skinned people in a manner delightful and acceptable to people who have never considered them often even as persons."

By 1949, a number of Negro dancers were making public appearances in the major concert halls. Janet Collins appeared that year with the Metropolitan Opera Company in *Aida*. Pearl Primus of Trinidad, a graduate of Hunter College, danced in New York after completing her studies, and moved into a dancing career through the Works Progress Administration. Liberian President Tubman invited her in 1959 to head the African Performing Arts Center in Monrovia. Carmen de Lavallade, described as "one of the most beautiful dancers in America both physically and technically," has performed with the New York City Ballet and in motion pictures. A number of other talented dancers— among them Arthur Mitchell, James Truitte, Alvin Ailey, Talley Beatty and Louis Johnson— have also earned critical acclaim for their artistry.

PAINTERS AND SCULPTORS

A current controversy rages among Negro artists over their choice of subject matter. Some insist that the artist should confine his energies to expressing Negro life and history on canvas, in sculpture and in all other art forms. Others argue that the true artist compromises his talents unless he transcends race.

Two who have fulfilled their promise as artists of the first school are Aaron Douglas and Hale Woodruff. Douglas' murals hang today in the Fisk University Library, the Harlem YMCA and the 135th Street Branch of the New York Public Library. These are paintings of the Negro's heritage and are of particular interest to black people. Woodruff illustrated Alain Locke's *The New Negro* and James Weldon Johnson's *God's Trombones*. His best-known oil painting is probably his slave ship scene, "*Amistad*." James L. Wells, winner of a Harmon Award for his paintings of religious subjects, also excels as a portrayer of nature. The author of *Modern Negro Art*, James Porter, has gained distinction for his oil paintings as well. Lois Jones received the Robert Woods Bliss Award at the 1941 exhibition of the Washington Society of Fine Arts, as well as honorable mention at the Negro Exposition in Chicago. Horace Pippin, too, ranks high among Negro painters. "Among self-taught painters of the world," Cedric Dover said of him, "Pippin ranks close to Rousseau, and in the company of Bombois, Peyronnet and Hippolyte."

Among those Negro artists who have won acclaim using subject matter not related to black culture, cartoonist E. Simms Campbell stands in the forefront. Campbell's illustrations, which rarely depict black people, have appeared regularly in *Esquire* and in many newspapers.

Probably the best-known American Negro artist, Henry O. Tanner, won fame as an interpreter of religious rather than racial themes. The son of an African Methodist Episcopal bishop, he studied art in France and in Palestine during the late nineteenth century. Tanner's "Flight into Egypt" and "The Return from Calvary" reside today at Howard University, while "The Two Disciples at the Tomb" hangs in the Chicago Institute of Art. Hampton Institute possesses "Banjo Lesson," and "Christ and Disciples" may be seen at Spelman College.

Jacob Lawrence, an outstanding painter, presents his themes with a power and simplicity and fine color sense that have profoundly affected his audience. An exhibition of his in the Downtown Gallery in New York illustrated the American Negro's migration North in sixty panels.

AUGUSTA SAVAGE

RICHMOND BARTHÉ

Other painters of note are Romare Bearden, Charles White, Norman Lewis, Harper Phillips, Gilbert Harris, Sam Middleton, Charles Alston, Virginia Cox, Charles Davis, Merton Simpson, Larry Compton, Walter Williams, Charles McGee, John Biggers, Larry Erskine Thomas, Sam Gilliam and Tom Feelings.

The first Negro sculptors to attract attention were Richmond Barthé and Augusta Savage. Barthé executed busts of celebrities, among them one of Booker T. Washington for the Hall of Fame at New York University. Well known are his "Head of a Tortured Negro," "West Indian Girl" and "The Boxer." Miss Savage has been praised for "Mother and Child." More recent sculptors include Todd Williams and Barbara Chase.

Ethiopian-born Skunder Boghossian has achieved unusual effects in oils, watercolors and pen-and-ink drawings. "African art created a condition in my mind," he has explained. "I learned that creation must be an immense and unceasing modulation of concept." Exhibitions of his paintings have been held in London, Rome, Paris, Frankfurt, Brussels, New York and Addis Ababa.

SCIENTISTS AND TECHNOLOGISTS

Shortages of men during World War II gave many Negroes a chance to become corporate laboratory researchers. The greatest Negro in the sciences, Dr. George Washington Carver, who died in 1943, had discovered and developed many uses for peanuts at Tuskegee Institute. Thanks to his work, the South's small peanut and sweet potato production became major industries. Other younger men were soon to follow in his footsteps. Dr. Percy Julian, for instance, served as a professor of chemistry and research chemist for the Glidden Paint Company's laboratories in Chicago. He later opened the Julian Laboratories and rapidly won acclaim for himself with his synthesis of products from soybeans. This research made possible a low cost means of producing cortisone, a drug now used in treating millions of arthritis sufferers.

Another Negro, Dr. Elmer S. Imes, engaged in research in molecular physics. As a professor of physics at Fisk University, he was one of the first to prove that the quantum theory could be expanded to include the rotational status of the molecule. Dr. Hildrus A. Poindexter, a graduate of Lincoln University, earned postgraduate degrees at Harvard and Columbia Universities. Later he became professor of bacteriology and preventive medicine at the Howard University School of Medicine. He has worked for the U.S. Public Health Service and has made major contributions to the treatment of tropical diseases. Another Negro scientist, Lloyd Hall, became a specialist in food products and chemical director of a large Chicago research laboratory.

A number of scientists have devoted themselves to training Negroes as laboratory researchers. Drs. Robert P. Barnes and Lloyd Ferguson, Howard University chemists, have led the way in their field. Dr. Hermon Branson, a Howard physicist, and Dr. N. O. Collaway, a Fisk and Tuskegee endocrinologist, have passed on their knowledge to future generations. Dr. Carver had sought to encourage young Negroes to enter the sciences. The Tuskegee chemurgist donated funds from many of the awards and prizes he received, and from his estate, to establish the George Washington Carver Foundation. This fund finances the continuing research in farm products and foods in which Dr. Carver had an interest. Another Negro scholar, Dr. Theodore K. Lawless, graduated from Talladega College and Northwestern University Medical School. A Chicago physician and lecturer at Northwestern University, the late Dr. Lawless had had remarkable success in treating skin diseases.

Other Negroes have become famous as engineers and architects. Archie Alexander, later governor of the Virgin Islands, laid out the blueprint for the Tidal Basin bridge from the nation's capital across the Potomac River to Arlington, Virginia. His firm constructed the bridge, as well as a sewage treatment plant in Des Moines, Iowa. His engineers also built airports and power plants. Paul Williams, the best-known Negro architect, designed the California homes of such Hollywood stars as Zasu Pitts, Grace Moore and many others. Williams has also designed the Beverly Wilshire Hotel, Twentieth Century Fox Studios, Sunset Plaza Apartments, Saks Fifth Avenue and the palatial home of William Paley.

THE CHURCH AND OTHER ORGANIZATIONS

Late in the Depression period, exactly one-third of those Negroes listed in *Who's Who in America* were clergymen. The same leadership pattern existed through the war years and into the era of the civil-rights struggle. Most of these churchmen were Baptist and Methodist ministers like Dr. Joseph H. Jackson of Chicago, Dr. Benjamin Mays of Morehouse College, Dr. James H. Robinson of New York, Dr. Howard Thurman of Boston University and Dr. Gardner Taylor of Brooklyn. Dr. Martin Luther King, Jr., of Atlanta, became the best-known of the Negro clergymen in the mid-fifties when he organized nonviolent protests against segregation in the Deep South. With a group of fellow Baptist ministers—the Revs. Ralph David Abernathy, Fred Shuttlesworth, Wyatt Tee Walker and Andrew Young—he organized the Southern Christian Leadership Conference. It became the vanguard of the civil-rights movement for more than a decade. After the tragic assassination of Dr. King in April, 1968, the Rev. Ralph Abernathy assumed the SCLC leadership. Other

PERCY JULIAN

GEORGE WASHINGTON CARVER

THEODORE K. LAWLESS

PAUL WILLIAMS

GARDNER TAYLOR

church leaders who took active roles in pressing for social reforms during the mid-century include a white Roman Catholic priest, the Rev. James Groppi of Milwaukee; the Rev. Milton A. Galamison, a Presbyterian minister in Brooklyn; and the Revs. Channing Phillips and Walter Fauntroy, two Baptist ministers in Washington, D.C.

Though Negroes were barred from college fraternities and sororities on most predominantly white campuses until the late 1960's, black students formed their own parallel social groups. These groups thrived on both black and integrated campuses, as well as in non-academic settings. Among these social fraternities and lodges are Alpha Phi Alpha, the Prince Hall Grand Lodge of Masons, the Supreme Grand Lodge of Pythians, the Improved Benevolent Protective Order of Elks of the World and the United Order of Odd Fellows. The National Association of Colored Women dates from 1895, when Mary Church Terrell was installed as the group's first president. The National Council of Negro Women, founded by Dr. Mary McLeod Bethune, has exerted great influence in community affairs.

The National Urban League expanded as a social welfare outlet under the direction of E. Kinckle Jones, Lester B. Granger and Whitney M. Young, Jr. The League worked for interracial amity in keeping with the advice of W. H. Baldwin, Jr., one of its founders: "Let us work not as colored people nor as white people for the narrow good of any group alone, but as American citizens for the common good of our common city, our common country."

The National Association for the Advancement of Colored People, with more than 1,500 branches across the nation, maintains its role as the Negro's largest pressure group to end second-class citizenship and to ensure equality in education, voting, housing, jobs, transportation, public accommodations and health care.

LABOR UNIONS

The changing attitude of the unions—both national and local—has been a vital factor in the economic advancement of the Negro. The new mood within labor's ranks was noted in December of 1955 when the American Federation of Labor and the Congress of Industrial Organizations agreed to merge. One of the aims of the AFL-CIO constitution was "to encourage all workers without regard to race, creed, color, national origin or ancestry to share equally in the benefits of union organization." The merger preceded the election of two Negro labor leaders as vice presidents of the new labor alliance. The Negro officials were A. Philip Randolph of the Brotherhood of Sleeping Car Porters and Willard S. Townsend of the United Transport Service Employees (formerly the Redcap union).

The united AFL-CIO promptly set up a civil-rights committee and a civil-rights department to help enforce the non-bias policy. Two regional panels were named to oversee union practices. The Southern Advisory Committee on Civil Rights, a gathering of the AFL-CIO's top southern officers, formed first. A Mid-Western Advisory Committee on Civil Rights was organized in 1960. It included top union spokesmen in Ohio, Indiana, Illinois, Michigan, Wisconsin and Minnesota. Each of these states had its own civil-rights committee as well. These groups brought concerted pressure to bear on those unions where "restrictive covenants" remained in force. The Brotherhood of Railway Trainmen voted four to one in 1960 to remove the "white only" clause from its constitution. Other international bodies appear on the verge of following suit. But many local unions still discriminate against Negro workers in various ways. They are refused membership, are closeted in separate unions of their own, or are barred from apprenticeship training in the skilled trades. Color has not always been the cause of such barriers. Often Negroes were simply not trained for these jobs and fared poorly in tests. This gave unions and employers an excuse for excluding Negroes from these trades.

To combat these conditions, a Negro-American Labor Council formed in 1959 under Randolph's leadership. Its goal was to secure equal treatment for Negroes in labor unions, whether in policy-making, in apprenticeship programs or in any other labor relationship. Other factors also worked to raise the Negro worker's status and wage level. By 1960 some sixteen states—with half the nation's population—had adopted Fair Employment Practices Acts banning racial

WILLARD S. TOWNSEND

exclusion or wage bias. These laws did much to improve the lot of black laborers.

The federal government had also moved to guard against race bias in work performed under government contract. The steps taken by Presidents Roosevelt and Truman provoked criticism in Congress—even from within the ruling Democratic Party. His support for FEPC laws meant that Truman had to overcome a strong coalition of conservative Republicans and Dixiecrats to remain in office in 1948. The Negro vote for the Democratic ticket, especially in the large northern cities, accounted for the surprise Truman victory. The conservative coalition in Congress, however, remained in power to thwart progressive bills from becoming law, until the liberals gained power in the 1960's.

A 1953 Executive order signed by President Eisenhower formed a nonpartisan President's Committee on Government Contracts. Vice-President Richard M. Nixon headed the sixteen-man panel of government, business and labor leaders, and Secretary of Labor James Mitchell served as vice-chairman. The committee was charged with pressing enforcement of the nation's antibias policy in government contracts. A later White House order made the policy apply to all future contracts as well. Between August of 1953 and mid-May of 1960—roughly the Eisenhower era—the committee received nearly one thousand bias complaints involving several thousand jobs and entire industries. Where possible, this committee and the Equal Employment Opportunities Commission which replaced it tried to negotiate voluntary compliance with the law. In 1967 President Johnson named Clifford Alexander to head the Commission. The President had earlier appointed Roger Wilkins director of another federal civil-rights mediation agency, the Community Relations Service, now a permanent arm of the Justice Department.

INTERNATIONAL AFFAIRS

The formation of the United Nations as a world peace-keeping body in 1945 created a new role for the Negro American in international affairs. He had been ignored by the old League of Nations. So had the dark continent of Africa,

HAILE SELASSIE I

so long under the thumb of Europe's colonial powers. When fascist Italy's air force strafed and bombed defenseless Ethiopia in 1936, Emperor Haile Selassie's appeal for League intervention fell on deaf ears. But under the new United Nations Charter, the role of the Negro American and that of the new African leaders became more and more influential. By the 1960's the Afro-Asian members, led by a Pan-Africanist grouping known as the Casablanca bloc, had come to hold the balance of UN power on vital questions before the General Assembly.

When the United Nations first met at New York City's Hunter College in 1946, only three of its fifty-one charter members represented African nations (Ethiopia, Liberia and South Africa). The General Assembly also included seven Middle-Eastern members, as well as three from Asian countries. By 1965, however, colonial shackles had been cast off. That year the General Assembly included thirty-five African nations, as well as twelve Middle-Eastern and fifteen Asian nations. The total United Nations membership had grown to 115 nations. By 1968 the total had risen to 124. And the affluent North

American-European bloc had lost its hold over General Assembly policy-making.

Since their entry into this world body, nations like Ghana, Guinea and Sudan have pressed for a united African front on the colonialism issue. Besides calling for a liberated "one Africa," the bloc has embraced "negritude," or pride in blackness, as have most black Americans. And the growth of African influence among the world's powers has certainly affected black culture and race relations in this country.

Well before the new African nations joined the General Assembly, American civil-rights workers used the United Nations as a forum to denounce racism in this country. The National Negro Congress petitioned the UN's Economic and Social Council in 1946 to aid in ending racial bias in the United States. The next year the NAACP sent a 154-page document to the United Nations appealing for redress for victims of discrimination. While these measures brought no concrete results, they did add the weight of world opinion to the domestic pressure against segregation. The same can be said of Paul Robeson's 1951 presentation to the UN on behalf of the Civil Rights Congress, charging the United States with racial genocide.

By 1960, with a host of new, sovereign African states like Chad, Cameroon, Mali and Upper Volta admitted to the General Assembly, the death knell had sounded for colonialism. "The tremendous upsurge of freedom which we have witnessed in the African continent during the last year or two," Pakistan's Zulfekor Ali Bhutto said in welcome to the new nations, "reaches culmination in the admission of all these states. Colonialism bows out of Africa."

Governor-General Nnamdi Azikiwe of Nigeria spoke pointedly at the time of the view shared by all the new African members. "We cannot concede that it is in our national interest to fraternize with . . . nations which practice race prejudice, and we must not acquiesce in such an outrageous insult on the black race. In fact, we must regard it as a mark of disrespect and an unfriendly act if any country with whom we have friendly relations indulges in race prejudice in any shape or form, no matter how it may be legally cloaked." By this time, federal officials in Washington, the foreign embassies and the United Nations had adapted to the General Assembly's power shift and were actively courting the African diplomats.

"The United States wants for Africa what Africa wants for itself," undersecretary of state for African affairs G. Mennen Williams declared in late 1961. African leaders such as the Congo's Foreign Minister Justin Bonboko commended Washington's new position. The Congo diplomat hailed the former Michigan governor's "foresight in understanding the role of Africa in the future."

At the same time, two thousand African and American UNESCO delegates met in Boston to discuss the new role of Africa. Professor Melville Herskovits, a Northwestern University anthropologist, warned at the UNESCO meeting: "As Africa moves to more and more active participation in the world scene, the American image of Africa must become richer in fact, more flexible in attitude. . . . In the coming years Africans will experiment with many different kinds of government—those we find distasteful to our tradition as well as those that are more to our liking."

In the same meeting a Southern Rhodesian journalist named Nathan Shamuyarira (editor-in-chief of African Newspapers, Ltd.) told delegates that racial inequality in the United States provided a serious handicap to the nation's diplomats in Africa.

"This [Negro] population is now American in every sense of the word," Shamuyarira declared. "If given full civil rights, it provides you with a definite psychological advantage in influencing people in Africa. But if treated in the way some 'freedom bus riders' have been, you should know that every newspaper report of an anti-integration incident throws mud in the face of your spokesmen—some of them very able ones—in Africa."

BLACK DIPLOMACY

The United States tried to improve its image in Africa—as well as among Negro Americans—by naming more black persons to diplomatic posts. The State Department witnessed the remarkable success of Ralph Bunche, a Negro in the United States delegation, whom the United Nations chose in 1948 as its acting mediator in the Palestine dispute. Dr. Bunche received the Nobel Peace Prize for his efforts in 1950. The one-time Howard University political science professor became his nation's highest official in the UN's own organization. He served as director of the Trusteeship Council and is now deputy secretary-general in charge of political affairs.

Many other Negroes have sat as alternate delegates to the General Assembly—among them, Chicago attorney Edith Sampson, New York YMCA executive Channing H. Tobias, concert artist Marian Anderson, musician Zelma George, Detroit insurance man Charles H. Mahoney, Chicago clergyman Archibald J. Carey, Jr., and Howard University President James M. Nabrit.

Negroes had served periodically as envoys to Haiti and Liberia (Ebenezer D. Bassett was the first in 1869). The State Department had confined Negro diplomacy to these black nations until President Eisenhower broke with this tradition in 1957. He assigned Clifton R. Wharton, a career foreign-service officer, as minister to Romania. President Kennedy later named Wharton ambassador to Norway. He became the first Negro to represent his country in a non-black nation. Minneapolis newsman Carl Rowan also earned a Kennedy appointment, as ambassador to Finland. Rowan later served as director of the U.S. Information Agency before resuming his newspaper career. President Johnson selected Patricia Roberts Harris to serve as ambassador to Luxembourg in 1965. Several black diplomats also drew lesser assignments to key world capitals. Rupert Lloyd held the post of first secretary of the United States Embassy in Paris. Frank Snowden, formerly the dean of Howard University's College of Liberal Arts, served as cultural attaché to the United States Embassy in Rome. Archie Alexander, W. C. Gordon and William H. Hastie fulfilled the duties of governor of the Virgin Islands. Many more headed Peace Corps teams in impoverished areas in Africa, Latin America and Asia. Franklin Williams, once chief of the African division of the Peace Corps, has served as ambassador to Ghana.

Scholars such as historian John Hope Franklin are chosen to lecture abroad and to study on Fulbright scholarships. A Negro clergyman, the Rev. James Robinson of New York, leads

JAMES H. ROBINSON

JOHN HOPE FRANKLIN

JAMES M. NABRIT, JR.

a work-study exchange called Crossroads Africa, which gives hundreds of North American young people a chance to work in the new African nations. In addition to the regular volunteer program, a second "seminar-safari" operation gives U.S. and Canadian adults a forum in which to meet with leaders of the African nations they visit. Many other non-governmental organizations have African ties—student exchange, agricultural and community development programs —enabling Americans to share in the African culture.

THE CONCEPT OF NEGRITUDE

The birth of African nations, as noted earlier, has given rise to a new pride in the cultural heritage of black people, a pride the French-speaking Africans speak of as negritude. In the words of St. Clair Drake, a black professor of sociology at Roosevelt University, negritude "rejects both white racialism and black chauvinism; it stands for racial coexistence on the basis of absolute equality and respect for human personality." The expatriate Guinean editor of *Présence Africaine*, Alioune Diop, sees it manifested in the Pan-African nationalism of Guinea's Sékou Touré and the toppled Ghanian strongman, Kwame Nkrumah.

"Our nationalism is a yell, a painful roar," Diop said in 1961. "It is a revolt against a power that grows without a conscience, that acts ferociously against the have-nots, whose breath of life is threatened if they don't respond to the challenge." Diop and other disciples of negritude see it as "an expression of the black man's inner genius," a genius of "those who never invented

anything, who never conquered anything—but who in awe give themselves up to the essence of things." This inner nature, they say, expresses "something richer and deeper than riveters erecting skyscrapers or designers of machinery bent over their drawing boards. . . . It deals with subtler matters of the soul." This outlook, as Professor Drake perceives it, "calls upon Negroes everywhere to feel confident and unashamed and even proud of their color, their hair, their lips, and of African cultures."

THE WORLD FESTIVAL OF NEGRO ART

It was with this spirit that Senegal's poet-president Leopold Senghor welcomed Negro artists from nations the world over to Dakar in 1966. The first World Festival of Negro Art displayed the works of black creative artists, writers, painters, sculptors, dancers, film-makers and skilled craftsmen—most of them previously unknown to the world public. The festival, which exhibited the works of many Negro Americans, included twenty participant nations, among which were the United States, France, Great Britain, India, Hungary and Cuba.

Explaining the presence of the white nations, Tchicaya U'Tamsi declared: "The fruits of negritude should not be picked by black hands alone, but also by the hands of men of goodwill throughout the world." And Senegalese President Senghor opened the festival with a call for human brotherhood. "Let us be to hand at the rebirth of the world as the leaven requisite to white flour," he pleaded. "For who will impart the rhythm to the soulless world of machinery and guns?"

CHAPTER FOURTEEN

The Burgeoning Black Middle Class— Its Supplies and Demands

EVER since freedom had been proclaimed, the virtues of education, thrift and hard work had been impressed on the Negro American. Benjamin Franklin's time-honored maxims "Diligence is the mother of good luck" and "God helps them that help themselves" were adopted by Booker T. Washington and his trade school movement. Even Washington's critics were impressed by his economic arguments for building a solid base of black business and, ultimately, a prosperous Negro middle class. Thus slowly— in the face of every form of racial bias—such a "black bourgeoisie" did evolve. A small, elite circle of business and professional people, it owed much to the Negro colleges founded after the Civil War. This bloc also formed the backbone of the protest against Jim Crow. For while it enjoyed many of the material signs of opulence, it shared in the indignities of second-class citizenship.

By the 1950's, however, this segment of black America had come under heavy attack from its own midst. Professor E. Franklin Frazier, the noted Howard University sociologist, shocked his fellow educators in 1956 with the publication of his *Black Bourgeoisie*. "Despite the tinsel, glitter and gaiety of the world of make-believe in which middle-class Negroes take refuge," Frazier wrote, "they are still beset by feelings of insecurity, frustration and guilt. As a consequence, the free and easy life which they appear to lead is a mask for their unhappy existence." The black intellectual community reacted in anger and disbelief to Frazier's bombshell.

Frazier attributed much of the outrage to his book's data on "the real economic position" of the Negro. Far from depicting Negro business as having vast purchasing power, he noted at one point that "the total assets of all Negro banks in the United States were less than those of a single small white bank in a small town in the state of New York." Not all black people shared the Negro Establishment's anger. After

E. FRANKLIN FRAZIER

reading reviews in both the black and white press, poor Negroes concluded that the Frazier book attacked "upper-class, light-skinned" Negroes. "As a consequence," the author later revealed, "I was even stopped on the street by working-class Negroes who shook my hand for having performed this long overdue service."

This last remark points up the widening gulf between the black "haves" and "have-nots." For the "haves," the "American way of life" still remained an attractive and attainable goal. For almost always the same values which have spurred the white middle class to prosperity have also influenced the black community. Even after generations of repression, the desire to "move up" remained. At the same time, however, an increasing number of Negroes felt estranged from society—black, as well as white. In a very literal sense they found themselves left out—poor in the midst of plenty. In every way they saw themselves as "have-nots."

This was particularly meaningful in the mid-twentieth century, as the white working class rose swiftly to the middle class economic level. Discrimination in labor and industry had left the mass of black workers behind, and education was still largely a luxury for the middle class. Not until ways might be found to give all blacks their fair share of America's plenty, starting with the basics of schooling and jobs, could the country be called truly democratic.

NEGRO COLLEGES AT THE CROSSROADS

For better or for worse, the black middle class evolved mainly through the efforts of the Negro colleges of the South. From humble beginnings (Fisk University was established in an old military hospital, Atlanta University in a railroad car, Central Tennessee College in an old gun factory), these schools had grown to form a vital network of higher education. The present head of the United Negro College Fund, Dr. Stephen J. Wright, has traced this growth. Dr. Wright, the former president of Fisk University, breaks the schools' history into four eras:

1. 1865-1885—The founding and early development years of private Negro colleges by northern church bodies.

STEPHEN J. WRIGHT

2. 1885-1916—More colleges founded by Negro churches and the southern states.

3. 1916-1938—The period in which those colleges that survived came "of age" and often achieved accreditation.

4. 1938-present—The period of developing and expanding graduate and professional study programs.

During the first period, Dr. Wright notes, most of the college teachers were missionaries from the northeastern states who received starvation wages. "Although called 'colleges' and 'universities,'" he maintains, "these institutions were little more than elementary and high schools," since qualified preparatory schools were totally lacking. Though the Morrill Act of 1890 opened many tax-supported "land grant" colleges, the southern states failed to maintain the black schools in accord with the "separate but equal" doctrine, and their major problem became that of merely surviving.

That 115 Negro colleges have survived despite handicaps is largely owing to private philanthropy. The Peabody Education Fund, the John F. Slater Fund, the Negro Rural School (Jeanes) Fund and the Virginia Randolph Fund gave generously through the years to support Negro schools. These merged in 1937 to become the Southern Education Foundation. But the black colleges suffered severely from financial crises, and most of them failed to achieve any measure of self-reliance. A group of Carnegie Foundation researchers, headed by Professor Earl McGrath, reported in 1965 that "many of the predominantly Negro colleges could eliminate or at least mitigate their present shortcomings and needs if they had additional financial resources." Nearly half of the Negro college presidents interviewed by McGrath pinpointed their financial condition as the most crucial weakness in their institutions.

As a result of fiscal strain, Negro colleges suffer other burdens. Not the least of these is the loss of academic freedom in those schools dependent upon southern state aid. This has prompted two leading educators to comment that "the great majority of Negro institutions stand near the tail end of the academic procession in terms of student aptitudes, faculty creativity, and intellectual and moral ferment." Even so, these scholars—David Riesman and Christopher Jencks—concede the stabilizing effect the black campus has had in the South until recent years.

> Negro colleges have for several generations been the major agency for selecting and socializing the prospective members of the black bourgeoisie. Their role here is even more important than the role of white colleges, for upward mobility among Negroes has depended more on professional credentials and less on . . . managerial talent. [But] the fact that these colleges often sift out the rebellious, the creative, and the alienated may do even more to explain the character of the black bourgeoisie and may do more damage to the Negro potential than the equivalent sifting does to the white. Those who have joined the Negro middle class, and even those who aspire to do so, have been extremely conservative on all issues other than racial equality, and sometimes even on that.

Professor Bernard Harleston of Tufts University, a graduate of Howard, has been even more critical. He wrote in 1965 that "the educational opportunities which many of these institutions offer are so limited in range and depth that what they call higher education is at best a cruel hoax." Harleston asserts that only a few of the Negro schools "have reached or can hope to reach full educational maturity."

"UNCLE TOM"—THE CAMPUS LEADERS' DILEMMA

Another Negro commentator, Louis Lomax, made the same point in 1962. "The Negro institutions that served their time well," he wrote, "have now fallen into disfavor because they are inextricably tied to the status quo." Lomax tells the poignant story of a Negro college president, Felton Grandison Clark of Southern University, torn between his school and his students.

Founded in Baton Rouge, Louisiana, by Dr. Clark's father, the campus now houses the largest predominantly Negro university in the world. In 1960, when Southern University students staged sit-ins, the all-white board of trustees ordered Dr. Clark to end the protest or expel the students. (The school, then run on a $7 million-a-year budget, depends on state support.) When the students failed to heed Dr. Clark's plea, he expelled eighteen campus leaders. "My dominant concern is to save Southern University," he said in explanation. A boycott of classes followed, forcing the school to close temporarily. When it reopened, Dr. Clark appeared to have won his battle—even though he had temporarily lost the respect of many of his students.

Dr. Clark is not the only Negro college president to be labeled an "Uncle Tom" for bowing to white trustees. The same epithet has been hurled at Dr. James M. Nabrit of Howard University, Dr. James Lawson of Fisk University and other heads of colleges with rebellious student bodies. Lomax, as early as 1962, reported that students "throughout the South" berated men like Dr. Clark who refused "to support the Negro revolt in clear, open terms."

Independent scholars conclude that Southern University and other Negro colleges in state capitals are pressured because of the nearness of white state lawmakers. Other black colleges have been able to resist a subservient role, and have even maintained their own traditions of dissent.

BLACK VERSUS MIXED CAMPUSES

In more recent years another important issue has surfaced: the role of the black college at a time when the nation is striving to ease out racially exclusive institutions of all kinds. The Negro psychologist Kenneth Clark stressed the irony of this role in 1967:

> The Negro colleges became symbols of American racism. They became testaments of the society's commitment to excluding Negroes from any meaningful role in society as a whole. They slowly but surely became machines; their role as educational institutions became seriously compromised, and they reflected the contamination and moral erosion and emptiness of white colleges and universities in an America that presented itself as a democratic society.

When the Supreme Court rulings in the Sweatt and McLaurin cases removed the barriers facing Negroes in southern white schools, therefore, some educators called for an end to "Negro" colleges as such. Those engaged in fund-raising for these schools strongly disagreed.

Dr. James A. Boyer, the president of St. Augustine's College in Raleigh, North Carolina, argued in 1960 that the Negro colleges were "part of the nation's educational mosaic." Dr. Boyer,

JAMES A. BOYER

a director of the United Negro College Fund, which assists thirty-six such schools, declared at a Boston fund-raising rally: "They are needed now, and they will continue to be needed even after they reach the stage where they can lose their racial identity."

A white scholar, former Dean John Munro of Harvard, was even more emphatic when serving as director of freshman studies at predominantly Negro Miles College in Birmingham during 1967. Commenting on a suggestion that the Negro schools should be phased out or merged with white colleges, Munro told a *U.S. News and World Report* interviewer: "I regard the idea as idiocy. We are taking students that no one else will take, and we're designing programs for the whole spread of students—remedial programs, reinforcement programs, enrichment programs, special curricula in black history, black culture, black problems. The University of Alabama isn't going to do this. Harvard isn't going to do this. We're doing things for our students that no one else will do and we're turning out strong, professional people who are going to be leaders in the Negro community."

THE "POOR RISK" PROGRAM

By the late 1960's, a number of the nation's leading colleges and universities were recruiting Negro students and faculty with new vigor. More important, some were seeking out so-called "high risk" youths—poor minority-group students with erratic high school records but who showed signs of profiting from college attendance. The Southern Education Reporting Service found that four large state-supported universities had developed exceptionally good programs of this kind. Many other schools, both public and private, have begun such "high risk" programs, and are firmly committed to the approach. The big state-supported universities now enroll nearly half of all black college students. They are all recruiting black faculty members, and many are adding Negro history and related courses to their curricula.

Now the debate over the Negro college role has revolved full cycle. Again the argument for upgrading these schools is heard, but this time on different terms. Each year a sizeable number of Negro students transfer from "white" to Negro colleges. Today's student activists have proven themselves implacable enemies of the old black bourgeoisie with its ties to the status quo. They demand a fresh approach to learning, one which speaks to them as black people.

NEW EMPHASIS ON "BLACK CULTURE"

In 1931 Dr. Carter Woodson found courses at Negro colleges drawn up "without much thought about the Negro." Thirteen years later John Van Deusen recalled Woodson's words and added: "Few courses appear to give the student any knowledge of his own people, any sense of group loyalty, or any appreciation of things Negroid." It is this void which black militants on campus resolve to see filled. They often ignore the crucial problem, however, of how to restructure their course of study so that they will

Johns Hopkins University in Baltimore plays a leading role in recruiting low-income, high-ability students.

graduate on a par with white collegians. In the flurry of rhetoric over black heritage, little attention is given to the task of preparing the student to compete successfully in a biracial society. The black activist today calls for an end to schooling directed toward that goal. Paradoxically, he is asking for the same sort of training program espoused by Booker T. Washington in the 1890's. In essence it is an inward-looking curriculum tailored to cope with the problems of the black ghetto. Despite its overtones of black nationalism, such a program may yet offer practical solutions to the woes of slum life. Still, the black man with a broader vision is doubtful. He asks whether a study structure which isolates and confines him—despite its worthy social goals—may not turn out to be as oppressive as the classrooms of the old black bourgeoisie.

Student demands for courses in black culture and history have been felt outside the Negro colleges as well. The Kentucky public school system and Harvard University were forerunners in announcing the inclusion of such courses in their curricula. San Diego State College was among the first schools to offer the degree of Associate of Arts in Negro history and culture. Other major colleges and universities have followed suit but have had difficulty securing qualified people to teach these courses.

Along with these educational innovations has come a totally new intellectual self-awareness among blacks. For one thing, educators are now beginning to question seriously the conventional "lily white" interpretation of history and the social sciences. Another positive change now seen, especially among Negro youth, is the demise of the black middle class bias favoring light over dark skin. "In the Negro colleges in the 1920's and 1930's," one black historian has recorded, "dark-skinned students were brazenly excluded from fraternities (and, even more, sororities), but twenty years later students and young colored intellectuals in general showed a mounting disposition to reject whiteness as a standard of excellence, and even to stress darker skin as evidence of superior moral inheritance." This trend, now irreversible, has laid new stress on the colorful dress and ancient culture that make up the legacy of the Afro-American.

THE SELF-HELP DOCTRINE IN EDUCATION

Just as the status quo has been toppled on the Negro college campuses, so too have anti-traditional feelings been shown in the public schools. When schools opened in the fall of 1967, violence erupted in high schools in Los Angeles, Philadelphia and Pittsburgh, and in Waukegan (Ill.) and other Chicago suburbs. "Take the top off all these ghetto high schools and you see the same sorry story," Los Angeles Councilman Billy C. Mills has said. Mills, a Negro, pointed to frayed community-school ties, rundown physical plant, short-sighted policies, outdated attitudes, angry black-power pressures, teacher fears, student frustration and heavy absenteeism. In this seething atmosphere, Negro parents in Harlem, Watts and elsewhere demanded a controlling role in running their neighborhood schools. Walter Bremond, chairman of the Watts area Black Congress, spelled out these demands early in 1968:

BILLY C. MILLS

Lawrence Simms lends a hand during lunch time at the Arlington, Virginia, Head Start program.

What we are asking is a redistribution of power as it relates to control of ghetto schools. We want black people to have the opportunity to influence as well as make decisions as to what goes on in our own educational environment. Traditionally we haven't had any say . . . about how the schools are run, what is taught, what is relevant and what isn't, what the attitudes of teachers should or shouldn't be.

The school board, teachers, and administrators now have a vested interest in things as they are now. They aren't going to change that without a struggle. We are prepared to engage ourselves in that struggle. The only way for us to influence the schools is to enjoin the issues and make things uncomfortable. If there is no struggle, there is no progress.

Students themselves have designed new curricula in some schools, several urban boards of education are experimenting with new teaching methods, and virtually every college and university has some working interest in the education of disadvantaged youth. Antioch, Howard, Yale, Michigan State and the University of California are but a few of the schools with outstanding self-help programs operating in city ghettos.

Many local groups have assumed responsibilities for educational self-help programs. There are examples of neighborhood cooperatives setting up tutoring centers, of students organizing summer programs—to help both themselves and younger children—and of such community agencies as recreation centers, libraries, schools and churches offering to supplement the regular school curricula.

These illustrate what can be done at the local level, through private initiative. State and urban governments also operate effective programs in many areas. By far the biggest thrust has come from the federal government's Office of Economic Opportunity working with the Departments of Labor and of Health, Education and Welfare. In conjunction with community agencies, self-help programs have been set up all over the country where local funds have been made available.

Project Head Start, Follow Through, Community Education, Upward Bound and the Job Corps are among the many government-organized, community-operated programs designed to help educate those of disadvantaged backgrounds from childhood through adulthood. Head Start operates as a pre-school program orienting children to the world outside the ghetto.

The McNamara Job Skills Center has given this trainee new, marketable skills as a machine operator.

The Upward Bound program at Johns Hopkins University gives this student an opportunity to train for leadership.

The McNamara Center conducts classes to assist the unemployed as part of Detroit's job counseling program.

ROY WILKINS

JAMES FARMER

BAYARD RUSTIN

A Follow Through program is designed to ensure that Head Start "graduates" maintain the gains they have made throughout the primary grades. Community Education, which can involve providing study centers, individual tutoring, small instructional classes, cultural and recreational programs, educational and vocational guidance or parental training programs in academics or skills, is just one example of the programs available to complement these projects.

It is usually in high school that youngsters actually come face to face with career decisions. To generate the skills and motivation necessary for success in education at university level, the Upward Bound pre-college preparatory program sponsors summer residence on college campuses throughout the country to introduce students to the academic world. When summer ends, a second supportive program follows which encourages the students to remain interested. Arrangements are then made to place the students in colleges. The Job Corps provides training in everything from forestry to cooking, automobile repair to accounting—paying a salary to the corpsmen and allowances to their families. For two years the corpsmen live in the training centers learning their lifetime skills.

All of these programs are based on cooperative action, and their success is wholly dependent on the desire of the young people involved to "seek a newer world" of their own making.

THE MOYNIHAN REPORT

President Lyndon Johnson paid a visit to Howard University on June 4, 1965, to make a memorable speech on the future of the nation's race relations. His address was based on a Department of Labor report marked "for official use only." Its presumed chief author, former Assistant Secretary of Labor Daniel Patrick Moynihan, made three major points. The report asserted:

—Negroes will encounter serious personal prejudice for at least another generation.

—As a group, at the present time, in terms of ability to win out in the competitions of American life, they are not equal to most of those groups with which they will be competing.

—The evidence—not final, but powerfully persuasive—is that the Negro family in the urban ghettos is crumbling.

The reaction among civil-rights leaders varied sharply. Roy Wilkins, executive secretary of the NAACP, was as profuse in his praise as James Farmer of CORE was in his criticism. Said Wilkins: "I think he deserves the highest thanks and commendation from the public for his courage in laying this delicate and touchy subject on the table. Most people want to sweep it underneath the carpet." Farmer, in contrast, writing in his column "The Core of It" late in 1965, condemned the report as "the most serious threat to the ultimate freedom of American Negroes to appear in print in recent memory."

Bayard Rustin, chief strategist for the civil-rights movement, took the middle ground. On one hand he lauded Dr. Moynihan as "a very honest man who is trying to do his best. He is not a racist, and he is not giving aid and comfort to racists." On the other hand, Rustin insisted, there is nothing basically wrong with the Negro family as such. "The problem is poverty," he declared. "If one were to use any other poverty-stricken group, the same pattern would emerge. What we need to give the Negro and other poor groups is economic security. It all goes back to this single item."

SELF-HELP IN "REBUILDING BLACK"

For those Negroes who had pinned their hopes on racial integration occurring promptly and smoothly after the Supreme Court rulings of the 1950's, the next decade was to prove a trying period. The white Harvard scholar Thomas Petti-grew estimated that Negroes would not reach equal status in clerical jobs until 1992, among skilled workers until 2005, among professionals until 2017, among sales workers until 2114, and among business managers and proprietors until 2130. Another researcher, Robert Dentler, fore-cast "deep and extensive racial segregation in [northern] urban schools as late as the middle of the next century."

The late Senator Robert Kennedy of New York observed that "obviously, we cannot wipe out the ghetto overnight. Therefore, we must de-vote our attention to improving living conditions and rebuilding the present Negro areas, to giving their residents new job skills and jobs to go with them, to improving the education of their chil-dren, to providing new cultural interests for those who live there."

ROBERT F. KENNEDY

When he was director of Harlem's large anti-poverty agency, Livingston L. Wingate explained what this outlook meant for the people served by the federally funded Harlem youth program (Haryou-Act) in terms of the future: "I see a situation of a thriving black community like the white, living in dignity, even in isolation. This falls far short of the American dream, of course. But I say don't worry about the physical integration of Harlem. To live next to a man doesn't mean acceptance."

Wingate, a long-time associate of former Congressman Adam Powell, tempered his re-marks with the pragmatism of a veteran poli-tician. "If overnight Harlem houses were palaces and all its streets were clean enough to eat upon," he argued, "Harlem would still be af-flicted by the by-products of 350 years of social injustice. The spirit of the people wouldn't con-form to the new physical conditions." Win-gate, like Harlem's black nationalists, was con-vinced of the need for a united Negro front.

"There must be black contracting firms, black bulldozer operations, and black ownership while we await the open society," he said. At the same

LIVINGSTON L. WINGATE

time he found white technicians needed and welcome. "I don't refer to any formal dogma or creed when I speak of black unity," he explained, "but I do see an ever sharper awareness that the plight of one black man is unavoidably the plight of the other.

"Social services and jobs are not enough," Wingate declared. "The Negro must be given equal opportunity to compete for jobs. These other things are in order, but only to help him compete."

While Wingate was outlining the strategy for his war on Harlem poverty, his counterpart in Newark, New Jersey, Cyril D. Tyson, was placing new stress on an economic structure to attack the problems of the poor. Tyson served as director of the United Community Corporation in predominantly Negro Newark. In 1966 he envisioned a bold assault on black poverty.

"We're after a more sophisticated, more creative, more efficient use of each antipoverty dollar," he said. "We want to make the dollar work for the poor man as it does for the rich.

"We're trying to organize the poor," Tyson went on, "so that we can achieve a multiplier effect." This was the stimulation of business by new money entering the economy via a central

banking system and being used over and over again within the same corporate structure.

"A dollar has to be worth more than a dollar in our society," the Newark official explained. "It has to hook back to serve another purpose. But the poor person's dollar purchases less today than the middle-class dollar. So through the multiplier effect and breaking through the economics of the poor, we're slowly putting the pieces together here in Newark."

A child in the Newark Preschool Council (Operation Headstart) program, for example, buys a meal with his antipoverty dollar, which in turn helps to pay the training salary of the cook's apprentice who prepared the meal. The apprentice would be urged to invest part of his salary in a corporation bank modeled after the Carver Federal Savings and Loan Association in Harlem. This bank would provide mortgage or home improvement loans to poor people in the city. Home repair work might be provided by specialists trained through another apprenticeship program. Thus the original funds would continue to draw interest.

"It's not a new idea," Tyson admitted, "except that we've never thought of applying this type of concept to the poor. We've thought of welfare as

This man is now the owner and manager of a modern restaurant thanks to a small business loan.

another kind of bird, but you have a new sort of leverage now . . . We need human renewal. The phrase 'maximum feasible participation of the poor' doesn't mean the poor are receiving hand-outs. They must take part in the planning, in the staffing. They're giving the services to them-selves."

Although both Wingate and Tyson departed from their posts under fire, their ideas have been put into effect more and more frequently. In the black Bedford-Stuyvesant section of Brooklyn, a twofold program has been established: the Bedford-Stuyvesant Restoration Corporation and the Development and Services Program. The lat-ter part is designed primarily to bring money into the black community, while the former centers around direct self-help and training programs; the board of directors is drawn from the com-munity itself.

In Harlem the black community owns and manages a cooperative supermarket. The self-help principle is also applied in business. In sev-eral major cities NEGRO (National Economic Growth and Reconstruction Organization), founded by Dr. Thomas Matthews of Harlem, recruits blacks to take jobs in any of its seventeen various business subsidiaries.

Other programs function under the auspices of the Department of Labor, which, in turn, works with the National Alliance of Business-men to promote black economic success. Under the JOBS program, businessmen in cities through-out the country have joined together to employ and train at least a hundred thousand hard-core unemployables in fifty major cities. Contracts are drawn up with local unions in an attempt to guarantee employment within their areas to those trained.

Universities have established small business guidance centers which often form valuable asso-ciations within the structure of the existing business community.

The Department of Commerce's Small Busi-ness Administration has helped Negro firms ob-tain capital and is currently expanding its efforts, particularly in ghetto areas. The Interracial Council for Business Opportunity, a privately funded national organization, gives management advice and counseling to black entrepreneurs.

ICBO also sponsors a business education pro-gram for high school and college students, and works to secure government funds for black busi-nessmen. It also arranges loans through both pri-vate and government sources.

The early 1970's saw new gains in the field of black business. Typical of these gains was the appointment of veteran journalist Stanley C. Scott, formerly a general assignment reporter for the New York bureau of United Press Inter-national, to the White House Communications Staff.

The appointment of Scott was particularly meaningful since his family has long been identi-fied with journalism. They publish several daily newspapers in the Deep South especially in the Atlanta area.

During the calendar year 1972, there were 13 black-owned firms whose sales exceeded $10, 000,000. In addition, many blacks rose to direc-torships on boards of major corporations. Four of the top ten among the Fortune 500 industrial corporations have black directors, but represen-tation is strongest on the boards of life insurance companies, banks and utilities. This may be due to the fact that these boards are larger than those of industry.

Another factor for the rise is the system of free enterprise itself. In areas with a predominately black population, it becomes "good politics"—not tokenism—to have black officers and direc-tors if the firm is out to attract black business. One such case is the National Bank of Washing-ton (D.C.) which has made no secret of its desire to attract more black depositors.

And still another reason is the elimination of many forms of racial prejudices which have kept these qualified individuals from attaining such positions in the past.

PROGRESS WITHIN THE AFL-CIO

Equally important to the future of the black community is an apprenticeship program break-through for young Negroes. To date, labor union critics like the NAACP's Herbert Hill have charged widespread discrimination against non-whites. Hill reported in 1960—five years after the

HERBERT HILL

merger of the AFL-CIO—that "efforts to eliminate discriminatory practices within trade unions have been piecemeal and inadequate and usually the result of protest by civil-rights agencies acting on behalf of Negro workers." The NAACP secretary accused the Seafarers International Union of running hiring halls in Duluth, Chicago, Detroit, Cleveland and Buffalo which "will dispatch Negro workers only for menial jobs as messmen in the galley departments of ships. . . ."

Hill aimed another reproach at the Union of Electrical Workers in Cleveland, which he claimed had brought about "token admission of a few Negroes . . . as public relations gestures but continued to exclude Negroes from membership by tacit consent." Moreover, in the crucial apprenticeship training programs, the NAACP official observed that Negro participation from 1950-1960 had increased only from 1.5 per cent to 2 per cent in the New York state building trades. Hill singled out the plumbers union (from which George Meany rose to become AFL-CIO president) as especially resistant to Negro apprentices. He also criticized the Sheet Metal Workers Union, the Ornamental and Structural Iron Work-

ers, the Glass Workers, the Tile Setters, the Machinists and the Bricklayers Unions.

Six years later the chairman of the New York City Commission against Discrimination repeated the same charges, this time pointing to Harry Van Arsdale, chairman of the New York Central Labor Council and a long-time champion of civil rights. By now, union resistance was thwarting federal programs such as the Neighborhood Youth Corps in their efforts to train Negroes in skilled trades. Department of Labor officials were working behind the scenes to bring pressure on unionist Van Arsdale and on Peter Brennan of the New York Building Trades Council; but these officers pleaded for more time. They contended that the white rank-and-file adamantly opposed the open apprenticeship programs and that only time and education could change their views. Meanwhile, unemployment among black males was generally more than double that of whites—and even higher among Negro youths.

Thomas O'Hanlon, writing in *Fortune* in January of 1968, presented a strong case against the unions' "moral ambiguity" in shunning the black workman.

Detroit's New Careers program trains young people in job skills. It also employs teacher aides, thus relieving overworked ghetto teachers.

In response to the O'Hanlon article, AFL-CIO civil-rights director Don Slaiman wrote an angry letter to *Fortune.* He decried O'Hanlon's "distortions, misrepresentations, and downright misstatements of fact." He noted that O'Hanlon neglected to mention progress since the fair employment section of the 1964 Civil Rights Act had become law. Hence, he said, O'Hanlon was "by definition out of date." Slaiman also recalled a quote by A. Philip Randolph, the black president of the sleeping car porters' union. "Negro leadership recognizes," Randolph had said in 1965, "that of all the mass institutions in the nation the labor movement holds out the greatest hope for progress in the daily conditions of life in the Negro community." A few years earlier, Randolph had lashed out at the " 'do nothing' civil-rights record in the House of Labor."

Despite Randolph's changed opinion, the late Walter Reuther remained dismayed by labor's slow pace in carrying out social reforms. Reuther, president of the United Auto Workers, withheld his union's dues to the AFL-CIO on this issue, thus daring the group's leaders to expel the UAW. When it voted to do just that in early 1968, the shaky merger of Meany's AFL and Reuther's CIO appeared about to topple over. One of the factors in the ideological dispute between Meany and Reuther was the issue of race. However, the old labor leadership has been attempting to put its house in order by placing Negroes in positions of leadership within the framework of the national organizations. Former redcap Walter Davis became AFL-CIO director of education, and both staff representatives of the Civil Rights Division are Negroes.

By early 1968, eighteen building trades unions gave Secretary of Labor Willard Wirtz a formal pledge to start actively recruiting Negroes as trainees and apprentices. The Washington *Evening Star,* in heralding the event, observed that "a long and shameful chapter of American race relations appears to be drawing to a close." Much of the credit belongs to the Department of Labor, which has long pressed for an end to "white only" labor standards.

The problems which undeniably exist for both the apprenticeship and recruiting programs are slowly being overcome. In 1964 the Workers Defense League, organized in the thirties to combat job discrimination, launched a program with a similar organization, the A. Philip Randolph Institute. The groups recognized the inability of the state employment services to provide adequate information about unions to prospective apprentices. Their Joint Apprenticeship Program was initiated in New York; offices were opened in ghetto areas for the recruitment of minority group apprentices. The JAP realized that these offices could not operate on a nine-to-five basis, but would have to gear their hours to those of the young people they hoped to recruit. It went to all possible lengths to ask assistance in distributing information in order to reach Negro and Puerto Rican youths. The program has been so successful that several offices have been opened in New York City and branches have been established in other cities.

Two government programs intended to aid the cause of the black worker are the Manpower Development and Training Act and the Model Cities program. Robert McGlotten, of the civil-rights section of AFL-CIO, has felt that by 1971 these programs, with the help of the schools, communities and mass news media, may be responsible for training some five hundred thousand minority group workers.

Many unions, notably in Shreveport, Louisiana, and in Chattanooga, Tennessee, requested that programs be established in their cities to train minority applicants for labor work. Much of the resentment and fear over Negro inclusion in trade and labor is a bitter affront to the Negro American. But the recognition by union officials and by government agencies, and, most important, by the laborers themselves, that the old system is unjust and untenable provides hope for the future.

CHAPTER FIFTEEN

Black Power in the Establishment— Elections and Appointments

I N spite of the air conditioning, the House of Representatives had grown hot and humid, and the nation's lawmakers were in a feverish mood. It was August 3, 1966, and the chamber was charged with emotion. The longest debate since Reconstruction was underway. The issue: the "open housing" section of an omnibus civil-rights bill which had finally been dislodged from the House judiciary committee.

Behind the brass rail to the rear of the chamber, Congressman Charles Cole Diggs, Jr., was taking a mental headcount of the pro-civil-rights members on hand from his party. Diggs, a liberal representative from Detroit, serves as civil-rights "whip" of the Democratic Study Group. Earlier that day the Negro congressman had confided to newsmen that the floor vote that day would be extremely close.

Now the critical test had come. The "teller vote" was in progress. First those in favor of the delicate open housing compromise marched up the center aisle to be counted. Then the opposition. Just over three hundred congressmen had been counted. Observers in the packed press gallery checked their tallies and found the measure losing by a dozen votes. At this point—with only a few uncounted members waiting to be added to the total—three more members raced in from the Democratic cloakroom. Then a few more. Finally a cluster of about fifteen—Charlie Diggs' reserves—dashed in to cast last-minute votes. At last Diggs himself rushed into the

CHARLES COLE DIGGS, JR.

chamber, down to the speaker's desk and up the center aisle to be counted. With the extra votes, the civil-rights camp's teller announced he had 179 "aye" votes, the same number as the "nays." The presiding officer of the House, Congressman Richard Bolling of Missouri, promptly cast his tie-breaking vote in favor of open housing.

EDWARD W. BROOKE   YVONNE B. BURKE   CARDISS COLLINS   AUGUSTUS HAWKINS

THE BLACK CAUCUS

A new power bloc, the Black Caucus, has housed itself within the Congress of the United States. The Black Caucus, comprised of sixteen of the seventeen Congressional members, was organized for the purpose of opening some line of communication between the Nixon administration and the black people of this country.

Yvonne Braithwaite Burke, California, an attorney, served in the California State Legislature for six years prior to coming to the Hill. She sits currently on the Public Works Committee and the Interior and Insular Affairs Committee.

Shirley Chisholm, New York, made political history by becoming the first woman and first black to seek the presidential nomination on a major party ticket. She sits on the House Education and Labor Committee.

William L. Clay, Missouri, is treasurer of the Caucus. He sits on the House Education and Labor Committee and the Post Office and Civil Service Committee.

Cardiss Collins, Illinois, is the newest member of the Caucus. She won a seat in the House in a special election to fill the Illinois 7th District vacancy caused by her husband's untimely death.

John Conyers, Jr., Michigan, is a sponsor of the Full Opportunity Act which would provide $30 billion a year to disadvantaged Americans. He authored the only amendment passed by the House which puts guts into the Fair Housing section of the 1966 Civil Rights Bill.

Ronald V. Dellums, California, is a former social worker and manpower consultant. He is currently a member of the House's District of Columbia and Armed Forces Committees.

Charles C. Diggs, Jr., Michigan, is Chairman of both the House Committee on the District of Columbia and the House Foreign Affairs Subcommittee on Africa. He is serving his 10th term for Detroit's 13th District.

Walter E. Fauntroy, District of Columbia, is one of the two Caucus' practicing ministers. He became the first delegate to the U.S. Congress representing the nation's capital since the nineteenth century.

Augustus F. Hawkins, California, had been a California assemblyman since 1934. He came to Congress in 1963 from Los Angeles' 21st District and is currently chairman of the House Subcommittee on Equal Opportunity.

Barbara Jordan, Texas, came to the House in 1972. Prior to coming to Washington, she had served in the Texas State Senate and her training as an attorney has prepared her well for her service as a member of the House Judiciary Committee.

Ralph H. Metcalfe, Illinois, a former Olympic sprint champion, came to Congress in 1970. He has served as a Ward Democratic Committeeman, an Alderman in 1969, and President pro tempore of the Chicago City Council.

Parren J. Mitchell, Maryland, represents the 7th Congressional District in Baltimore. He is a former professor at Morgan State College and has a history of active civil rights participation.

Robert N. C. Nix, Pennsylvania, is the second senior Caucus member, coming to Congress in 1958. He has been a practicing attorney since 1925 and is currently chairman of the Asian and Pacific Affairs Subcommittee.

Charles B. Rangel, New York, came to Congress from the 18th Congressional District by defeating Adam Clayton Powell. He serves on the House District of Columbia Committee and has been a moving force in the Congressional fight for anti-drug legislation.

CHARLES C. DIGGS, JR. ROBERT N. C. NIX JOHN CONYERS, JR. WALTER WASHINGTON

Louis Stokes, Ohio, is the new Chairman of the Black Caucus. He became the first black member of Congress from Ohio when he was elected in 1968—in his first run for public office. He was the first black appointed to sit on the House Appropriations Committee.

Andrew Young, Georgia, is the first black Congressman from that state since Reconstruction. He was a practicing minister in Alabama and Georgia before going to work for the National Council of Churches in 1957.

Although not a member of the Caucus, Edward W. Brooke, Massachusetts, is a close friend in the U.S. Senate. In 1966, he became the first black elected to that body since Reconstruction. Prior to his entrance into the Senate, he served for three years as Massachusetts Attorney General. He is the recipient of numerous honorary degrees and awards including the Bronze Star.

"NEW BREED" IN CITY HALL

The likelihood of the black politicians improving the lives of their constituents seems more dependent on a rising crop of "new breed" mayors like Carl B. Stokes of Cleveland, Richard Hatcher of Gary and Walter Washington of the District of Columbia. The black congressmen seldom exercise city-wide leverage, although Dawson was a notable exception. But as the black social analysts St. Claire Drake and Horace R. Cayton observed in *Black Metropolis* (1945), the black voter has not usually opted for social change but has stayed with organization politics.

"Negroes [in Chicago] have seldom supported the reformers," Drake and Cayton point out. "They have preferred to deal with hardheaded realists who are willing to trade political posi-

tions and favorable legislation for votes. A cynical realism has pervaded Black Metropolis which sees democracy as something granted to Negroes on the basis of political expediency rather than as a right. In the past this has meant dealing with the 'corrupt' machines, and even the clergy have not hesitated to play the game." Though this statement was written over twenty years ago, it seems nearly as applicable today.

When a black has won a big-city mayor's seat, however, he has usually done it by bucking his party organization. The victories of Stokes and Hatcher came about only after bitter factional struggles against "bossism."

Just as Michigan has led the way in electing black congressmen, so it has moved ahead in selecting black mayors. These have included Floyd J. McCree of Flint, Henry Marsh of Saginaw and John Burton of Ypsilanti. Voters in Lansing elected thirty-year-old Joel Ferguson, a former local basketball star, to a councilman-at-large post. In each of these cities, whites lent needed support to the Negroes' election.

The current trend is toward electing young blacks with progressive programs for dealing with urban ills. Many white voters apparently agree that black leaders are better equipped to deal with the problems that cause unrest in the ghettos. This theory helps explain the victories of Boston Councilman Tom Atkins, Compton (Calif.) Mayor Doris Davis, Atlanta Mayor Maynard Jackson and a number of other newly elected blacks. But the vast majority of black officeholders have won their seats with the aid of bloc voting by nonwhites.

An exception to this was the 1973 election of Thomas Bradley as mayor of Los Angeles. Bradley won the election in a city whose total black population was only slightly over 15 per cent.

LUCIUS AMERSON

WILLIAM L. TAYLOR

THE BLOC VOTE

The potential of this tactic was shown in 1961 in the municipal election in Atlanta. A former mayor, Ivan Allen, Jr., swamped Lester Maddox, gaining at least 99.9 per cent of the vote in black precincts. Maddox, of course, was well known to Negroes as the owner of a restaurant which refused to serve black customers. He eventually closed the eating place rather than bow to the federal Civil Rights Act of 1964.

Lucius Amerson, the sheriff of Macon County, Alabama, is one of many black southerners who thinks bloc voting is here to stay. "I might as well tell it like it is," he said. "As long as whites are going to bloc-vote against any Negro, well, we might as well bloc-vote against any white."

The thirty-three-year-old lawman inspired awe in many youthful militants when he arrested a white police chief and a state trooper in 1968 on charges of threatening and beating a Negro man they had arrested. Though white local officials predicted an early end to his good relations with the Alabama highway patrol, the black sheriff shrugged off the suggestion. Despite later difficulties, Amerson managed to retain his post in 1971. Amerson, a postal worker in 85 per cent black Macon County before he ran for sheriff, is one of a growing number of blacks who have sought public office in the South in the middle 1960's.

Much of the current progress in registering black voters in the South began after Congress passed the Voting Rights Act of 1965. Although the Student Nonviolent Coordinating Committee had pressed registration campaigns in Lowndes County, Alabama, Greenwood,

Mississippi, and other strongholds of segregation, the 1965 statute placed the full force of federal law behind its efforts. In its 1968 report, the U.S. Civil Rights Commission noted that over half of the Negroes in the southern states—about three million people—had registered to vote since passage of the Voting Rights Act.

During 1966 and 1967, the report found, over a thousand Negroes sought state, local and party office in the South. Almost 250 were elected to public office. But when he released the report, the commission's staff director, William L. Taylor, underscored subtler means now appearing to thwart black voters.

"While we found that there has been an increase in the number of registered Negro voters and a corresponding increase in the number of black candidates seeking public and party office," he said, "there are new forms of discrimination and new election contrivances to prevent Negroes from participating fully and freely in the political and electoral processes."

Taylor cited state or party rules to dilute Negro votes, discrimination against Negroes who tried to register, vote fraud, interference with Negro poll watchers, harassment and intimidation of Negro voters—particularly economic and physical. The commission warned that much of the progress the southern black had made at the ballot box since 1965 could be wiped out in the next few years without continued vigilance against discriminatory tactics by local white politicians and election officials.

Still, southern "lily white" politics have been giving way before tough-minded black office seekers like Amerson and Robert Clark, the first black to gain a seat in the Mississippi house of representatives in seventy-four years. Clark, a teacher who graduated from Michigan State University, indicated that his white colleagues showed him widespread surface courtesy but did not go out of their way to teach him the parliamentary ropes.

A young black elected in 1965, former SNCC worker Julian Bond, was refused his seat by the Georgia legislature because of his anti-war views. He was later seated by a ruling of the Supreme Court. Seven other black legislators joined Georgia's lower house in 1965 and two

JULIAN BOND   BARBARA JORDAN   W. FERGUSON REID   GILBERT MASON

(Leroy Johnson and Horace Ward) joined the state senate. All but two of these legislators came from Fulton County (Atlanta).

Georgia had moved far ahead of other southern states in forming a "black bloc" in its state capitol. Alabama, Arkansas, Florida, North Carolina and South Carolina still had all-white state legislatures in the late 1960's.

Tennessee ranked next to Georgia in number of blacks in state office. Memphis, Knoxville and Nashville have all sent blacks to the state house of representatives. Texas Senator Barbara Jordan of Houston is the first black woman to sit in a southern legislature. Other black Texans are members of the house of representatives in Austin. Ernest Morial of Orleans Parish was the first black to enter the Louisiana statehouse in Baton Rouge since Reconstruction. The same is true of Virginia State Representative W. Ferguson Reid of Richmond.

Many blacks—more than two hundred—hold local public office in the South. These officials range from mayors and councilmen to tax collectors and county coroners. Blacks in influential positions now include school board members (over thirty Negroes sit on school boards in Arkansas alone), justices of the peace, sheriffs, constables, county supervisors and police jurymen. In addition, more Negroes are taking part in party politics—mostly Democratic—in the South. Dr. Gilbert Mason of Biloxi, for instance, was chosen in June, 1968, to attend the Democratic National Convention as part of Mississippi's first integrated delegation since Reconstruction. The move was regarded as an effort to sidetrack the Mississippi Freedom Democrats' expected challenge to seating a "lily white" delegation. The MFD Party tried that tactic in the 1964 Democratic National Convention but was ruled out of order. The all-Negro Freedom Democrats are the foremost champions of the Negro bloc vote in the South.

THE BLACK VOTE IN THE NORTH

As a result of the new southern upsurge in black voting strength, there are now a good many state senators, state representatives, and city councilmen, and more than 200 other black elected officials across the nation. With only a dozen or so exceptions, all of these are Democrats. Of equal importance, blacks have proved a decisive factor in electing whites with moderate-to-liberal records in races where no blacks are entered. Examples have been the victories of Mayors John V. Lindsay of New York City (the first Republican to enter City Hall in over twenty years), Jerome Cavanagh of Detroit, Kevin White of Boston and Joseph Alioto of San Francisco. For the Negroes seeking big-city office, the problems of campaigning for both black and white votes are immense.

On the eve of the November election of 1967, Dr. Kenneth B. Clark spoke to the National Conference of Negro Elected Officials about this dilemma. Dr. Clark, the Negro president of the Metropolitan Applied Research Center, said the black candidate has to make it seem "as if America had in fact reached that stage of racial maturity where race and color are irrelevant and where a candidate would be judged and selected by the electorate in terms of his intelligence, competence, experience, and integrity." Too much stress on race may lose the white vote because of "the racism inherent in America," Dr. Clark warned. But an irresolute stand on black principles can lose the black vote just as easily. Many blacks, Clark said, may view

J. ERNEST WILKINS

SAMUEL Z. WESTERFIELD

ALFRED L. EDWARDS

CARL B. STOKES

such a candidate "as a traitor . . . willing to sell his own race down the river in order to enhance his chances of personal advancement." Moreover, once elected, Mayor Stokes of Cleveland and Mayor Hatcher of Gary faced problems no less critical than those of their white predecessors. Clark suggested that they must find a formula "whereby there can be a reasonable working relationship with some elements of Negro nationalism."

For officials like Mayor Stokes, this has meant returning often to the slums of their childhood to shoot a game of pool with jobless black youths. White mayors like Lindsay of New York have also tried to establish rapport with the black community. Their aim is to overcome the alienation of Hough and Harlem through political and economic reforms. Though the gigantic task of urban reorganization seems nearly hopeless, Stokes, Lindsay and others of like mind are making determined efforts to change the ghetto mood. They are perhaps mindful of C. Eric Lincoln's judgment that "the 'nationalism' of the American Negro is not voluntary, prompted by a desire to set himself apart in order to preserve some cultural values. It is, rather, a defensive response to external forces—hostile forces which threaten his creative existence. It is a unity born of the wish not to conserve, but to escape a set of conditions." If they can change those conditions, men like Stokes and Lindsay can win back the suspicious ghetto and make its people useful citizens again. In the event that they fail, the "sullen brooding" of the Harlems and Houghs appears certain to rekindle those fires of lawlessness that flared across the nation during the 1960's.

THE INCREASE IN BLACK APPOINTEES

Owing largely to ghetto outbreaks, the executive branches of governments at all levels (the President, governors and mayors) have turned more and more to Negroes to help cure urban ills. President Eisenhower had earlier named J. Ernest Wilkins as assistant secretary of labor in 1954 and 1958, and made E. Frederick Morrow his administrative assistant in 1955. Morrow was the first black executive to join the White House staff. This trend was greatly accelerated during the Kennedy and Johnson administrations.

When President Kennedy took office in 1961 (having attracted 70 per cent of the nation's Negro vote in his contest with Richard M. Nixon), he appointed San Francisco newsman Andrew Hatcher his associate press secretary. Hatcher, the first New Frontier Negro appointee, remained until 1964, when he left the Johnson administration to become a business executive. Soon after entering office, President Kennedy made two more Negro appointments:

CLIFFORD L. ALEXANDER   CHARLOTTE M. HUBBARD

Robert C. Weaver as administrator of the Housing and Home Finance Agency and George L. P. Weaver as assistant secretary of labor. He later named Roy Davenport his deputy undersecretary of the army and Alfred L. Edwards his deputy assistant secretary of agriculture. Before his assassination in 1963, the President tapped Howard Jenkins, Jr., to serve as a member of the National Labor Relations Board. He said publicly that he would appoint Dr. Robert Weaver the first secretary of the proposed Department of Urban Affairs. But southern opposition to naming a Negro to the Cabinet temporarily killed the new department. When Congress approved it in 1965 as the Department of Housing and Urban Development, however, President Johnson broke with tradition in asking Dr. Weaver to head HUD. Despite grumbling from the southerners, the Senate confirmed the Negro's appointment.

After taking office in November of 1963, Lyndon Johnson made a record number of Negro appointments. The first was Chester C. Carter, who served briefly as the State Department's deputy chief of protocol. In 1964 he named Arthur Christopher, Jr., to the trial examiner post on the National Labor Relations Board. Christopher thus became the first trial examiner of his race in the federal government. The same year Charlotte M. Hubbard became deputy assistant secretary of state; this was the highest federal post held by a Negro woman. Campbell C. Johnson, a graduate of Howard and Columbia Universities, was also chosen during 1964 to serve as assistant director of the selective service. And Ambassador to Finland Carl T. Rowan became President Johnson's choice to head the United States Information Agency. The President named other Negroes to high-ranking posts while he was finishing out John F. Kennedy's term. These appointees included Samuel Z. Westerfield (deputy assistant secretary of state), Ronald D. Palmer (staff assistant to the assistant secretary of state for educational and cultural affairs), Hobart Taylor, Jr. (associate special counsel to the President), Mrs. Frankie Muse Freeman (a member of the U.S. Civil Rights Commission), Clifford L. Alexander (Presidential assistant for personnel and administration) and Charles Patterson (deputy director for the Peace Corps, Africa office).

Then, in November 1964, the President won a landslide victory over Senator Barry Goldwater of Arizona, to remain in the White House for a full term. Goldwater alienated Negroes by the millions when he cast a vote against the Civil Rights Act of 1964 (a measure to ensure equal access to all public accommodations). It surprised nobody when Negroes gave President Johnson 94 per cent of their vote. It was the greatest support ever given a Democratic presidential candidate by Negroes.

During his next four years, President Johnson continued to choose Negroes for jobs never before open to them. In 1965 alone he named Howard Woods as associate director of the United States Information Agency, Eileen Hernandez and Samuel Jackson to serve on the Equal Employment Opportunity Commission, Thurgood Marshall as solicitor general of the

RONALD D. PALMER   CARL T. ROWAN   HOWARD JENKINS, JR.   HOBART TAYLOR, JR.

A. LEON HIGGINBOTHAM   JAMES B. PARSONS   JOSEPH WADDY

United States, Hobart Taylor, Jr., as director of the Export-Import Bank, Clifford Alexander as associate special counsel to the President and Roger Wilkins as director of the Community Relations Service. Andrew Brimmer, who had been assistant secretary of commerce, was appointed to the Federal Reserve Board in 1966. The following year Clifford Alexander was named chairman of the Equal Opportunity Commission.

NEGROES IN THE JUDICIARY

Since 1945—when President Harry Truman named Irvin C. Mollison to the bench of the United States Customs Court—an increasing number of Negroes have been appointed federal judges in the North. President Truman also tapped Judge William H. Hastie in 1949 to serve on the U.S. Court of Appeals, Third Circuit. During his eight years in the White House, President Eisenhower appointed only one Negro judge, Scovel Richardson, who was named to a life term on the United States Customs Court bench.

The judicial appointments of Presidents Kennedy and Johnson, however, numbered many Negroes. In his "thousand days" in the White House, President Kennedy chose six Negroes for federal judgeships. In 1961 he named Judge James B. Parsons to the U.S. District Court (Illinois) and Judge Wade McCree to the U.S. District Court (Michigan). That year he also nominated Judge Thurgood Marshall to sit on the U.S. Circuit Court of Appeals. In 1962 he appointed Joseph Waddy to the Washington, D.C., District Court. Before his assassination, the President had

selected two other Negroes for judgeships, but they received recess appointments from President Johnson until confirmed by the Senate. These two were A. Leon Higginbotham and Spottswood W. Robinson, III. Higginbotham joined the U.S. District Court (eastern Pennsylvania), and Robinson sits on the U.S. Court of Appeals for the District of Columbia.

President Johnson appointed Damon J. Keith in 1964 as a judge of the U.S. District Court in eastern Michigan. He followed this with other lower court nominations of Negroes, among them: James L. Watson (Customs Court of New York); Aubrey E. Robinson, Jr., and William Benson Bryant (U.S. District Court in the District of Columbia); and Constance Baker Motley (U.S. District Court in southern New York). Mrs. Motley, an NAACP attorney since 1946, had just been elected borough president of Manhattan, after having served in the New York state senate.

These appointments caused little sensation, and there was only token resistance from southern senators before the judges won confirmation. But this mood changed in 1967, when the President nominated Judge Thurgood Marshall to fill the U.S. Supreme Court vacancy created when Justice Tom Clark retired. The high court had been delicately balanced between liberals and conservatives, with Justice Clark often casting the swing vote. Though the court usually voted with near unanimity on civil-rights issues, it often rendered five–four decisions in cases dealing with the rights of the accused. When Solicitor General Marshall went before the Senate judiciary committee for several days of questioning,

CONSTANCE B. MOTLEY   DAMON J. KEITH   SPOTTSWOOD W. ROBINSON

THURGOOD MARSHALL

Senator Sam Ervin, Jr., of North Carolina, baited the former NAACP counsel unmercifully. In the end, though, only a scattering of die-hard southerners voted against confirming the court's first Negro appointee. Though Justice Marshall has been a lifetime champion of civil rights, observers expected him to compile a conservative voting record on other issues.

The few judicial posts which remain "lily white" today are located, predictably, in the South. The President who names a Negro to the U.S. Court of Appeals' Fourth or Fifth Circuit can expect a storm of protest from the solid South. Together, the area of jurisdiction of these courts includes all of the former Confederate states except Tennessee. The Fifth Circuit, however, has in recent years rendered by far the most progressive decisions on civil-rights issues of any of the federal Courts of Appeals.

THE NEGRO VOTER IN THE CITY

After his narrow loss of the Presidency in 1960, former Vice-President Richard M. Nixon blamed his fate on his inability to attract a larger Negro vote. Nixon said that he had simply not campaigned correctly. Nixon's ally, Republican National Chairman Thruston B. Morton, came

to the same conclusion. Senator Morton noted at a post-election news conference that Nixon "took only 10 to 12 per cent of the Negro vote, compared to the 26 per cent President Eisenhower attracted." Morton observed that the Republicans had "taken too much for granted" in 1960 and added: "We should have done a lot more in that area three months before."

Nevertheless, in 1964 Republicans handed the party's presidential nomination to Senator Barry Goldwater, an action which affronted roughly 95 per cent of the black voters. Though the Goldwater campaign was geared to a possible "white backlash," this failed to materialize. The Arizona Senator carried only five southern states—Alabama, Mississippi, Louisiana, South Carolina and Georgia—in addition to his home state. Goldwater's campaign, like Nixon's 1960 "southern strategy," had obviously backfired.

As the 1968 presidential elections approached, the candidates of both parties were more aware than ever of the Negro voter—especially in the big industrial states of the North with their large electoral votes. In the big cities, where the black ballot could tip the scales for the entire state, early attempts had been made to attract the Negro vote. The crucial nature of this undertaking can be seen in the table shown here, which is based on 1960 census statistics.

Key Negro Political Cities Based on
State Electoral Vote

State Electoral Vote	City	Population	Negro Population	Negro Percentage of Population
45	New York	7,781,984	1,087,931	14.0
32	Philadelphia	2,002,512	529,240	26.4
32	Los Angeles	2,479,015	334,916	13.5
32	San Francisco	740,316	74,383	10.0
27	Chicago	3,550,404	812,637	22.9
25	Cleveland	876,050	250,818	28.6
25	Cincinnati	502,550	108,754	21.6
20	Detroit	1,670,144	482,223	28.9
13	St. Louis	750,026	214,377	28.6
12	Atlanta	487,455	186,464	38.3
11	Memphis	497,524	184,320	37.0
11	Nashville	170,874	64,570	37.8
10	Louisville	390,639	70,075	17.9
9	Baltimore	939,024	326,589	34.8

FLOYD McKISSICK

STOKELY CARMICHAEL

In each of these cities the Negro vote has risen markedly since 1960. This is due to Negro registration drives and to a continuing white exodus from the big cities to their suburbs. Before his assassination in June of 1968, Senator Robert F. Kennedy of New York had proven himself a favorite of black voters in Democratic primary election victories in Indiana, Nebraska, California and the District of Columbia. In the wake of the Kennedy tragedy, saddened Negro Democrats debated the question of whether to support the party's frontrunner, Vice-President Hubert H. Humphrey, or a new challenger, Senator George McGovern of South Dakota. Both had championed the cause of equal rights and had supported broad social-welfare reforms in the Senate.

At the same time, Richard Nixon was hoping to cut sharply into the Negro vote if, as expected, he should gain the GOP nomination. His only real challenge came from Governor Nelson Rockefeller of New York, a liberal whose campaign centered on the weakness of Nixon's appeal to Negro and independent white voters.

At this point, many prominent black leaders across the nation formed a national "committee of inquiry" to study the presidential candidates and their platforms. Among the committee's prime movers were the Rev. Ralph Abernathy (successor to Dr. Martin Luther King as head of the Southern Christian Leadership Conference), Floyd McKissick (national director of the Congress of Racial Equality), James Farmer (former CORE director and a Liberal-Republican candidate for Congress in Brooklyn), Stokely Carmichael (former chairman of the Student Nonviolent Coordinating Committee), Mayor Richard Hatcher of Gary, Indiana, Congressman John Conyers, Jr., of Detroit, and State Representative James Del Rio of Lansing, Michigan. Congressman Conyers urged Negroes to remain uncommitted until the committee had interviewed all candidates. The Rev. Ralph Abernathy said SCLC was thinking of dropping its nonpolitical tradition in 1968. The wait-and-see strategy naturally appealed to Republican liberals, who saw it as an invitation to bid heavily for black support. The only candidate now obviously out of the running (in terms of Negro backing) was George Wallace of Alabama, who was at the head of the American Independent Party's ticket. Any votes he might get, however, as a conservative Democrat, could seriously affect the election's outcome.

Congressman Conyers, a liberal Democrat and "dove" on the Vietnam War issue, told a Chicago press conference in October of 1967 that his party appeared vulnerable to a Negro bolt in 1968. The statement followed a three-day convention of the National Conference of Negro Officials at the University of Chicago. "The Democratic Party can be defeated in at least half a dozen states by Negroes' staying home," Conyers told the press. "It's no secret that the Republican Party has been attracting a large number of disaffected Negroes."

"We are dealing with a new kind of Negro, an articulate, dedicated and qualified one," State Senator Mervyn Dymally of Los Angeles explained at the same conference. "We feel that this is the beginning of a new age for the Negro politician, an age in which he learns how to harness political power into meaningful changes in the black community."

As the time of political decision-making arrived in 1968, the "new age" had indeed dawned for the black political leaders. Sensing the pivotal nature of the Negro ballot across the nation, these leaders were prepared to strike a hard bargain for the black vote. For the Negro had at last entered the mainstream of American politics. Once having reached the age of political independence he could confer his favor on the party which offered him and his race the best hope for advancement. Traditional voting patterns would be cast aside. And neither party would dare to take his support for granted again.

CHAPTER SIXTEEN

Direct Action and Passive Resistance— The Struggle To Let Freedom Ring

DURING war-torn 1942, a strange protest occurred on the home front—a fore-runner of the civil-rights demonstrations of the 1950's and 1960's. An integrated group known as the Congress of Racial Equality (CORE) formed in Chicago and staged the first "sit-in" in a restaurant in the busy Loop area. When Negro patrons were refused service, CORE members of both races remained seated, thereby bringing business to a standstill. Although the young organization was thoroughly committed to nonviolence, CORE believed in forcing a direct confrontation with the degrading racial policies then legally sanctioned in North and South. After the Chicago test, CORE later succeeded in desegregating St. Louis and Baltimore lunch counters. The sit-in had proved a highly effective pressure tactic. Not until 1960, however, did it find widespread use as a means of cracking the wall of segregation.

In the interim, a series of lawsuits—many of which were argued by the NAACP—paved the way for a greater assault on racial bias. An early suit, *Mitchell* v. *United States,* occurred in 1941—a year before CORE's birth. Congressman Arthur W. Mitchell, a black Chicagoan elected in 1935 to succeed Oscar De Priest, was compelled to move to a second-class car while traveling by rail through Arkansas because the railroad offered no first-class cars for Negroes. When the Interstate Commerce Commission ruled against Mitchell's complaint, he appealed to the U.S. Supreme Court. Chief Justice Charles Evans Hughes, in stating the majority opinion, held that denial of equal accommodations "because of his race would be an invasion of a fundamental individual right which is guaranteed by the Fourteenth Amendment." This decision, while favoring Mitchell's argument, failed to challenge the "separate but equal" doctrine which had been held constitutional by the Supreme Court in *Plessy* v. *Ferguson* in 1896. It simply restated that the separate facilities must be equal.

Again, in 1949-50, the Supreme Court faced this issue in *Henderson* v. *United States.* Elmer W. Henderson, an employee of the President's Fair Employment Practices Commission, took a train trip from Washington, D.C., to Alabama to investigate race bias in war industries. Henderson encountered no seating problems on the Southern Railway as far as Atlanta. But he was refused service in the dining car at tables reserved for Negroes when white passengers were seated at them. The Interstate Commerce Commission admitted that Henderson had been discriminated against but dismissed his complaint. It contended that prosecution would undercut any future remedial legislation. When Henderson appealed to the federal District Court in Maryland in 1948, it too dismissed his case. When he appealed to the Supreme Court in 1950, with the NAACP filing a "friend of the court" brief in his behalf, Henderson asked that "the United States Court strike down once and for all the myth of separate but equal and . . . destroy once and for all the badge of inferiority suffered so long by the Negro."

Once more the high court evaded a direct ruling on the Plessy doctrine while upholding Henderson's "right to be free from unreasonable discrimination." Justice Harold H. Burton noted that "where a dining car is available to passengers holding tickets entitling them to use it, each such passenger is equally entitled to its facilities in accordance with reasonable regulations. The denial of dining car service to any such passenger by the rules before us subjects him to a prohibited disadvantage. . . . The curtains, partitions and signs [designating the tables for Negroes] emphasize the artificiality of a difference in treatment, which serves only to call attention to a racial classification of passengers holding identical tickets and using the same public dining facilities."

The fact that Attorney General J. Howard McGrath associated himself with Henderson's plea reflected the Truman administration's approval of his stand. The White House directed the Interstate Commerce Commission to issue an order abolishing dining-car segregation. That order became a milestone of progress in the civil-rights struggle. While the Henderson case awaited a Supreme Court verdict, President Truman's Committee on Civil Rights urged the states to enact laws "guaranteeing equal access to places of public accommodation, broadly defined, for persons of all races, colors, creeds and national origins." At the time, eighteen states had such laws in force. Oregon added itself to that list in 1953 and Montana and New Mexico did the same. Vermont passed such a law in 1957, as did Maine and Alaska in 1959. Idaho, New Hampshire, North Dakota and Wyoming all followed suit in 1961, bringing the total to twenty-eight states. This principle became nationwide policy with adoption of the Civil Rights Act of 1964.

BREAKTHROUGH IN THE COURTS

Throughout the postwar 1940's, other civil-rights victories had occurred in the courts. The Supreme Court had outlawed the white primary in its 1944 ruling in *Smith* v. *Allwright*. By mid-1946, the court had banned segregation in interstate bus travel. The following April, CORE and its parent organization, the pacifist Fellowship of Reconciliation, sent the first Freedom Rider buses through Virginia and North Carolina.

Then, in 1948, the Supreme Court handed down the first of a series of decisions regarding school segregation. It held in *Sipuel* v. *University of Oklahoma* that a state must offer schooling for Negroes "as soon as it provides it for whites," thereby opening the colleges to Negro admissions. Within two months, the same court ruled in *Shelley* v. *Kraemer* that federal and state courts were not to enforce "restrictive covenants" in housing. Two years after the Sipuel ruling, the court struck another blow at segregation in the companion test cases *Sweatt* v. *Painter* and *McLaurin* v. *Oklahoma*. In the Sweatt case, a Negro sued for admission to the University of Texas Law School, holding that the state's law school for Negroes was inferior not only in facilities and study program but in its professional reputation as well. The court upheld him. It also supported a Negro's plea in the McLaurin case in protesting the University of Oklahoma's practice of requiring isolated seating in classrooms and cafeterias for Negro students. Such a practice promoted inequality in education, the court ruled. These decisions set the stage for the landmark ruling in *Brown* v. *Board of Education* in 1954, which finally reversed the Plessy doctrine of "separate but equal." This case involved a Kansas statute requiring segregated classrooms in both elementary and high schools. "Slavery is perpetuated in these statutes," insisted Thurgood Marshall, the NAACP's chief counsel, who had successfully argued the Sweatt and McLaurin cases. The court unanimously agreed.

"We cannot turn the clock back to 1868 when the Amendment was adopted, or even to 1896 when *Plessy* v. *Ferguson* was written," Chief Justice Earl Warren stated on May 17, 1954.

"We must consider public education in the light of its full development and its present place in American life throughout the Nation. . . . We conclude that in the field of public education, the doctrine of 'separate but equal' has no place." The Court relied heavily on the testimony of Negro psychologist Kenneth B. Clark and Sweden's Gunnar Myrdal, long a champion of black rights. It noted that "to separate [Negro pupils] from others of similar age and qualifications solely because of their race generates a feeling of inferiority as to their status in the community that may affect their hearts and minds in a way unlikely ever to be undone."

"MASSIVE RESISTANCE"

The court followed up the Brown decision in mid-1955 by ordering the lower courts to oversee local moves to carry out its integration policy. A unanimous court decreed that the transition occur "with all deliberate speed." Voluntary integration did take place in Delaware, Maryland, West Virginia, Kentucky, Missouri and Oklahoma. Cities like Baltimore, Louisville and Washington, D.C., moved swiftly to comply. But in the Deep South a reaction best described as "massive resistance"—a phrase coined by Senator Harry Flood Byrd of Virginia—set in. Only North Carolina and Texas among the former Confederate states made any moves toward desegregation.

In Congress a declaration of principles known as the "Southern Manifesto" was made public in March of 1956. Over one hundred southern members of Congress signed it. The statement charged the Supreme Court with "a clear abuse of judicial power" and pledged "to use all lawful means to bring about a reversal of this decision." Southern lawyers conferred as White Citizens Councils sprang up in such strongholds of bigotry as Indianola, Mississippi.

Soon state legislatures were busy passing laws intended to circumvent the new law of the land. They proposed these "acts of interposition" or assertions of states' rights to thwart what they regarded as federal encroachment on their sovereignty.

The Ku Klux Klan boosted its membership. "Resistance groups . . . have spread across the South," the *New York Times* reported. "Gunpowder and dynamite parades and cross burnings have been the marks of their trade." The New York *Herald Tribune* later noted the rise in racial violence had accounted for 530 killings, beatings and bombings since 1955—all laid to "tension." Teachers known to be NAACP members or to favor integration found their jobs in jeopardy. In Elloree, South Carolina, twenty-five Negro teachers were dismissed when they refused to sign disclaimer statements.

DIRECT ACTION RENEWED

While the NAACP was mounting its court-room attack on segregation, CORE was testing the tactics soon to be employed widely in the South. The biracial group conducted a "wade-in" in 1947 at a Palisades Park (N.J.) swimming pool from which Negroes were excluded. Police used billy clubs to eject the CORE team, arresting fifty of its members. When New Jersey passed its civil-rights law, called the Freeman Act, in 1949, CORE renewed its pressure. The group filed a test suit against the pool's proprietor. He soon agreed to let Negroes swim there. Across the Hudson River another big step was taken. The New York City council passed an ordinance in 1951 banning racial bias in any city-assisted housing developments. A few months later the municipal Court of Appeals outlawed segregation in the District of Columbia's restaurants. The decision came after several years of pressure by a coalition of civil-rights groups led by Mary Church Terrell. By 1952, CORE had succeeded in desegregating seventeen St. Louis restaurants. That same year the Supreme Court upheld the District of Columbia restaurant desegregation order.

Not until 1955, however, did the Interstate Commerce Commission ban segregation in buses and bus terminals where they engaged in inter-state travel. This order occurred two weeks after the Supreme Court ruled in a Baltimore case that the Constitution did not permit segregated public facilities. Within a month, the arrest of Mrs. Rosa Parks for refusing to vacate her seat in a city bus for a white man touched off the celebrated Montgomery boycott. The bus boycott in Alabama's capital made the Baptist clergyman Dr. Martin Luther King, Jr., the key figure in the civil-rights movement.

PASSIVE RESISTANCE

Mrs. Parks, a meek but determined garment worker, related at a later date that the bus incident had not been prearranged. It seemed almost an accident. "I was quite tired after spending a full day working," she recalled. "The section of the bus where I was sitting was what we called

ROSA PARKS

the colored section. . . . Just as soon as enough white passengers got on the bus to take what we consider their seats and then a few over, that meant that we would have to move back for them even though there was no room to move back. It was an imposition as far as I was concerned."

The Negro clergy hastily formed the Montgomery Improvement Association, with Dr. King at its head. It called for a bus boycott which proved almost 100 per cent effective in terms of Negro riders. The boycott introduced a new philosophy to counter the "massive resistance" of the South. Dr. King, a disciple of Mohandas Gandhi, called it "passive resistance." He described it in his book *Stride toward Freedom*.

"The term 'passive resistance,' " he wrote, "often gives the false impression that this is a sort of 'do-nothing method' in which the protester quietly and passively accepts evil. But nothing is further from the truth. For while the nonviolent resister is passive in the sense that he is not physically aggressive toward his opponent, his mind and emotions are always active, constantly seeking to persuade his opponent that he is wrong. . . ." Within two months of the boycott's inception, Dr. King's home was bombed. But his patient method showed results. Thirteen months after the boycott began, after a federal court order, the Montgomery "back of the bus" policy was put down.

In the meantime, the bus boycott movement had spread to Tallahassee, Florida, and then to Birmingham, Alabama. On Christmas Day of 1956, the home of the Birmingham protest leader, the Rev. Fred L. Shuttlesworth, was dynamited and destroyed. The next day twenty-one Negroes were arrested for defying the Jim Crow bus laws. The courts re-entered the fray the following day. Federal Judge Dozier Devane issued an injunction in Tallahassee restraining officials from barring integration of the city bus system. "Every segregation act of every state or city is as dead as a doornail," Judge Devane declared. But enforcing this judicial decree would prove a much harder task.

The focus of the civil-rights movement now shifted to the more emotional issue of school integration. In February of 1956 Autherine Lucy tried to enter the University of Alabama. The coed was admitted but then suspended and expelled after a campus riot. In August of the same year a white mob in Mansfield, Texas, blocked a group of Negro high school students from enrolling in an all-white public school. And in Clinton, Tennessee, a white rabble-rouser named John Kasper led another mob protesting racial mixing in the schools. It became necessary for the Tennessee National Guard to disperse the unruly element. The National Guard was needed in Sturgis, Kentucky, to quell another mob uprising as schools opened to all races there. Kentucky troops helped Negro children enroll in a Clay elementary school on September 12, only to see them suspended the following week.

By 1957 southern integrationists had mounted a regional attack on Jim Crow. They formed the Southern Christian Leadership Conference in New Orleans in mid-February. Dr. King was elected its president. Its first move was a shopping boycott of white stores in Tuskegee, Alabama; this was a protest against a new state gerrymander directed at Tuskegee's Negro citizens. The Tuskegee boycott began in June of 1957,

two weeks after Negroes converged on Washington in a "prayer pilgrimage," the largest civil-rights demonstration yet staged. Dr. King spelled out the SCLC program shortly after assuming its leadership. "We must not get involved in legalism, needless fights in lower courts," he warned, apparently criticizing the NAACP. "That's exactly what the white man wants the Negro to do. Then he can draw out the fight into what he has already called a 'Century of Litigation.' The court has spoken. The legal basis of segregation has been destroyed. Our job now is implementation of the decision. We must move on to mass action."

CONFRONTATION AT LITTLE ROCK

The showdown Dr. King sought was soon at hand. As the summer of 1957 drew to a close, the South prepared itself for another school enrollment crisis. In Nashville, "the Athens of the South," the new Hattie Cotton Elementary School was blown to pieces by a dynamite blast on September 9. The explosion occurred because the school was soon to have received its first black student. The same day, a mob accosted the Rev. Fred Shuttlesworth when he tried to enter his daughters in an all-white Birmingham school. But these were only the preliminaries.

The main event took place at Central High School in Little Rock, Arkansas. When a federal court ordered that Negroes be admitted to the all-white school, Governor Orville E. Faubus countered by placing state troopers there with orders to resist desegregation. Then President Eisenhower responded by federalizing the Arkansas National Guard to enforce the court order. The President went on nationwide television to explain why he had also dispatched units of the 101st Airborne Division under Major General Edwin Walker to Little Rock. It was the first time in eighty-one years—since Reconstruction had ended in the withdrawal of Union troops from the South—that federal armed forces had been used to protect Negro citizens' rights. On September 25, the paratroopers escorted the nine black students into Central High School.

"The streets were blocked off," Daisy Bates, then president of the Arkansas NAACP, later re-

DAISY BATES

called. "The soldiers closed ranks. Neighbors came out and looked. The street was full, up and down. Oh! It was beautiful. And the attitude of the children at that moment: the respect they had. I could hear them saying, 'For the first time in my life I truly feel like an American.' I could see it in their faces: 'Somebody cares for me—*America cares.*'"

Even after their safe entry, though, the Negro students found themselves harassed by classmates and adult diehards alike. Nor was their student life eased when the federal troops departed in late November. President Eisenhower recalled the National Guardsmen the next May. Yet, with the skillful counsel of Mrs. Bates and the youths' own heroic forbearance, the crisis passed. The following May 27, the oldest of "the Little Rock nine," Ernest Green, received his diploma. The young Negro entered Michigan State University the next fall. The NAACP paid tribute to the courage of Mrs. Bates and the students by awarding the Spingarn Medal to them in 1958.

After the federal show of force in Little Rock,

a lull occurred. Little in the way of planned protest gained national attention during 1958, aside from a series of sit-ins staged by the NAACP Youth Council at Oklahoma City eating places. By 1959, though, three unrelated events refocused national attention on racial injustice. The first was the April lynching of Mack Parker in Poplarville, Mississippi—the first such atrocity since fourteen-year-old Emmett Till had been kidnapped and lynched in Mississippi in 1955. A second action took place in Prince Edward County, Virginia. In keeping with the "massive resistance" strategy, the board of supervisors closed the public schools. White pupils were enrolled in newly created private schools in a device to circumvent the Supreme Court's ruling in the Brown case. A third event occurred just before Christmas in Deerfield, Illinois. Citizens there approved a plan to thwart builders of a proposed interracial housing development. The Illinois incident served to remind civil-rights forces that the North also remained deeply prejudiced against Negroes, despite the moral lessons of Montgomery and Little Rock.

THE SIT-INS

As a new decade, the 1960's, opened, CORE's sit-in tactics found new use in every corner of the South. The revival occurred first at Greensboro, North Carolina. Four North Carolina A. & T. students entered Woolworth's there on February 1, and sat at the lunch counter which served whites only. Within ten days the practice had spread to Negro campuses in fifteen southern cities covering a five-state area. In Chattanooga a race riot flared during a sit-in. In Nashville, police arrested one hundred student sit-in demonstrators. Finally, on February 25, a student group from Alabama State College staged the first Deep South sit-in at the cafeteria in the state courthouse in Montgomery. A few days later, over a thousand students joined them in a protest meeting. The state board of education promptly expelled nine of the student demonstration leaders, and a few days later Montgomery police broke up a campus protest. They arrested thirty-five students and a teacher. In Tallahassee, Florida, police used tear gas to quell another student gathering.

The movement showed results. On March 16 San Antonio became the first major southern city to integrate its lunch counters. In Charlotte, North Carolina, where college students picketed local and chain store merchants, the businessmen felt a sharp financial pinch. The previous year Negroes had spent an estimated $25 million in the shopping district! The same pressure occurred in other southern cities. In the North, CORE and the NAACP led pickets in New York and elsewhere, boycotting chain stores whose southern affiliates refused to serve Negroes. Northern students staged sympathy demonstrations. Campus fund-raising drives helped pay court costs for those jailed. Finally, in October of 1960, a crucial breakthrough occurred. Four national chain firms announced that lunch counters had been integrated in roughly 150 stores in the South. These stores were scattered through 112 cities in North Carolina, Maryland, Virginia, West Virginia, Texas, Kentucky, Tennessee, Oklahoma, Missouri and Florida. But in the Deep South states —Mississippi, Louisiana, Georgia, Alabama and South Carolina—the store owners were still saying "Never!"

White segregationists like John Kasper continued to stir up racial hatred, even in cities like Nashville, which prided itself on its harmonious race relations. The home of NAACP counsel Z. Alexander Looby, attorney for 153 Fisk and Tennessee A. & I. students arrested for sit-in protests, was destroyed by a bomb in mid-April, 1960. Over two thousand students marched on city hall to deliver a protest to Mayor Ben West. The homeless lawyer, Looby, had been elected to the Nashville city council in 1951. He was the first Negro to attain such a post in the post-Reconstruction South.

Other acts of violence also marred the record of gradual progress below the Mason-Dixon line. A race riot exploded in Biloxi, Mississippi, after Negroes attempted a wade-in at a local beach in April 1960. Another riot occurred in Jacksonville, Florida, following sit-ins in August. Whites armed with axe handles beat and injured many young Negroes during the melee. If the southerners thought they would crush the spirit of the civil-rights workers, however, they were mistaken.

THE FREEDOM RIDES

CORE, under the direction of pacifist James Farmer, decided to revive an old tactic—the Freedom Ride, which it had introduced briefly in 1947. On May 4, 1961, CORE's first two integrated buses left Washington, D.C., for Birmingham, Alabama, to test laws integrating travel and terminal facilities. The group met its first resistance at Rock Hill, South Carolina, where on May 14 the Greyhound bus received a hostile reception at the city bus station. The other, a Trailways bus, was stoned and burned by a white mob the same day near Anniston, Alabama. Twelve of the Freedom Riders were hospitalized, but the CORE members continued on another bus to Birmingham. Again they met a surly mob which assaulted them. Again police were conspicuously absent, though they had been notified of the bus's arrival.

The following day another group of Freedom Riders—this one under SCLC leadership—left Nashville for Birmingham. Police greeted this group at Birmingham's city limits, arrested two SCLC members for interracial seating and sent the bus back to the Tennessee line the next day. But the Freedom Riders returned to Birmingham via another bus and pressed on to Montgomery. There, on May 20, a mob met the second bus and assaulted the passengers. Twenty riders, including a *Life* photographer, were beaten. A Justice Department agent, John Seigenthaler, was mauled unconscious. The ensuing riot conditions compelled Governor John Patterson to declare martial law and U.S. Attorney General Robert Kennedy to send in four hundred federal marshals.

Under heavy federal escort, the Freedom Riders proceeded on May 24 to Jackson, Mississippi. Here James Farmer and twenty-six other passengers were arrested and charged with disturbing the peace when they tried to desegregate the terminal lunchroom and rest rooms. More Freedom Riders journeyed to Jackson. Police promptly arrested them. Over a hundred passengers had been jailed by June 23, severely overcrowding the local jails. By the end of June a total of 279 Freedom Riders had been arrested at the Jackson depot. However, the national publicity gained by this tactic and by the sit-ins was molding public opinion in the riders' favor. And the pressure increased.

The Southern Regional Council, an organization which documents civil-rights activities, noted that from early 1960 to the fall of 1961 the sit-in movement had affected more than one hundred cities in twenty states. No less than seventy thousand persons of both races had taken part, of whom roughly thirty-six hundred were arrested. But in the process the demonstrators forced or persuaded 108 cities to drop some racial barriers.

The Freedom Riders accomplished their purpose. The Interstate Commerce Commission acted in September of 1961 to ban segregation on all buses and in all bus stations. Despite the ICC ruling, white mobs attacked Freedom Riders at a Macomb, Mississippi, bus station on December 1. A similar white challenge had taken place earlier in the Trailways terminal in Albany, Georgia. Arrests of college students there brought about formation of the Albany Movement. This group joined forces with Dr. King's SCLC to plan mass protests against all acts of racial bias. The Student Nonviolent Coordinating Committee had been founded a year and a half earlier on the Shaw University campus for much the same reasons. Despite arrests of its members, the Albany Movement marched in protest during much of 1962, singing the spiritual *We Shall Overcome* for inspiration.

UNREST IN THE NORTH

For a brief period in early 1962, national attention returned to the North. In January a New York citizens' group filed suit in the U.S. District Court against the board of education. It charged that the board used "racial quotas" for Negro and Puerto Rican students in the school system. Later that month CORE marched to protest a housing bias at the University of Chicago. It contended that the university owned nearly a hundred segregated apartment houses. In February a biracial group was arrested in Englewood, New Jersey, after an all-night vigil in City Hall. A few days later parents filed a court suit against the racial segregation in this fashionable suburb's elementary schools. At the same

time, Negro mothers in Chicago staged a sit-in in an elementary school. Although they were arrested and given $50 suspended fines, the mothers continued to picket against de facto segregation —that is, segregation not condoned by law but resulting from housing patterns. The NAACP in Rochester, New York, also alleged that de facto segregation existed in local schools when it sued the board of education in May. Rochester was but one of thirty-two "non-southern" cities that the NAACP charged permitted this form of segregation. The next month, civil-rights workers launched a "passive resistance" sit-in in Cairo, Illinois. The protest deplored the segregated swimming pool, skating rink and restaurants there. Then, as another school enrollment period approached, the eyes of the nation shifted again to the South.

PROGRESS AT A SNAIL'S PACE

The *Southern School News* had reported in May that roughly 247,000 or 7.6 per cent of Negro public school pupils in the southern and border states and the District of Columbia were attending integrated classes. To some the trend meant progress. But to many others the pace was discouragingly slow. In early 1963 Negro newsman Carl Rowan summed up their views in a *Saturday Evening Post* article entitled "The Travesty of Integration."

> It bothers me—and it should bother lawyers, judges, and all who treasure a society based on justice under law, that in the current school year only 901 of North Carolina's 339,840 Negro school children have secured relief from a practice that, according to our highest tribunal, "generates a feeling of inferiority . . . that may affect their hearts and minds in a way unlikely ever to be undone." . . . In Texas they may boast about "the peaceful transition" to "integration" in Dallas or Houston, but the meaningful thing to me is that a "whopping" 2.16 per cent of the Negro children in that state attended integrated schools last year. . . . Alabama, South Carolina and Mississippi have yet to free a single Negro child from this stigma of state-imposed racial isolation.

At the college level, integration was proceeding at the same snail's pace. A riot had occurred in January of 1961 when two Negro students entered the University of Georgia. When the two were suspended a federal court ordered them reinstated, and they returned to classes later that month. This sequence of events was typical of the integration battle throughout the South.

SHOWDOWN AT "OLE MISS"

It was against this backdrop that Supreme Court Justice Hugo Black, an Alabaman, overruled a lower court on September 10, 1962, in ordering the University of Mississippi to admit James H. Meredith. The Negro air force veteran's application had been on file and before the courts for fourteen months. Three days later, Governor Ross Barnett went on statewide television to announce in a fiery speech that he would "interpose" the state's authority between "Ole Miss" and the federal courts. "There is no case in history where the Caucasian race has survived social integration," the Governor declared. He vowed to go to jail, if need be, to block Meredith. True to his word, Barnett personally refused the Negro applicant admission on September 20.

In Washington, President Kennedy conferred with his brother, Attorney General Robert Kennedy, to map a step-by-step federal strategy to aid Meredith. The U.S. Court of Appeals on September 24 ordered Mississippi's board of higher education to admit Meredith or be held in contempt. The board agreed to comply. But the next day Governor Barnett again defied the court by personally denying Meredith admission. This act was reinforced by Lieutenant Governor Paul Johnson and a force of state patrolmen the following day, when they turned back Meredith and an escort of federal marshals in front of the university's gate. Within the next few days, the Fifth Circuit Court of Appeals ordered both Barnett and Johnson to purge themselves of contempt or face arrest and daily fines of $10,000 and $5,000 respectively.

Then on September 30 a phalanx of federal marshals accompanied Meredith to the "Ole Miss" campus. President Kennedy federalized the Mississippi National Guard and asked the state to accept the court's order in a national television address. But Mississippi students and adults from the town of Oxford—goaded by retired U.S. army Major General Edwin Walker —rioted on the campus. Two persons, including a French newsman, were killed, and over a hundred wounded. General Walker, who had led the federal troops at Little Rock, now called for "volunteers" to resist these federal troops. By October 1, however, a force of twelve thousand troops had restored order on campus and in Oxford. James Meredith, with federal marshals at his side, filed for registration and was enrolled as a student.

James Meredith receiving his degree from "Ole Miss."

TERRORISM ON THE RISE

The mob violence which had followed the Freedom Riders in 1961 had not slackened. Nor had the brutal tactics of the police. Negroes had had a taste of the latter late in 1961 when police in Baton Rouge, Louisiana, unleashed dogs and used tear gas to subdue fifteen hundred demonstrators.

In the summer of 1962, a Negro Baptist church in Leesburg, Georgia, was burned by arsonists. When within a month two more Negro churches were set aflame near Sasser, Georgia, a group of black leaders asked President Kennedy to end "the Nazi-like reign of terror in southwest Georgia." A few days later shotgun blasts wounded two Negro youths working to register Mississippi Negro voters. After this incident, SNCC's executive secretary, James Forman, called on the President to "convene a special White House Conference to discuss means of stopping the wave of terror sweeping through the South, especially where SNCC is working on voter registration." President Kennedy spoke out a few days later, denouncing the Negro church burnings and supporting the voter registration drives. Yet four days afterward a fourth Negro church burned near Dawson, Georgia. Three white men who later admitted the crime received seven-year prison sentences for arson. Then, on September 25, fire destroyed another Negro church in Macon, Georgia—the eighth such burning in forty days. It seemed an anticlimax when President Kennedy issued a long-awaited executive order on November 20. It was this "stroke of a pen" that barred racial and religious discrimination in all federally financed housing

Although violence continued, the civil-rights workers remained undaunted. On the centennial of the Emancipation Proclamation on March 3, 1963, they inaugurated a massive voter-registration campaign in Greenville, Mississippi. In April Dr. King opened his SCLC drive against segregation in Birmingham; it resulted in the arrest of over two thousand demonstrators, including Dr. King himself. It was during this campaign that terrorists bombed the SCLC headquarters, the Gaston Motel and the home of the Rev.

A. D. King, brother of Dr. Martin Luther King. Birmingham police commissioner Eugene "Bull" Connor ordered his forces to turn high-powered fire hoses on the demonstrators, washing them down the streets. State troopers swung billy clubs at Negroes sitting on their own porches. Police dogs growled at the Negro protesters.

On the night after the Gaston Motel bombing, to Dr. King's dismay, "passive resistance" reached its limits. Twenty-five hundred angry activists tossed bricks at police and firemen, overturned police cars and taxis and set them ablaze. On the previous day, the Rev. Fred L. Shuttlesworth had announced an agreement with Birmingham officials on a modified integration plan that ended the SCLC campaign. Yet Birmingham had not had its fill of violence. In mid-September of 1963, four Negro girls died when the 16th Street Baptist Church was bombed. The rest of the South was no less troubled.

A new wave of terrorism had still to run its tragic course that year. A white Baltimore postal worker, William Moore, began a one-man freedom march to Jackson, Mississippi, on April 22. The next day he was found shot to death along U.S. Highway 11, his hand-made pro-integration sign across his body. He had planned to hand-deliver a letter to Governor Barnett. Mississippi, he had written, had earned its reputation as "the most backward and most bigoted state in the land. Those who truly love Mississippi must work to change this image."

Less than two months later, the NAACP Mississippi field secretary Medgar Evers fell to an assassin's bullet as he stepped from his car in his own driveway. The top leaders of the civil-rights movement, as well as United Nations Undersecretary Ralph Bunche, attended his funeral. After the service ended, a group of Negro youths sang the Negro spiritual:

> Before I'd be a slave
> I'd be buried in my grave
> And go home to my Lord and be free.

The emotion pent up in those words, the sweltering heat in Jackson that day and the loss of Evers all combined to bring the crowd to near fever pitch. It flowed quickly into the main business district where a blockade of riot-helmeted police

MEDGAR EVERS

met it. Only the timely intercession of the Justice Department's John Doar at that moment prevented a full-scale bloodbath. But as one sullen police officer remarked: "He didn't stop it. He just postponed it."

Before the Evers slaying, President Kennedy had made a nationwide television plea for reason. He called segregation "morally wrong," and said it was "time to act in the Congress, in your state and local legislative body and, above all, in all of our daily lives." The President and his brother, the attorney general, had outmaneuvered Governor George C. Wallace a day before the Jackson tragedy, to see two Negro students enrolled at the University of Alabama. But President Kennedy himself was to be struck down by an assassin within five months, his New Frontier beyond reach. Before that fateful day in Dallas, however, he lived through both the first warning of the northern racial holocaust to come and the finest hour of the civil-rights movement: first the race riot in Cambridge, Maryland, and then the historic March on Washington.

A month after Evers' death, the Cambridge conflict came to a head. For several months an anti-bias campaign led by Gloria Richardson had been forming in this Eastern Shore cannery town. As one reporter noted, on July 11: "Cambridge abandoned the formalities and went to war. All through that night, there were sounds of warfare—careening cars, screaming men, shattering glass, sirens, yells and the short angry barks of rifles and pistols." Eventually the National Guard arrived on the scene to still the gunfire, but for more than a year Cambridge lived under limited martial law. It was an omen of the days ahead.

"I HAVE A DREAM"

Month after month of 1963 passed with no dramatic shift in the national conscience, and impatience with "passive resistance" grew. In northern cities, Malcolm X drew thousands of new converts to Elijah Mohammad's Nation of Islam. In Harlem and other black ghettos across the country, the Black Muslim theme song, *A White Man's Heaven Is a Black Man's Hell*, skyrocketed in popularity. And the established civil-rights groups found it wise to whistle the tune themselves in the interests of their own survival.

John Lewis and James Forman of SNCC now began to talk in tougher tones. So did CORE's James Farmer. Even the more conservative NAACP's Roy Wilkins, and Whitney Young of the Urban League, spoke impatiently. All were becoming aware of the tinderbox in the northern ghettos—the raw ingredients to set off "the fire next time."

With these thunderclouds overhead, the civil-rights leaders laid plans for a stepped-up campaign for equal opportunity. Labor, government and the clergy became more active in pressing for racial reform. "Some time or other we are all going to have to stand and be on the receiving end of a fire hose," declared the Presbyterian church leader Eugene Carson Blake. Together this coalition planned the massive March on Washington, an assembly of roughly 250,000 Americans which converged on the nation's capital in late August. About 60,000 of the marchers were white. Meeting at the Washington Monument on August 28, the largest crowd of demon-

WHITNEY M. YOUNG, JR.

JOHN LEWIS

strators ever to mass in the federal city moved on to the Lincoln Memorial. Everywhere the marchers wore "Freedom Now" buttons. For nearly three hours the gathering of blacks and whites heard speakers demand prompt passage of the civil-rights bill pending before Congress. Then Dr. Martin Luther King walked to the lectern to deliver the day's most memorable address. After completing the prepared text, Dr. King launched into an impromptu oration on his "dream" for America.

"In spite of the difficulties and frustrations of the moment," he told an audience in rapture, "I still have a dream. It is a dream deeply rooted in the American dream.

"I have a dream that one day this nation will rise up and live out the true meaning of its creed: 'We hold these truths to be self-evident; that all men are created equal.' "

Dr. King's dream, unrealized in life, was to remain unfulfilled in death. The words of the spiritual calling for a nation of "black and white together" were muted by the turmoil that followed in the cities.

Legions of Dr. King's followers continued to inflict heavy damage on Jim Crow—but suffered severe casualties in the process. Efforts to extend Dr. King's "passive resistance" campaign in the North met with only limited success. Even Dr. King's confrontation with blue-collar whites in the Chicago suburb of Cicero in 1966 ended in a draw, at best.

Dr. King counseled his race to turn the other cheek and valiantly preached against despair. But many began to doubt the power of nonviolent persuasion in what was perceived as the dawning of a new era.

By 1966, patience with pacifism was waning in both SNCC and CORE. James Farmer stepped down as CORE's national director in early 1966 and was succeeded by Floyd B. McKissick, a younger and more militant activist. Shortly afterwards, an even more militant figure, Stokely Carmichael, a native of Trinidad, replaced Baptist minister John Lewis as SNCC's national chairman. Carmichael had formed the all-black Lowndes County Freedom Organization in Alabama, using the now famous black panther as its symbol.

Dr. Martin Luther King, Jr., addressing a huge crowd during the 1963 March on Washington.

"BLACK POWER"

In June of 1966, James Meredith began a walking crusade through Mississippi in hopes of overcoming the ingrained fear shared by blacks in the "closed society" in the state, and also to spur voter registration among Mississippi blacks. In its second day, this pilgrimage was interrupted by three shotgun blasts, and Meredith fell, wounded by an ambusher.

During this march, Carmichael and his followers began to chant "black power"—a cry that soon sounded across the nation.

"I'm not anti-white," Carmichael insisted. He described the phrase as denoting a political strategy. Soon thereafter, CORE endorsed the black power concept. Explaining the decision in eco-nomic terms, McKissick said, "As long as the white man has all the power and money, nothing will happen, because we have nothing. The only way to achieve meaningful change is to take power."

More importantly, CORE reversed its position on nonviolence. "The right of self-defense is a constitutional right," McKissick contended, "and you can't expect black people to surrender that right while whites maintain it . . . you can't have white people who practice violence and expect black people to remain passive."

Defining the mid-1960s shift from pacifism to militancy, the President's National Advisory Commission on Civil Disorders reported in early 1968:

The militants began to turn away from American society and the "middle-class way of life." Cynical about the liberals and the leaders of organized labor, they regarded compromise, even as a temporary tactical device, as anathema. They talked more of "revolutionary" changes in the social structure, of retaliatory violence, and increasingly rejected white assistance. They insisted that Negro power alone could compel the white "ruling class" to make concessions.

Bayard Rustin, the Harlem civil-rights strategist who had masterminded the 1963 March on Washington, saw the shift in a somewhat different light:

The civil-rights movement is evolving from a protest movement into a full-fledged *social movement* —an evolution calling its very name into question. It is now concerned not merely with removing barriers to full *opportunity* but with achieving the fact of *equality*. From sit-ins and freedom rides we have gone into rent strikes, boycotts, community organization, and political action.

Meanwhile, the unrest which erupted in Cambridge, Maryland, in 1963 triggered a series of urban riots along the eastern seaboard. Ghetto neighborhoods whose names were unknown nationally would become imprinted on the American conscience. First, Harlem exploded, followed by Brooklyn's Bedford-Stuyvesant section, then by Rochester, New York, by the New Jersey slum sections of Elizabeth, Paterson and Jersey City, and by Philadelphia.

After the "long hot summer" of 1964, there was a brief respite during which passions were recharged. Then in August 1965, the worst riot since the 1943 Detroit race war broke out in the Watts district of Los Angeles. Rioters, their tempers pushed to the breaking point by claims of "police brutality," went on a rampage, smashing windows, looting and fire bombing. Damage was estimated at some $35 million.

An eight-member commission headed by John A. McCone, former director of the Central Intelligence Agency, called the pillage of Watts "not a race riot in the usual sense . . . what happened was an explosion—a formless, quite senseless, all but hopeless violent protest—engaged in by a few but bringing great distress to all."

In 1966 another flareup occurred in Watts, followed by July uprisings in Chicago and the Hough section of Cleveland. The intensity of the riots led to charges that "outside agitators," including Communists and black extremists, may have exploited socially tense situations in areas ripe for explosion.

By 1967 urban riots had become a way of life in the United States. In the spring of that year massive demonstrations, largely confined to black college campuses, rocked Nashville, Jackson (Mississippi) and Houston. By the summer months Tampa, Cincinnati, Atlanta, Newark and Detroit had joined the list of riot-torn cities.

Following the slaying of Dr. King in 1968, an epidemic of rioting broke out in black neighborhoods in cities across the nation, including the District of Columbia, where rioters vented their anger and sorrow only a few blocks away from the White House.

For black Americans, it was a case of too little change coming too slowly. SNCC Chairman H. Rap Brown caught the mood of the times, asserting, "Violence is as American as cherry pie."

Concerning the rioters, looters and arsonists, Tom Wicker, Washington bureau chief of the *New York Times,* wrote:

By and large the rioters were young Negroes, natives of the ghetto (not of the South), hostile to the white society surrounding and repressing them, and equally hostile to the middle-class Negroes who accommodated themselves to that white dominance. The rioters were mistrustful of white politics, they hated the police, they were proud of their race, and acutely conscious of the discrimination they suffered. They were and they are a time-bomb ticking in the heart of the richest nation in the history of the world.

But more than that, the rioters are the personification of that nation's shame, of its deepest failure, of its greatest challenge. They will not go away.

The fire was not "next time." It was now. And it would take a massive effort—one demanding the energy and goodwill of every American—to put out the blaze.

CHAPTER SEVENTEEN

Epilogue

The black revolution of the 1960s was one of violence, militancy, pride in race and sense of power. By 1970 the civil rights movement had changed in spirit, direction and leadership. Passions had waned as battles were won and segregation laws were wiped off the books. It was a time of transition, and the new decade signaled a turning point in black American history.

A resolution adopted by the 62nd annual convention of the NAACP in 1971 stated:

> The turmoil, conflict, cross-purpose, and divided counsel of the past decade are coming to be seen in their true perspective: not as the blueprint for a future of violence and withdrawal, but as the understandable byproducts of transition, of re-evaluation, and of regrouping of forces.

James Baldwin observed the past and immediate present with a different vision:

> Black power was always a slogan. It was not a reality, but it was a very important slogan leading one in a certain direction. Now the direction in which it pointed was perfectly valid and we're still on that same road, but the road is longer than one thought, and always much more complex in any case. It is very rare that the goals of a generation are accomplished within that generation.

MARTIN LUTHER KING, JR.

Strategy, considerably less dramatic and visible than the massive rallies, public protests and civil disorders, was now focused on the consolidation of past gains and on bringing more blacks into the political and corporate sectors. The shift was from open militancy to "working within the system."

This did not mean that blacks had achieved their objectives, but simply that they had reached another plateau in their historic march towards total freedom and full equality.

Discrimination—legally, at least—was outlawed: blacks could eat in restaurants and swim in public pools anywhere in the Deep South; they could enroll at schools and universities which had formerly barred them or accepted them on a quota basis; the horizons of employment had been broadened for them; and they were breaking out of black enclaves and moving into integrated neighborhoods.

But subtle discrimination against blacks still existed. They were excluded from many private clubs and associations, stymied in attempts to attain high-level, responsible positions, and kept out of many residential areas by real estate compacts, expressly or tacitly agreed upon.

More importantly, many poor blacks had less food and worse housing than ever, and the number of jobless blacks was disproportionately high in relation to their percentage of the United States population.

Twenty years after the Supreme Court ordered an end to public school segregation, 11.2 per cent of the nation's black children still attended all-black schools. "The full achievement of equal educational opportunity for all Americans is still before us," declared HEW Secretary Caspar W. Weinberger on the twentieth anniversary of the landmark Supreme Court decision.

The Senate Select Committee on Nutrition and Human Needs reported, "Five years after President Nixon's promise to end hunger in America . . . the nation's needy are hungrier and poorer." The committee pointed to substantial increases in food stamp distribution and welfare allotments, while noting that inflation and higher prices had more than offset the federal assistance programs. Also, an NAACP study showed that unless white-dominated labor unions and the construction industry opened up to black workers, "a large part of an entire generation of young blacks will never enter the labor force." Thus, while the black movement had made significant strides, human and institutional problems remained, blocking black development.

The question for blacks on the threshold of the 1970s was whether to integrate into the system or to develop separate black institutions.

Meanwhile, the 1970 census showed there were 22,580,289 blacks in the United States, representing more than 10 per cent of the total population. Many black spokesmen maintained the figure was higher. In any event, no longer would blacks remain "invisible" on the American scene.

PATTERNS

The 1970s ushered in a change in the life pattern of most blacks. It was characterized by the pulse of soul music, Afro hair styles and flamboyant dress fashions—all distinctive with the black community. Black Americans had paid their dues and now sought individuality. They did not seek assimilation, as many white Americans had wrongly feared, but acceptance on their own merits without the handicap of discrimination.

Progress had been made, but few blacks were complacent about it. Indeed, many contended that some of the advancement had been illusionary. They underscored the number of blacks living below the poverty level, the overcrowded housing and the discrimination and exploitation by merchants and landlords.

"Conditions are as bad today, or worse than they were yesterday," said Percy Sutton, black borough president of Manhattan. "The unhappiness is still here. The frustration is still here. The people are poorer now than they were then [the mid-1960s]. More people are now entitled to public housing than were then and at that time more public housing was being constructed."

Furthermore, drug peddling among low-income blacks created new problems in heavily congested urban centers. And while racial violence—by blacks and whites—had subsided, it did not end with the advent of the 1970s.

On April 7, 1970, a courtroom escape attempt at San Rafael, California, led to the death of

Superior Court Judge Harold J. Haley and three convicts after a gunman invaded the trial of black convict James McClain and passed guns to the defendant and three convict witnesses. Angela Davis, a black political activist and a former philosophy instructor at UCLA, was arrested as an accomplice. She was subsequently acquitted after spending almost two years in jail.

In Pontiac, Michigan, on August 30, 1971, ten empty school buses were blown up eight days before the start of a program calling for the transportation of 8,700 children to non-neighborhood schools, a move bitterly opposed by organized white parents in the area.

At the Attica State Correctional Facility in New York State, more than 1,000 state troopers and police on September 13, 1971, stormed the maximum security prison, where 1,200 prisoners held 38 guards hostage during a four-day rebellion against "inhuman" conditions. Nine hostages and 28 convicts, mostly black, were killed in the assault.

Simmering racial tensions aboard the aircraft carrier *Kitty Hawk* off Vietnam, October 12-13, 1972, led to a fight between black and white sailors, leaving 46 injured. Navy officials preferred charges against 25 participants, nearly all of them black.

On November 16, 1972, two black students were killed by rifle buckshot on the Southern University campus, in Baton Rouge, Louisiana, as state police and sheriff's deputies were clearing demonstrators from the administration building. The incident occurred during a day of violence following weeks of unrest stemming from student demands for more of a voice in academic decisions and for better housing. An investigating panel said in a report that the students were killed by a single shotgun blast fired from an area where several sheriff's deputies had been stationed.

Then, on June 30, 1974, Mrs. Alberta Williams King, sixty-nine, mother of the martyred Dr. King, was shot and killed while playing the organ during Sunday services in Atlanta's Ebenezer Baptist Church, where her son once preached nonviolence and her husband, Martin Luther King, Sr., was pastor for more than four decades. Also killed was Edward Boykin, a church deacon. The accused assassin, Marcus Wayne Chenault, a twenty-three-year-old student from Dayton, Ohio, said he was serving on a mission for "the God of Jacob."

LEADERSHIP

With the deaths of Dr. King and Malcolm X and the evolutionary shifts in the black struggle, civil rights leadership underwent vast changes and became fragmented. Militant leaders such as H. Rap Brown, formerly head of the Student Nonviolent Coordinating Committee, and Huey P. Newton, cofounder of the Black Panther party, no longer attracted the wide attention they once did. Ralph David Abernathy, successor to Dr. King as president of the Southern Christian Leadership Conference, resigned July 8, 1973, charging that affluent blacks were no longer giving the organization financial support. Radical leader Eldridge Cleaver virtually vanished from view after fleeing to Algiers.

The transformation within the movement was reflected in still other shifts. In a major departure, the NAACP in February 1973 agreed to a minimum desegregation plan for Atlanta's public schools in exchange for a maximum integration of administrative positions in the city's educational system. "The settlement was further evidence of a new pragmatism in the civil rights movement," the *New York Times* reported.

NAACP executive director Roy Wilkins said, "Our general position has been there is no sacrifice of racial pride or loss of education if blacks go to school with blacks. If the school board agrees to the improvement in education and a program that leads to meaningful equalization of the educational process, black children will not suffer by attending an all-black school."

The Black Panthers, meanwhile, sought to change their image by channeling the organization's energies into community service, including give-away meals, voter registration drives and free tests for sickle cell anemia, a fatal blood disease which afflicts blacks.

A Black Nationalist party, espousing separatism, flickered and then faded.

What happened to the militants of yesteryear, once in the vanguard of the black revolution?

Dr. Kenneth Clark, noted black psychologist, offered this view: "It was just a matter of time before the essential emptiness (of the militant movement) became manifest. Pride is not something you can sustain by verbality. Pride comes out of solid achievement."

The wave of the future was in politics, particularly at the local level in direct competition with whites.

Election of black mayors during 1972–73 in a number of major cities in all sections of the country typified the political prominence of blacks. Thomas Bradley, fifty-five, a veteran police officer and son of a Texas field hand, defeated Mayor Sam Yorty to become the first black mayor of Los Angeles. In Atlanta, Maynard Jackson, thirty-five-year-old attorney, captured 59 per cent of the vote, defeating the incumbent to become the first black mayor of that Southern city. Significant mayoralty victories were also registered by Coleman Young in Detroit and Clarence Lightner in Raleigh, North Carolina. In another political breakthrough, Wilson C. Riles, a black educator, was elected California state superintendent of public instruction, one of the most prestigious positions in the state.

The Joint Center for Political Studies, Washington, D.C., reported that as of July 1, 1973, there were 82 black mayors, 928 black city councilmen, 211 elected county officers, 42 state senators, 196 state representatives, 1 United States senator and 15 United States representatives. There were 2,621 blacks holding elected office, according to the Center, an increase of 315 over the previous year and twice the number four years ago.

In Congress, black representation reached a total of 16 members, the highest number since Reconstruction. Among the black congressional delegation were four women, Shirley Chisholm of New York, Yvonne B. Burke of Los Angeles, Barbara Jordan of Houston, and Cardiss Collins of Chicago.

On the national appointee level, Benjamin Hooks was appointed in 1972 as the first black member of the Federal Communications Commission. Samuel L. Gravely, Jr., who served in World War II, in Korea and in Vietnam, became the first black admiral in 1971. Other black ap-

pointees included: Jewel Lafontant, deputy solicitor general; Constance E. Newman, member of the Consumer Product Safety Commission; and Robert Duncan, judge of the United States Court of Military Appeals.

But overall, blacks could take small comfort from the number of black appointments to policy positions by President Nixon. The sentiment of many blacks was expressed by Augustus Adair, director of the Congressional Black Caucus: "We are never going to be happy until the appointment of blacks reflects their proportion of the population. This is certainly not manifested in this Administration's appointments. There are no black Cabinet Secretaries, department heads or commission chairmen, with the exception of the head of the Equal Employment Opportunity Commission." The present EEOC chairman, John H. Powell, Jr., succeeded another black, William H. Brown, III.

Meanwhile, the distribution of blacks in the federal bureaucracy continued to rise. In 1973, an estimated 20.4 per cent of federal employees were from minority groups, as opposed to 19.3 per cent in 1969.

First established in 1970 as national spokesman for blacks and a clearinghouse for black concerns, the black caucus decided that it could best serve its people through its legislative efforts. Representative Louis Stokes (D-Ohio), the caucus chairman, reported that the group is now recognized in Congress as a "legitimate power pocket." He said the caucus would focus on reviving social programs abandoned by President Nixon.

On July 25, 1974, advocates of school integration received a setback when the Supreme Court by a 5–4 vote handed down a decision which would ban busing of children across school district lines for desegregation purposes, except where both districts were found to be discriminating.

Justice Thurgood Marshall charged the majority with "emasculation of our constitutional guarantees of equal protection" and called the ruling "a giant step backward."

The court's decision served as a reminder, if any was needed, that full equality lies somewhere in the future.

PICTURE ALBUM

EDUCATION AND LIVING CONDITIONS IN THE SOUTH

Such one-room schoolhouses as these provided little warmth or comfort, little light, few facilities and even less incentive to learn; yet until recently these schools were the only source of education for many southern Negroes. In time, there came a demand for better education—and better education meant integrated education.

The 1954 Supreme Court decision to integrate schools was greeted, on the whole, without incident. Yet in 1957 Little Rock, Arkansas, resisted change. Mrs. Daisy Bates, president of the Little Rock NAACP, led the courageous students, who came to be known as the Little Rock Nine, in challenging the community and registering at Little Rock's Central High School. Above, white students look on as the Negro students climb the steps on the second day of classes, under the protection of paratroopers of the 101st Airborne Division. Below, six of the students sit with Daisy Bates and Thurgood Marshall in front of the Supreme Court a year later, when the NAACP requested emergency action which would permit the Negro children to return to Central High School.

In June of 1959 school authorities in Prince Edward County, Virginia, closed public schools in order to avoid integration. For five years, until a court order opened and integrated the schools, white children attended private schools (above) financed by state, county and private funds, while Negroes attended schools in one-room shacks like that shown below.

The Negro discontent so much in evidence in the 1960's stemmed partly from deplorable living conditions. These scenes—a crust of bread for lunch, a back yard littered with trash, match-box homes—show little advance over the log cabin of 1903 (bottom right).

CIVIL-RIGHTS STRUGGLE IN THE SOUTH

As the South became aware of its racial crisis, both integrationists and segregationists resorted to action. Above, Negro demonstrators stage a sit-in at a Woolworth's lunch counter in North Carolina. Below, members of the Ku Klux Klan attend a cross-burning held as a warning to two Negroes who planned to integrate the University of Alabama.

By 1963 the fight for civil rights had reached a high pitch: tempers were short on both sides, and black demonstrators were constantly subjected to indignities and brutal assaults. Here, demonstrators are seen trying to escape the high-pressure hoses directed on them during a protest in Birmingham, Alabama.

On September 15, 1963, hatred erupted into cold-blooded murder in Alabama. A bomb planted in the back of the 16th Street Baptist Church in Birmingham exploded during a service, killing four small Negro girls. Below, at left, a crowd numbering six thousand attends the mass funeral for the victims; at right, FBI bomb experts search the rubble for clues.

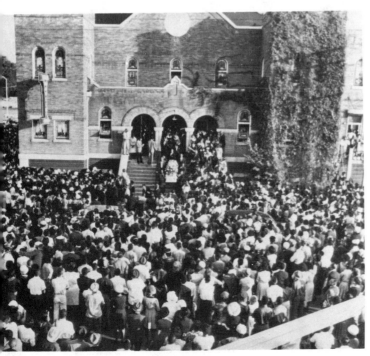

At left, a hearse carrying the body of Jimmie Lee Jackson drives through the rain to the cemetery, with an estimated seven hundred mourners following. Jackson was shot during a night demonstration in Marion, Alabama, on February 18, 1965, and died in a Selma hospital several days later. Dr. Martin Luther King gave the eulogy at the two funerals held for the civil-rights worker.

Civil-rights demonstrators (below) kneel in prayer before the caskets placed in front of the Alabama state capitol in Montgomery during the March 1965 rally. The caskets were used to symbolize the deaths of those participating in the recent Alabama civil-rights campaign.

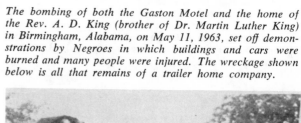

The bombing of both the Gaston Motel and the home of the Rev. A. D. King (brother of Dr. Martin Luther King) in Birmingham, Alabama, on May 11, 1963, set off demonstrations by Negroes in which buildings and cars were burned and many people were injured. The wreckage shown below is all that remains of a trailer home company.

The first Negro graduate of "Ole Miss," James Meredith (left), urged Negroes to participate' in civil-rights demonstrations. In June 1966 he organized a march from Memphis, Tennessee, to Jackson, Mississippi. After twenty-eight of the projected 220 miles, Meredith was shot in an ambush (above). Dr. Martin Luther King (second from the left, below) then assumed the leadership of the march.

Arrested in front of the Dallas County courthouse in Selma, Alabama, on February 3, 1965, hundreds of schoolchildren march down the street under police guard (above), singing "freedom songs."

A sheriff's posse (below) breaks up a group of civil-rights demonstrators sitting-in at a Montgomery, Alabama, intersection in March 1965.

Above, a long line of marchers, led by SNCC representative John Lewis (right) and the Rev. Hosea Williams, proceeds across an Alabama River bridge past state troopers and a "welcome-to-Selma" sign declaring it "The City with 100% human interest!" Fifty yards further on they were halted by state troopers, who used clubs and tear gas to break up their 1965 march to Montgomery.

DISCONTENT
IN THE NORTH

Frustration and anger persisted, but so did conditions provoking them. Run-down, overcrowded neighborhoods were constant reminders of apathy toward the real problems.

As black frustration grew and lack of communication between Negroes and whites persisted, sudden outbursts of racial violence took place in nearly every major city in the United States. In Jersey City, New Jersey, a night of rioting in August 1964 ended with the injury of thirty-two persons and the arrest of fourteen. In attempts to clear the streets, white policemen stopped cars and challenged their occupants (top left). Some of the worst rioting of the 1960's took place in August 1965 in the Watts area of Los Angeles (top right). As most of Watts went up in flames, courts prepared to handle the cases of some two thousand people arrested for looting and burning (bottom left). In North Philadelphia (bottom right) mass looting and destruction occurred in August 1964, when ghetto occupants gave vent to their resentment of police and the white community.

272

In July 1967 black activist groups from all over the United States gathered in Newark, New Jersey, for a national Black Power conference. Seated at the conference table (above) are some of the leaders of the meeting. From left to right are: Ron Karenga, head of US, a West Coast group; H. Rap Brown, national chairman of SNCC; Ralph Featherstone of SNCC; the Rev. Jesse Jackson of the Southern Christian Leadership Conference.

As delegates to the national Black Power conference entered Cathedral House, members of the Harlem Mau-Mau Society stood guard (left).

Although Negroes continued to make legal gains, the old problems and fears—poverty, hunger and frustration—remained. Again and again in the late 1960's the anger of the black ghetto spilled over into the nation's streets and cities. In July 1967, in Detroit, snipers and rock throwers drove off firemen who were attempting to put out a fire caused by the rioting. When the firemen left, members of the black community picked up the hose and fought the fire (top left). Throughout the night members of the 101st Airborne Division patrolled Detroit's uneasy streets (top right). In Memphis, Tennessee, on March 28, 1968, the protest march led by Dr. King erupted into bloody street fighting (bottom left). Four thousand National Guardsmen were rushed to the city. More than a hundred persons were arrested. The next day marchers appeared to protest in the streets of Memphis, walking between lines of National Guardsmen and tanks (bottom right).

Violence finally erupted in the nation's capital. The assassination of the Rev. Martin Luther King, Jr., in April 1968, touched off three days of rioting, burning and looting. When troops were brought into the city an uneasy peace was restored, and residents came into the streets to view the destruction.

After attending a memorial service for Dr. King, Senator Robert F. Kennedy, Mrs. Kennedy and the Rev. Walter E. Fauntroy walked through the devastated areas of Washington.

Black city officials from across the nation attend the second annual Southern Conference of Black Mayors in Tuskegee, Alabama. Shown here during a break in the three day meeting are (from left to right) Mayor Ed Bivins, Inkster, Michigan; Robert Blackwell, Highland Park, Michigan, founder of the National Black Caucus of Local Elected Officials; Mayor David R. Humes, Hayti, Missouri; and John F. Bass, Comptroller, St. Louis, Missouri.

Barbara Jordan listens intently to testimony during a session of the House Judiciary Committee's impeachment inquiry into the relationship of former President Nixon and the Watergate conspirators.

Bibliography

ARMED FORCES

AMERICAN TEACHERS ASSOCIATION. *The Black and White of Military Service.* Montgomery, Ala., 1944.

BEECHER, JOHN. *All Brave Sailors.* New York, 1945.

BRAITHWAITE, WILLIAM S. *The Story of the Great War.* New York, 1919.

BROWN, EARL, and LEIGHTON, GEORGE R. *The Negro and the War.* Washington, 1942.

BYERS, JEAN. *Study of the Negro in Military Service.* Washington, 1950.

CADE, JOHN B. *Twenty-two Months with Uncle Sam.* Atlanta, 1929.

COUNCIL FOR DEMOCRACY. *The Negro and Defense.* New York, 1941.

DELSARTE, WALTER WILLIAMS. *The Negro, Democracy and the War.* Detroit, 1919.

EVANS, JAMES C., and LANE, DAVID A., JR. "Integration in the Armed Services," *Annals of the American Academy of Political and Social Science,* CCCIV (March 1956), 78–85.

FAHY, CHARLES, et al. *Freedom To Serve: U.S. President's Committee on Equality of Treatment and Opportunity in the Armed Forces.* Washington, 1950.

FRANCIS, CHARLES E. *The Tuskegee Airmen: The Story of the Negro in the U.S. Air Force.* Boston, 1956.

FRAZIER, E. FRANKLIN. "Ethnic and Minority Groups in Wartime: With Special Reference to the Negro," *American Journal of Sociology,* XLVIII (November 1942), 369–77.

FURR, ARTHUR F. *Democracy's Negroes.* Boston, 1947.

GLASS, EDWARD L. *A History of the Tenth Cavalry, 1866–1921.* Tucson, Ariz., 1921.

GRANGER, LESTER B. "Negroes and War Production," *Survey Graphic,* XXXI (November 1942), 469–71, 534–44.

GUTHRIE, JAMES M. *Campfires of the Afro-American: Or the Colored Man as Patriot.* Philadelphia, 1899.

HEYWOOD, CHESTER D. *Negro Combat Troops in the World War.* Worcester, Mass., 1928.

JOHNSON, EDWARD A. *A History of Negro Soldiers in the Spanish-American War.* Raleigh, N.C., 1899.

JOHNSON, GUION G. "The Impact of War upon the Negro," *Journal of Negro Education,* X (July 1941), 596–611.

LEE, IRVIN H. *Negro Medal of Honor Men.* New York, 1967.

LITTLE, ARTHUR W. *From Harlem to the Rhine.* New York, 1936.

LYNK, MILES V. *The Black Troopers: Or the Daring Heroism of the Negro Soldiers in the Spanish-American War.* Jackson, Tenn., 1899.

MANDELBAUM, DAVID G. *Soldier Groups and Negro Soldiers.* Berkeley, 1952.

MARSHALL, THURGOOD. *Report of Korea.* New York, 1951.

McINTYRE, W. IRWIN. *Colored Soldiers.* Macon, Ga., 1932.

MULZAC, HUGH. *A Star To Steer By.* New York, 1963.

"The Negro's War," *Fortune,* XXV (June 1942), 77–80, 157–64.

NELSON, DENNIS D. *The Integration of the Negro into the U.S. Navy.* New York, 1951.

NICHOLS, LEE. *Breakthrough on the Color Front.* New York, 1954.

ROSS, WARNER A. *My Colored Battalion.* Chicago, 1920.

SCHOENFELD, SEYMOUR J. *The Negro in the Armed Forces: His Value and Status, Past, Present, and Potential.* Washington, 1945.

SCOTT, EMMETT JAY. *The American Negro in the World War.* Chicago, 1919.

SHANNON, F. A. *The Organization and Administration of the U.S. Army.* Cleveland, 1928.

SHERMAN, GEORGE R. *The Negro as a Soldier.* Providence, R.I., 1913.

SILVERA, JOHN D. *The Negro in World War II.* Baton Rouge, 1946.

SWEENY, W. ALLISON. *The History of the American Negro in the Great World War.* Chicago, 1919.

U.S. COMMISSION ON CIVIL RIGHTS. SOUTH DAKOTA ADVISORY COMMITTEE. *Negro Airman in a Northern Community.* Washington, 1963.

WASHINGTON, BOOKER T. *The Colored Soldier in the Spanish-American War.* Chicago, 1899.

WEAVER, ROBERT C. "The Negro Veteran," *Annals of the American Academy of Political and Social Science,* CCXXXVIII (March 1945), 127–32.

WELLIVER, WARMAN. "Report on the Negro Soldier," *Harper's Magazine,* CXCII (April 1946), 333–39.

WHITE, WALTER F. *A Rising Wind.* New York, 1945.

WILLIAMS, CHARLES H. *Sidelights on Negro Soldiers.* Boston, 1923.

WILLIAMS, JOHN HENRY. *A Negro Looks At War.* New York, 1940.

WILSON, RUTH DONNENHOWER. *Jim Crow Joins Up: A Study on Negroes in the Armed Forces of the United States.* New York, 1944.

YERKES, R. M. *Psychological Examining in the United States Army.* Washington, 1921.

YOUNG, CHARLES. *Military Morale of Nations and Races.* Kansas City, Kan., 1912.

BIOGRAPHICAL WORKS

ANDERSON, MARIAN. *My Lord, What a Morning.* New York, 1956.

ANGELL, PAULINE K. *To the Top of the World: The Story of Peary and Henson.* Chicago, 1964.

BARTON, REBECCA. *Witnesses for Freedom: Negro Americans in Autobiography.* New York, 1948.

BATES, DAISY. *The Long Shadow of Little Rock.* New York, 1962.

BENNETT, LERONE, JR. *What Manner of Man: A Biography of Martin Luther King, Jr.* Chicago, 1964.

BONTEMPS, ARNA W. *The Story of George Washington Carver.* New York, 1954.

BRAWLEY, BENJAMIN G. *The Negro Genius.* New York, 1937.

BRODERICK, FRANCIS L. *W. E. B. Du Bois: Negro Leader in a Time of Crisis.* Palo Alto, 1959.

BUCKLER, HELEN. *Dr. Dan: Pioneer in American Surgery.* Boston, 1954.

CANNON, POPPY. *A Gentle Knight.* New York, 1956.

CHEW, ABRAHAM. *A Biography of Colonel Charles Young.* Washington, 1933.

CRONON, EDMUND D. *Black Moses: The Story of Marcus Garvey and the Universal Negro Improvement Association.* Madison, Wis., 1955.

CUNEY HARE, MAUD. *Norris Wright Cuney.* Washington, 1923.

DABNEY, WENDELL P. *Maggie L. Walker . . . the Woman and Her Work.* Cincinnati, 1927.

DU BOIS, W. E. B. *Dusk of Dawn: An Essay toward an Autobiography of a Race Concept.* New York, 1940.

EDWARDS, ADOLPH. *Marcus Garvey, 1887–1940.* London, 1967.

EMBREE, EDWIN R. *Brown Americans.* New York, 1943.

FLIPPER, HENRY O. *The Colored Cadet at West Point.* New York, 1878.

FRAZIER, E. FRANKLIN. "Garvey: A Mass Leader," *Nation.* CXXIII (August 18, 1926). 147–48.

GARVEY, AMY JACQUES. *Garvey and Garveyism.* Kingston, Jamaica, 1963.

———— (ed.). *Philosophy and Opinions of Marcus Garvey.* New York, 1923.

HARRIS, SARA. *Father Divine: Holy Husband.* New York, 1953.

HENSON, MATTHEW A. *A Negro Explorer at the North Pole.* New York, 1912.

HOLT, RACKHAM, *George Washington Carver.* New York, 1943.

HOSHOR, JOHN. *God in a Rolls Royce: The Rise of Father Divine, Madman, Menace or Messiah.* New York, 1936.

LANGSTON, JOHN MERCER. *From the Virginia Plantation to the National Capitol.* Hartford, Conn., 1894.

LORD, WALTER. *Peary to the Pole.* New York, 1963.

MALCOLM X. *The Autobiography of Malcolm X.* New York, 1965.

MATHEWS, BASIL. *Booker T. Washington: Educator and Interracial Interpreter.* Cambridge, Mass., 1948.

OTTLEY, ROI. *The Lonely Warrior: The Life and Times of Robert S. Abbott.* Chicago, 1955.

PATTERSON, HAYWOOD, and CONRAD, EARL. *Scottsboro Boy.* Garden City, N.Y., 1950.

PONTON, M. M. *The Life and Times of Henry M. Turner.* Atlanta, 1917.

REDDING, J. SAUNDERS. *The Lonesome Road.* New York, 1958.

RICHINGS, G. F. *Evidences of Progress among Colored People.* Philadelphia, 1897.

RUDWICK, ELLIOTT M. *W. E. B. Du Bois: A Study in Minority Group Leadership.* Philadelphia, 1960.

SIMMONS, WILLIAM J. *Men of Mark, Eminent, Progressive, and Rising.* Cleveland, 1887.

SPENCER, SAMUEL R., JR. *Booker T. Washington and the Negro's Place in American Life.* Boston, 1955.

TERRELL, MARY CHURCH. *A Colored Woman in a White World.* Washington, 1940.

WASHINGTON, BOOKER T. *Up from Slavery: An Autobiography.* 5th ed. Garden City, N.Y., 1931.

WATERS, ETHEL. *His Eye Is on the Sparrow.* Garden City, N.Y., 1951.

Who's Who in Colored America. 7 vols. New York, 1927–1950.

WRIGHT, RICHARD. *Black Boy.* New York, 1945.

YOUNG, A. S. "DOC." *Great Negro Baseball Stars.* New York, 1953.

CIVIL RIGHTS

BELFRAGE, SALLY. *Freedom Summer.* New York, 1965.

BRINK, WILLIAM J., and HARRIS, LOUIS. *The Negro Revolution in America: What Negroes Want, Why and How They Are Fighting, Whom They Support, What Whites Think of Them and Their Demands.* New York, 1964.

BROOKS, ALEXANDER D., and ELLISON, VIRGINIA. *Civil Rights and Liberties in the United States: An Annotated Bibliography.* New York, 1962.

BURNS, W. H. *Voices of Negro Protest in America.* Oxford, England, 1963.

CLAYTON, EDWARD (ed.). *The SCLC Story.* Atlanta, 1964.

HENTOFF, NAT. *The New Equality.* New York, 1965.

HOLT, LEN. *The Summer That Didn't End.* New York, 1965.

HUGHES, LANGSTON. *Fight for Freedom: The Story of the NAACP.* New York, 1962.

JACK, ROBERT L. *History of the National Association for the Advancement of Colored People.* Boston, 1943.

KELLOGG, CHARLES FLINT. *NAACP.* Baltimore, 1967.

KING, MARTIN LUTHER, JR. *Stride toward Freedom: The Montgomery Story.* New York, 1958.

LEWIS, ANTHONY, and THE NEW YORK TIMES. *Portrait of a Decade: The Second American Revolution.* New York, 1964.

McCORD, WILLIAM. *Mississippi: The Long Hot Summer.* New York, 1965.

OVINGTON, MARY W. *How the National Association for the Advancement of Colored People Began.* New York, 1914.

———. "The National Association for the Advancement of Colored People," *Journal of Negro History,* IX (April 1924), 107–16.

POWELL, ADAM CLAYTON, JR. *Marching Blacks.* New York, 1945.

ST. JAMES, WARREN D. *The National Association for the Advancement of Colored People: A Case Study in Pressure Groups.* New York, 1958.

STERLING, DOROTHY. *Tear Down the Walls! A History of the American Civil Rights Movement.* Garden City, N.Y., 1968.

U.S. COMMISSION ON CIVIL RIGHTS. *Freedom to the Free: A Century of Emancipation, 1863–1963.* Washington, 1963.

WESTIN, ALAN F. (ed.) *Freedom Now! The Civil Rights Struggle in America.* New York, 1964.

WYNN, DANIEL WEBSTER. *The NAACP versus Negro Revolutionary Protest.* New York, 1955.

ZINN, HOWARD. *The New Abolitionists.* Boston, 1964.

EDUCATION

AMERICAN COUNCIL ON RACE RELATIONS. "Memorandum on Racial Segregation in Higher Education." Chicago, 1948. (Mimeographed.)

BOND, HORACE M. *The Education of the Negro in the American Social Order.* New York, 1934.

BRICKMAN, WILLIAM W. *The Countdown on Segregated Education.* New York, 1960.

BUMSTEAD, HORACE. *Secondary and Higher Education in the South for Whites and Negroes.* New York, 1910.

CALIVER, AMBROSE. *A Background Study of Negro College Students.* Washington, 1933.

CLIFT, VIRGIL A., ANDERSON, ARCHIBALD W., and HULLFISH, H. GORDON (eds.). *Negro Education in America: Its Adequacy, Problems, and Needs.* New York, 1962.

CONANT, JAMES B. *Slums and Suburbs: A Commentary on Schools in Metropolitan Areas.* New York, 1961.

FLORIDA, UNIVERSITY OF. COLLEGE OF EDUCATION. *Segregation and Desegregation in American Education: A Bibliography.* 3rd ed. Gainesville, 1962.

GALLAGHER, BUELL G. *American Caste and the Negro College.* New York, 1938.

GLAZIER, HARLAN E. *The Color Line in Our Public Schools.* Washington, 1937.

HOLMES, DWIGHT O. W. *The Evolution of the Negro College.* New York, 1934.

HUMPHREY, HUBERT H. (ed.). *Integration vs. Segregation.* New York, 1964.

JENCKS, CHRISTOPHER, and RIESMAN, DAVID. "The American Negro College," *Harvard Educational Review,* XXXVII (Winter 1967), 3–60.

JOHNSON, CHARLES SPURGEON. *The Negro College Graduate.* Chapel Hill, N.C., 1938.

JOHNSON, GEORGE M., and LUCAS, JANE MARSHALL. "The Present Legal Status of the Negro Separate School," *Journal of Negro Education,* XVI (July 1947), 280–89.

KENT, RAYMOND A. (ed.). *Higher Education in America.* Boston, 1930.

KILPATRICK, JAMES J. *The Southern Case for School Segregation.* New York, 1962.

LONG, HOWARD H. "Federal-Aid-to-Education Legislation: Current Trends," *Journal of Negro Education,* XIII (April 1944), 252–54.

McGRATH, EARL J. *The Predominantly Negro Colleges and Universities in Transition.* New York, 1965.

McMILLAN, LEWIS K. *Negro Higher Education in the State of South Carolina.* Orangeburg, S.C., 1952.

MILLER, ARTHUR S. *Racial Discrimination and Private Education.* Chapel Hill, N.C., 1957.

RANSOM, LEON A. "Education and the Law: Current Trends," *Journal of Negro Education,* XI (April 1942), 224–28.

REDDICK, L. D. "The Education of Negroes in States Where Separate Schools Are Not Legal," *Journal of Negro Education,* XVI (July 1947), 290–300.

STAUPERS, MABEL K. *No Time for Prejudice.* New York, 1961.

STOWELL, JAY S. *Methodist Adventures in Negro Education.* New York, 1922.

TAYLOR, IVAN. "Negro Teachers in White Colleges," *School and Society,* LXV (May 24, 1947), 370.

U.S. BUREAU OF EDUCATION. *Negro Education.* Washington, 1917.

U.S. COMMISSION ON CIVIL RIGHTS. *Civil Rights U.S.A.: Public Schools, Cities in North and West, 1962, Staff Reports.* Washington, 1962.

———. *Civil Rights U.S.A.: Public Schools, Southern States, 1962, Staff Reports.* Washington, 1962.

U.S. OFFICE OF EDUCATION. *Biennial Survey of Education in the United States. Statistics of State School Systems, 1943–44*. Washington, 1946.

WEY, HERBERT, and COREY, JOHN. *Action Patterns in School Desegregation: A Guidebook*. Bloomington, Ind., 1959.

WILKERSON, DOXEY A. *Special Problems of Negro Education*. Washington, 1939.

GENERAL NEGRO HISTORY

ALEXANDER, WILLIAM T. *History of the Colored Race in America*. Kansas City, Mo., 1887.

APTHEKER, HERBERT. *A Documentary History of the Negro People in the United States*. Vol. II. New York, 1964.

BARDOLPH, RICHARD. *The Negro Vanguard*. New York, 1959.

BENNETT, LERONE, JR. *Before the Mayflower: A History of the Negro in America, 1619–1962*. Chicago, 1962.

BONTEMPS, ARNA W. *Story of the Negro*. New York, 1962.

BRAWLEY, BENJAMIN. *A Short History of the American Negro*. New York, 1919.

CAUGHEY, JOHN W., FRANKLIN, JOHN HOPE, and MAY, ERNEST R. *Land of the Free: A History of the United States*. New York, 1966.

CHALMERS, ALLAN K. *They Shall Be Free*. Garden City, N.Y., 1951.

EPPSE, MERLE R. *The Negro, Too, in American History*. Nashville, 1939.

FRANKLIN, JOHN HOPE. *From Slavery to Freedom*. 3rd. ed. New York, 1967.

HUGHES, LANGSTON, and MELTZER, MILTON. *A Pictorial History of the Negro in America*. New York, 1963.

JOHNSON, EDWARD A. *A School History of the Negro Race in America from 1619 to 1890*. Chicago, 1893.

JOHNSON, JAMES WELDON. *Along This Way*. New York, 1933.

Journal of Negro History (Washington). 1916–

POWELL, ADAM CLAYTON, SR. *Against the Tide*. New York, 1938.

QUARLES, BENJAMIN. *The Negro in the Making of America*. New York, 1964.

RHODES, JAMES FORD. *History of the United States from the Compromise of 1850*. 7 vols. New York, 1893–1906.

SALK, ERWIN A. (ed.). *A Layman's Guide to Negro History*. Chicago, 1966.

WASHINGTON, BOOKER T. *Story of the Negro*. New York, 1940.

WHEADON, AUGUSTA AUSTIN. *The Negro from 1863 to 1963*. New York, 1963.

WILLIAMS, GEORGE W. *History of the Negro Race in America from 1619 to 1880*. New York, 1883.

WOODSON, CARTER G. *The Negro in Our History*. Washington, 1922.

HOUSING

ABRAMS, CHARLES. *Forbidden Neighbors*. New York, 1955.

———. "The Housing Problem and the Negro," *Daedalus*, XCV (Winter 1966), 64–76.

BURGESS, E. W. "Residential Segregation in American Cities," *Annals of the American Academy of Political and Social Science*, CXL (November 1928), 110.

CARTER, ROBERT L., KENYON, DOROTHY, MARCUSE, PETER, and MILLER, LOREN. *Equality*. New York, 1965.

COMMITTEE ON NEGRO HOUSING. PRESIDENT'S CONFERENCE ON HOME BUILDING AND HOME OWNERSHIP. *Negro Housing*. Washington, 1932.

DEUTSCH, MORTON, and COLLINS, MARY E. *Interracial Housing: A Psychological Evaluation of a Social Experiment*. Minneapolis, 1951.

JONES, WILLIAM H. *The Housing of Negroes in Washington, D.C.* Washington, 1929.

MILLER, LOREN. "Supreme Court Covenant Decision—An Analysis," *Crisis*, LV (September 1948), 265–66.

RAPKIN, CHESTER, and GRIGSBY, WILLIAM G. *The Demand for Housing in Racially Mixed Areas: A Study of the Nature of Neighborhood Change*. Berkeley, 1960.

ROSEN, ELLSWORTH E., and NICHOLSON, ARNOLD. "When a Negro Moves Next Door," *Saturday Evening Post*, CCXXXI (April 1959), 32–33.

U.S. HOUSING AUTHORITY. "Report on Employment of Negro Workers in Construction of USHA-Aided Projects." Washington, 1941. (Mimeographed.)

LABOR AND ECONOMICS

ALEXANDER, RICHARD D., et. al. *Management of Racial Integration in Business*. New York, 1964.

BAILER, LLOYD H. "The Negro Automobile Worker," *Journal of Political Economy*, LI (October 1943), 415–28.

BARIL, V. S., and LAKENAN, A. C. "Earnings of Negro Workers in the Iron and Steel Industry, April 1938," *Monthly Labor Review*, LI (November 1940), 1139–49.

BARNES, CHARLES B. *The Longshoremen*. New York, 1915.

"Bi-Racial Cooperation in the Placement of Negroes: Indiana Plan," *Monthly Labor Review*, LV (August 1942), 231–34.

BRAZEAL, BRAILSFORD R. *The Brotherhood of Sleeping Car Porters*. New York, 1946.

BROWNING, JAMES B. "The Beginnings of Insurance Enterprise among Negroes," *Journal of Negro History*, XXII (October 1937), 417–52.

CAYTON, H. R., and MITCHELL, G. S. *Black Workers and the New Unions*. Chapel Hill, N.C., 1939.

CORSON, JOHN J. *Manpower for Victory*. New York, 1943.

CROSSLAND, W. A. *Industrial Conditions among Negroes in St. Louis.* St. Louis, 1915.

DU BOIS, W. E. B. (ed.). *Economic Cooperation among Colored Americans.* Atlanta, 1907.

FELDMAN, HERMAN. *Racial Factors in American Industry.* New York, 1931.

FLEMING, WALTER L. *The Freedmen's Savings Bank.* Chapel Hill, N.C., 1927.

FRANKLIN, CHARLES L. *The Negro Labor Unionist of New York.* New York, 1936.

GINZBERG, ELI (ed.). *The Negro Challenge to the Business Community.* New York, 1964.

GREENE, LORENZO J., and CALLIS, MYRA COLSON. *The Employment of Negroes in the District of Columbia.* Washington, 1931.

GREENE, LORENZO J., and WOODSON, CARTER G. *The Negro Wage Earner.* Washington, 1930.

"Half a Million Workers," *Fortune,* XXIII (March 1941), 96–98, 163–66.

HARMON, JOHN H., LINDSAY, ARNETT G., and WOODSON, CARTER G. *The Negro as a Business Man.* Washington, 1929.

HARPER, SAMUEL. "Negro Labor in Jacksonville," *Crisis,* XLIX (January 1942), 11, 13, 18.

HARRIS, ABRAM L. *The Negro as Capitalist: A Study of Banking and Business among American Negroes.* Philadelphia, 1936.

———, and SPERO, STERLING. *The Black Worker.* New York, 1931.

HAYES, L. G. W. *The Negro Federal Government Worker.* Washington, 1941.

HAYNES, GEORGE E. *The Negro at Work in New York City.* New York, 1912.

———. *The Negro at Work during the World War and the Reconstruction.* Washington, 1921.

HENDERSON, E. W. "Employment of Negroes by the Federal Government," *Monthly Labor Review,* LVI (May 1943), 889–91.

———. "Negroes in Government Employment," *Opportunity,* XXI (July 1943), 118–21, 142–43.

HINES, GEORGE WASHINGTON. *Negro Banking Institutions in the United States.* Washington, 1924.

HOFFSOMMER, HAROLD. *The Resident Laborer on the Sugar Cane Farm.* Baton Rouge, 1941.

JACKSON, GILES B., and DAVIS, D. WEBSTER. *The Industrial History of the Negro Race of the United States.* Richmond, 1911.

JOHNSON, CHARLES SPURGEON. *The Negro in Baltimore Industries.* Baltimore, 1932.

KELSEY, CARL. "The Evolution of Negro Labor," *Annals of the American Academy of Political and Social Science,* XXI (January 1903), 55–76.

KINZER, ROBERT H. *The Negro in American Business.* New York, 1950.

LEWIS, EDWARD E. *The Mobility of the Negro: A Study in the American Labor Supply.* New York, 1931.

MARSHALL, RAY F. *The Negro and Organized Labor.* New York, 1965.

———. *The Negro Worker and the Trade Unions: A Foot in the Door.* New York, 1965.

MITCHELL, G. S. "The Negro in Southern Trade Unionism," *Southern Economic Journal,* II (January 1936), 26–33.

———., and CAYTON, HORACE R. *Black Workers and the New Unions.* Chapel Hill, N.C., 1939.

MITCHELL, JAMES B. *The Collapse of the National Benefit Life Insurance Company.* Washington, 1939.

Monthly Labor Review (Washington). 1915–1940.

NATIONAL CONFERENCE ON SMALL BUSINESS. *Problems and Opportunities Confronting Negroes in the Field of Business.* Washington, 1961.

NATIONAL MANPOWER COUNCIL. *A Policy for Skilled Manpower.* New York, 1954.

NATIONAL URBAN LEAGUE. *Unemployment Status of Negroes.* New York, 1931.

"Negro Employment in Airframe Plants," *Monthly Labor Review,* LVI (May 1943), 888–89.

"Negro Workers in Skilled Crafts and Construction," *Opportunity,* XI (October 1933), 296–300.

"Negroes in a War Industry: The Case of Shipbuilding," *Journal of Business,* XVI (July 1943), 160–72.

NORGREN, PAUL. *Employing the Negro in American Industry: A Study of Management Practices.* New York, 1959.

NORTHRUP, HERBERT R. "The Negro and Unionism in the Birmingham, Ala., Iron and Steel Industry," *Southern Economic Journal,* X (July 1943), 27–40.

———. *Organized Labor and the Negro.* New York, 1944.

OAK, VISHNU VILLHAL. *The Negro Entrepreneur.* Yellow Springs, Ohio, 1948.

PADMORE, GEORGE. *The Voice of Colored Labor.* Manchester, England, 1945.

PERLMAN, JACOB. "Earnings of Negro Workers in Independent Tobacco Stemmeries in 1933 and 1935," *Monthly Labor Review,* XLIV (May 1937), 1153–72.

PIERCE, JOSEPH A. *Negro Business and Business Education.* New York, 1947.

PINCHBECK, R. B. *The Virginia Negro Artisan and Tradesman.* Richmond, 1926.

PRESIDENT'S COMMITTEE ON FAIR EMPLOYMENT PRACTICES. *Minorities in Defense.* Washington, 1941.

RANDOLPH, A. P. "The Crisis of the Negro Railroad Worker," *American Federationist,* XLVI (August 1939), 807–21.

REID, IRA DE A. *Negro Membership in American Labor Unions.* New York, 1930.

ROMERO, PATRICIA W. "Willard S. Townsend and the International Brotherhood of Red Caps." Unpublished Master's thesis. Miami University, Oxford, Ohio, 1964.

ROSS, ARTHUR M. "The Negro Worker in the Depression," *Social Forces,* XVIII (May 1940), 550–59.

RUCHAMES, LOUIS. *Race, Jobs, and Politics: The Story of the FEPC.* New York, 1953.

RUSSELL SAGE FOUNDATION. *The Negro in Industry.* New York, 1924.

SHORTER, C. A. "Philadelphia's Employers, Unions and Negro Workers," *Opportunity,* XX (January 1942), 4–7.

SOUTHALL, SARA E. *Industry's Unfinished Business.* New York, 1950.

STERNER, RICHARD. *The Negro's Share.* New York, 1943.

STUART, M. S. "Insurance a Natural," *Crisis,* XLVIII (April 1941), 110–44.

SWANSTROM, EDWARD E. *The Waterfront Labor Problem.* New York, 1938.

TAFT, PHILIP. *Organized Labor in American History.* New York, 1964.

TOWNSEND, WILLARD S. "One Problem and a Possible Solution," in RAYFORD W. LOGAN (ed.), *What the Negro Wants.* Chapel Hill, N.C., 1944.

TRENT, W. J., JR. "Development of Negro Life Insurance Enterprises." Unpublished Master's thesis. University of Pennsylvania, Philadelphia, 1932.

U.S. DEPARTMENT OF THE INTERIOR. *Urban Negro Workers in the United States, 1925–1936.* 2 vols. Washington, 1939.

VALIEN, PRESTON. "The Brotherhood of Sleeping Car Porters," *Phylon,* I (Fall 1940), 224–38.

WALKER, ARNOLD B. "St. Louis' Employers, Unions, and Negro Workers," *Opportunity,* XIX (November 1941), 336–38, 348.

WASHINGTON, BOOKER T. *The Negro in Business.* Chicago, 1907.

WEAVER, ROBERT C. "Detroit and Negro Skill," *Phylon,* IV (Summer 1943), 131–43.

———. *Negro Labor: A National Problem.* New York, 1946.

WEBSTER, THOMAS A. "Employers, Unions, and Negro Workers," *Opportunity,* XIX (October 1941), 295–97.

WEISS, HARRY, and ARNOW, PHILIP. "Recent Transition of Redcaps from Tip to Wage Status," *American Labor Legislation Review,* XXXII (September 1942), 134–43.

WESLEY, CHARLES H. *Negro Labor in the United States.* New York, 1927.

WOLFE, F. E. *Admission to American Trade Unions.* Baltimore, 1912.

WOODSON, CARTER G. "Insurance Business among Negroes," *Journal of Negro History,* XIV (April 1929), 209–11.

LEGAL

Books, Pamphlets and Articles

BICKEL, ALEXANDER M. *The Least Dangerous Branch: The Supreme Court at the Bar of Politics.* Indianapolis, 1962.

BLAUSTEIN, ALBERT P., and FERGUSON, CLARENCE C., JR. *Desegregation and the Law: The Meaning and Effect of the School Segregation Cases.* New Brunswick, N.J., 1957.

BUREAU OF NATIONAL AFFAIRS. *The Civil Rights Act of 1964: Text, Analysis, Legislative History, What It Means to Employers, Businessmen, Unions, Employees, Minority Groups.* Washington, 1964.

CARR, ROBERT K. *Federal Protection of Civil Rights.* Ithaca, N.Y., 1947.

COTTERALL, HELEN J. *Judicial Cases concerning American Slavery and the Negro.* 2 vols. Washington, 1926.

FELLMAN, DAVID. *The Supreme Court and Education.* New York, 1961.

GREENBERG, JACK. *Race Relations and American Law.* New York, 1959.

GUILD, JUNE PURCELL. *Black Laws of Virginia.* Richmond, 1936.

HALE, R. L. *Freedom through Law.* New York, 1952.

HARRIS, ROBERT J. *The Quest for Equality: The Constitution, Congress and the Supreme Court.* Baton Rouge, 1960.

HILL, HERBERT, and GREENBERG, JACK. *Citizen's Guide to Desegregation.* Boston, 1955.

LESKES, THEODORE, "A Study of State Laws against Discrimination," in MILTON KONVITZ (ed.), *A Century of Civil Rights.* New York, 1961.

LEVI, EDWARD H. *An Introduction to Legal Reasoning.* Chicago, 1949.

MANGUM, CHARLES S. *The Legal Status of the Negro.* Chapel Hill, N.C., 1940.

McCLELLAN, GRANT S. (ed.). *Civil Rights.* New York, 1964.

MILLER, LOREN. *The Petitioners: The Story of the Supreme Court of the United States and the Negro.* New York, 1966.

STEPHENSON, GILBERT T. *Race Distinctions in American Law.* New York, 1911.

U.S. SUPREME COURT. *The Supreme Court on Racial Discrimination,* ed. Joseph Tussman. New York, 1963.

VOSE, CLEMENT E. *Caucasians Only: The Supreme Court, the NAACP and the Restrictive Covenant Cases.* Berkeley, 1959.

WASHINGTON, BOOKER T. "My View of Segregation Laws," *New Republic,* V (December 4, 1915), 113–14.

WHITE, WALTER. "The Negro and the Supreme Court," *Harper's Magazine,* CLXII (January 1931), 238–46.

ZEIGLER, BENJAMIN M. (ed.). *Desegregation and the Supreme Court.* Boston, 1958.

Court Cases

Aaron v. Cooper, 261 F. 2d 97 (8th Cir. 1958), order on remand, 169 F. Supp. 325 (E.D. Ark. 1959).

Aaron v. McKinley, 173 Supp. 944 (E.D. Ark.), aff'd sub nom., Faubus v. Aaron 361 U.S. 197 (1959). *See also Cooper v. Aaron.*

Abstract Inv. Co. v. Hutchinson, 204 Cal. App. 2d 242, 22 Cal. Rptr. 309 (1962).

Adkins v. Children's Hospital, 261 U.S. 525 (1923).

Alston v. *Board of Ed. of City of Norfolk*, 112 F. 2d 992 (4th Cir. 1940).

Anderson v. *Martin*, 375 U.S. 399 (1964).

Anderson v. *Moses*, 185 F. Supp. 727 (S.D. N.Y. 1960).

Arizona Employers' Liab. Cases, 250 U.S. 400 (1919).

Armstrong v. *Board of Educ.*, 220 F. Supp. 217 (N.D. Ala. 1963), mandate issued ordering district court to issue preliminary injunction pending appeal, 323 F. 2d 333 (5th Cir. 1963), petition for cert. filed, 32 U.S.L. Week 3223 (U.S. Dec. 11, 1963) (No. 670).

Associated Press v. *N.L.R.B.*, 301 U.S. 103 (1937).

Associated Press v. *U.S.*, 326 U.S. 1 (1945).

Augustus v. *Board of Pub. Instruction*, 306 F. 2d 862 (5th Cir. 1962).

Bailey v. *Patterson*, 369 U.S. 31 (1962).

Baker v. *Carr*, 369 U.S. 186 (1962).

Balaban v. *Rubin*, 40 Misc. 2d 249 N.Y.S. 2d 973 (Sup. Ct.), motion to vacate ex parte order granting injunction denied, 19 App. Div. 2d 790, 243 N.Y.S. 2d 472 (2d Dept. 1963).

Baldwin v. *Morgan*, 251 F. 2d 780 (5th Cir. 1958).

Baltimore v. *Dawson*, 350 U.S. 877 (1955).

Banks v. *Housing Authority*, 120 Cal. App. 2d 1, 260 P. 2d 668 (1953), cert. denied, 347 U.S. 974 (1954).

Barnes v. *City of Gadsen*, 268 F. 2d 593 (5th Cir. 1959).

Barrows v. *Jackson*, 346 U.S. 249 (1953).

Batt Scott v. *J. Harvey Netter, et al.*, Civ. Dis. Ct., Parish of Orleans, Louisiana, March 2, 1942.

Beal v. *Missouri Pac. R. R. Corp.*, 312 U.S. 45 (1941).

Beckett v. *School Bd.*, 185 F. Supp. 459 (E.D. Va. 1959), aff'd *sub nom.*, *Farley* v. *Turner*, 281 F. 2d 131 (4th Cir. 1960).

Bell v. *School Bd.*, 321 F. 2d 494 (4th Cir. 1963).

Bell v. *State*, 227 Md. 302, 176 A. 2d 771 (1962), cert. granted, 374 U.S. 805 (1963).

Berman v. *Parker*, 348 U.S. 26 (1954).

Betts v. *Easley*, 161 Kan. 459, 169 P. 2d 831 (1946).

Block v. *Hirsch*, 256 U.S. 135 (1921).

Bob-Lo Excursion Co. v. *Michigan*, 333 U.S. 28 (1948).

Borders v. *Rippy*, 195 F. Supp. 732 (N.D. Tex. 1961).

Boson v. *Rippy*, 285 F. 2d 43 (5th Cir. 1960).

Bowman v. *Birmingham Transp. Co.*, 280 F. 2d 531 (5th Cir. 1960).

Bowman v. *Chicago & Northwestern Ry.*, 115 U.S. 611 (1885).

Boynton v. *Virginia*, 364 U.S. 454 (1960).

Bradley v. *School Bd.*, 317 F. 2d 429 (4th Cir. 1963).

Branche v. *Board of Educ.*, 204 F. Supp. 150 (E.D. N.Y. 1962).

Brooks v. *U.S.*, 267 U.S. 432 (1925).

Brotherhood of R. R. Trainmen v. *National Mediation Board*, 88 F. (2d) 757 (1936).

Brotherhood of R. & S. Clerks v. *United Transport Service Employees*, U.S.C.C.A., D.C. Circuit, August 2, 1943; U.S. Sup. Ct., December 6, 1943.

Browder v. *Gayle*, 142 F. Supp. 707 (M.D. Ala.), aff'd, 352 U.S. 903 (1956). *See also Gayle* v. *Browder*.

Brown v. *Board of Educ.*, 347 U.S. 483 (1954).

Brown v. *Board of Educ.*, 349 U.S. 294 (1955).

Bruce v. *Atlantic Coast Line Railway, et al.*, Virginia State Court, Richmond, Va., September 12, 1932.

Brunson v. *Board of Trustees*, 311 F. 2d 107 (4th Cir. 1962), cert. denied, 373 U.S. 933 (1963).

Buchanan v. *Warley*, 245 U.S. 60 (1917).

Bull v. *Stichman*, 189 Misc. 597, 72 N.Y.S. 2d 488 (Supp. Ct. 1947), aff'd, 273 App. Div. 311, 78 N.Y.S. 2d 279 (3d Dept.), aff'd, 298 N.Y. 516, 80 N.E. 2d 661 (1948).

Burks v. *Poppy Constr. Co.*, 57 Cal. 2d 463, 476, 370 P. 2d 313, 320, 20 Cal. Rptr. 609, 616 (1962).

Burton v. *Wilmington Parking Authority*, 365 U.S. 715 (1961).

Bush v. *Orleans Parish School Bd.*, 138 F. Supp. 337 (E.D. La. 1956), aff'd, 242 F. 2d 156 (5th Cir.), cert. denied, 354 U.S. 921 (1957).

Bush v. *Orleans Parish School Bd.*, 308 F. 2d 491 (5th Cir. 1962).

Calhoun v. *Latimer*, 321 F. 2d 302 (5th Cir. 1963), cert. granted, 32 U.S.L. Week 3254 (U.S. Jan. 13, 1963) (No. 623).

Camp-of-the-Pines Inc. v. *N.Y. Times Co.*, 184 Misc. 389, 53 N.Y.S. 2d 475 (Supp. Ct. 1945).

Carson v. *Warlick*, 238 F. 2d 724 (4th Cir. 1956), cert. denied, 353 U.S. 910 (1957).

Casey v. *Plummer*, 353 U.S. 924 (1957).

Catlette v. *U.S.*, 132 F. 2d 902 (4th Cir. 1943).

Champion v. *Ames*, 188 U.S. 321 (1903).

City of Columbia v. *Barr*, 239 S.C. 395, 123 S.E. 2d 521 (1961), cert. granted, 374 U.S. 804 (1963).

City of Columbia v. *Bouie*, 239 S.C. 570, 124 S.E. 2d 322 (1962), cert. granted, 374 U.S. 805 (1963).

City of Greensboro v. *Simkins*, 246 F. 2d 425 (4th Cir. 1957).

City of Richmond v. *Deans*, 281 U.S. 704 (1930).

Civil Rights Cases, 109 U.S. 3 (1883).

Clemons v. *Board of Educ.*, 228 F. 2d 853 (6th Cir.), cert. denied, 350 U.S. 1006 (1956).

Clyatt v. *U.S.*, 197 U.S. 207 (1905).

Coke v. *City of Atlanta*, 184 F. Supp. 579 (N.D. Ga. 1960).

Collins v. *Hardiman*, 341 U.S. 651 (1951).

Colorado Anti-Discrimination comm'n v. *Continental Air Lines Inc.*, 372 U.S. 714 (1963).

Conley v. *Gibson*, 355 U.S. 41 (1957).

Conn. College for Women v. *Calvert*, 87 Conn. 421, 88 Atl. 633 (1913).

Cooper v. *Aaron*, 358 U.S. 1 (1958).

Corfield v. *Coryell*, 6 Fed. Cas. 546 (No. 3230) (C.C.E.D. Pa. 1832).

Council of Defense v. *International Magazine Co.*, 267 Fed. 390 (8th Cir. 1920).

Covington v. *Edwards*, 264 F. 2d 780 (4th Cir.), cert. denied, 361 U.S. 840 (1959).

Davis v. *Board of Educ.*, 216 F. Supp. 295 (E.D. Mo. 1963).

Davis v. *East Baton Rouge Parish School Bd.*, 219 F. Supp. 876 (E.D. La. 1963).

Dept. of Conservation & Dev. v. *Tate*, 231 F. 2d 615 (4th Cir.), cert. denied, 352 U.S. 838 (1956).

Derringer v. *Plummer*, 240 F. 2d 922 (5th Cir. 1956), cert. denied, 335 U.S. 924 (1957).

Dillard v. *School Bd.*, 308 F. 2d 920 (4th Cir. 1962), cert. denied, 374 U.S. 827 (1963).

District of Columbia v. *John R. Thompson Co. Inc.*, 346 U.S. 100 (1953).

Dorsey v. *Stuyvesant Town Corp.*, 299 N.Y. 512, 87 N.E. 2d 541 (1949), cert. denied, 339 U.S. 981 (1950).

Dove v. *Parham*, 196 F. Supp. 944 (E.D. Ark. 1961).

Dove v. *Parham*, 282 F. 2d 256 (8th Cir. 1960).

Dowell v. *School Bd.*, 219 F. Supp. 427 (W.D. Okla. 1963).

Easterly v. *Dempster*, 112 F. Supp. 214 (E.D. Tenn. 1953).

Eaton v. *Bd. of Managers of James Walker Memorial Hospital*, 261 F. 2d 521 (4th Cir. 1958), cert. denied, 359 U.S. 984 (1959).

Eaton v. *Grubbs*, 216 F. Supp. 465 (E.D.N.C. 1963).

Engel v. *Vitale*, 370 U.S. 421 (1962).

Estes v. *Union Terminal Co.*, 89 F. 2d 768 (1937).

Evans v. *Buchanan*, 195 F. Supp. 321 (D. Del. 1961).

Evans v. *Buchanan*, 207 F. Supp. 820 (D. Del. 1962).

Farmer v. *Phila. Electric Co.*, 215 F. Supp. 729 (E.D. Pa. 1963).

Flax v. *Potts*, 218 F. Supp. 254 (N.D. Tex. 1963). *See also Potts* v. *Flax*.

Flemming v. *S.C. Elec. & Gas Co.*, 224 F. 2d 752 (4th Cir. 1955), appeal dismissed, 351 U.S. 901 (1956).

Florida ex rel. Hawkins v. *Board of Control*, 350 U.S. 413 (1956).

FTC v. *R. F. Keppel & Bros., Inc.*, 291 U.S. 304 (1934).

Gaines v. *Dougherty County Bd. of Educ.*, 222 F. Supp. 166 (M.D. Ga. 1963).

Garner v. *Louisiana*, 368 U.S. 157 (1961).

Garrett v. *Faubus*, 230 Ark. 445, 323 S.W. 2d 877 (1959).

Gayle v. *Browder*, 352 U.S. 903 (1956).

Ghioto v. *Hampton*, 371 U.S. 911 (1962).

Gibbons v. *Ogden*, 9 Wheat 1 (1824).

Gibson v. *Board of Public Instruction*, 272 F. 2d 763 (5th Cir. 1959).

Gomillion v. *Lightfoot*, 364 U.S. 339 (1960).

Gordon v. *Gordon*, 332 Mass. 197, 124 N.E. 2d 228 (1955), cert. denied, 349 U.S. 947 (1958).

Goss v. *Board of Educ.*, 373 U.S. 683 (1963).

Green v. *School Bd. of the City of Roanoke, Va.*, 304 F. 2d 118 (4th Cir. 1962).

Griffin v. *Board of Supervisors*, 322 F. 2d 332 (4th Cir. 1963), cert. granted, 32 U.S.L. Week 3242 (U.S. Jan. 6, 1964) (No. 592).

Griffin v. *State*, 225 Md. 422, 171 A. 2d 717 (1961), cert. granted, 370 U.S. 935 (1962), restored to calendar for argument, 373 U.S. 920 (1963).

Grovey v. *Townsend*, 295 U.S. 45 (1934).

Guillory v. *Administrators of Tulane U.*, 203 F. Supp. 855 (E.D. La. 1962).

Hackley v. *Art Builders Inc.*, 179 F. Supp. 851 (D. Md. 1960).

Hall v. *DeCuir*, 95 U.S. 485 (1877).

Hall v. *St. Helena Parish School Bd.*, 197 F. Supp. 649 (E.D. La. 1961), aff'd per curiam, 368 U.S. 515 (1962).

Hampton v. *City of Jacksonville*, 304 F. 2d 320 (5th Cir. 1962).

Harmon v. *Tyler*, 273 U.S. 668 (1927).

Harris v. *City of St. Louis*, 223 Mo. App. 911, III S.W. 2d 995 (1938).

Harris v. *Gibson*, 322 F. 2d 780 (5th Cir. 1963).

Harrison v. *Day*, 200 Va. 439, 106 S.E. 2d 636 (1959).

Harrison v. *Murphy*, 205 F. Supp. 449 (D. Del. 1962).

Heckman v. *U.S.*, 224 U.S. 413 (1912).

Henderson v. *U.S.*, 340 U.S. 846 (1950).

Henry v. *Godsell*, 165 F. Supp. 87 (E.D. Mich. 1958).

Hodges v. *U.S.*, 203 U.S. 1 (1906).

Hoke v. *U.S.*, 227 U.S. 308 (1913).

Holland v. *Board of Public Instructors*, 258 F. 2d 730 (5th Cir. 1958).

Holmes v. *City*, 350 U.S. 879 (1958).

Holt v. *Raleigh City Bd. of Educ.*, 265 F. 2d 95 (4th Cir.), cert. denied, 361 U.S. 818 (1959).

Hughes Tool Co. v. *Motion Picture Assn. of America*, 66 F. Supp. 1006 (S.D. N.Y. 1946).

Hurd v. *Hodge*, 334 U.S. 24 (1948).

Ill. ex rel. McCollum v. *Board of Educ.*, 333 U.S. 203 (1948).

Iowa-Des Moines National Bank v. *Bennett*, 284 U.S. 239 (1931).

Jackson v. *Pasadena City School Dist.*, 59 Cal. 2d 876, 382 P. 2d 878, 31 Cal. Rptr. 606 (1963).

Jackson v. *School Bd.*, 321 F. 2d 230 (4th Cir. 1963).

James v. *Almond*, 170 F. Supp. 331 (E.D. Va. 1959).

James v. *Duckworth*, 170 F. Supp. 342 (E.D. Va.), aff'd, 267 F. 2d 224 (4th Cir.), cert. denied, 361 U.S. 835 (1959).

Jeffers v. *Whitley*, 309 F. 2d 621 (4th Cir. 1962).

Johnson v. *Levitt & Sons*, 131 F. Supp. 114 (E.D. Pa. 1955).

Jones v. *Marva Theaters Inc.*, 180 F. Supp. 49 (D. Md. 1960).

Jones v. *School Bd.*, 278 F. 2d 72 (4th Cir. 1960).

Kates v. *Lefkowitz*, 28 Misc. 2d 210, 216 N.Y.S. 2d 1014 (1961).

Kerr v. *Enoch Pratt Free Library*, 149 F. 2d 212 (4th Cir.), cert. denied, 326 U.S. 721 (1945).

Lane v. *Wilson*, 307 U.S. 268 (1939).

Lathrop v. *Donahue*, 367 U.S. 820 (1961).

Lawrence v. *Hancock*, 76 F. Supp. 1004 (S.D. W. Va. 1948).

Local No. 231, International Longshoremen's Association v. *Ross*, 180 La. 293, 156 So. 357 (1934).

Loewe v. *Lawlor*, 208 U.S. 274 (1908).

Lynch v. *U.S.*, 189 F. 2d 476 (5th Cir. 1951).

Mannings v. *Board of Pub. Instruction*, 277 F. 2d 370 (5th Cir. 1960).

Mapp v. *Bd. of Educ.*, 319 F. 2d 571 (6th Cir. 1963).

Marsh v. *Alabama*, 326 U.S. 501 (1946).

Marsh v. *County School Bd.*, 305 F. 2d 94 (4th Cir. 1962).

Maxwell v. *County Bd. of Educ.*, 301 F. 2d 828 (6th Cir. 1962), rev'd on other grounds, 373 U.S. 683 (1963).

Mayor & City Council of Balt. v. *Dawson*, 350 U.S. 877 (1955).

McCabe v. *Atchison, Topeka & Santa Fe Ry.*, 235 U.S. 151 (1914).

McCoy v. *Greensboro City Bd. of Educ.*, 283 F. 2d 667 (4th Cir. 1960).

McCulloch v. *Maryland*, 4 Wheat 315 (1819).

McDermott v. *Wisc.*, 228 U.S. 115 (1913).

McNeese v. *Bd. of Educ.*, 373 U.S. 668 (1963).

Ming v. *Horgan*, 3 Race Rel. L. Rep. 633 (Sacramento Cty., Cal. Super. Ct. 1958).

Missouri ex rel. Gaines v. *Canada*, 305 U.S. 337 (1938).

Mitchell v. *Boys Club of Metro. Police*, 157 F. Supp. 101 (D.D.C. 1957).

Monroe v. *Board of Comm'rs*, 221 F. Supp. 968 (W.D. Tenn. 1963).

Monroe v. *Pape*, 365 U.S. 167 (1961).

Morgan v. *Virginia*, 328 U.S. 373 (1946).

Muir v. *Louisville Park Theatrical Ass'n.*, 347 U.S. 971 (1954).

National Federation of Railway Workers v. *National Mediation Board*, 110 F. 2d 529; cert. denied, 310 U.S. 628 (1940).

National Labor Relations Board v. *Jones & Laughlin Steel Corp.*, 301 U.S. 1 (1936).

National Labor Relations Board v. *Newport News Shipbuilding and Dry Dock Co.*, 308 U.S. 241 (1939).

National Labor Relations Board v. *Sun Shipbuilding and Dry Dock Co.*, U.S.C.C.A., (3d Cir.), March 30, 1943.

Nebbia v. *N.Y.*, 291 U.S. 502 (1934).

New Orleans City Park Improvement Ass'n. v. *Detiege*, 358 U.S. 54 (1958).

Nixon v. *Condon*, 286 U.S. 73 (1932).

Nixon v. *Herndon*, 273 U.S. 536 (1927).

Nord v. *Griffen*, 86 F. 2d 281; cert. denied, 300 U.S. 673 (1937).

Norris v. *Mayor and City Council of Balt.*, 78 F. Supp. 451 (D. Md. 1948).

Northcross v. *Board of Educ.*, 302 F. 2d 818 (6th Cir.), cert. denied, 370 U.S. 944 (1962).

Novick v. *Levitt & Sons Inc.*, 200 Misc. 694, 108 N.Y.S. 2d 615 (Supp. Ct.), aff'd, 279 App. Div. 617, 107 N.Y.S. 2d, 1016 (1951).

O'Neil v. *Vermont*, 144 U.S. 323 (1892).

Overnight Motor Transp. Co. v. *Missel*, 316 U.S. 572 (1942).

Parham v. *Dove*, 271 F. 2d 132 (8th Cir. 1959).

Park v. *Detroit Free Press Co.*, 72 Mich. 560, 566, 40 N.W. 731, 733 (1888).

Penn. v. *Board of Directors of City Trusts*, 353 U.S. 230 (1957).

Peterson v. *City of Greenville*, 373 U.S. 244 (1963).

Plessy v. *Ferguson*, 163 U.S. 537 (1896).

Potts v. *Flax*, 313 F. 2d 284 (5th Cir. 1963).

Public Utilities Comm'n v. *Pollak*, 343 U.S. 451 (1952).

Railway Mail Association v. *Corsi*, 326 U.S. 88 (1945).

Railway Mail Association v. *Murphy*, N.Y. Sup. Ct., Albany Cy., November 4, 1943.

Robinson v. *State*, 144 So. 2d 811 (Fla. 1962), prob. juris. noted, 374 U.S. 803 (1963).

Ross v. *Ebert*, 275 Wis. 523, 534–37, 82 N.W. 2d 315, 321–22 (1957).

Ross v. *Peterson*, 5 Race Rel. L. Rep. 703 (S.D. Tex. 1960).

Saia v. *New York*, 334 U.S. 558 (1948).

Sanitary Dist. v. *U.S.*, 266 U.S. 405 (1925).

Schine Chain Theaters Inc. v. *U.S.*, 334 U.S. 110 (1948).

School Bd. v. *Atkins*, 246 F. 2d 325 (4th Cir.), cert. denied, 355 U.S. 855 (1957).

Screws v. *U.S.*, 325 U.S. 91 (1945).

Sealy v. *Dept. of Pub. Instruction*, 159 F. Supp. 561 (E.D. Pa. 1957), aff'd, 252 F. 2d 898 (3d Cir.), cert. denied, 356 U.S. 975 (1958).

Shelley v. *Kraemer*, 334 U.S. 1 (1948).

Shepard v. *Bd. of Educ.*, 207 F. Supp. 341 (D.N.J. 1962).

Shuttlesworth v. *Birmingham Bd. of Educ.*, 162 F. Supp. 372 (N.D. Ala.), aff'd per curiam, 358 U.S. 101 (1958).

Simkins v. *Moses H. Cone Memorial Hosp.*, 323 F. 2d 959 (4th Cir. 1963), cert. denied, _____ U.S. _____ (1964).

Sipuel v. *Board of Regents*, 332 U.S. 631 (1948).

Smith v. *Allwright*, 321 U.S. 649 (1944).

Smith v. *Holiday Inns of America Inc.*, 220 F. Supp. 1 (M.D. Tenn. 1963).

Statom v. *Board of Comm'rs*, 195 A. 2d 41 (Ct. App. Md. 1963).

Steele v. *Louisville & Nashville Railroad Co.*, 323 U.S. 192 (1944).

Steele v. *Louisville & Nashville Railroad Co., et al.*, Cir. Ct., 10th Judicial Circuit, Alabama. In equity, No. 52,279 (1943).

Stell v. *Savannah-Chatham County Bd. of Education*, 220 F. Supp. 667 (S.D. Ga. 1963) (Scarlett, J.), mandate issued ordering district court to issue preliminary injunctions pending appeal, 318 F. 2d 425 (5th Cir. 1963).

Strauder v. *W. Va.*, 100 U.S. 303 (1879).

Sweatt v. *Painter*, 339 U.S. 629 (1950).

Syres v. *Oil Workers*, 350 U.S. 892 (1956), reversing 223 F. 2d 739 (5th Cir. 1955).

Taylor v. *Board of Educ.*, 195 F. Supp. 231 (S.D. N.Y.), aff'd, 294 F. 2d 36 (2d Cir.), cert. denied, 368 U.S. 940 (1961).

Teague v. *Brotherhood of Locomotive Firemen*, 127 F. 2d 53 (1942).

Terry v. *Adams*, 345 U.S. 461 (1953).

Testa v. *Katt*, 330 U.S. 386 (1947).

Texas & N.O.R. Co. v. *Brotherhood of Ry. & Steamship Clerks*, 281 U.S. 548 (1930).

Thompson v. *County School Bd.*, 204 F. Supp. 620 (E.D. Va. 1962).

Thornhill v. *Alabama*, 310 U.S. 88 (1940).

Trowbridge v. *Katzen*, 14 A.D. 2d 608, 218 N.Y.S. 2d 808 (3d Dept. 1961).

Truax v. *Corrigan*, 257 U.S. 312 (1921).

Truax v. *Raich*, 239 U.S. 33 (1915).

Tunstall v. *Brotherhood of Locomotive Firemen & Enginemen*, 323 U.S. 210 (1944).

Turner v. *City of Memphis*, 369 U.S. 350 (1962).

U.S. v. *American Bell Tel. Co.*, 128 U.S. 315 (1888).

U.S. v. *Beaty*, 288 F. 2d 653 (6th Cir. 1961).

U.S. v. *Beebe*, 127 U.S. 338 (1888).

U.S. v. *Biloxi Municipal School Dist.*, 219 F. Supp. 691 (S.D. Miss. 1963).

U.S. v. *Bossier Parish School Bd.*, 220 F. Supp. 243 (W.D. La. 1963).

U.S. v. *City of Jackson*, 318 F. 2d 1, petition for rehearing denied per curiam, 1320 F. 2d 870 (5th Cir. 1963).

U.S. v. *City of Montgomery*, 201 F. Supp. 590 (M.D. Ala. 1962).

U.S. v. *City of Shreveport*, 210 F. Supp. 36, 210 F. Supp. 708 (W.D. La. 1962).

U.S. v. *Classic*, 313 U.S. 299 (1941).

U.S. v. *County School Bd.*, 221 F. Supp. 93 (E.D. Va. 1963).

U.S. v. *Cruikshank*, 92 U.S. 542 (1875).

U.S. v. *Darby*, 312 U.S. 100 (1941).

U.S. v. *Harris*, 106 U.S. 629 (1882).

U.S. v. *Klearflax Linen Looms*, 63 F. Supp. 32 (D. Minn. 1945).

U.S. v. *Lassiter*, 203 F. Supp. 20 (W.D. La.), aff'd, 371 U.S. 10 (1962).

U.S. v. *Macdaniel*, 32 U.S. (7 Pet.) 1 (1833).

U.S. v. *Madison City Bd. of Ed.*, 219 F. Supp. 60 (N.D. Ala. 1963).

U.S. v. *McElveen*, 177 F. Supp. 355 (E.D. La. 1959), aff'd, 362 U.S. 58 (1960).

U.S. v. *New Orleans Pac. Ry.*, 248 U.S. 507 (1919).

U.S. v. *Raines*, 362 U.S. 17 (1960).

U.S. v. *San Jacinto Tin Co.*, 125 U.S. 273 (1888).

U.S. v. *Sullivan*, 332 U.S. 689 (1948).

U.S. v. *U.S. Klans*, 194 F. Supp. 897 (M.D. Ala. 1961).

U.S. v. *Wallace*, 218 F. Supp. 290, 222 F. Supp. 485 (M.D. Ala. 1963).

U.S. v. *Williams*, 341 U.S. 70 (1951).

Vick v. *County Bd. of Educ.*, 205 F. Supp. 436 (W.D. Tenn. 1962).

Vickers v. *Chapel Hill City Bd. of Educ.*, 196 F. Supp. 97 (M.D. N.C. 1961).

Watchtower Bible & Tract Soc. v. *Metropolitan Life Ins. Co.*, 297 N.Y. 339, 79 N.E. 2d 433 (1948).

Watson v. *City*, 373 U.S. 526 (1963).

Werner v. *Southern Calif. Assoc. Newspapers*, 35 Cal. 2d 121, 144, 216 P. 2d 825, 839 (1950).

West Coast Hotel Co. v. *Parrish*, 300 U.S. 379 (1937).

Wheeler v. *Durham City Bd. of Educ.*, 309 F. 2d 630 (4th Cir. 1962).

Wickard v. *Filburn*, 317 U.S. 111 (1942).

Williams v. *Howard Johnson's Inc.*, 323 F. 2d 102 (4th Cir. 1963).

Williams v. *U.S.*, 341 U.S. 97 (1951).

Wright v. *Georgia*, 373 U.S. 284 (1963).

Zorach v. *Clauson*, 343 U.S. 306 (1952).

LITERATURE AND THE ARTS

ALLEN, WILLIAM FRANCIS, WARE, CHARLES P., and GARRISON, LUCY McKIM. *Slave Songs of the United States.* New York, 1867.

BALDWIN, JAMES. *Another Country.* New York, 1962.

———. *The Fire Next Time.* New York, 1963.

———. *Go Tell It on the Mountain.* New York, 1953.

———. *Nobody Knows My Name.* New York, 1961.

———. *Notes of a Native Son.* Boston, 1955.

———. *Tell Me How Long the Train's Been Gone.* New York, 1968.

BONE, ROBERT A. *The Negro Novel in America.* New Haven, 1958.

BRAITHWAITE, WILLIAM STANLEY. *Anthology of Magazine Verse.* New York, 1913–1925.

BRAWLEY, BENJAMIN. *The Negro in Literature and Art in the United States.* New York, 1929.

BROOKS, GWENDOLYN. *A Street in Bronzeville.* New York, 1945.

BROWN, STERLING A. *The Negro in American Fiction.* Washington, 1937.

———, DAVIS, ARTHUR P., and LEE, ULYSSES (eds.). *The Negro Caravan.* New York, 1941.

CUNEY HARE, MAUD. *Negro Musicians and Their Music.* Washington, 1936.

DOVER, CEDRIC. *American Negro Art.* Greenwich, Conn., 1960.

DU BOIS, W. E. B. *The Souls of Black Folk.* Chicago, 1903.

DUNBAR, PAUL LAURENCE. *Candle-Lightin' Time.* New York, 1901.

———. *The Fanatics.* New York, 1901.

———. *Folks from Dixie.* New York, 1898.

———. *Howdy, Honey, Howdy.* New York, 1905.

———. *In Old Plantation Days.* New York, 1903.

———. *The Love of Landry.* New York, 1900.

———. *Lyrics of Love and Laughter.* New York, 1903.

———. *Lyrics of Lowly Life.* New York, 1896.

———. *Poems of Cabin and Field.* New York, 1899.

———. *Sport of the Gods.* New York, 1902.

———. *The Strength of Gideon.* New York, 1900.

———. *The Uncalled.* New York, 1901.

ELLISON, RALPH. *Invisible Man.* New York, 1952.

FAUSET, JESSIE REDMON. *The Chinaberry Tree.* New York, 1931.

———. *Comedy: American Style.* New York, 1933.

———. *Plum Bun.* London, 1928.

———. *There Is Confusion.* New York, 1924.

FISCHER, RUDOLPH. *The Conjure Man Dies.* New York, 1932.

HUGHES, JOHN M. *The Negro Novelist, 1940–1950.* New York, 1953.

HUGHES, LANGSTON. *First Book of Jazz.* New York, 1955.

———. *Not without Laughter.* New York, 1930.

ISAACS, EDITH J. *The Negro in the American Theatre.* New York, 1947.

JOHNSON, JAMES WELDON. *God's Trombones.* New York, 1927.

JONES, LEROI. *Blues People: Negro Music and White America.* New York, 1963.

———. *The Dutchman.* New York, 1964.

LARSEN, NELLA. *Quicksand.* New York, 1928.

LOCKE, ALAIN. *Negro Art: Past and Present.* Washington, 1936.

LOGGINS, VERNON. *The Negro Author.* New York, 1931.

McKAY, CLAUDE. *Banjo.* New York, 1929.

———. *Harlem Shadows.* New York, 1922.

———. *Home to Harlem.* New York, 1927.

———. *Songs of Jamaica.* London, 1912.

MOTLEY, WILLARD. *Knock on Any Door.* New York, 1947.

PETRY, ANN LANE. *The Street.* Boston, 1946.

PORTER, JAMES AMOS. *Modern Negro Art.* New York, 1943.

REDDING, J. SAUNDERS. *To Make a Poet Black.* Chapel Hill, N.C., 1939.

RICHARDSON, WILLIS (ed.). *Plays and Pageants from the Life of the Negro.* Washington, 1930.

TOOMER, JEAN. *Cane.* New York, 1923.

WHITE, WALTER. *The Fire in the Flint.* New York, 1924.

———. *Flight.* New York, 1926.

WHITEMAN, MAXWELL. *A Century of Fiction by American Negroes, 1853–1952.* Philadelphia, 1955.

WRIGHT, RICHARD. *Black Boy.* New York, 1945.

———. *Native Son.* New York, 1940.

YERBY, FRANK. *The Foxes of Harrow.* New York, 1946.

MIGRATION

BONTEMPS, ARNA, and CONROY, JACK. *Anyplace but Here.* Garden City, N.Y., 1966.

FANNING, JOHN WILLIAM. *Negro Migration.* Athens, Ga., 1930.

FLORANT, LYONEL C. "Negro Internal Migration," *American Sociological Review,* VII (December 1942), 782–91.

KENNEDY, LOUISE V. *The Negro Peasant Turns Cityward: Effects of Recent Migrations to Northern Centers.* New York, 1930.

KLINEBERG, OTTO. *Negro Intelligence and Selective Migration.* New York, 1935.

LEWIS, EDWARD E. *The Mobility of the Negro.* New York, 1931.

ROSS, FRANK A., and KENNEDY, LOUISE V. *A Bibliography of Negro Migration.* New York, 1934.

SCOTT, EMMETT J. *Negro Migration during the World War.* Washington, 1918.

SHRYOCK, HENRY S., JR., and ELDRIDGE, HOPE TISDALE. "Internal Migration in Peace and War," *American Sociological Review,* XII (January 1948), 32.

WOODSON, CARTER G. *A Century of Negro Migration.* Washington, 1918.

WOOFTER, THOMAS JACKSON. *Negro Migration.* New York, 1920.

POLITICS AND POLITICIANS

ALILUNAS, LEO. "Legal Restriction on the Negro in Politics," *Journal of Negro History,* XXV (April 1940), 152–202.

ARNETT, A. M. *The Populist Movement in Georgia.* New York, 1922.

BACOTE, CLARENCE ALBERT. *The Negro in Georgia Politics, 1880–1908.* Chicago, 1955.

BAKER, RAY STANNARD. *Following the Color Line: American Negro Citizenship in the Progressive Era.* New York, 1908.

BREWER, JOHN MASON. *Negro Legislators of Texas and Their Descendants.* Dallas, 1935.

CLARK, JOHN B. *Populism in Alabama.* Auburn, Ala., 1927.

CLAYTON, EDWARD T. *The Negro Politician: His Success and Failure.* Chicago, 1964.

DU BOIS, W. E. B. "The Republicans and the Black Voter," *Nation,* CX (June 5, 1920), 757.

EDMONDS, HELEN G. *The Negro and Fusion Politics in North Carolina, 1894–1901.* Chapel Hill, N.C., 1951.

HICKEY, NEIL, and EDWIN, ED. *Adam Clayton Powell and the Politics of Race.* New York, 1965.

HICKS, JOHN D. *The Populist Revolt.* Minneapolis, 1931.

MERRIAM, CHARLES E. *Four Party Leaders.* New York, 1926.

MOON, HENRY LEE. *Balance of Power: The Negro Vote.* Garden City, N.Y., 1948.

MORTON, RICHARD L. *The Negro in Virginia Politics, 1865–1902.* Charlottesville, Va., 1919.

MOSLEY, J. H. *Sixty Years in Congress and Twenty-eight Out.* New York, 1960.

NOWLIN, WILLIAM FELBERT. *The Negro in American National Politics.* Boston, 1931.

ODEGARD, P. H. *Pressure Politics.* New York, 1928.

PRICE, HUGH DOUGLAS. *The Negro and Southern Politics.* New York, 1957.

RECORD, WILSON. *Race and Radicalism: The NAACP and the Communist Party in Conflict.* Ithaca, N.Y., 1964.

REID, IRA DE A. "Georgia Negro Vote," *Nation,* CLXIII (July 6, 1946), 14.

SMITH, SAMUEL D. *The Negro in Congress, 1870–1901.* Chapel Hill, N.C., 1940.

WHITE, M. J. "Populism in Louisiana during the Nineties," *Mississippi Valley Historical Review,* V (June 1918), 3.

WILSON, JAMES Q. *Negro Politics: The Search for Leadership.* Glencoe, Ill., 1960.

THE PRESS

BENNETT, LERONE, JR. "Founders of the Negro Press," *Ebony,* XIX (July 1964), 96–98.

BROOKS, MAXWELL. *The Negro Press Reexamined: Political Content of Leading Negro Newspapers.* Boston, 1959.

GORE, GEORGE WILLIAM. *Negro Journalism.* Greencastle, Ind., 1922.

"The Negro Press: 1955," *Time,* LXVI (November 7, 1955), 64.

PENN, I. GARLAND. *The Afro-American Press and Its Editors.* Springfield, Mass., 1891.

ROSEN, BERNARD C. "Attitude Changes within the Negro Press toward Segregation and Discrimination," *Journal of Social Psychology,* LXII (February 1964), 77–84.

U.S. DEPARTMENT OF COMMERCE. *Negro Newspapers and Periodicals in the United States: 1943.* Washington, 1944.

U.S. LIBRARY OF CONGRESS. *Negro Newspapers on Microfilm.* Washington, 1953.

WATERS, ENOCH P. "The Negro Press: A Call for Change," *Editor and Publisher,* XCV (May 1962), 67–68.

RECONSTRUCTION

ALEXANDER, THOMAS B. *Political Reconstruction in Tennessee.* Nashville, 1950.

ALLEN, JAMES S. *Reconstruction: The Battle for Democracy, 1865–1876.* New York, 1937.

BUCK, PAUL H. *The Road to Reunion, 1865–1900.* Boston, 1937.

BURGESS, JOHN W. *Reconstruction and the Constitution, 1866–1876.* New York, 1905.

CARTER, HODDING. *The Angry Scar: The Story of Reconstruction.* Garden City, N.Y., 1959.

COULTER, ELLIS MERTON. *The South during Reconstruction, 1865–1877.* Baton Rouge, 1947.

COX, LAWANDA, and COX, JOHN H. *Politics, Principle, and Prejudice, 1865–1866: Dilemma of Reconstruction America.* New York, 1963.

DAVIS, W. W. *Civil War and Reconstruction in Florida.* New York, 1913.

DU BOIS, W. E. B. *Black Reconstruction.* New York, 1935.

ECKENRODE, HAMILTON J. *The Political History of Virginia during the Reconstruction.* Baltimore, 1904.

FERTIG, JAMES W. *The Secession and Reconstruction of Tennessee.* Chicago, 1898.

FICKLEN, JOHN R. *History of Reconstruction in Louisiana (through 1868).* Baltimore, 1910.

FLEMING, W. L. (ed.). *Documentary History of Reconstruction.* 2 vols. Cleveland, 1906–1907.

FRANKLIN, JOHN HOPE. *Reconstruction after the Civil War.* Chicago, 1961.

GARNER, JAMES W. *Reconstruction in Mississippi.* New York, 1901.

HAMILTON, JOSEPH G. DE R. *Reconstruction in North Carolina.* New York, 1914.

HILL, T. ARNOLD. *The Influence of Reconstruction on Education in the South.* New York, 1913.

———. *The Negro and Economic Reconstruction.* Washington, 1937.

KRUG, MARK M. "On Rewriting the Story of Reconstruction in the United States History Textbooks," *Journal of Negro History,* XLVI (July 1961), 133–53.

LONN, ELLA. *Reconstruction in Louisiana.* New York, 1919.

LYNCH, JOHN R. *The Facts of Reconstruction.* New York, 1913.

McGINTY, GARNIE W. *Louisiana Redeeemed: The Overthrow of the Carpetbag Rule, 1876–1880.* New Orleans, 1941.

McKITRICK, ERIC. *Andrew Johnson and Reconstruction.* Chicago, 1960.

McPHERSON, JAMES M. *The Struggle for Equality: Abolitionists and the Negro in the Civil War and Reconstruction.* Princeton, 1964.

NUNN, W. C. *Texas under the Carpetbaggers.* Austin, 1962.

PATTON, JAMES W. *Unionism and Reconstruction in Tennessee, 1860–1869.* Chapel Hill, N.C., 1934.

RAMSDELL, CHARLES W. *Reconstruction in Texas.* New York, 1910.

RANDALL, JAMES G., and DONALD, DAVID. *Civil War and Reconstruction.* Boston, 1961.

REYNOLDS, JOHN S. *Reconstruction in South Carolina, 1865–1877.* Columbia, S.C., 1905.

RIDDLEBERGER, PATRICK W. "The Break in the Radical Ranks: Liberals vs. Stalwarts in the Election of 1872," *Journal of Negro History,* XLIV (April 1959), 136–57.

———. "The Radicals' Abandonment of the Negro during Reconstruction," *Journal of Negro History,* XLV (April 1960), 88–102.

SIMKINS, FRANCIS B., and WOODY, R. H. *South Carolina during Reconstruction.* Chapel Hill, N.C., 1932.

SPROAT, JOHN G. "Blueprint for Radical Reconstruction," *Journal of Southern History*, XXIII (February 1957), 25–44.

STAMPP, KENNETH M. *The Era of Reconstruction, 1865–1877*. New York, 1965.

STAPLES, THOMAS S. *Reconstruction in Arkansas, 1862–1874*. New York, 1923.

TAYLOR, ALRUTHEUS A. *The Negro in the Reconstruction of Virginia*. Washington, 1926.

———. *The Negro in South Carolina during the Reconstruction*. Washington, 1924.

———. *The Negro in Tennessee, 1865–1880*. Washington, 1941.

THOMAS, DAVID Y. *Arkansas in War and Reconstruction*. Little Rock, 1926.

THOMPSON, C. MILDRED. *Reconstruction in Georgia*. New York, 1915.

THOMPSON, HENRY T. *Ousting the Carpetbaggers from South Carolina*. Columbia, S.C., 1927.

WARMOUTH, HENRY CLAY. *War Politics and Reconstruction*. New York, 1930.

WEISBERGER, BERNARD A. "The Dark and Bloody Ground of Reconstruction Historiography," *Journal of Southern History*, XXV (November 1959), 427–47.

WHARTON, VERNON LANE. *The Negro in Mississippi, 1865–1890*. Chapel Hill, N.C., 1947.

WILLIAMSON, JOEL. *After Slavery: The Negro in South Carolina during Reconstruction, 1861–1877*. Chapel Hill, N.C., 1965.

WOODWARD, C. VANN. *Reunion and Reaction: The Compromise of 1877 and the End of Reconstruction*. Boston, 1951.

WOOLLEY, E. C. *The Reconstruction of Georgia*. New York, 1901.

RELIGION

ANDERSON, MATTHEW. *Presbyterianism in Its Relation to the Negro*. Philadelphia, 1897.

BLYDEN, EDWARD W. *Christianity, Islam, and the Negro Race*. London, 1887.

BRAGG, GEORGE F. *History of the Afro-American Group of the Episcopal Church*. Baltimore, 1922.

BRAWLEY, EDWARD M. *The Negro Baptist Pulpit*. Philadelphia, 1890.

CLARK, ELMER TALMAGE. *The Negro and His Religion*. Nashville, 1924.

CROMWELL, W. "The First Negro Churches in the District of Columbia," *Journal of Negro History*, VII (January 1922), 64–106.

DANIEL, W. A. *The Education of Negro Ministers*. New York, 1925.

DAVENPORT, FREDERICK M. *Primitive Traits in Religious Revivals*. New York, 1917.

DU BOIS, W. E. B. (ed.). *The Negro Church*. Atlanta, 1903.

EARNEST, J. B. *The Religious Development of the Negro in Virginia*. Charlottesville, Va., 1914.

FRAZIER, E. FRANKLIN. *The Negro Church in America*. New York, 1964.

GILLARD, JOHN T. *The Catholic Church and the American Negro*. Baltimore, 1929.

HAMILTON, C. HORACE, and ELLISON, JOHN M. *The Negro Church in Rural Virginia*. Blacksburg, Va., 1930.

HOOD, J. W. *One Hundred Years of the African Methodist Episcopal Zion Church*. New York, 1895.

JORDAN, LEWIS G. *Negro Baptist History U.S.A., 1750–1930*. Nashville, 1930.

MAYS, B. E., and NICHOLSON, J. W. *The Negro's Church*. New York, 1933.

MOORE, J. J. *History of the African Methodist Episcopal Zion Church*. York, Pa., 1884.

PAYNE, DANIEL A. *History of the African Methodist Episcopal Church*. Nashville, 1891.

SIMPSON, MATTHEW. *A Hundred Years of Methodism*. New York, 1885.

STEWARD, T. G. *Fifty Years in the Gospel Ministry*. Philadelphia, 1922.

TANNER, BENJAMIN T. *An Apology for African Methodism*. Baltimore, 1867.

WASHINGTON, JOSEPH R. *Black Religion: The Negro and Christianity in the United States*. Boston, 1964.

WEATHERFORD, WILLIS D. *American Churches and the Negro: An Historical Study from Early Slave Days to the Present*. Boston, 1957.

WOODSON, CARTER G. *History of the Negro Church*. Washington, 1921.

SOCIAL STUDIES

ALEXANDER, CHARLES C. *The KKK in the Southwest*. Lexington, Ky., 1965.

ALEXANDER, SADIE TANNER MOSSELL. *Standards of Living among 100 Negro Migrant Families in Philadelphia*. Philadelphia, 1921.

BAKER, RAY STANNARD. *Following the Color Line*. New York, 1908.

BECKER, GARY S. *Economics of Discrimination*. Chicago, 1957.

BEECHER, JOHN. "Problems of Discrimination," *Science and Society*, VII (Winter 1943), 36–44.

BRACKETT, JEFFREY R. *The Negro in Maryland*. Baltimore, 1889.

BRAWLEY, BENJAMIN. *Social History of the American Negro*. New York, 1921.

BRODERICK, FRANCIS L., and MEIER, AUGUST (eds.). *Negro Protest Thought in the Twentieth Century*. Indianapolis, 1966.

BROOM, LEONARD, and GLENN, N. D. *Transformation of the Negro American*. New York, 1965.

BROTZ, HOWARD. *The Black Jews of Harlem: Negro Nationalism and the Dilemmas of Negro Leadership*. New York, 1964.

BROUGH, CHARLES H. *The Clinton Riot*. Oxford, Miss., 1902.

CARROLL, CHARLES. *The Negro: A Beast or in the Image of God?* Merrimac, Mass., 1967.

———. *The Tempter of Eve: Or the Criminality of Man's Social, Political and Religious Equality with the Negro and the Amalgamation to Which These Crimes Inevitably Lead.* St. Louis, 1902.

CARTER, WILMOTH A. *The Urban Negro in the South.* New York, 1962.

CHADBOURN, JAMES HARMON. *Lynching and the Law.* Chapel Hill, N.C., 1933.

CHALMERS, DAVID M. *Hooded Americanism: The First Century of the Ku Klux Klan, 1865–1965.* Garden City, N.Y., 1965.

CHICAGO COMMISSION ON RACE RELATIONS. *The Negro in Chicago.* Chicago, 1922.

CLARK, KENNETH B. *Dark Ghetto: Dilemmas of Social Power.* New York, 1965.

COLLINS, WINFIELD H. *The Truth about Lynching and the Negro in the South.* New York, 1918.

COMMONS, JOHN R. *Races and Immigrants in America.* New York, 1907.

COUNCIL, W. H. *Lamp of Wisdom or Race History Illuminated.* Nashville, 1898.

COX, OLIVER C. *Caste, Class, and Race: A Study in Social Dynamics.* Garden City, N.Y., 1948.

CROGMAN, W. H. *Progress of a Race.* Naperville, Ill., 1920.

CUTLER, JAMES E. *Lynch Law: An Investigation into the History of Lynching in the United States.* New York, 1905.

DANIELS, JOHN. *In Freedom's Birth-Place.* Boston, 1914.

DAVIS, ALLISON, GARDNER, BURLEIGH B., and GARDNER, MARY R. *Deep South: A Social Anthropological Study of Caste and Class.* Chicago, 1941.

DeCORSE, HELEN. *Charlottesville: A Study of Negro Life and Personality.* Charlottesville, Va., 1933.

DIXON, THOMAS. *The Clansman: An Historical Romance of the Ku Klux Klan.* Ridgewood, N.J., 1967.

———. *The Leopard's Spots: A Romance of the White Man's Burden, 1865–1900.* Ridgewood, N.J., 1967.

DOLLARD, JOHN. *Caste and Class in a Southern Town.* New Haven, 1937.

DOWD, JEROME. *The Negro in American Life.* New York, 1926.

DOYLE, BERTRAM W. *The Etiquette of Race Relations in the South.* Chicago, 1937.

DRAKE, ST. CLAIR, and CAYTON, HORACE R. *Black Metropolis: A Study of Negro Life in a Northern City.* New York, 1945.

DU BOIS, W. E. B. *The Philadelphia Negro.* Philadelphia, 1899.

ESSIEN-UDOM, E. U. *Black Nationalism: A Search for an Identity in America.* Chicago, 1962.

FAUSET, ARTHUR H. *Black Gods of the Metropolis.* Philadelphia, 1944.

FERGUSON, CHARLES W. *Fifty Million Brothers.* New York, 1937.

FISH, CARL R. *The Rise of the Common Man.* New York, 1927.

FRAZIER, E. FRANKLIN. *Black Bourgeoisie.* Glencoe, Ill., 1957.

———. "Durham: Capital of the Black Middle Class," in ALAIN LOCKE (ed.), *The New Negro.* New York, 1925.

———. *The Negro Family in the United States.* Chicago, 1939.

GALLAGHER, BUELL G. *Color and Conscience: The Irrepressible Conflict.* New York, 1946.

GARVEY, MARCUS. *The Tragedy of White Injustice.* New York, 1927.

GILLETTE, PAUL J. *Ku Klux Klan: The Invisible Empire.* New York, 1964.

GINZBERG, ELI, and BRAY, DOUGLAS W. *The Uneducated.* New York, 1953.

GRODGINS, MORTON. *The Metropolitan Area as a Racial Problem.* Pittsburgh, 1958.

HAYNE, JOSEPH E. *The Ammonian or Hamitic Origin of the Ancient Greeks, Cretans and All the Celtic Races.* Brooklyn, N.Y., 1905.

HELPER, HINTON ROWAN. *Nojoque: A Question for a Continent.* New Orleans, 1867.

HERRON, GEORGE DAVIS. *The New Redemption.* New York, 1893.

HERSKOVITS, MELVILLE J. *The Myth of the Negro Past.* New York, 1941.

HOFFMAN, FREDERICK L. *Race Traits and Tendencies of the American Negro.* New York, 1896.

HOLMES, S. J. *The Negro's Struggle for Survival.* Berkeley, 1937.

ISAACS, HAROLD R. *The New World of Negro Americans.* New York, 1963.

JACKSON, HELEN HUNT. *A Century of Dishonor.* New York, 1881.

JOHNSON, CHARLES SPURGEON. *The Negro in American Civilization.* New York, 1930.

———. *Patterns of Negro Segregation.* New York, 1943.

JOHNSON, GUY B. "Negro Racial Movements and Leadership in the United States," *American Journal of Sociology,* XLIII (July 1937), 57–71.

JOHNSON, JAMES WELDON. *Black Manhattan.* New York, 1930.

JUNKER, BUFORD H., and ADAMS, WALTER A. *Color and Human Nature.* Washington, 1941.

KATZ, IRWIN. *Conflict and Harmony in an Adolescent Interracial Group.* New York, 1955.

KERLIN, ROBERT T. *The Voice of the Negro.* New York, 1920.

KILLIAM, LEWIS M., and GRIGG, CHARLES. *Racial Crisis in America: Leadership in Conflict.* Englewood Cliffs, N.J., 1964.

LEAP, WILLIAM L. *Red Hill: Neighborhood Life and Race Relations in a Rural Section.* Charlottesville, Va., 1933.

LINCOLN, C[HARLES] ERIC. *The Black Muslims in America*. Boston, 1961.

———. *My Face Is Black*. Boston, 1954.

LOCKE, ALAIN. "Harlem: Dark Weather-Vane," *Survey Graphic*, XXV (August 1936), 457–62, 493–95.

LOGAN, RAYFORD W. *The Betrayal of the Negro*. New York, 1965.

———. *The Negro and the Post-War World*. Washington, 1945.

LOMAX, LOUIS. *The Negro Revolt*. New York, 1962.

———. *When the Word is Given: A Report on Elijah Muhammad, Malcolm X, and the Black Muslim World*. Cleveland, 1963.

MAYOR'S COMMISSION ON CONDITIONS IN HARLEM. "The Negro in Harlem." Unpublished report. New York, 1936.

McCORD, CHARLES H. *The American Negro as a Dependent, Defective and Delinquent*. Nashville, 1914.

McGILL, NETTIE P., and MATTHEWS, ELLEN N. *The Youth of New York City*. New York, 1940.

MEIER, AUGUST. *Negro Thought in America, 1880–1915: Racial Ideologies in the Age of Booker T. Washington*. Ann Arbor, Mich., 1963.

MITCHELL, GLENFORD E., and PEACE, WILLIAM H., III (eds.). *Angry Black South*. New York, 1962.

MYRDAL, GUNNAR. *An American Dilemma*. New York, 1962.

NEW JERSEY CONFERENCE OF SOCIAL WORK. *The Negro in New Jersey*. Newark, 1932.

NORTHWOOD, LAWRENCE K., and BARTH, E. A. T. *Urban Desegregation*. Seattle, 1965.

POWDERMAKER, HORTENSE. *After Freedom*. New York, 1939.

POWELL, ADAM CLAYTON, SR. *Riots and Ruins*. New York, 1945.

PRESLEY, SAMUEL. *Negro Lynchings in the South*. Washington, 1899.

RANDALL, WILLIAM P. *The Ku Klux Klan: A Century of Infamy*. Philadelphia, 1965.

RAPER, ARTHUR F. *The Tragedy of Lynching*. Chapel Hill, N.C., 1933.

REDDING, J. SAUNDERS. *On Being Negro in America*. Indianapolis, 1951.

REUTER, EDWARD B. *The American Race Problem*. New York, 1927.

RICE, ARNOLD S. *The Ku Klux Klan in American Politics*. Washington, 1962.

RUDWICK, ELLIOTT M. *Race Riot at East St. Louis, July 2, 1917*. Carbondale, Ill., 1964.

SCHEINER, SETH M. *Negro Mecca: A History of the Negro in New York City, 1865–1920*. New York, 1965.

SHANNON, A. H. *The Negro in Washington: A Study in Race Amalgamation*. New York, 1930.

SHAPIRO, FRED C., and SULLIVAN, JAMES W. *Race Riots, New York, 1964*. New York, 1964.

SHERWIN, MARK. *The Extremists*. New York, 1963.

SHOGAN, ROBERT, and CRAIG, TOM. *The Detroit Race Riot: A Study in Violence*. Philadelphia, 1964.

SILBERMAN, CHARLES E. *Crisis in Black and White*. New York, 1964.

STANDING, T. G. "Nationalism in Negro Leadership," *American Journal of Sociology*, XL (September 1934), 180–92.

STONE, ALFRED H. *Studies in the American Race Problem*. New York, 1908.

THOMAS, WILLIAM HANNIBAL. *The American Negro: What He Is, and What He May Become*. New York, 1901.

THOMPSON, EDGAR T. (ed.). *Race Relations and the Race Problem*. Durham, N.C., 1939.

TOURGEE, ALBION W. *An Appeal to Caesar*. New York, 1884.

———. *A Fool's Errand*. Cambridge, Mass., 1961.

TUMIN, M. *Desegregation: Resistance and Readiness*. Princeton, 1958.

VAN EVRIE, JOHN H. *White Supremacy and Negro Subordination*. New York, 1870.

VOORHIS, HAROLD VAN BUREN. *Negro Masonry in the United States*. New York, 1940.

WARNER, ROBERT A. *New Haven Negroes*. New Haven, 1940.

WEATHERFORD, W. D. *Negro Life in the South*. New York, 1910.

WEAVER, ROBERT C. *Dilemmas of Urban America*. Cambridge, Mass., 1965.

WHITE, WALTER F. *Rope and Faggot: A Biography of Judge Lynch*. New York, 1929.

WILLIAMS, ROBERT F. *Negroes with Guns*. New York, 1962.

WOODSON, CARTER G. *The Negro Professional Man and the Community*. Washington, 1934.

WOODWARD, C. VANN. *The Strange Career of Jim Crow*. New York, 1955.

Picture Credits

The author is grateful to the following for their aid in the search for unusual and interesting photographs with which to illustrate the text. Those pictures which have not been listed are in the private collection of United Publishing Corporation, Washington, D.C.

Key: T: Top; B: Bottom; L: Left; R: Right; C: Center

American Oil Company, Chicago: 175B, 211TR
Blackstone Studios: 218L
Chase Studios, Ltd.: 231, 237BR, 238TR
Chicago Historical Society, Chicago: 58
Cincinnati Historical Society, Cincinnati: 32B
Corcoran Gallery of Art, Washington: 47B
Down Beat Magazine, New York: 204B
Duncan Schiedt, Indianapolis: 157BR, 204T
Fabian Bachrach: 183TL
General Services Administration, Washington: 234R, 236BL
Harris and Ewing, Washington: 239TR
Historical Society of Pennsylvania, Philadelphia: 63BR, 102
Historical Society of Pennsylvania-Simon Gratz Collection, Philadelphia: 38, 72T, 106
Historical Society of Pennsylvania-Society Portrait Collection, Philadelphia: 23T, 92, 137R
J. Edward Bailey: 239TC
John Di Joseph, Washington: 261BR, 276
James Lewis, Washington: 275T
M. Knoedler & Co., Inc., New York: 82
Library of Congress, Washington: iiTL, CL, 1, 3, 7C, 11TR, 13, 15RC, 25, 29, 34B, 39, 41, 45TL, TR, 47TR, 50, 54, 62, 77, 88, 89, 93B, 107R, 120, 124TL, TR, 127, 131, 136, 137L, 155L, 157TL, 163, 167B, 168, 169, 171TL, TR, 177B, 201L, LC, 265BR,
Langston Hughes: 205BL, 207T
Merkle Press, Washington: 129
National Archives, Washington: iiTR, 83, 90B, 94, 95L, 141, 143, 145, 146, 147, 171B, 179, 183B, 187, 188TL
National Association for the Advancement of Colored People, New York: 229L, 248, 253
New York Historical Society, New York: 2, 9
New York Public Library, New York: 44, 61, 69, 71, 72B, 81B, 87, 91, 93T, 95R, 97, 104
New York Public Library-Schomburg Collection, New York: iiCR, 5C, 12, 21, 45B, 51L 55, 66, 113, 133, 139, 157TR, BL, 158B, 160TR, 201R, 205BR, 209L, 214
Office of Economic Opportunity, Washington: iiBL, BR, 221, 223, 224, 227, 229R
Scurlock Studios, Washington: 80, 98
United States Army, Washington: 180, 185TL, B, 188TR, 189, 190, 191, 192, 193, 195, 197, 198
United States Department of Agriculture, Washington: 236TRC
United States Maritime Administration, Washington: 81TL, 188B
Washington Post, Washington: 225TR, 241, 254B
Wilhelmina Robinson, Wilberforce: 262
UPI: 251, 261TL, CL, C, CR, BL, BC, 263, 265TL, TR, BL, 266-74, 275B

Index

Page numbers in *italic type* refer to illustrations.

Treasury Department
  and segregation, 151
Trotter James, 117
Trotter, Monroe, 112, 117, 151, *118*
  and Washington, Booker T., 119
Truitte, James, 208
Truman, Harry S, 186, 196, 213, 244
  and civil rights, 186
  and Negro appointments, 238
Tucker, Henry, 67
Tucker Act, 67
Tulsa, Oklahoma
  riots, 134
Tunnell, Elijah H., 89, *90*
Turner, Henry MacNeal, 6, 74, *7*
Tuskegee Institute (Alabama), 75, 112,
  114, 128, 146, 159, 161, 182, 210
  and lynching studies, 73, 107
Twenties, the, 151-162
25th Combat Team, *192*
25th Infantry, 80, 82, 86, 89, 92, 180
  discharge without honor of 3 com-
    panies, 105, *93*
24th Infantry, 86, 88, 92, 180
23rd Kansas Regiment, 88
Tyson, Cicely, 207
Tyson, Cyril D., 227-228

Unemployment
  and Depression (1930's), 168, 169,
    172, 178
UNESCO, 215
Union, the
  provisions for readmission of the South,
    2, 4
Union Army
  Negro chaplains, 6, 12
  and occupation of the South, 2, 4, 7,
    33
Union Baptist Church (Baltimore), 48
Union Labor Party, 36
Union of Electrical Workers, 229
United Aid and Insurance Company, 64
United Auto Workers, 174, 230
United Community Corporation (New-
  ark), 227
United Mine Workers, 173
United Nations, 151, 213-215
  General Assembly, 196, 214, 215
  and Negro delegates, 215
United Negro College Fund, 218, 220
United Shoe Machinery Company
  and Matzeliger invention, 58
United States
  and Central America, 96
  and Colombia, 96
  and Cuban oppression, 85-94, 96
  and imperialism, 96, 98
  and Indians, 103-104
  and Latin America, 84-86
  and Philippines, 95, 96, *95*
  and Puerto Rico, 95, 96
United States Air Force
  Negroes in, 198
United States Army
  Negroes in, 189-198
    Indian wars, 80-84
    Korean conflict, 196
    Mexican War, 139-140
    Spanish-American War, 85-86
    Vietnamese conflict, 196-198
    World War I, 140-146
    World War II, 180-196
United States Coast Guard
  Negroes in, 187, 198
United States Congress
  and bill to equate representation with
    civil rights, 153

and civil rights, 15, 21, 35, 151
and "Force Acts," 28, 68
and lynch laws, 152
Negroes in, 231, 232
and Reconstruction Acts, 3, 4
and Spanish-American War, 86, 88
and Voting Rights Act of 1965, 234
and World War I, 140
See also United States House of Representatives; United States Senate
United States Constitution, 23, 26, 68,
  73, 135, 150
  amendments, 7, 31
  Fifteenth Amendment, 12, 19, 24-25,
    27, 33, 99, 136, 138
  Fourteenth Amendment, 12, 18, 22, 24,
    25, 26, 32, 153, 243
  Nineteenth Amendment, 152
  Thirteenth Amendment, 22, 26
United States Court of Appeals, 238, 240,
  251
United States Customs Court, 238
United States District Court, 238, 244,
  250
United States House of Representatives
  and anti-lynching bill, 152
  and civil-rights bill, 231-232
  committee on education and labor, 232
  judiciary committee, 231
  and open housing, 231
  Reconstruction
    Negroes in, 6, 14-18
  subcommittee on Africa, 232
United States Information Agency, 215,
  237
United States Marine Corps
  Negroes in, 181, 187, 198
United States Military Academy, 79-80,
  142, 182
United States Musical Review (magazine),
  52
United States Naval Academy, 80, 187
United States Navy
  Negroes in, 180, 181, 182, 184, 187,
    198, *143, 183, 185, 188*
United States Public Health Service, 210
United States Senate
  judiciary committee, 238
  Negroes in, 8, 10, 12-14, 232
  and open housing, 232
United States Supreme Court, 220, 238,
  263
  Bailey v. *Alabama* (compulsory serv-
    ice), 136-137
  Brown v. *Board of Education* (public
    school integration), 244-245
  Buchanan v. *Warley* (closed housing),
    138
  Butts v. *Merchants . . .* (public trans-
    portation), 137
  decision on strikes and boycotts, 42
  and Fifteenth Amendment, 12, 19, 24-
    25, 27, 33, 99, 136, 138
  and Fourteenth Amendment, 22, 24,
    25, 26, 138
  Gibson v. *Mississippi* (all-white juries),
    25
  Giles v. *Harris* (voting), 136
  Guinn v. *United States* (voting), 138
  Hall v. *DeCuir* (public transportation),
    22
  and Harlan, John Marshall, the "great
    dissenter," 23, 26, 136, *23*
  Henderson v. *United States* (public
    transportation), 243-244
  invalidation of Civil Rights Act of
    1875, 22-23, 24, 67, 137
  invalidation of National Recovery Act,
    175

McCabe v. *Atchison, Topeka & Santa
  Fe Railroad* (public transportation),
  137-138
McLaurin v. *Oklahoma* (public school
  integration), 244
Mitchell v. *United States* (public trans-
  portation), 243
Plessy v. *Ferguson* (public transporta-
  tion), 25, 37, 136, 243, 244
  and poll tax, 27
  and school integration, 220, 263
Shelley v. *Kraemer* (open housing),
  244
Sipuel v. *University of Oklahoma* (pub-
  lic school integration), 244
Smith v. *Allwright* (voting), 244
Sweatt v. *Painter* (public school inte-
  gration), 244
Williams v. *Mississippi* (voting), 27
United States Volunteers (7th-10th), 88
United Transport Service Employees, 212
Universal Negro Improvement Associa-
  tion, 162
University Commission on Race Ques-
  tions, 126
University of Alabama, 247, 253
University of Chicago, 242, 250
University of Georgia, 250
University of Mississippi, 251
University of Oklahoma, 244
University of Pennsylvania, 7
University of Texas Law School, 244
Upper Volta, 214
Upward Bound school program, 223, 225,
  224
Urban disorders. *See* Riots
Urban League. *See* National Urban
  League
U.S. News and World Report, 220

Van Arsdale, Harry, 229
Van Deusen, John, 221
Van Evrie, John
  *White Supremacy and Negro Subordi-
    nation,* 69
Vanderhorst, Bishop Richard H., 46
Vann, Robert L., 112
Vardaman, James K., 120, 125
Vaughan, Sarah, 204
Verrett, Shirley, 203, *202*
Victory Life Insurance Company, 168
Vietnamese conflict, 196, 198, 242
Villa, Pancho, 139
Villard, Oswald Garrison, 120, 151, *121*
Virginia
  disfranchisement laws, 99
  Reconstruction
    constitutional convention, 28
    Negro congressmen, 16
Virginia (battleship), 145
Virginia Normal and Collegiate Institute,
  16
Virginia Randolph Fund, 219
Virginia State College, 43
Virginius (ship), 85
Voice of the Negro (newspaper), 116
Voting
  first in postwar South, 3
  and the Negro vote, 3, 25, 31-38, 117,
    123, 149, 150, 152, 154, 213, 240-
    242, *2*
    methods for barring, 27, 28, 67
  southern campaigns for registering, 234
  See also Disfranchisement
Voting Rights Act of 1965, 234, 255